EVERYMAN'S MODERN PHRASE & FABLE

Gyles Brandreth

EVERYMAN'S MODERN PHRASE & FABLE

J. M. Dent & Sons Ltd, London

© Complete Editions Limited 1990

All rights reserved. No part of this publication may be
reproduced, stored in a retrieval system, or transmitted,
in any form or by any means, electronic, mechanical,
photocopying, recording or otherwise, without the prior
permission of the publishers.

This book is set in 9pt Plantin Light and Bold by
Deltatype Ltd, Ellesmere Port, Cheshire

Printed in Great Britain by
Butler & Tanner Ltd, Frome, for J. M. Dent & Sons Ltd,
91 Clapham High Street, London SW4 7TA.

British Library Cataloguing in Publication Data

Everyman's modern phrase and fable. – (Everyman reference)
    1. English language. Idoims – Dictionaries
    I. Brandreth, Gyles, *1948–*
    423'.1

Paperback ISBN 0 460 02911 8
Hardback ISBN 0 460 03045 0

Foreword

While this collection of phrases and sayings is described as a 'modern' Phrase and Fable', in it you will find dozens of intriguing expressions dating back hundreds of years, each one with a remarkable origin and still in regular use.

Some phrases have been well-documented through the years. Others remain something of a mystery and we can only guess at their origin. I was particularly eager to unearth a definitive source for the expression the 'bee's knees', but my researches drew a blank and I can offer you nothing more than the somewhat obvious suggestion that the phrase originated because of the nifty way in which bees gather pollen for honey using their knees. Quite how this snippet of apiarists' knowledge came into common usage to describe someone who thinks themselves specially clever I cannot tell you. Could it be even that once upon a time a wag of a wordsmith conjured up the phrase from nowhere simply to ensure that over the years zealous word detectives have wasted hours on a 'wild goose chase' (which, happily, has a less elusive history)?

Other ancient phrases in current use can offer a special perspective on the way our ancestors lived and thought. Take the case of 'pin money', for example; a phrase we use without much thought today when we refer to an insignificant sum of money. Five hundred or so years ago, when the phrase was first recorded, 'pin money' was a far from insignificant sum. In the days before mass production pins were an expensive investment, and only available for sale on a couple of days each year. So it came to pass that every January those husbands who could afford it gave their wives some 'pin money' – and though pins soon became more freely available the phrase stuck and was applied to a sum of money given to a woman for her own personal expenditure.

The other day, with my wife (or 'better half'), I was watching a tennis match on television and remarked that one of the players couldn't 'hold a candle' to his opponent. Imagine now, if you will, a dark 17th-century street through which nocturnal travellers made their way by following servants who carried candle lanterns. This job was considered very menial and such servants were pretty low on the 'pecking order' (another fascinating derivation) but even they managed to get lost from time to time – at which their frustrated masters would declare that they 'couldn't hold a candle' to them.

If candle-holding had its problems, working as a hatter was positively dangerous. Hat-makers were gradually poisoned by the mercuric nitrate they used for working their felt. As a result they became deranged and confused – as 'mad as hatters', in fact.

I must 'speak as I find' and tell you that, in 'my humble opinion', many of the more recent words and phrases that have been included in this book lack the picturesque qualities of their more ancient counterparts. (That said, perhaps in a century or two etymologists may point to a current word, 'loadsamoney', as being of historical interest for the gloss it casts on British society in the late 1980s). My overriding impression of the contemporary words and phrases that have found their way into this collection is that the majority of them are to do with categorizing and defining people. Take the Yuppie phenomenon, for example. Not long after the archetypal Young Urban Professionals had been identified and named, related groups began to spring up. There were Buppies and Woopies, Swells, and Glams, and foodies and deccies. There was even a category for failed Yuppies, known to demographers as Droppies. No sooner had we revealed the 'bimbo' than we uncovered her 'toy-boy' equivalent, the 'himbo'. And in the United States the 'now generation' includes that bizarre phenomenon, the 'kidult', a young adolescent who, while outwardly a child, has absorbed so much information and so many sophisticated attitudes from television and the media that he or she is, in mind and spirit if not body, an adult. As well as an excess of television, which may turn them into 'couch potatoes', such children may also be in danger of suffering from 'muesli-belt malnutrition', a debilitating condition brought about by a diet based largely on high-fibre health food.

Computers and business have also had a significant influence on the development of our vocabulary. From the 'electronic virus', a bug inserted into computer software which leads to its gradual destruction, to such phrases as 'catching a cold' and 'golden parachute' which hail from the business world, our language inevitably reflects the technical and socio-economic changes of the recent past.

Some concerns have remained consistent over the centuries. The most predictable of these is death. While our ancestors talked with brutal frankness of 'kicking the bucket' (alluding to the way in which pigs were hung up to be killed) or euphemistically of 'going to Abraham's bosom', the newer phrases tend to be more clinical. In American hospitals a patient who defies the best efforts of his doctors is said to have suffered a 'negative patient care outcome' or to have 'flatlined' – this last phrase referring to the fatally flat line shown on a screen monitoring the heart and other vital functions.

If the evidence of recent phrase-making is to be relied on, a peculiarly modern fixation is prejudice – and, more specifically, the need to combat it. Racism and sexism are two obvious and well-established examples, but how about 'ageism' and 'ableism' and 'fattism'? And what about 'heightism' – defined as prejudicial treatment of a person on the grounds of their height? My favourite-ism is 'alphabetism', discrimination, believe it or not, against someone on the grounds of the initial letter of their surname. As a privileged B who never has to wait long in alphabetically-arranged lines and who is always towards the top of the list, I have discovered a new sympathy for all those Walkers, Youngs and Zimmermans who are waiting for their turn. Despite having 'turned over a new leaf' with this recent conversion to a non-alphabetist attitude to life, in the pages that follow I have decided to be somewhat 'old hat' and give you the words and phrases in traditional 'apple-pie order', running all too predictably from A to Z. To those of you who spot my errors of omission and commission, I say 'Please pardon by BOOBS.' To the gentleman reader, I say 'Right on, man'; and to the ladies, 'wham, bang, thank you, ma'am'. To one and all, whether kidult or Crumbly, 'common or garden punter' or 'man on the Clapham omnibus', I say 'ENJOY!'

A

A1 means first-rate, the very best, and derives from the rating given to ships in *Lloyd's Register of British and Foreign Shipping*, where the letters denoted the state of the ship itself and the figures the state of the ship's fittings – A1 therefore being the mark of the best. The expression was used at Lloyd's at least from the 1770s. Charles Dickens was the first person to use it in reference to people. In *The Pickwick Papers* Sam Weller describes a character as a 'first-rater'. 'A1', is the response of Mr Roker.

AC/DC. Bisexual, practising both homosexual and heterosexual intercourse – by analogy with electrical devices which are capable of operating with either type of electric current. *See also* AMBIDEXTROUS and SWING BOTH WAYS.

ADA. A computer programming language – the standard language adopted by the US Department of Defense – named after Ada Augusta, Countess Lovelace, who was Lord Byron's daughter and, as the colleague of Charles Babbage, was the first female computer scientist.

A.I.D. Artificial Insemination by Donor. A process used by women and couples in which the man is unable to father a child, whereby the woman is artificially impregnated with donated sperm, often from a sperm bank. Not to be confused with AIDS.

à la carte. A menu of varied dishes offered in a restaurant, each of them prepared to order. It is French for 'according to the menu card' and is the opposite of the **table d'hôte** menu, translated as 'the table of the host'. The table d'hôte menu consists of a limited selection of dishes, mostly prepared in advance. Dining à la carte is more expensive. Recently the expression has been used in the names of a number of businesses keen to promote the image of personal attention and unique results. Among other things, one can now buy cosmetics, clothing and interior decoration and hairdressing services à la carte, i.e. to suit individual requirements. Such services are not cheap.

A-O.K. means 'first-class', 'great', 'better than O.K.'. It is widely believed to have originated from the American astronaut Alan Shepard during the first suborbital space flight (1961). In fact Shepard simply said 'O.K.', but did so with so much zest that the NASA public relations officer heard it as A-O.K. and reported it as such. Even though this expression came into being by accident, it was subsequently consciously cultivated by Shepard's fellow astronauts and others involved in the space programme. *See also* BAD, CRUCIAL, FAB.

ableism. Discrimination against the disabled and in favour of the able-bodied, specifically in the workplace.

Coined in the 1980s by analogy with racism, SEXISM etc, it is said to have originated in America and, according to *The Daily Telegraph*, was first used in Britain in a press release issued by London's Haringey Council. Haringey having the reputation of being a LOONY LEFT borough, both the word ableism and the concept behind it were greeted with ridicule. *See also* AGEISM.

Abominable Snowman. Also known as the YETI, an elusive (some would say mythical) hairy man-like creature living among the snowy peaks of the Himalayas. The term came into popular use following Eric Shipton's Everest Expedition of 1951. Shipton, with his companions Michael Ward and Sen Tensing, discovered tracks in the snow at an altitude of 18,000 feet. The tracks, of a creature that walked like a man and must have been about eight feet tall, continued for a mile and then disappeared in some ice. Since then many other Himalayan explorers have discovered similar tracks. In 1970 the well-known British mountaineer Don Whillans, after photographing similar tracks in the mountains of Nepal, saw in the bright moonlight a creature like an ape moving on all fours. There are also many reports from natives of the area concerning a race of giant wild men. *See also* BIGFOOT.

above-board, meaning honest, is an expression originally used in 16th-century gambling circles. In an attempt to prevent cheating and promote an honest game, card players were encouraged to keep their hands above the table, or board, at which they played. Those whose hands strayed **under the table** were suspected of dishonestly swapping their cards. The word **underhand** may also have originated in this card-playing setting; it has been suggested that it refers to the habit of 'palming' a playing card that has been hidden on the underside of the hand.

above the line is a term used in the business world to describe marketing activity through the mass media. This includes advertising on television, in the Press and on posters. **Below the line** advertising is, in contrast, selective marketing activity through on-pack sales promotions and direct mail. In the media world these phrases have a different meaning. Above the line is used to describe the indispensable creative force behind a film, TV advert or production including directors, producers, writers and stars. Below the line is used to refer to the dispensable personnel who work on such projects – hairdressers, lighting technicians etc, all of whom can be easily replaced.

abracadabra. A magical charm believed to be made up of the Hebrew initials for the words Father, Son and Holy Spirit. The earliest reference to it occurs in the second century AD, in the writings of Severus Sammonicus who used it as a charm against malaria. It survives today as a popular incantation for those doing magic tricks.

abuse. A 1980s vogue word much abused by sociologists to describe various social problems – e.g. alcohol abuse (drunkenness), solvent abuse (glue-sniffing), drug abuse, child abuse, etc.

Acapulco gold. The name given to marijuana of a very high quality, which is grown near Acapulco in Mexico, and has leaves of a golden colour. *See also* GRASS, POT, REEFER.

accidentally on purpose. Something that is done deliberately, or even maliciously, but in such a way that it appears to be accidental. This expression, which seems thoroughly modern, in fact dates back to the 1880s.

according to Hoyle. Following the rules or established procedures; in the usual or correct way. Edmond Hoyle wrote *A Short Treatise on the Game of Whist* which was published in 1742. This book was very popular and became established as the absolute authority on the rules of the game. The name of the author thus became synonymous with the correct procedure to be followed, not just in the game of whist, but in any field of activity.

ace. (1) A unit or single point, as in cards, dice, dominoes, etc. – derived from the Latin word *as*, meaning 'unity'. (2) During World War I the French word *as*, applied to an airman who had shot down ten or more enemy aircraft, was imported into English as ace. Thence it came to be applied to any expert or someone of distinguished achievement in any field of activity. (3) In the early 1980s ace was a vogue word used by young people to express approval – in the long tradition of words like 'super', 'smashing', 'fab', 'brill', etc.

ace in the hole. Something important or of special effectiveness – a clever stratagem or argument, for example – that is not revealed and is kept in reserve for use when the time is right to bring success or victory. The expression comes from the game of stud poker. In this game, five cards are dealt to each player, the first round of cards being dealt face down and the remainder face up. So each player's hand consists of four cards visible to his opponents plus one – the 'hole' card – which he alone sees. If a player has one or more exposed aces plus an 'ace in the hole' he has a hand that is hard to beat.

Achilles' heel. One's only vulnerable spot. In Greek mythology Thetis, chief of the Nereids or sea-nymphs, in order to make her infant son Achilles invulnerable, took him by the heel and dipped him in the river Styx. The heel by which she held him, however, was untouched by the water, and so remained liable to injury. Later, when Achilles was fighting in the Trojan War, his mortal enemy Paris learned of this weak spot and deliberately aimed an arrow at Achilles' unprotected heel, thus causing his death.

acid. A term for the hallucinogenic drug LSD (lysergic acid diethylamide) which had a great vogue in the late 1960s.

acidfreak or **acidhead.** One who uses LSD habitually.

acid pad. A place, particularly someone's home, where LSD is used.

acid rock. A form of rock music, played very loudly, and often accompanied by weird lighting effects to suggest the hallucinatory effects of LSD. *See also* PSYCHEDELIC.

acid test. (1) A test that proves the worth, genuineness or reliability of something beyond all doubt. The phrase goes back to the Middle Ages when an object that might or might not be made of gold was tested by applying acid to it. Gold, the 'royal metal', is not affected by most acids but does react to 'aqua regia' – a mixture of concentrated nitric and hydrochloric acids. (2) In the 1960s in America an acid test was a party at which ACID (LSD) was added to the food or drink. The verb phrase 'to acid test' meant to provide PSYCHEDELIC effects such as strobe lighting. (3) In business jargon, the acid test is a measure of business solvency, involving the ratio of cash to liabilities.

acid – to put the acid on someone. An Australian slang phrase meaning to put pressure on someone for a loan or favour, particularly to do so in such a way as to yield immediate results.

3

actress – as the actress said to the bishop is an innuendo added after a perfectly ordinary statement to draw attention to its sexual double meaning. 'Actress' is here used as euphemism for 'prostitute' or HOOKER. Such innocent remarks as, 'It's too big to fit in,' or 'You can't have it both ways at once,' could be followed by, 'As the actress said to the bishop.' Although the phrase was first in recorded use in RAF circles in the 1940s it is said to be Edwardian in origin.

actressocracy is a derogatory term applied to those female members of the aristocracy who were once actresses, models or starlets and who have been ennobled only by virtue of marriage. Members of the actressocracy, the term implies, are not real aristocrats.

Adam's Ale (or, in Scotland, **Adam's Wine**) is a fanciful term for water as a beverage.

Adam's Apple. The protuberance of the thyroid cartilage in the front of the throat. The name derives from the legend that when Adam ate the forbidden fruit in the Garden of Eden a piece of the fruit stuck in his throat.

adult. In some modern contexts, a euphemism for 'obscene' or 'pornographic' – e.g. 'adult books', 'adult movies', 'adult entertainment'.

adultify, to. This new verb, which originated in the USA, describes the way in which, in recent years, the period of childhood has been steadily reduced. Today's children are adultified by exposure to television and the media and develop a degree of worldliness at an increasingly early age. *See also* KIDULT.

advertorial. Advertising material in a newspaper that is designed to resemble editorial matter. The name is a portmanteau word, combining 'advertisement' and 'editorial'.

aerial pingpong. An Australian term for Australian Rules football in which, unlike the European version of the game, high leaps and kicks feature strongly. Its first recorded use was in 1965.

aerobic is a scientific term used to describe those organisms or tissues which require free oxygen for respiration. According to sports scientists, aerobic exercise is useful in developing the heart muscles and lungs and improving the efficiency of the body's oxygen take-up. Jogging, swimming and cycling are said to be effective aerobic exercise if effort is maintained for a period of thirty minutes without a break. Other sports such as tennis, football and squash, though physically demanding, do not have the same beneficial aerobic effect. Aerobics is a shortened version of 'aerobic exercises,' part of the diet and exercise craze that swept the world during the 1980s. Popularised by the actress Jane Fonda, whose workout videos and books sold in their millions, it is a form of strenuous non-stop exercise to music practised mainly by women. The craze waned after 1986 with reports of injuries to the feet and shins and rumours that Miss Fonda, the aerobics guru, was herself suffering from heart problems.

Affluent Society, The. This was the title of a book published in 1958 by John Kenneth Galbraith, a Canadian political economist. In this book, which reached a wide readership, Galbraith commented on the contrast between 'private affluence and public squalor' in Western industrial democracies. The term passed into general usage as an encapsulated criticism of modern society.

affluenza. An American term coined by psychologists to describe the sometimes bizarre and disturbing changes that occur in an individual's personality as a result of their tremendous wealth.

Afro-Saxon. A black person considered by other blacks to be servile to whites or to be too anxious to emulate or adopt the standards of white society – in other words, a modern synonym for UNCLE TOM.

aftermath. Consequences – particularly, in current usage, the consequences of some destructive action. The original meaning, and one still in use in some rural areas, is 'a second crop of hay after one crop has already been cut in the same season'. *Math* comes from an old Teutonic root, meaning 'a mowing'. An alternative form of the word, in its agricultural sense, is 'lattermath'.

ageism. Discrimination against an individual on the grounds of age. Coined by Robert Butler, M.D., while he was director of the Institute of Aging, using analogy with racism and SEXISM. Ageism is most often applied to discrimination against those of advanced age, particularly in the job market. An extreme example occurred in 1986 when it was revealed that at its factory in Wales the Japanese company Hitachi was attempting to arrange early retirement for workers over the age of thirty-five. *See also* ABLEISM.

agonizing reappraisal. This popular cliché originated in a speech made at a NATO meeting in December 1954 by US Secretary of State John Foster Dulles.

ahead of the game. A common cliché in modern American English, it means simply 'in a position of advantage; in a winning position'.

Aids. An acronym for Acquired Immune Deficiency Syndrome (or Acquired Immunodeficiency Syndrome as it should more accurately be called.) A serious and often fatal disease that leads to the breakdown of the body's auto-immune system. Aids was first properly recognised in Africa in 1980 and was later found to have spread to New York and San Francisco, where its prevalence among the gay community led to the nickname 'the gay plague'. Further research showed that the disease was being transmitted in blood and other body fluids, and that while haemophiliacs and intravenous drug users were among those most at risk, heterosexual sex with an infected person was also dangerous. In 1986–7 there were widespread Aids education campaigns throughout Europe and America aimed at educating people about what has been called 'the greatest threat to human life since the Black Death.' Nowhere was the campaign more hard-hitting than in Britain, where the word CONDOM has subsequently achieved a new respectability. As yet there is no cure for the disease, though medical research suggests that it may be caused by a virus.

Aids terrorist. A person infected with the Aids virus who knowingly has unprotected sex with the intention of infecting their partners.

album. This word comes from the neuter form of the Latin adjective meaning 'white'. Among the Romans an album was a white tablet on which edicts and other public notices were recorded. In English, it came to mean a book containing blank pages in which things were to be inserted – a stamp album, photograph album, autograph album, etc. Later it came to mean a book-like folder containing two or more gramophone records. Later still it came to be used of any long-playing gramophone record (earlier called an L.P.) as opposed to a **single** which contains only one song or musical track on each side.

alibi. A Latin word simply meaning 'elsewhere'. It came to be used as a legal term for a defence by an accused person that he was elsewhere at the time of the offence with which he is charged. From this legal usage, it came into colloquial use meaning loosely any excuse or pretext.

Alice blue. The blue-grey shade named after Alice Roosevelt, daughter of President Theodore Roosevelt. Her fondness for this colour was celebrated in a popular song of the day, 'Alice Blue Gown', and brought the phrase into common use.

all chiefs and no Indians. A catch phrase used of a business or other organisation in which there are perceived to be too many people wanting to give orders and not enough people to do the actual work. The phrase is common in Britain and America, but the first recorded use is from Australia – it dates from around 1940.

All my eye and Betty Martin. This phrase, which means simply 'nonsense', is a bone of contention among etymologists. One account of the origin of this phrase, staunchly defended by some, ridiculed by others, is that it originated when a British sailor visited a church in Italy and overheard a beggar offering a prayer to St Martin beginning with the words 'O mihi, beate Martine' ('O grant me, blessed Martin') which sounded to the sailor like the nonsensical 'All my eye and Betty Martin'. Another improbable theory is that the phrase derives from 'O mihi, Britomartis', Britomartis being the name of a Cretan goddess associated with the sun worship of the Phoenicians who had trading links with ancient Cornwall. Variations of this phrase have been common in England since about 1770. Eric Partridge, in his *Dictionary of Catch Phrases*, is of the opinion that Betty Martin was a 'character' in the London of the 1770s, who left her mark on history only in this phrase.

all systems go is the phrase used by technicians and scientists at Cape Canaveral to describe the state of readiness of a rocket prior to launching. It was first used in the 1960s and came into popular use when the launches were broadcast on television. It is often used humorously, indicating a readiness to undertake some minor task. *See also* A-O.K.

allergy. An abnormally sensitive reaction to something. When used as a medical term it refers to the physical sensitivity of some people to certain foods, fabrics, dust, pollen or other substances. Hay fever is one of the most common allergies. Although medically recognised since the First World War, growing interest in environmental issues and the boom in alternative medicine brought allergies into fashion in the 1970s and 80s. In popular usage the word has come simply to mean an aversion to something. For example, 'Richard is allergic to exams.'

almighty dollar, The. This phrase may refer to the power of money to rule people's actions – or, in other contexts, to the ability of the USA to use its financial strength to influence world events. The phrase was first used by Washington Irving in his sketch *Wolfert's Roost, Creole Village* in 1837: 'The almighty dollar, that great object of universal devotion throughout our land . . .', although the phrase 'almighty gold' had been used by Ben Jonson in a similar sense almost two hundred years earlier.

alphabetism. Coined originally as a parody of other 'isms', alphabetism – discrimination on the grounds of the first letter of one's surname – has turned out to have a surprisingly serious side. The Atkinsons, Brewers and Collins' of the world have, it seems, an unfair advantage over the Unwins, Vernons, Walkers and Youngs. The As, Bs and Cs are always at the top of the list, the first to be dealt with in queues that have been organised by alphabet, the first to be called to interviews or receive announcements and the first in telephone and address books; while the Us, Vs, Ws and Ys (not to mention the Xs and Zs) suffer the psychological disadvantage of always coming last. Whether their cause will be taken up by the LOONY LEFT remains to be seen, but the effects of alphabetism are already being studied by academics who have coined their own vocabulary to describe the alphabetical position of names. Thus those whose surnames begin with the letters A–F and U–Z are known as extremilexics, those beginning A–M are summilexics, while N–Z are fundilexics and G–T are medilexics. *See also* ABLEISM, AGEISM, SEXISM etc.

Alpha man. The idealised, fantasy male found in fiction but never in real life. The phrase was invented by psychologists to describe the classic romantic heroes of books such as *Pride and Prejudice*, *Jane Eyre* and *Gone With the Wind*. The Alpha man is by definition more attractive, more fascinating and more attuned to the female psyche than any real man could ever be.

also-ran. A loser, a competitor who didn't come close to winning the contest. It originated in the world of horse-racing, where racing results listed the first three horses past the post in order and then, under the heading Also-ran, mentioned the number of other competitors in the race. In America in 1904 it was used in a political context for the first time and since then has come into popular use to describe failed politicians, job candidates, sportsmen and anyone else who doesn't make the grade.

alternative. A vogue word used to describe anything novel, unconventional, fashionable or faddy – e.g. alternative lifestyle, alternative comedy, alternative diet, alternative religions.

Amazon. In Greek mythology, the Amazons were a race of female warriors, located variously in Scythia, Asia or Africa. They had their right breasts burnt off or cut off in order to make it easier to draw a bow. In Greek the word Amazon means 'without a breast'. In current usage, the word is used of a female soldier or a strong, vigorous or manlike woman. The river Amazon in South America was so called because the early Spanish explorers who discovered it claimed to have seen a race of female warriors in the region.

ambidextrous. As well as its traditional meaning of a person who is able to use both right and left hands with equal dexterity, it is also a modern euphemism for 'bisexual' – one who is sexually attracted to both men and women. This has in turn led to the punning variation ambisextrous. *See also* AC/DC.

ambulance chaser. The phrase originated in the USA in the late 1880s when unscrupulous lawyers started following ambulances from the scene of accidents in the hope of persuading the victims to let them represent them in a case for damages. They are still in action today. After the Union Carbide chemical factory disaster in Bhopal, India in December 1984 it was reported that a number of American lawyers had flown to India. Their intention was to persuade victims to sue Union Carbide through the American courts where they could expect to receive massive damages – and where the lawyers could rake-off a lucrative percentage of the award.

Amen corner. An American phrase referring to any group of devoted followers or fervent believers. The term derives from the custom in some churches of placing a bench for the deacons in a corner at the front of the congregation near the pulpit,

7

from which corner fervent cries of 'Amen' would be elicited by the preacher.

amok or **amuck.** In a frenzy – especially in the phrase 'to run amok' meaning to rush about in a murderous frenzy. The origin is the Malay word *amoq* meaning 'frenzied'. *See also* BERSERK.

anathema. In current usage, anything rejected as hateful or obnoxious. This word has an interesting history. In the original Greek it means 'an offering to the gods'. It later came to mean an evil offering, an execration or curse, and in the Catholic and Calvinistic Churches it was a solemn ecclesiastical denunciation involving excommunication and damnation.

And now for something completely different. This catch phrase, used with humorous intent to introduce a change of topic, originated with the BBC television series *Monty Python's Flying Circus*, in the late 1960s and early 1970s, in which it was used as a link between comedy sketches. For another catch phrase from the same series, *see* NUDGE NUDGE, WINK WINK.

Andrew, The. The British Royal Navy has become known as 'The Andrew' since the mid-1800s. Before that it was more specifically nicknamed The Andrew Miller in memory of an infamous press-gang leader who rounded up many a reluctant sailor to join the fleet.

Andromeda strain. Any strain of micro-organism, previously unknown to scientists, which could have catastrophic effects if disseminated. The expression comes from the title of a novel by American author Michael Crichton about a deadly new type of bacteria introduced into the environment by a space probe returning to earth.

angel. In the theatre world an angel is the name given to those who put the money up to finance the production of a play. It is probably derived from the phrase 'guardian angel'.

angel dust. A narcotic – the powdered form of PCP (phencyclipine) which is either sniffed or mixed with marijuana and smoked. The phrase is also sometimes used for a form of synthetic heroin.

angel – to write like an angel. *See under* WRITE.

angels on horseback. A dish consisting of oysters rolled in bacon, cooked on skewers, and served on toast. The name, which dates from the early 20th century, is a straight translation of the French *anges à cheval* – and doubtless refers to the 'heavenly' taste of this dish.

Angry Brigade, The. Name used by a radical group responsible for a number of bomb and firearm attacks in London in the early 1970s.

angry young man. A young man outspoken in his disgust at the social order and what his elders have made of it. The archetype was the character Jimmy Porter in John Osborne's 1956 play *Look Back In Anger*. The phrase did not occur in the play, but was first used in 1957 by a reporter in *The Daily Telegraph* to describe Osborne. It soon came into general use, often applied to a group of young writers of the time, several of them from provincial and working-class or lower middle-class backgrounds, who criticised or satirised the Establishment – writers such as John Wain, Colin Wilson and Kingsley Amis.

Annie Oakley. In America, any complimentary ticket or pass. Annie Oakley was the stage-name of Ohio-born Phoebe Annie Oakley Mozee (1860–1926). She was an expert markswoman, and toured in the 1880s and 1890s with the Wild West Show of William F. Cody, better known as Buffalo Bill. One of her famous feats of marksmanship was to toss a playing card (usually the five of hearts) into the air and shoot holes through all of its pips. The card thus ended up looking like a much-punched theatre ticket. The term was first used by circus performers to refer to their punched meal tickets, and then passed into general usage to refer to free railroad and press passes and subsequently to any free ticket or pass.

antimacassar. When fashionable Victorian gentlemen adopted the habit of dressing their hair with Macassar oil, originally imported from Makassar in Indonesia, Victorian housewives responded with antimacassars. These were pieces of washable fabric, often embroidered or decorated with lace, that were pinned to the backs of armchairs to protect the upholstery from being stained by the Macassar oil. They remained an essential part of drawing-room furnishings long after the disappearance of the hair oil for which they were originally named. In view of the latest fashion for slicked-back hairstyles, they may well be due for a revival.

antsy. Probably derived from the earlier phrase 'to have ants in one's pants', this expression originated in the USA in the late 1960s and means 'restless', 'disturbed', 'jittery' or 'nervous' – or, in some contexts, it may mean 'lustful' or 'sexually aroused'.

anything that can go wrong, will go wrong. Depending on where you come from this expression is known either as Murphy's Law (named, presumably after some inept person of that name) or Sod's Law. The phrase began life in scientific and engineering circles but has spread into common use among pessimists in all spheres.

apartheid. From the Afrikaaner word for 'apartness', apartheid is the official system of racial segregation maintained in South Africa for the purpose of preserving white supremacy. Policies have included the prohibition of mixed marriages, the creation of separate black townships and tribal homelands, the compulsory teaching of Afrikaans in African schools and the notorious 'pass laws', by which freedom of movement around the country was curtailed for blacks. Apartheid is, appropriately, correctly pronounced 'apart-hate'.

apparatchik. A staff member, aide or worker in a bureaucratic or political organisation – originally a Russian word meaning a Communist Party bureaucrat as distinct from an ordinary Party member.

apple of one's eye. Anything or anyone cherished and protected. Originally, the apple of the eye was the pupil and was so called because it was supposed to be a solid spherical object like an apple. Because it is an indispensable part and essential for sight, the apple of one's eye came to have its figurative meaning.

apple-pie bed. A bed in which, as a practical joke, the bottom sheet is doubled over so that the person using the bed cannot stretch out his legs in the normal way. The phrase is said to be a corruption of the French *nappe pliée* meaning 'a folded sheet'.

apple-pie order. Perfect order, with everything in its right place. The origin of the phrase is uncertain. It has been suggested that the origin is the French *nappes pliées* – 'folded linen' – compare apple-pie bed above. Other theories are that it comes from the old English phrase 'cap-à-pie' which came from the French and means 'from head to foot'; that it comes from 'alpha beta order'; or that it simply originated in the meticulous and methodical way in which New England housewives

9

made their apple pies, with perfectly crimped edges to the crust. I think we have to agree with the Oxford English Dictionary that the origin of the phrase is uncertain.

applesauce. An American expression, meaning nonsense, lies, exaggeration, pretentious talk or insincere flattery. The term originated in the early 1900s and derives from the custom of boarding-house keepers serving large portions of cheap apple sauce with meals, to make up for the lack of choicer (and more expensive) food.

Après moi le déluge is translated as 'After me the deluge', meaning 'I don't care what happens when I'm dead'. The phrase originated in a letter from Madame de Pompadour to Louis XV of France in which she wrote '*Aprés nous le déluge*', ('After us the deluge'). In her opinion, after Louis' reign, the existing order would collapse – as it did when Louis XVI was overthrown during the French Revolution.

Archer, London slang for a sum of £2,000, was named after Jeffrey Archer, novelist, playwright and one-time deputy chairman of the Conservative Party, who resigned from this position after being accused of paying a prostitute £2,000. Despite the fact that Mr Archer subsequently won a libel action against his accusers and received record damages in the process, his alleged indiscretion lives on in the English language.

Are you sitting comfortably? A jocular catch phrase used to introduce a speech or story. The full phrase is 'Are you sitting comfortably? Then I'll begin'. These words were invariably used to introduce the story that was a regular feature of the BBC children's radio programme *Listen With Mother* which began in January 1950. The phrase quickly passed into popular usage and is still current.

Armageddon is the name given in the Apocalypse (Revelations xvi, 14–16) to the site of the final battle on Judgement Day between the forces of good and evil. The name comes from the Hebrew *har megiddón*, 'mountain of Megiddon', near Samaria in Israel, which has been the scene of several real battles from pre-Christian times to World War I. In modern use, Armageddon is often used to refer to the prospect of a nuclear conflict which will annihilate all human life on earth.

Arthur or Martha. In Australian slang, 'not to know whether one is Arthur or Martha' means to be in a state of confusion.

artificial intelligence. Also known as A I, this is a computer term for programs that will enable machines to perform tasks such as understanding language, translating and communicating with people. For this the machines will need, to a certain extent, to 'think' for themselves and it is this capacity for thought that is described as 'artificial intelligence'. *See also* FIFTH GENERATION.

Ashes, The. A mythical prize contended for in cricket Test Matches between England and Australia. The phrase originated in 1882 when an English cricket team was beaten by Australia. *The Sporting Times* published a humorous obituary for English cricket, which included the words 'The body will be cremated and the ashes taken to Australia'. In the following year, however, England won and some Melbourne ladies presented the victorious English team with an urn containing the ashes of the stumps and bails. This urn was retained by the MCC at Lord's cricket ground – and it remains there still, even when Australia win a Test Match and 'regain The Ashes'.

aspro. Australian academic slang for

'associate professor' – a pun on the brand-name of a form of aspirin.

assassin. The original assassins were a sect of Muslim fanatics founded in Persia in the 11th century by Hassan ben Sabbah, who was known as the Old Man of the Mountain. They sought to dominate the Islamic world by a campaign of terrorism which spread through Persia and Iraq to Syria, until their reign of terror was ended in 1273. Their Arabic name was *hashishin*, derived from their habit of dosing themselves with hashish in preparation for their murderous attacks. An assassin, nowadays, is one who murders by surprise or secretly for reward or for political reasons, the victim usually being someone important such as a political leader. Assassination is regarded as a legitimate expression of dissent by many modern terrorists and extremist political groups.

assertiveness training is a form of training aimed at teaching people to act and express themselves with assertion, i.e. neither aggressively nor passively, but with straightforward confidence. Over the last decade it has become increasingly popular among women, with the result that it has been attacked by MALE CHAUVINIST PIGS who see it merely as a means of justifying female bossiness.

at sixes and sevens, meaning to be in a state of confusion, arose from a dispute between two of the great livery companies in medieval London, the Merchant Taylors and the Skinners. Both companies received their charters within a few days of each other in 1327, and because of this there was uncertainty about which of them should be sixth and which seventh in the order of precedence. The dispute lasted more than 150 years, during which time there were numerous fights and battles in which lives were lost. Eventually on 10 April 1484 the Mayor, Sir Robert Billesden, ended the conflict by deciding that the two companies should alternate between sixth and seventh places annually, and that each company should entertain the other at dinner each year. This tradition still holds and the sixth and seventh positions in the order of precedence are exchanged annually on Easter Sunday.

athlete's foot. In 1928 a copywriter was set the task of creating a catchy advertisement for a product called Absorbine Jr. This remedy was used for treating the unbearable itch of ringworm, which usually affected the skin of the feet and toes. Reasoning that this condition was often caught in the gym or the changing-room at sports venues, he coined the euphemism 'athlete's foot', which gave a glamorous image to a most unglamorous problem. The name caught on immediately and has been in use ever since.

-athon or -thon. A suffix, said to derive from 'marathon' and coined in the USA in the 1930s, indicating a feat of endurance. Such events are most often associated with raising money for charity. Examples of its use include telethon, swimathon and readathon.

Atlantic Charter. The name given to a declaration of war aims agreed between Roosevelt and Churchill in 1941. The phrase has since been revived from time to time to describe any agreement between the United States and its European allies.

Auld lang syne. Long ago; old times, particularly times remembered with fondness; old or long-established friendships. The literal meaning of this Scottish phrase is 'old long since'.

Auld Reekie. A nickname of Edinburgh old town, so called because it usually appeared to be covered by a cloud of 'reek' or smoke.

Aunt Tom. A woman who does not agree with or support the Feminist movement. This phrase is obviously derived by analogy from UNCLE TOM.

Auntie. Nickname, in Britain, of the British Broadcasting Corporation or, in Australia, of the Australian Broadcasting Commission.

Australian salute. A wave of the hand in front of the face to brush away flies – a common gesture in parts of Australia where insects are a great nuisance.

awshucksness. A lovely American word meaning modesty or bashfulness.

axel. A type of jumping movement in ice-skating. The term comes from the name of a Norwegian ice-skater Axel Paulsen (1855–1938).

Aztec two-step. Diarrhoea, especially as a result of eating foreign food – traditionally suffered by visitors to Mexico. Also known as **Montezuma's revenge**. The Mexicans themselves call the affliction *turista*. Various names are given to the same affliction suffered when visiting different countries – e.g. **Delhi belly**, **Hong Kong dog**.

B

B.O. stands for body odour – or, more specifically, bad body odour. It was first used in radio advertisements for Lifebuoy Health Soap in 1933.

baby boomer. A person born in the first ten years after World War II, when there was a rise in the birth-rate – a baby boom.

back-hander (1) The traditional shortened version of a back-handed compliment, meaning a badly-phrased compliment that sounds like criticism. This may be derived from the basic meaning of back-hand, a blow with the back of the hand, as in tennis; a back-handed compliment is an unorthodox blow that turns out not to be a blow after all. (2) Back-hander is also used for a bribe or payment made to obtain a service from, for example, a corrupt official. Used in this sense its meaning is probably derived from the way such a bribe is passed, with the money concealed in the palm and the back of the hand offered publicly to the individual accepting the bribe. *See also* UNDERHAND under ABOVE-BOARD.

back-seat driver. A car passenger who issues the driver with unwanted advice from the back seat.

back to square one means starting over; doing something again from the beginning because the previous attempt has failed. According to some authorities, this phrase derives from the early days of radio commentaries on football matches. To make the commentary easier to follow, a diagram of the pitch, divided into numbered squares, would be printed in the *Radio Times*, and the commentator would refer to these numbered squares. It seems much more likely, however, that the phrase originally had reference to the game of hopscotch or to games such as Snakes and Ladders which are played on boards with numbered squares, and in which an unlucky fall of the dice can take one back to the beginning – literally back to square one.

backlist is an expression used in publishing and marketing worlds to describe basic items that sell regularly throughout the year, year in and year out, without being affected by fashion or season.

backroom boys. People who work 'behind the scenes', particularly those engaged in research work. The phrase arose as a result of a speech made in 1941 by Lord Beaverbrook, Britain's Minister for Aircraft Production during World War II. Referring to the Research Department of the Air Ministry, he said, 'To whom must praise be given? I will tell you. It is the boys in the back room. They do not sit in the limelight, but they are the men who do the work'.

backwards at coming forward. Someone who is backwards at coming forward is shy and retiring, reluctant to draw attention to themselves. This phrase is usually used negatively ('He's not backwards at coming forward') to imply over-confidence.

backwards, to bend over. *See under* BEND.

bacon – to bring home the bacon means to win a prize or succeed at something. It probably dates back several centuries to the time when country fairs held competitions in which contestants tried to catch a greased pig. The winner took the animal home with him. It may also refer to the Dunmow Flitch, a tradition said to have been instituted by a noblewoman called Juga in the year 1111. Custom had it that any man who knelt on the stones outside Dunmow Church in Essex, and swore that for a year and a day his marriage had been entirely without strife, could claim a side of bacon (known as a flitch).

bacon – to save one's. This may refer to the centuries-old practice of carefully preserving bacon throughout the winter months, and in particular to saving it from the hungry household dogs. However, in modern usage it means to get oneself out of trouble or difficulty – often physical difficulty. It has therefore been suggested that 'bacon' was originally the Old English word *baec*, meaning back or body, and to save one's bacon originally had meant 'to avoid punishment'.

bad. Normally used to mean 'evil' and 'wicked', the use of the word bad to connote excellence began in black American jazz clubs in the 1950s and was adopted into teenage culture. In Britain it was adopted into use in the late 1980s, particularly after the success of Michael Jackson's hit album 'Bad'. *See also* CRUCIAL and WICKED.

bad egg. A nasty or disreputable person. Although there is no conclusive proof, the phrase may have derived from the metaphorical bad smell such a person leaves behind them – much as a real bad egg creates a bad smell. Appropriately enough, a **good egg** means a nice, reliable person.

bad news. A colloquial expression, originating in American, to describe any object, person or event that is disagreeable or an unpleasant surprise.

bad trip. An expression originating in the drug culture of the 1960s, it originally meant the experience of unpleasant, depressing or disturbing effects as a result of taking drugs, particularly LSD. It later came to be used of any unpleasant experience, occasion or situation. The expressions **bum trip** and **bummer** have the same origin and are used in the same sense.

badger game. The cruel old 'sport' of badger-baiting consisted of putting a badger in a hole or barrel and setting dogs on it to 'draw' or 'worry' it out. This was repeated over and over until the badger died. From this cruel practice came the verb 'to badger' meaning to pester, worry, annoy or importune persistently. In criminal slang it also meant to blackmail. Much later the name badger game was given to a particular form of blackmail that became prevalent in the United States. It was practised by a pair of male and female accomplices. A wealthy man is selected as the victim, and the woman entices him into an intimate relationship. When they are in bed together the male accomplice surprises them and pretends to be an outraged husband. The victim is then badgered into paying sums of money to avoid the disgrace of publicity or involvement in divorce proceedings.

badmouth. In American slang, to badmouth someone is to say uncomplimentary or libellous things about that person.

Baedeker. Karl Baedeker (1801–59) published his first travel guide book at Coblenz in 1839, the first of many. His authoritative guide books were the first to use one or more stars to indicate objects or places of interest. By the time of his death, his guide books covered most of Europe and had been published in several languages. In 1941–2 bombing raids by the Luftwaffe over England were called Baedeker raids, because the Germans – in revenge for British raids on Cologne and Lübeck – selected as targets sites of historical and cultural importance such as might be listed in Baedeker (e.g. Bath, Canterbury, Norwich).

baffle. Today this means simply to confuse or bewilder someone. Originally, however, it was a humiliating punishment meted out to medieval knights who had committed perjury or other misdeeds. Part of their punishment was to be hung upside down from a tree; a treatment guaranteed to leave anyone in a bewildered and confused state of mind.

bag lady is a female vagrant who carries her worldly goods around with her in shopping bags. The phrase was first coined in America in the 1960s and was originally shopping bag lady.

bag-man. In Britain this is a now little-used term for a commercial traveller. In the USA the word has the more sinister meaning of a person who collects money on behalf of extortionists or mobsters, maybe as part of a protection racket.

baggage. Applied to a woman, the word means a scheming or artful female. This dates from the time when armies went into action accompanied by their families and other camp-followers, including prostitutes. These women did not march with the men but moved with the baggage-train, hence the term.

Bailey bridge. A bridge made of prefabricated steel sections that are easily portable and capable of being erected very speedily. It was an invention of the British engineer Sir Donald Coleman Bailey, and was of great importance to the Allied war effort in World War II, particularly in the Normandy landings. Bailey is said to have first sketched his bridge on the back of an envelope. According to Field Marshal Montgomery, 'Without the Bailey bridge we should not have won the war'. Bailey bridges are still in use today, mainly for relief operations in flood and disaster areas.

baker's dozen. Thirteen instead of twelve. The phrase, according to most authorities, derives from a custom that developed in England in the 13th century. In 1266 the English parliament issued a law regulating the price and weight of bread. The penalties for giving short weight were very severe. Since bakers were not able to determine accurately the weight of every loaf they baked, it became a custom to add a thirteenth loaf – the 'inbread' or 'vantage loaf' – to every batch of a dozen ordered by a customer. This ensured that they did not inadvertently break the law.

baksheesh. A Persian word for a tip, present or gratuity. Travellers and businessmen in the Near East have found over the years that it is demanded as of right by servants, officials, etc., and it must be regarded as a necessary rather than a voluntary payment in order to obtain service or co-operation. *See also* BACK-HANDER, SLUSH FUND.

balaclava. *See under* CARDIGAN.

balance of power. A distribution and opposition of forces among sovereign states such that no single state has the power to dominate or endanger the independence of the others. Although this phrase seems particularly relevant to the modern situation in world politics, it goes back to at least the 16th century. The phrase appears in Sir Geoffrey Fenton's *The History of Guicciardini, Conteining the Warres of Italie* published in 1579. A modern variation of the phrase, with reference to the nuclear arms race, is the 'balance of terror'.

bald as a coot. This term is not so frequently heard now as it once was, but it is still used to describe someone who is completely bald. The expression is derived from the common coot, a bird whose distinctive white bill extends to form a shield on its head, giving the erroneous impression that it is bald. Some sources trace the origin of the phrase back as far as the 15th century.

balderdash. A polite euphemism for BALLS.

ball of fire. An expression, originating in the USA, used to describe someone with a great deal of energy and ability.

ball, to play. An Americanism meaning to co-operate or participate in something. It entered the language in the 1930s and derives from the playground, where kids often requested others to play ball with them, i.e. co-operate in a game of baseball.

balloon – when the balloon goes up means 'the first sign of trouble'. It is said to have originated during the First World War when the sight of observation balloons going up signalled to the men in the trenches that action was about to start.

ballpark figure. This expression originated in American business circles, but is now used much more widely. It means 'a rough estimate' or 'an approximate figure'.

balls has long been slang for 'testicles' in both Britain and America. It was in the USA in the 1930s that another meaning, that of having courage or guts, came into use. In Britain it can also mean 'rubbish' or 'nonsense', as

in the phrase, 'You're talking a load of balls.'

ballyhoo. Sensational publicity or advertising. There are several theories about the origin of the word, one being that it derives from the village of Ballyhooly in County Cork, Ireland, whose inhabitants had a reputation for rowdiness and noise. This gave rise to a common music-hall catchphrase 'the ballyhooly truth', which in turn was abbreviated to ballyhoo. Another theory is that it originated among circus performers, being a corruption of 'ballet whoop'. Yet another theory points to the cry of dervishes, '*B'allah hoo*' ('through God it is') who performed at the 1893 World Fair in Chicago. According to the Oxford English Dictionary, however, the origin of the word is *ballahou*, a native Central American word for a type of wood from which clumsy sailing vessels were made. The term was then applied to any badly-rigged vessel and gave rise to the expression 'ballyhoo of blazes' (a term that appears in one of Herman Melville's works in 1847) used by sailors to describe any ship they disliked.

balmy. *See* BARMY.

bamboo curtain. A phrase created by American publicists in the 1950s to describe the invisible barrier of secrecy between the West and China. It is the oriental parallel of the IRON CURTAIN, a phrase that dates back as far as 1817 but became popular when used by Winston Churchill in 1946. It denotes the barrier that exists between the west and the USSR and her Communist allies.

banana oil in American and Australian slang means cajolery; insincere flattery with an ulterior motive – equivalent to the English expression **soft soap**.

banana republic can be applied to any small and unstable country, particularly in Central or South America, whose economy is largely under the control of foreign companies and often reliant on fruit-growing. It was first used to describe Panama, where the American-owned United Fruit Company virtually controlled the country.

bandy. This word, used to describe a bow-legged person, can be traced back to the 17th century Irish game called Bandy. An early version of hockey, Bandy was played with curved sticks which resembled the shape of bow legs and thus the association came about. The game got its name from the way in which the ball was 'bandied' about the pitch as each team tried to get it into the opponent's goal. This gave rise to the phrases 'bandying words', meaning, 'having an argument' and 'I don't want to bandy words with you', meaning 'I don't want to wrangle with you.'

bang on. Something that is dead accurate or absolutely right for the occasion. The phrase was coined during World War II by bomber pilots and was originally 'bang on target' – meaning that a bomb had been dropped (and presumably gone 'bang') exactly as planned.

bank holiday. The Oxford English Dictionary defines the term, in use since 1871, as a statutory public holiday when banks are closed. In Britain there are currently eight regular days of holiday each year. The phrase apparently had its American origins in the 1932 Depression when a run on American banks put many of them out of business and fuelled financial panic. In an attempt to stabilise the situation, President Roosevelt announced that all American banks would be closed for a period of four days to give time for the Emergency Banking Act to be passed.

bankable. A bankable movie star is one whose popularity is riding so high that simply by casting him or her in a role the producers can guarantee raising enough money to make the film. Among the most bankable stars of the last few years have been Clint Eastwood, Robert Redford, Harrison Ford, Sylvester Stallone and Eddie Murphy.

bankrupt. In medieval Italy, moneylenders ran their businesses from a bench or table. The word for this item was *banco*, from which the English word bank is derived. When a moneylender went out of business he was legally required to break up the bench and became *bancorotto*, which was later Anglicised as bankrupt. Although not on record, it seems likely that the phrase **to go broke** may also originate from the practice of breaking up the dealing table.

banshee. An Irish ghost or spirit who usually takes the form of a woman, sometimes a beautiful young girl and at other times an ancient crone. When the banshee wailed Irish families were filled with dread, for the sound is a warning that one of their number will soon die. Belief in banshees having waned somewhat, the expression is usually applied as a derogatory description of a woman's shouts or screams or sometimes even of a bad singing voice. A shrill cry or an off-key singer may elicit the response, 'Stop wailing like a banshee!'

banzai. A traditional Japanese felicitation meaning 'May you live forever', it took on a new shade of meaning in World War II when it was used as a war-cry by Japanese soldiers making bayonet charges. Apparently it may also mean 'forward!' or 'attack!'.

baptism of fire. This expression referred originally to those Christian martyrs who were burned for their beliefs. It retained this meaning until, according to some sources, an incident in 1870 when Napoleon III decided to give his fourteen-year-old son a taste of war by sending him into battle. Anticipating the worst, the French referred to this decision as the boy's baptism of fire. Fortunately he survived and since that time the phrase has been used to describe a soldier's first experience of battle. It is also loosely applied to any rude introduction to something new.

barbarian. Today we use the word to describe an uncultured or destructive person, but when it was originally coined by the Greeks it was used simply to denote foreigners who spoke in an unintelligible babble.

barbecue. An outdoor meal cooked over an open fire or the apparatus for producing such a meal. The word comes from the language of the Haitian Taino tribe, now extinct. Spanish pirates visiting Haiti in the 17th century found the natives cooking meat on a framework of sticks that they called a *barbecoa*. The word passed into the Spanish language, and then into English as barbecue. A recent development has been the use of the (often spelled Bar-B-Q) in the marketing of JUNK FOOD – e.g. 'Barbecue-flavour Crisps', 'Bar-B-Q Steakettes'.

barbie doll. American slang, dating from the late 1960s, for a bland, mindless, conformist person. The term is derived from the trade name of a blonde blue-eyed teenaged doll very popular with little girls.

bare – to go bare is a phrase from the world of insurance and applied mainly in the business area. It means to be without insurance cover.

bark up the wrong tree. To choose the wrong course of action or to misdirect one's effort. This phrase originated in America and was common in the early 19th century. It comes from the practice of using dogs to hunt racoons. Since racoons are nocturnal creatures they have to be hunted at night. When pursued by a 'coon dog' the racoon takes refuge in a tree, and the dog is trained to remain at the foot of the tree and bay until its master arrives to shoot the cornered prey. But if the dog mistakes the tree in which the racoon has hidden or if, in the dark, the racoon escapes through the branches to another tree, the dog is literally left 'barking up the wrong tree'. Davy Crockett used the phrase in 1833 in his *Sketches and Eccentricities*: '. . . he reminded me of the meanest thing on God's earth, an old coon dog, barking up the wrong tree'.

barley sugar. A variety of boiled sweet which takes its name not from barley but from the French phrase *sucre brûlé*, meaning 'burnt sugar'. Interestingly enough, barley sugar is sold in France not as *sucre brûlé* but as *sucre d'orge*, meaning literally 'barley sugar'.

barmy or **balmy.** A slang word meaning silly, stupid or mad. There are a couple of interesting but incorrect theories as to the derivation of the word. One is that it is a corruption of 'Bartholomew', St Bartholomew being the patron saint of the feeble-minded. The other theory is that it comes from the name of the Barming Heath lunatic asylum near Maidstone in Kent. The true derivation, according to the Oxford English Dictionary, is from an old English word 'barm' meaning yeast or froth; hence barmy meaning full of froth, and this seems to have been applied in a figurative sense to mean 'crazy'. The earliest recorded use of the word used in this way dates from the 1850s.

barnstormer. A strolling player; a second-rate actor, particularly one who badly overacts. The original barnstormers were groups of actors who roamed the countryside giving performances wherever they could attract an audience. Often a village barn was used as their temporary theatre. Towards the end of the 19th century the term was also applied to American political speakers who went on tour during election campaigns.

barrack. To barrack means to shout boisterously and derisively against a person or side engaged in a contest – particularly in the context of a cricket or football match. To barrack *for* someone, however, means to shout encouragement and approval. The expression seems to have originated in Australia in the 1880s. There is no evidence of any connection with the military term 'barracks' but the true origin is not exactly clear. The probable origin is the Australian Aboriginal word 'borak' meaning 'banter', but other suggestions are the Cockney slang word 'barickin' meaning 'nonsense' or the Northern Ireland dialect word 'baraking' meaning 'boastfulness'.

BASIC. A widely-used computer programming language. It was originally designed at Dartmouth College as a teaching aid to introduce students to the elements of programming, but it became so popular that it was adopted as the preferred programming language for many computers. The name is an acronym, standing for Beginners' All-purpose Symbolic Instruction Code.

bastard is an illegitimate child. It is derived from the Old French word *bast* for a pack-saddle. When mule drivers made camp for the night they would lay out the saddle and use it for a bed, and we must assume that on this makeshift mattress many an illegitimate child was conceived. The expression **born on the wrong side of the blanket** is a euphemism for

bastard, implying as it does an illicit liaison snatched on top of the bedcovers, while respectable married sex takes place beneath them.

bat – like a bat out of hell. This evocative phrase simply means 'to move extremely fast' – as, perhaps, one might expect bats to fly from hell. Its origin has yet to be discovered.

bats in one's belfry, to have. To be crazy, to have wild ideas. This alliterative phrase, which dates from around 1907, has clear parallels with another similar expression: to have a BEE IN ONE'S BONNET.

bath chair. A substantial, enclosed wheelchair made originally of wickerwork and used for transporting invalids or the infirm from their residences to the treatment baths in the English spa town of Bath. They gained popularity and were soon seen at other spas and seaside resorts frequented by invalids.

Bath Oliver. A dry biscuit invented in the 18th century by Dr William Oliver who founded the Royal Mineral Water Hospital in the spa town of Bath. On his death the recipe for these popular biscuits was left to his coachman. They are still manufactured today.

bathroom record. In American radio stations a disc jockey who experiences a call of nature may put on a bathroom record – a record or tape that will play for at least ten minutes, thus giving him time to UTILISE THE FACILITIES. British disc jockeys may use this method too, but as far as we know they have yet to invent a suitable expression for it.

battle-axe. A formidable, domineering woman. This slang word originated in America at the end of the 19th century. It has been suggested that the origin is the name of an American journal devoted to the women's rights movement, *The Battle Axe*.

battle royal. An expression used to

refer to a fracas or free-for-all contest. There are at least two conflicting theories about its derivation. One is the phrase was first used to describe medieval jousting tournaments in which each of the two competing sides was led by a king. However, according to Brewer it was originally a term used in cockfighting circles to describe a contest in which a number of birds were thrown into the ring at the same time. The lone survivor of the mêlée was said to be winner of the battle royal.

batty. This word, meaning 'crazy', is supposed by some to be derived from the name of an eccentric barrister in Spanish Town, Jamaica, called Fitzherbert Batty. He apparently attracted some public attention in London in 1839 when he was certified to be insane. Since there are no recorded uses of this word before 1927, however, the connection with Fitzherbert Batty must be judged to be rather dubious. It is much more likely that the word is simply derived from the expression TO HAVE BATS IN ONE'S BELFRY, perhaps influenced by other slang words with the same meaning which have the same '-tty' ending: potty, nutty, scatty, dotty.

beach bunny. This American slang expression is used to describe a girl who frequents beaches not to swim but to show off her figure in a swimsuit. It is also used of any girl who associates with surfers, whether or not she herself is a surfer.

beans, to spill the. No one is certain about the origin of the phrase, but it is known that an older expression, 'to know one's beans', means 'to know what's what'. It is perhaps from this that we get the idea of spilling the beans, meaning to reveal a secret, TO LET THE CAT OUT OF THE BAG. One source suggests that the phrase alludes to a person cooking a meal and refusing to tell the diners what to expect, then revealing the contents of the pot by accidentally spilling the beans. Another suggests that the phrase goes back to Greek times when members of secret societies would indicate whether they wanted a nominated new member to join by placing beans in a jar. A white bean was a yes vote, a black bean a no vote. Occasionally, it has been suggested, the jar would get knocked over and the beans would be spilled. Attractive though it is, most authorities suggest that it is just a load of POPPYCOCK.

bear is the Stock Exchange description of a dealer who predicts a fall in the market and consequently sells shares that he does not have. He gambles on the fact that by the time he has to deliver these shares the market will have fallen and he can buy them at a cheaper price than the one he sold at. It has been speculated that this use of the word may be connected with the old saying 'Selling the skin before you have caught the bear', i.e. ensuring a buyer before committing oneself. *See also* BULL and STAG.

bear the brunt. To take the main stress or force. Brunt can mean a blow, an onslaught or attack, but the origin of the word is not known. An early use of the phrase occurs in Robert Barret's *The Theorike and Praktike of Modern Warres* of 1598: 'The first three, five or seven rankes . . . do beare the chiefe brunt'.

bear trap. CB (citizen's band radio) jargon for a police radar unit designed to catch speeding drivers. *See also* SMOKY BEAR.

beard the lion in his den. To take on a brave or dangerous task; to defy a powerful foe on his own ground. Among many peoples, past and present, the beard has been seen as a sign of manly dignity. To pluck or touch someone's beard was an affront, hence the phrase 'to beard someone' came to mean to offer defiance. The first recorded example of the current phrase is in *Marmion*, written by Sir Walter Scott in 1808:

> . . . And dar'st thou then
> To beard the lion in his den,
> The Douglas in his hall?

Beat. The Beats or Beat Generation were a group of young people in California and elsewhere, belonging to the generation that came of age in the 1950s. The writer Jack Kerouac claimed to have invented the name Beat – it combined the senses of 'jazz rhythm' and 'exhausted' or 'frustrated', and according to Kerouac it also meant 'beatific' or 'blissfully happy'. The Beats adopted a bohemian lifestyle, wandered restlessly and rootlessly and resorted to oriental techniques of meditation, particularly Zen Buddhism. In some respects they were the forerunners of the HIPPIES of the 1960s. The word **Beatnik** was coined as an alternative to Beat by columnist Herb Caen of the *San Francisco Chronicle* in 1958.

beat about the bush. To approach an objective indirectly, cautiously or in a roundabout way, or to fail to come to the point; to prevaricate. The expression probably derives from the practice of hunters employing beaters who would flail at bushes, 'starting' birds or other game for the hunters to shoot at. The phrase was used as early as 1572 by the English author George Gascoigne:

> He bet about the bush, whyles other caught the birds.

Beatnik. *See under* BEAT.

beaver has several different meanings. In the USA it can mean a man's beard or the pubic hair and/or genitals of a woman. In the jargon of Citizen's Band radio it stands for any female, particularly one operating a CB radio. It is also slang for pornographic pictures and films. Phrases such as 'busy beaver' and 'beavering away', both of which are applied to busy, active people, have an obvious link with the animal of the same name, which spends so much of its time building and rebuilding its dam.

bed of roses and **bed of thorns.** The phrase of 'bed of roses' is used figuratively to describe a pleasant easy, comfortable life while a 'bed of thorns' means an extremely uncomfortable, worrying situation. Quite why a bed of roses should not also be a bed of thorns – for, after all, roses are known for their vicious thorns – is not clear.

bedlam. A scene of wild uproar, disorder and confusion. The word is a corruption of 'Bethlehem' and was originally the colloquial name given to the Hospital of St Mary of Bethlehem, a hospital for lunatics in the City of London. In the 17th century it was a popular pastime to visit the hospital (for an admission fee of twopence) where one could watch, jeer at and bait the unfortunate inmates.

bee in one's bonnet, to have a. To be somewhat crazy, especially on one particular topic; to be idiosyncratic or eccentric. Someone who has a bee in his bonnet is not quite as crazy as someone who has BATS IN THE BELFRY. The original expression, which dates back to the early 16th century, was 'to have a head full of bees'. The poet Robert Herrick (1591–1674), with his poem *Mad Maid's Song*, is said to be the source of the current expression.

bee's knees. Someone who thinks he is the bee's knees considers himself to be very clever or important. Quite where this saying originated is a mystery. It has been suggested that it refers to the clever way bees flex their knees in order to gather pollen from flowers. It seems equally likely that it is just a playful rhyming phrase which caught on because of the striking image it evokes.

beef. As a verb it means to complain or to make an unnecessary fuss; as a noun, a complaint or grievance. The word apparently originated in 19th century English criminal slang. The traditional cry of 'Stop thief!' was parodied as 'Hot beef!', and thus 'beefing' came to mean making a fuss.

Beefburger. *See under* HAMBURGER.

beefcake. *See under* CHEESECAKE.

Beefeaters. The nickname given to the Yeomen of the Guard (first formed as a royal bodyguard at the coronation of Henry VII in 1485) or the Yeomen Warders of the Tower of London (first appointed by Edward VI). It has been suggested that the word is a corruption of the French word *buffetier* – an official who served at a side table – but it is much more likely that it means simply 'an eater of beef'.

beef, where's the. This Americanism entered the language via a highly-successful advertising campaign for Wendy hamburgers. It featured a variety of characters, the most memorable being a little old lady, opening up hamburger buns, finding little or no meat, and demanding 'Where's the beef?' The expression is now in general use as an expression of disappointment at something that is weak, lacking punch.

begorra and **bejabbers.** Irish euphemisms for 'by God' and 'by Jesus' respectively. As they are both extremely mild epithets, even when used together they fail to make a great impact.

behind the eight-ball. This American phrase, meaning to be in a difficult or losing situation, comes from the game of Pool where it applies to the situation in which a player's ball is trapped behind the black eight ball which must not be hit. In Britain there is a direct parallel in the expression **snookered.**

below the line. *See under* ABOVE THE LINE.

belt, to hit below the. To deliver a mean blow; to fight unfairly. The expression dates from 1867 when the QUEENSBERRY RULES were introduced to regulate boxing matches. One of the new rules prohibited hitting an opponent below the belt line of his trunks.

bench warmer. A sporting term used to describe the substitute(s) in, for example, a football team, who is not required to play and thus spends his time sitting on the bench on the sidelines, keeping it warm.

bend over backwards, to. An exceptional effort to please or assist someone. It can carry the implication of going too far for one's own good.

benidormification. Coined in 1988, benidormification is a word used by those concerned with travel and tourism to describe the commercial spoiling of holiday resorts. Benidorm, once an attractive fishing village on the Spanish Costa Blanca, is the prime example of how over-commercialisation can ruin a place. Its proliferation of fish and chip shops, bars, cheap hotels and British-style pubs have spoiled any atmosphere or charm the resort once had and now succeed in drawing large numbers of low-budget tourists, many of them LAGER LOUTS, who have no interest in anything except sunbathing and cheap alcohol. Alarmed travel writers have recently accused Turkish entrepreneurs of benidorming their previously undeveloped resorts to attract tourists. Benidormification, it seems, is the inevitable price to be paid for mass tourism.

Benny. A stupid, slow-talking, slow-witted person. The expression derives from the now defunct British soap opera *Crossroads*, set in a Midlands motel, which featured a dim-witted but lovable character called Benny. The word is used by British troops stationed on the Falkland Islands to describe any native islander – a fact which causes understandable resentment.

berk is a British word meaning 'idiot'. It is commonly used by many people who would perhaps avoid it if they knew its origins. Berk is an abbreviation of the Cockney rhyming slang phrase Berkeley (or Berkshire) Hunt, meaning 'cunt'.

berserk. To be berserk is to be in a violent frenzy. The word can be traced back to Norse mythology, where Berserker was a furious warrior who went into battle without weapons or armour, wearing only his bearskin shirt. This characteristic gave him his name; Berserker in Norse means, literally, 'bear shirt'. This frenzied warrior had twelve sons who were all named Berserker and who fought in the same unusual manner. Hence, in Old English, the name Berserk or Beserker came to be applied to any fierce and reckless fighter. *See also* AMOK.

best bib and tucker. One's best or smartest clothes. In the 17th century a bib was a cloth, such as the upper part of an apron, worn by men or women, and extending from throat to waist. A tucker was a piece of lace worn by women within or around the top of the bodice. The expression was originally used only of women but later, when the literal meaning of the words were forgotten, it became applicable equally to men and women.

best years of our lives, the. An expression most used to describe retirement; the golden years of tranquillity after a lifetime's work. However, this romantic use of the phrase has sometimes annoyed retired people who, taking into account the aches and pains of old age, the lack of money and the loss of friends and a rewarding job, look back to their youth or childhood as the best years of their lives. Whatever its application, the phrase was penned by Robert Browning. He was fifty-two years old when he wrote it – not old enough, perhaps, to be qualified to pass judgment.

better – no better than she ought to be. A classic example of British understatement, for a woman described as such is sexually promiscuous, loose, a slag.

between the devil and the deep blue sea. In a hazardous or precarious position; between two equally severe dangers or difficulties; on the horns of a dilemma. This phrase was listed by James Kelly in his *Complete Collection of Scottish Proverbs* in 1721, but its earliest recorded use was a century earlier in Colonel Robert Monro's account of his service under Gustavus Adolphus of Sweden from 1621 to 1632: *His Expedition with the worthy Scots Regiment called Mac-Keyes Regiment.* Describing a situation in which he found himself being fired on not only by the enemy but also by the guns of his own side, he says: 'I with my partie, did lie on our poste, as betwixt the devill and the deep sea'. The devil referred to in the expression is not Satan, as one might suppose, but is a naval term for the seam between two planks in the deck of a wooden ship, specifically the long seam nearest either side of the ship. A sailor caulking the seams who was between the devil and the deep blue sea would be in an awkward position and in imminent danger of falling overboard.

beyond the pale. Socially or morally unacceptable. The word 'pale' (from the Latin *palus*, meaning a stake) means a fence or enclosure – hence, figuratively, any limit. In this phrase it means the limit of what is accepted as decent or tolerable.

bidet, which these days means a low basin over which one squats to wash one's genitals, has an amusing derivation. Originally the word applied to a horse so small that its riders were forced to draw up their legs or leave them dragging along the ground. When the new-fangled basins were introduced in the 17th century a perceptive person noticed the similarity between the squatting position necessary to ride such a horse and the posture adopted to use the basin – and thus the bidet got its name.

Big Apple, The. A nickname for the city of New York, current since the 1960s. It probably derives from the 1930s slang word 'apple' which, especially among jazz musicians, meant any district in which excitement was to be found or, more generally, any town or city.

Big Bang. (1) The cosmic explosion that marked the beginning of the universe, according to the Big Bang theory now accepted by most astrophysicists, as opposed to the Steady State theory, which says that the universe has always existed and has always been expanding with matter being created continuously and spontaneously. (2) The deregulation of the London Stock Exchange in October 1986 that allowed foreign institutions to become full members of the Stock Exchange for the first time, replaced fixed charges on securities trading by negotiated commissions, abandoned rigid distinctions between banking, broking and jobbing, and introduced dealing via computer networks instead of on the floor of the Exchange.

Big Brother. Personification of a police state or authoritarian regime, as in 'Big Brother is watching you'. The phrase comes from George Orwell's anti-utopian novel *1984*, which was first published in 1949.

big cheese. This common American expression meaning 'the boss' or a person of importance, has nothing at all to do with cheese. It is derived from a now obsolete British term 'the cheese', meaning 'the best thing'. This was in turn an import from India, where the Urdu word *chiz*, meaning 'thing', had been corrupted to 'cheese'. Other 'big' words which mean the same are big gun, big noise, BIG SHOT and BIG-WIG.

big deal. A colloquial expression, originating in America, to express the fact that one is unimpressed by some information. For example, 'So you're a pop star – big deal!'.

Big Ditch, The. American epithet which may apply to the Atlantic Ocean, the Erie Canal or the Panama Canal.

big shot. A person of importance. This is perhaps the most common of many similar expressions with the same meaning – e.g. big bug, big-dome, big doolie, big enchilada, big fish, big frog, big gun, big man, big noise, big wheel, big-wig. *See also* BIG CHEESE.

big-time, to hit the. In any profession or walk of life, someone who is said to have hit the big-time has made it to the top. He or she is likely to be making big money and dealing with BIG-WIGS, BIG CHEESES, big guns or BIG SHOTS. Those who fail to 'make it big' remain small-timers, and if such people are contented with their lot they may simply shrug their shoulders and say BIG DEAL! i.e. 'So what?'

big-wig, used to describe a person of importance, dates from the time when only judges, bishops and members of the aristocracy were allowed to wear the long wigs that are still worn by British judges today. Anyone who wore such a wig was, necessarily, important.

Bigfoot. The name given to a legendary race of hairy giants inhabiting the western parts of North America, and similar in many respects to the ABOMINABLE SNOWMAN or Yeti. Early settlers in the region were told by local tribes about this creature, which is inclined to abduct human beings, and which the Indians of British Columbia called the Sasquatch. There have been many reported sightings in British Columbia, Oregon, Washington and California, and the evidence for the existence of these creatures has been investigated by eminent anthropologists, but – as in the case of the Loch Ness Monster – there yet remains ample scope for scepticism.

bikini. An abbreviated two-piece swimsuit for women. Bikini Atoll in the Marshall Islands of the Pacific was the location for a series of American atomic bomb tests in 1946. While these tests were being conducted – and making newspaper headlines – this new daring style of swimwear (originally called *le minimum*) appeared in France. The name bikini became applied to the swimsuit – probably because of its 'explosive effect, but there may also have been some idea of a connection between the smallness of the atom and the brevity of the costume. More recently, with the increasing acceptance of women going 'topless' on beaches, we have seen the introduction of the 'monokini', which consists of only the lower part of a bikini.

billion. In American English a billion is a thousand million. In British English a billion, until recently, has always been a million million – and this is in line with the usage of other European countries. In fact there is a little-used English word – milliard –

which means a thousand million. However, there seems to be an increasing trend in Britain for acceptance of the American meaning which means that the word is virtually useless in most contexts unless it is made clear which meaning is intended. Related words such as 'trillion' and 'zillion' have no precise meaning.

bimbo is an American slang term dating from the early 1900s. Originally a corruption of the Italian word *bambino*, meaning little child, it has several uses. It may mean a baby. It may mean a man, a guy, a bozo – 'He's one helluva mean bimbo.' In modern usage it most commonly means a young, empty-headed, sexy woman, or a prostitute, a HOOKER.

Bingo. A popular gambling game requiring no skill. The origin of the name is not known, but it has had several other names. Before 1914 it was known variously as Keno, Beano or Loo. During World War I, as Housey-Housey, it was a popular pastime for soldiers. It was later a popular parlour game under the name Lotto. In the 1960s a Bingo craze swept Britain, and many cinemas were converted to Bingo Halls. It is still today a regular pastime for a large number of people who play it in Bingo Clubs, Working Men's Clubs, church halls, etc.

birder. A fanatical ornithologist or bird-watcher. He may also, but not necessarily, be a 'twitcher' or 'ticker', an equally fanatical bird enthusiast who is mainly concerned with collecting sightings of rare species. The twitcher or ticker keeps lists and ticks off each type of bird he spots. Most keep a year list, aiming to see as many species as possible within twelve months. Others keep a national list, with the aim of ticking off every breed of bird known to visit their country, while the wealthiest members of the clique keep what is known as a 'PE list', PE standing for Planet Earth. Their aim is to travel the world and tick off every known species.

biro. The proprietary name for a particular make of ball-point pen, also applied loosely to any make of ball-point pen. Laszlo Biro was a Hungarian who patented his invention of a ball-point pen in that country in 1938. Forced to flee from the Nazis, he emigrated to Argentina, continued his research and took out a patent there in 1943. At the end of World War II he found a British manufacturer to undertake production, but before this scheme got off the ground the company was taken over by the French firm of Bic, headed by Baron Biche. Thus the ballpoint pen came to be known in England as a Biro and in France as a Bic.

biscuit gets its name from the fact that it was cooked twice to make it hard and crisp, *bis cuit* being the French for 'cooked twice'. Biscuits were a staple part of the diet on board a ship and this special cooking enabled them to be kept for a considerable length of time.

bistro. Originally a small, unpretentious French cafe which served good, quickly prepared food at reasonable prices. In Britain in the 1960s and 70s it was fashionable to name any trendy restaurant with French-influenced food and decor (most notably red-and-white-checked tablecloths) a bistro. In the 1980s it went into decline as another French import, the brasserie, came into vogue. Definitions aside, the word bistro has an interesting derivation. It is said by some authorities to have originated when the Russians entered Paris in 1815. Restaurant owners anxious for custom would shout the Russian word *bistro*, meaning 'quick', in the hope of attracting diners who wanted a quick and cheap meal. This theory is questioned by other authorities who point out that the word is not to be found in written form until the 1880s. They suggest *bistouille* – the cheap, rough alcohol available in such cafes – as the bistro's origin.

bit. The basic unit of information in computing and telecommunications. It is a contraction of the phrase 'binary digit'. *See also* BYTE.

bite the dust. To be killed in battle; to fall in defeat. This phrase, so popular in stories about the Wild West, was popularised during World War II, particularly in RAF slang. The phrase has a longer history than one might imagine, and seems to have originated as a translation of a phrase in Homer's *Iliad*. William Cowper in his translation of 1791 has

. . . his friends around him, prone in dust, shall bite the ground . . .

The American poet William Cullen Bryant in his 1870 translation has

. . . his fellow warriors, many a one, Fall round him to the earth and bite the dust.

black books, to be in someone's. To have one's name recorded in someone's black books means to be in disgrace with them. The phrase may perhaps date back to the time when Oxford University undergraduates who misbehaved or broke college rules had their names written in the Proctor's black book. No one whose name appeared in it was allowed to receive a degree. Another theory points to the fact that around 1536 Henry VIII's agents compiled a number of critical reports on the English monasteries. These reports were known collectively as the Black Book. They were sent to Parliament where their influence was such that a law leading to the dissolution of the monasteries was passed, just as the king had intended. *See also* BLACK LIST.

black is beautiful. This slogan has been used by black people in the USA since the 1950s. There would seem to be little truth in the theory that it is derived from the biblical Song of Solomon: 'I am black but beautiful'.

black list. To be on such a list is to be out of favour with a person or organisation. Its source has been traced back to a list compiled by Charles II and containing the names of those judges and officials who had been involved in his father's trial and execution in 1649. When he was restored to the throne in 1660, after the death of Oliver Cromwell, Charles II set about tracing the people who appeared on his list. As a result thirteen of them were executed and others imprisoned for life.

Black Maria. A police van used for the conveyance of prisoners. The name is said to be derived from that of Maria Lee, a huge powerfully-built negress who was known familiarly as 'Black Maria' and who kept a boarding-house for sailors in Boston, Massachusetts in the early 1800s. She is said to have often assisted the police in removing drunk and disorderly customers and in escorting them to jail.

black sheep. A person who brings disgrace to his community or family (hence the expression 'black sheep of the family'). The phrase originated because black sheep were less valuable than white, their wool being too dark to dye. Popular superstition also had it that they carried the devil's mark and they were therefore unwelcome members of the flock.

blackball. To vote against or to veto; to ostracise; to reject someone as a member of a club or society. When candidates were proposed for membership of certain clubs in the 18th century, it was the custom for members to vote by dropping coloured

balls into an urn. A white ball signified a vote for the candidate, a black ball signified a vote against.

blanket. According to some authorities, blanket was coined eponymously for one Thomas Blanket, a 14th-century Bristol weaver who was one of the first people to weave the soft, thick woollen cloth that people adopted for covering their beds. In modern times, prisoners in Northern Ireland have drawn attention to their solitary confinement by staging 'on the blanket' protests. Such prisoners break their beds, foul their cells with urine and excreta and destroy their clothes, retaining just their blanket to wear and sleep in. **blanket, to be born on the wrong side of the.** *See* BASTARD.

blarney. In 1602 Cormach Macarthy was besieged in Blarney Castle near Cork, Ireland, by British forces led by Sir George Carew. Legend has it that during the negotiations Macarthy continually made promises to surrender; promises which Carew believed and relayed back to England, but which were inevitably broken. After some months of this persuasive talk Carew was a laughing stock and 'blarney' had become a by-word for smooth, flattering speech. Set high into the wall of the castle there is a stone with an inscription commemorating this event. Since the 17th century it has been said that anyone who climbs the wall and kisses the stone will inherit Cormach Macarthy's smooth tongue, and to this day anyone who has been gifted with unusual eloquence and persuasive skill may be said to have 'kissed the blarney stone.'

Blighty. A soldier's name for England or the homeland. Although the expression became widely used during World War I, it was first used by soldiers serving in India long before that. It comes from the Hindu word

27

bilayati, meaning 'foreign' or 'far away'.

blitz. Any sudden, overwhelming attack. In German, *blitzkrieg* means 'lightning war'. The word was used to describe the type of warfare planned by Hitler, using his superior airpower and armoured divisions to defeat his enemies at lightning speed. The contracted form blitz was first adopted into English to describe the series of air raids on London and other cities, and subsequently came to be used in a more figurative sense.

blockbuster. The British term for a giant bomb capable of destroying a whole 'block' during the Second World War. In modern usage it is applied to a hugely successful film (that may have people 'queuing around the block') or popular (and usually very thick) novel. It is tempting to link 'blockbuster' with 'bomb'. In Britain 'bomb' is traditionally used to denote the success of something: 'Tickets are going a bomb'. In the USA, however, a bomb means a disaster – the exact opposite of blockbuster.

blood and thunder. An epithet applied to novels, films, etc. that are melodramatic, violent and sensational. For particularly inept examples of this genre the Spoonerism 'Thud and Blunder' has been coined.

bloody is an expletive meaning 'very' or 'extremely'. It is used to emphasise the fact that one is angry or to add intensity to one's speech. There have been a number of theories for the derivation of the word, one of the most convincing being that it is a corruption of the phrase 'By our Lady', or that it is in some way connected with the 'bloods', aristocratic hooligans of 18th century London. It may also be derived from the idea of being covered in blood. Whichever definition is correct, it is interesting to note that it was an acceptable 18th century word and was not considered objectionable until the early 1800s. If it is true that bloody is a corruption of 'By our Lady' it would not be the only expletive to be derived from religious words or oaths. Crikey, it has been suggested, is a softened form of 'Christ'. Drat started life as 'God rot'. Gee may be an abbreviation of 'Jesus'. Gosh stands for 'God' and heck is a euphemism for 'hell'.

bloomer. In English slang, a mistake. It is derived from the phrase 'blooming error', in which blooming is a euphemism for BLOODY.

bloomers. Wide-legged, baggy trousers gathered at the ankle and named after the American woman who fought to make them fashionable, Amelia Jenks Bloomer. She is often falsely credited with having invented them, but that honour goes to Elizabeth Smith who designed them in 1850. Mrs Bloomer was an early and ardent feminist who encouraged a 'rational' style of dressing that included a loose skirt worn over bloomers to give greater freedom of movement. Rational dressing did not win many converts either in America or Britain, where she led a crusade, but the tendency of Mrs Bloomer's pantaloons to 'bloom out' in the wind *did* catch the attention of the public and the name stuck.

blotto. *See under* BRAHMS AND LISZT.

blow hot and cold, to. Someone who is inconsistent, forever changing their mind. The expression is said to be derived from one of the fables reputedly told by Aesop and involving a satyr who comes across a traveller blowing on his hands. 'Why are you doing that?' asks the satyr. The traveller explains that he is trying to keep his hands warm. Later the satyr offers him a hot drink and watches in amazement as he blows on that, too. 'I'm trying to cool it down,' explains the guest. The satyr throws him out of the cave on the grounds that he wants nothing to do with a person who can blow hot and cold from the same mouth. The expression caught on and now refers to an individual who says or does first one thing, then the opposite.

blow the whistle. To do this on someone means to betray them or inform against them. Although the origins of this phrase have not been recorded, it conjures up the image of a policeman with a whistle surprising a criminal whose plans have been betrayed by a WHISTLE-BLOWER.

blow up a storm. A phrase used by jazz musicians meaning to play an instrument with a great deal of skill and spirit.

blue, in the sense of 'obscene' or 'pornographic' (for example, blue movies), is said to be derived from a series of erotic books published in France in the early 19th century under the imprint *La Bibliothèque Bleu.*

blue-blooded, meaning 'aristocratic' and 'pure bred', was originally a Spanish term, *sangre azul*, used to distinguish the native, pale-skinned Castilian nobility from the darker-skinned Moors who ruled their country for several centuries. The expression refers to the fact that the Castilians' veins showed blue through their lighter skin.

blue chip. The highest-value chips in a game of poker are blue ones, and so it is that on the Stock Exchange the term for stock that performs consistently well and is a valuable investment is known as a 'blue chip'. Other phrases that originated around the gambling table include **the chips are down**, which we use to describe a testing situation. In the game of poker, once the chips are down, i.e. the bets have been laid, each player has to show his cards and discover who has won. From the same game comes the phrase **to cash in one's chips**, meaning 'to die'.

blue collar. *See under* PINK COLLAR.

blue-eyed boy. Why should people with blue eyes be considered better than those with brown or green ones? No one knows, for the origin of the phrase 'blue-eyed boy' has not been traced. We don't even know when it entered the language, simply that in figurative use it means a favourite man or boy, one destined for better things than his brown-eyed colleagues. In the USA the phrase 'fairhaired boy' means the same thing, which perhaps indicates that fair hair and blue eyes have long been considered a more attractive combination than other colourings. A blue-eyed boy is therefore more handsome than others and, by extension, considered superior in other ways.

blue meany. A cruel and unpleasant person. The term comes from the characters the Blue Meanies in the Beatles' animated film *Yellow Submarine.*

Blue Peter. A blue flag with a white rectangle in the centre, hoisted as a signal when a ship is about to sail. The word 'Peter' in this expression is not derived from the man's name but is a corruption of 'repeater' – the flag was originally used as a signal that a message had not been read and to request that the message be repeated.

Blue ribbon. Originally the ribbon of the Order of the Garter, Britain's highest order of knighthood, the term came to be applied to any high distinction or honour in any profession or field of endeavour. *See also* CORDON BLEU.

Blue sky laws. American state laws regulating the sale of securities and designed to protect investors from the promotion of fraudulent stocks. The first legislation to be so described

29

was in Kansas in 1912. The expression implies that without the protection of the legislation, naïve investors would be tricked into buying securities with as much value as a patch of 'blue sky'.

blue-stocking is a derogatory term used to describe an intellectual woman. It derives from a club founded in Venice in 1400 whose members, both male and female, wore blue stockings. In 1590 a similar society was founded in Paris and attracted a membership of female intellectuals who also wore blue hosiery. Then around 1750 the spotlight turned on London, where Mrs Elizabeth Montagu established a *salon* along French lines, inviting leading thinkers of the day to give talks and encouraging the discussion of ideas. Only one member of her clique wore blue stockings, and he was a man – Benjamin Stillingfleet. This fact was ignored by those who disapproved of Mrs Montagu and her feminist friends, all of whom were labelled 'blue-stockings'.

bluegrass. A type of grass with a bluish tinge that is found in the United States. This feature of the landscape gave Kentucky its nickname of 'the bluegrass state'. The term came to be applied to country music based on the songs and dances of the southern Appalachians, played at a fast tempo by unamplified string instruments, with the banjo playing a leading part.

blues. A state of depression or despondency. The term originated as a shortening of the expression 'blue devils', current in the 18th century and meaning 'low spirits'. Blues was used in this sense as early as 1807 by the American writer Washington Irving. Towards the end of the 19th century the term was first applied to a form of jazz music in the Southern states of the USA, that was based in part on traditional forms of Negro folk-songs about slavery and oppression. Traditionally blues music dealt with melancholy themes and was improvised.

bluff, to call someone's. This expression originated with the game of poker, in which players have to 'call' to make bets and attempt to bluff or deceive each other that they have a good hand of cards. To call someone's bluff means to make him reveal his hand and either prove he is genuine or expose his deception.

blurb. The publisher's promotional material on the dustjacket or cover of a book, purporting to describe the book, and often of a laudatory or eulogistic nature. The word was invented in 1907 by American humorist Gelett Burgess (1866–1951). He later defined it as 'self-praise, the noise made by a publisher'. The original blurb was designed for a special edition of his book *Are You A Bromide?* which was to be presented to booksellers attending the annual dinner of their trade association. Burgess designed a special bookjacket, featuring a portrait of a sickly-sweet young woman who was identified by the accompanying humorous text as a Miss Belinda Blurb. As a result of this book-jacket the word passed into the English language.

board, to go by the. Originally a nautical expression meaning 'to go overboard', the board being the side of the ship. Most things that went overboard were not retrieved, and it is in this sense that we use the phrase today. Something that goes by the board is abandoned; for example, 'In view of the latest statistics, our expectations have gone by the board.'

boards, to tread the. To act or appear on stage (the boards in question forming the stage itself).

bobby. Colloquial term for a British policeman. The name derives from

Sir Robert Peel (1788–1850) who established the Metropolitan Police in London in 1829. *See also* PEELER.

Bob's your uncle is a British catch phrase that has been in use since around 1890. It is used to mean 'everything will be all right' or applied when things turn out well, as in, for example, 'I'd just missed the bus and was going to be late when Bob's your uncle – another one turned up.' The phrase originated in 1887 when Arthur Balfour was appointed Secretary for Ireland by his uncle, Robert Cecil, the Prime Minister. Balfour was not highly regarded at the time and the appointment was interpreted as an act of nepotism. There was a great deal of adverse comment, which doubtless gave rise to the belief that so long as Bob's your uncle, everything is guaranteed to turn out all right.

bodice-ripper. A sensational historical novel in which the heroine normally has her bodice ripped from her by a series of villains, until at last the hero rescues her from a FATE WORSE THAN DEATH. *See also* ALPHA MAN and BLOCKBUSTER.

body worker. A modern American euphemism for a prostitute or HOOKER. In Britain prostitutes are sometimes known as **working women**. These terms have been coined by feminists as objective and non-derogatory alternatives to the dozens of existing euphemisms. Among them are 'whore', 'harlot', 'street-walker', 'tart', 'model', 'business girl' and 'call girl', an American euphemism dating back to 1935 when the widespread introduction of the telephone allowed a customer to call up when he required a prostitute's services. Such a client is known in the business as a 'trick', a 'punter' or a 'John', probably from the American **John Doe**, meaning 'the average guy'.

bogey. (1) in golfing circles a bogey signifies one stroke over par – par being the least number of strokes that a theoretical good average player would require to complete the hole. In Britain this theoretical golfer was given the name Colonel Bogey, after a popular song of the 1890s, and bogey came to mean par. However, American players preferred to stick with the original term. They used bogey to signify a score of one over par, i.e. one stroke more than a good average player would require, and this definition has since been adopted in Britain. (2) Bogey can also mean a cause of terror, whether of something imaginary like the bogeyman, a spooky figure often used as a threat against children, as in 'The bogeyman will get you', or something real as in, for example, examinations: 'I'm not bad at Maths, but Chemistry is my real bogey.' Used in this way, bogey is probably derived from the old word 'bug', meaning a ghost or hobgoblin. (3) A bogey is also English slang for a piece of solidified nasal mucus.

bogus. The derivation of this word, meaning 'false' or 'counterfeit', has been explained in so many different ways that some of them are bound to be bogus themselves. It could possibly have originated from the French word *bagasse*, meaning 'rubbish'. It may also, according to a newspaper published in Boston, Massachusetts in 1857, refer to the activities of a con-artist called Borghese who in the 1830s gained a reputation for supplying bank drafts made out to non-existent banks. His name was shortened to Bogus and, according to this account, his bank bills were known as Bogus currency. Other experts have traced a direct link to the Romany language of the gypsies in which *boghus* means a counterfeit coin, while those who like a more complicated explanation turn to a story in an Ohio paper in 1827. It reported the discovery of counterfeit coins so uncannily like the real thing that the counterfeiter was described as a BOGEYMAN. *See* BOGEY (2).

boloney. Most authorities agree that boloney in this American phrase refers to a kind of sausage called a bologna – Bologna in Italy being its place of origin. By the 1870s 'bologna' was being widely mispronounced as boloney and by the 1920s it was in general use to mean 'nonsense' or 'rubbish'. Whether this was because, like so many modern sausages, boloney contained nothing of nutritious value is not on the record. We do, however, know that Governor Alfred E. Smith of New York often used boloney to describe legislation he didn't like, and that his use of the word caught on. In Britain the word is often used in the phrase 'a load of boloney'.

bomb. In the figurative sense, as used in reference to the success or otherwise of a theatrical production or launch of a product, for example, bomb has traditionally had different meanings in Britain and America. In the USA a play that bombs (or is a bomb) is a total flop. In Britain it is a great success. However, this distinction seems to be changing and the American meaning is these days widely used on both sides of the Atlantic. *See also* BLOCKBUSTER.

bombay duck is not a duck, but a fish that is dried and eaten with curries. Although it was indeed originally exported from Bombay, its name is derived from the native word *bombila*, which also gives the fish its alternative English name of 'bummalo'.

bon viveur. In French bon viveur (or, sometimes bon vivant) means a 'good liver' – someone who lives well. It is often applied to those who enjoy fine food, wine and stimulating company, and who live life to the full.

bones – to make no bones about something means to accept it without hesitation or fuss. It may be an allusion to the ease with which a boneless piece of meat can be swallowed – while something containing bones takes more effort to get down.

bonk is a slang word meaning 'to hit lightly', as in 'a bonk on the head.' This traditional meaning of the word should not be confused with its more modern use in a phrase such as 'having a bonk', which means 'having sex'.

bonk journalism. The pages of the GUTTER PRESS are full of bonk journalism, stories purporting to reveal the private lives and sexual activities of well-known individuals. Bonk journalism is the staple material of tabloid newspapers and, as has been proved on several occasions, often has little basis in fact. Some of the most famous victims include Gary Hart and Sir Ralph Halpern, who hit the tabloid headlines because of their association with BIMBOS, Elton John, Russell Harty and England cricketers Ian Botham and Mike Gatting. *See also* BIMBO, GUTTER PRESS and KISS AND TELL.

booby. A fool or stupid person, the word dating from around 1600.

booby prize. A worthless item awarded to the person who comes last in a contest or event.

booby trap. Originally a practical joke played on an unsuspecting victim who, if the trick worked, was made to look a BOOBY. After World War I the phrase took on a new and more sinister meaning when it was applied to cleverly rigged explosive devices that were designed to go off unpredictably – for example, a booby-trapped bomb.

boogie-woogie. A type of jazz piano music popularised by black musicians in which the bass keeps up a steady rhythm of eight beats to the bar while the right hand improvises. Among its many other meanings in American slang, boogie stands for a black person.

bookworm. A person who spends a great deal of time reading books. The phrase is an allusion to the sustenance books provide both for the human bookworm and the various insects that live in and eat books.

boom, boom! A verbal flourish added after the punch line of a joke. It probably originated as an imitation of the drum beats from the orchestra used, particularly in American vaudeville, to add emphasis to a punch line. Billy Bennett, the British music-hall star, may have been the first to use the phrase. In the early 1970s it was popularised by its use on television by comedian Eric Morecambe and by the fox puppet Basil Brush.

boondocks. In the USA, wild isolated uncivilised country; any remote rural area; the 'sticks'. In Tagalog, the Indonesian language of the Philippines, *bundok* means 'mountain'. This word, corrupted to Boondocks, was adapted by American troops during the US occupation of the Philippines to mean wild, inaccessible terrain. When the troops returned to the US they used the word to describe the remote rural areas in which many training camps and military bases were situated.

boondoggle. A useless, unnecessary and wasteful task; work of little value, particularly 'make-work' projects provided by government to relieve unemployment. This word was coined by an American scoutmaster, Robert Link of Rochester, New York, for a lanyard made of plaited leather strips. The term was applied to any product of simple manual skill that was of little practical use and

later applied to the relief work provided by the US government under the New Deal to counter unemployment caused by the Great Depression of the 1930s.

boot, to get the. *See under* TO BE GIVEN ONE'S CARDS.

bootleg. A term used in Britain, in the rock music industry, to describe an illegally made and sold tape of a concert or recording session, while in the USA it is used to describe a move in American football.

bootlegger. It is often said that the American word bootlegger came into use during Prohibition in America, when smugglers hid illegal alcohol in the legs of their boots, but the word actually originated in the 1850s and is likely to have been coined when this method of concealment was used by people who traded with the Indians.

bootstraps, to pick oneself up by the. Tight-fitting, knee-length riding boots have always been difficult to pull on, which is why most of them come with two tabs at the top of the boot, one on each side. These enabled the wearer to pull them on more easily by hand or with the help of boot hooks which could be slipped through the tabs to give a better grip. The effort required for this operation might give one the sensation of being lifted off the ground, and it has been speculated that it was this feeling that inspired the phrase to pick oneself up by one's bootstraps, meaning to haul oneself up the social ladder, to raise oneself in the world by personal effort.

booze. Slang for alcohol. A boozer is a person who regularly drinks it. It has been in use since the 17th century and is probably derived from the Middle English word *bousen*, meaning 'to drink deeply', which itself is likely to have come from the same German word meaning 'to drink too much'. American sources also point to the existence of one Mr E. Booze, who in the 1840s was said to have distilled and sold alcohol under his own name. Since the word was in use before this time, it seems an unlikely but fascinating explanation of the word.

born-again. A born-again Christian is one who has undergone a renewal of faith so intense that it makes them feel a new person. Although used by evangelists for many years, the phrase only came into common use when Jimmy Carter, as presidential candidate, described himself as a born-again Christian. Some are so enthusiastic about their new lives that they make strenuous and not always welcome efforts to convert others. The phrase has therefore developed a facetious meaning. Born-again is also applied to anyone who has changed their life, or beliefs in other ways and wants others to do the same – for example, born-again vegetarians, non-smokers and exercise enthusiasts.

born on the wrong side of the blanket. *See under* BASTARD.

born on the wrong side of the tracks. When railroads were built throughout America they sometimes split a town into two halves, or at other times towns would spring up on either side of the track. In some of these places the wealthy people would find themselves congregating on one side of the line while the poorer inhabitants gathered on the other. If this happened, a child born to a family living in the seedier district could be said to have been born on the wrong side of the tracks. The phrase generally describes someone who is born poor and without social advantages.

born with a silver spoon in one's mouth. A lucky child born to wealthy parents. At christenings god-parents have traditionally presented a gift of a silver spoon to the baby, but the child of a wealthy family, where its inheritance is guaranteed from birth, is lucky enough not to need those gifts.

boss, meaning 'chief' or 'person in charge', has its origins in the Dutch word *baas,* for 'head of the household.' It caught on quickly in 18th century America where immigrant settlers were anxious to rid themselves of the hierarchical overtones of 'master'. From it we get the phrase **to boss someone about** or be **bossy,** i.e. to take charge and tell others what to do. In American slang it has been used for the last century to mean 'the greatest' or 'the best', hence the nickname of rock star Bruce 'The Boss' Springsteen.

bottle. This is a Cockney slang word with two opposite meanings. At one time it was used to mean 'fear' – from the rhyming slang phrase 'bottle of beer'. In current usage it means 'nerve' as in 'Don't lose your bottle'.

bottle, hit the. *See under* BRAHMS AND LISZT.

bottle, on the. *See under* BRAHMS AND LISZT.

bottom drawer. *See under* TOP DRAWER.

bottom line, the. Literally, the bottom line of a company's annual financial report, showing net profit. Figuratively, the final result of any activity; the basic or most important factor; the 'nitty gritty'.

bottom out. A business term to describe the point at which a slump hits its lowest point and, from there, can only recover. 'The fall is bottoming out' means that things will soon get better.

bottoms up. A traditional toast referring to the way in which the bottom of a glass is raised as it is emptied. **Cheers** is a similar toast and the two are sometimes linked in a phrase such as 'Cheers and bottoms up, everyone'. The phrase **Chin chin**, a synonym for Cheers, was popular in Britain around the 1920s and 30s and is still sometimes heard today. It derives from the Chinese phrase *t'sing t'sing*.

bowdlerize. In 1818 Dr Thomas Bowdler ensured his immortality by editing the works of Shakespeare so savagely that since his time to bowdlerize has been a synonym for prudish censorship. In the preface to his ten-volume work Dr Bowdler explained to his readers that, 'nothing is added to the original text; but those words are omitted which cannot with propricty bc rcad aloud in a family.' As might be imagined, this included a great deal of the Bard's text.

bowie knife. A strong hunting knife, with a blade ten to fifteen inches in length, curved and double-edged near the tip, with a hilt and cross-piece, and balanced for throwing. It was named after Colonel Jim Bowie (1796–1836), friend of Davy Crockett and hero of the battle of the Alamo. Although Jim Bowie popularised this type of knife and had his name associated with it, the actual inventor was his brother Rezln Pleasant Bowie.

bowler hat. Less commonly seen on London streets than in the past, a bowler hat is a hard rounded hat with a shallow brim, traditionally worn by city gentlemen and recently back in vogue among YOUNG FOGEYS. They came into being in 1850 when a Norfolk landowner called William Coke asked his hatter to make him a riding hat with a low crown so that it would not be knocked off by overhanging branches, as his ordinary tall riding hat was. Locks, the famous London hat-makers, obliged by producing the bowler, which took its name from the felt with which it was covered,

supplied by Thomas and William Bowler. This seems the most likely origin for the word but others have been suggested, including the possibility that it was invented by a hatmaker called Bowler and that its stiff, circular brim allows it to be bowled along the ground.

boycott. To coerce by combining to prevent any social or commercial dealings with a person, group or country. The term dates from 1880 when such tactics were used by the Irish Land League under Charles Parnell as part of the struggle for land reform. Landlords and their agents were much hated by the majority of the Irish people for their exploitation of the peasants. In a speech in September 1880 Parnell proposed that anyone who took over a farm from which a tenant had been evicted should be 'isolated from his kind as if he were a leper of old'. Charles Cunningham Boycott (1832–97), a retired English army captain, was land agent to Lord Erne for 1500 acres in County Mayo, on which there were thirty-eight tenant farmers. He was the first person on which the Land League's new tactics were tried. As he later reported to *The Times*, his servants were intimidated into leaving, local shopkeepers refused to supply his household, his crop and stock were stolen or destroyed, he received threatening letters and he was shot at on three occasions. Despite support from other landlords, Boycott was eventually forced to leave Ireland altogether. Thus Boycott gave his name to the English language.

bra. Delightful though it would be to believe that the bra was invented in 1912 by one Otto Titzling to provide support for a well-endowed opera singer, there is, sadly, no evidence to support the tale. Nor is there any proof of the accuracy of another theory which has it that the word was derived directly from the name of a French designer called Brassière, who sold them under his own name in the late 1920s. It seems more likely, though less interesting, that the word came from the French *bras* for 'arm'.

Brahms and Liszt. Cockney rhyming slang for pissed, i.e. drunk. It is just one of hundreds, possibly thousands, of English-language euphemisms relating to drinking and getting drunk. Following the rhyming example there are 'elephant's trunk' and 'tiddly' (from tiddlywinks, for 'drinks'). World War II was the origin of the words 'blitzed' and 'bombed', both describing the devastating effects of booze, while World War I gave us the less commonly used 'gassed', which turns on the similarity between someone paralytically drunk and a soldier gassed in the trenches. **Blotto** originated around the turn of the century and presumably alludes to the blotting paper-like way in which drinkers absorb alcohol. A heavy drinker may be **sozzled** or **on the bottle**; a nondrinker who **hits the bottle** in times of stress may be said to have **fallen off the wagon**. On a more up-beat note, a jolly drinker can be described as being **in his cups** – cups originally relating both to the drinking-vessel and the concoction it contained. Some who are merely merry rather than blind drunk can be said to be happy, tipsy, mellow or perhaps even tight, but not wrecked or ripped as young Americans might describe the experience of being smashed. Euphemisms alluding to the physical effects of alcohol include **to have a nose to light candles at**, **to have a nose that glows in the dark** or to be **lit up like a christmas tree**, while the American phrase **walking on rocky socks** goes some way to describing the gait of someone who is **pissed as**

a newt. The fact that this is just a small selection of the euphemisms applied to drinking and drunkenness goes some way to indicating its importance as a human activity.

brain drain. The continuing loss of a country's highly educated and qualified people (particularly scientists, technologists, doctors and university teachers) through emigration to other countries where they are paid more and facilities are better. This phenomenon has been noted in Britain since the 1950s, and the exodus has been mainly to the USA.

brainstorm. A fit of sudden craziness, forgetfulness or inspiration. **Brainstorming** is a method used in the business and marketing world for solving problems and coming up with new ideas. It is said to have been developed in the USA around 1953, when groups of people associated with a particular product or problem were for the first time gathered together for a session of 'thinking aloud'. Such creative, unstructured sessions are used today for, among other things, thinking up names for new products.

brainwashing. The process by which a person is systematically persuaded and indoctrinated in order to make them change their opinions. The expression came into use during the Korean War of 1950–3, when it was practised by the Chinese and North Koreans on American prisoners of war, some of whom transferred their loyalties to the other side. The phrase is a literal translation of the Mandarin Chinese *his* (to wash) *nao* (brain).

brand awareness. A phrase used in the marketing world to describe the degree to which consumers and retailers are aware of a brand's excellence or value. It is sometimes tested by means of market surveys before a product is heavily advertised and again afterwards, to see how much more awareness has been generated. In some cases advertising does not improve brand awareness. Several years ago in Britain the manufacturers of a well-known alcoholic drink produced several amusing and highly-regarded advertisements featuring soap-opera star Joan Collins and the late comic actor Leonard Rossiter. Despite the overwhelming popularity of these adverts they were withdrawn from the TV screen because research showed that very few viewers could remember the name of the drink they advertised.

branwagon. A jocular variation on the word 'bandwagon'. It is used sardonically to describe the growing trend towards healthy eating and high-fibre foods. *See also* MACRO-BIOTICS, MUESLI-BELT MALNUTRITION and WHOLEFOOD.

brass hat. A high-ranking military officer, so called because the masses of gold braid and gilt insignia on such an officer's dress cap made it shine like brass. One of the earliest literary uses of the phrase was in Rudyard Kipling's *Many Inventions* of 1893.

brass monkey weather. Extremely cold weather. The phrase is a shortened and polite version of 'It's cold enough to freeze the balls off a brass monkey.' There have been no truly convincing explanations of the origins of this expression, but one suggests that it might date back to the days when cannons were used aboard ships and the cannon balls were stored on a brass tray known as a monkey. In very cold weather, it's argued, ice would form and the tray would contract, pushing the stack apart.

brassed off. Disgruntled, bored, fed up. This expression, originally 1940s services slang, is a later variant of the expression BROWNED OFF.

brass tacks, to get down to. To get down to the essentials of something.

There are several theories about the origin of this phrase. One is that it is rhyming slang for 'hard facts'. Another points to the practice of using brass-headed tacks in upholstery; when an item of furniture was sent for reupholstering it was stripped down to brass tacks. It's more likely, however, that the expression dates back to the time when the counter in a draper's shop was marked off at intervals with brass tacks, each tack representing a measure against which cloth could be cut – at one yard, one-and-a-half yards, and so on. Customers might come into the shop to look at the fabrics, but only when they had decided to buy did the assistant get down to brass tacks by actually cutting and selling the required length.

Brat Pack. It can't have escaped the notice of many movie-goers in the mid-1980s that the most BANKABLE male movie stars were becoming distinctly middle-aged; Newman, Eastwood, Redford, Harrison Ford, Burt Reynolds – all of them were immensely popular but none of them had much youth following. Hollywood responded to this with a number of youth-orientated movies starring a new generation of YOUNG TURKS such as Emilio Estevez, Sean Penn, Charlie Sheen, Tom Cruise and Kiefer Sutherland, several of them being the offspring of ageing film stars. Together these youngsters were known as the Brat Pack and became renowned for their drinking, fights and other anti-social habits. This was nothing new, of course; in many ways they were only mirroring the exploits of earlier turbulent screen idols. But after the sedate style of Redford, Eastwood *et al.* the Brat Pack's headline-hitting exploits made them heroes with young audiences.

bread. This word is used in a wide

variety of expressions. Bread can be used generally to mean 'food' or the bare necessity for existence – hence the 17th century saying, **bread is the staff of life**. The phrase **to know which side one's bread is buttered** means to be aware of one's own best interests, while someone whose **bread is buttered on both sides** is a lucky person guaranteed to win either way. A **bread and butter letter** is a routine thank-you letter, perhaps for a gift or visit, written by those who know which side their bread is buttered. The bread and butter letter butters up the donor and ensures that there will be further gifts in the future. **To take the bread out of someone's mouth** means to deprive them of their income and therefore their food. And finally, since Roman times governments have offered their people **bread and circuses**, meaning food and entertainment, to distract them from rebellion. The slang word 'bread', meaning money, is derived from the Cockney rhyming phrase 'bread and honey'. *See also* BUTTER.

breadline, to be on the, means to be poor and on the verge of starvation. It is said by at least one authority that the word originated in New York during the 1870s when a bakery run by the Fleischmann family gained publicity for the freshness of its produce by giving away unsold bread to the needy each night. A queue of eligible poor formed each evening in the hope of receiving a loaf – hence the breadline.

breadwinner. The word, meaning a person who works to earn money to buy necessities, can be traced back to the Anglo-Saxon language in which *winnan* meant 'to work'. From this source we get 'win' and 'winner', meaning those who work hardest to achieve something. A breadwinner was originally a person who worked hard to obtain his daily bread.

brill. A vogue word among teenagers of the early 1980s, derived from 'brilliant', and used to describe anything admirable. *See also* BAD, CRUCIAL, FAB.

brinkmanship. Diplomacy or statesmanship that takes a nation to the brink of war in order to achieve its objectives. The expression was coined in 1956 by American statesman Adlai Stevenson to describe the policy of J. Foster Dulles.

broke, to go. *See under* BANKRUPT.

broker. A middle-man; one who buys in order to sell again, or one who buys and sells as an agent for others. This term is derived from the word 'broach', and originally meant someone who broached or opened up wine casks in order to sell the wine in smaller quantities.

Bronx cheer. A 'razz' or 'raspberry' – a vulgar sound of disapproval made by blowing with the tongue between the lips. The first recorded use of this expression was in 1929. It may have originated at baseball games at the Yankee Stadium in the Bronx area of New York City or at the National Theater there. There is another theory, however, that the origin of the expression has nothing to do with the Bronx but is a corruption of the Spanish word *branca*, meaning 'a rude shout'.

broom – A new broom sweeps cleanest. *See under* TO MAKE A CLEAN SWEEP.

brothel creepers. A British phrase to describe men's shoes, often made of suede, with thick crepe soles. They have always been associated with traditional rock and roll music and were worn in the 1950s by Teddy Boys. Elvis Presley's 'Blue Suede Shoes' may well have been brothel creepers. Quite where their colourful name originated is not clear, but the crepe soles were useful for creeping about silently.

brown-bagger. In British universities a brown-bagger was a studious undergraduate – a 'swot'. The expression was derived from the brown briefcase habitually carried by the serious student. In America a brown-bagger is a person who takes their lunch to work with them in a brown paper bag. The phrase is also used to describe a person so ugly that they should wear a brown paper bag over their head.

brown goods. Retailing industry jargon for furniture. **White goods** are refrigerators, washing machines and ovens.

browned off. Disgruntled, bored, fed up. This expression originated as army slang in about 1915. One theory for the origin of the phrase is that a 'brown' used to be Cockney slang for a penny and, originally, to be browned off meant to be given a penny to go away and stop being a nuisance.

brumby. An Australian term for a wild horse or, figuratively, someone with the characteristics of a wild horse – a MAVERICK. One theory for the origin of the expression is that it derives from the name of a Major William Brumby, a noted breeder of horses in Australia in the 19th century, some of whose stock escaped and ran wild. It is more likely, however, that it derives from the Aborigine word *booramby*, meaning 'wild'.

buck, to pass the. To avoid responsibility for something by passing it on to someone else. Although it seems generally accepted that the expression comes from the game of poker, there are two different explanations for it. According to one authority a buck was a marker passed from player to player during games to remind everyone of whose turn it was to deal next. Brewer, however, says that 'passing the buck' meant 'pas-

sing', or refusing to bid, in the game. From the same source we have the phrase **the buck stops here**, used famously by President Harry S. Truman. It indicates the acceptance of a person or an organisation that ultimate responsibility for a decision or policy lies with them – they can pass the buck no further.

bucket shop. In Britain today an agency selling cheap air tickets. Typically such agencies deal over the telephone from small offices and thus have a slightly shady image. In the USA the phrase is still used in its original sense of an illegal or shady brokerage operation in which dubious stocks, shares and real estate are sold to the public. There are two theories about its origin. The first is that it began in 1882 when the Chicago Board of Trade banned dealings in grain for quantities of less than 5,000 bushels. As a result, illegal brokerage firms began trading in smaller amounts or 'bucketfuls'. The second explanation is that it derives from an older American slang word, now obsolete, 'to bucket' meaning 'to cheat'.

buckle down. In modern English, to buckle down to something means to get on with it, however unpleasant it may be, without fuss. It is derived from the time when English knights would buckle on their armour in preparation for battle. *See also* BUTTON-DOWN.

Buckley's Chance. A forlorn hope; an extremely remote chance or no chance at all. It has been suggested that this Australian expression is derived from the name of William Buckley, a convict who escaped from the penal settlement of Port Philip in 1803 and lived for thirty-two years among the Aborigines. There is another, more convincing, theory that it originated as a pun on the name of the Melbourne business house of Buckley and Nunn – hence 'Buckley's chance or none'.

budget. Today it means the distribution of funds, but is derived from the word for a small leather bag known to the Romans as a *bulga*. This term passed into Old French as a *bouge*, known familiarly as a *bougette*. From here the word was borrowed into English where it became 'budget', the leather wallet from which a medieval Englishman counted out his cash. Centuries later, when the Chancellor of the Exchequer started the tradition of carrying the papers containing his annual estimate of revenues and expenditure into the House of Commons in a leather bag, he was said to 'open the Budget'.

bug. For such a small word, bug has an exceptionally long and varied history. It is likely to have been derived originally from the Welsh word *bwg* meaning a terrifying ghost or goblin-like creature. How it came to mean an insect is unclear, but the connection may be that in the past such things as spiders and earwigs terrified people much as they do now. The use of bug to mean a listening device may go back to the original idea of a ghost; an invisible entity that listens to conversations and, as a consequence, alarms people. The phrase 'bitten by a bug,' used to describe people who become obsessed by something ('She's been bitten by the aerobics bug') probably derives from the crazed itching that afflicted people infested with fleas. A person who repeatedly annoys another may be told 'don't bug me'. Some authorities trace this back to the West Indian word *bugu*, meaning 'annoy', or to an abbreviated version of BUGGER, but it may simply refer to the persistent annoyance caused by a flea or other biting bug. The use of bug to mean a defect or problem ('We have a bug in the new computer system') can prob-

ably be traced right back to the original Welsh meaning of a ghost or BOGEY. *See also* GREMLIN.

bugger. The word originates from the medieval Latin word *Bulgarus*, meaning a Bulgarian sodomite. It was first applied to Bulgarian heretics of the 11th century who were believed to be capable of any wickedness, including sodomy. From this specific meaning it came to be applied to anyone who practised sodomy, bestiality or other unnatural acts. So offensive was this word that for many years it was illegal even to print it. More recently it has fallen into robust colloquial use, and although in some areas it still causes offence, in the USA, Australia and northern England it is commonly used as an expletive or even with a mildly affectionate meaning, as in 'He's a little bugger', meaning 'He's a little scamp.' It also appears in phrases such as 'buggering about', meaning 'messing about', and 'bugger off', meaning to go away ('He's just buggered off home'), while 'to bugger something up' means to do it badly or make a mess of it.

buick. *See under* CHUNDER.

bull. (1) A speculator on the Stock Exchange who buys shares anticipating a rise in prices – the opposite of a BEAR. *See also* STAG. (2) Originally Army slang – a contraction of BULL-SHIT – for excessive spit and polish.

bull – to take the bull by the horns. Though people have been taking the bull by the horns for many centuries – for example, in ancient Crete bull-jumpers grabbed the horns and vaulted over them onto the bull's back – the expression seems only to have originated at the end of the last century and it is widely agreed refers to Spanish matadors who attempt to seize the bull by the horns as they make their passes. Applied figuratively, it means to approach something dangerous head-on; to bravely get to grips with something difficult or unpleasant.

bulldoze. To Negro slaves working on American plantations, a 'bulldosing' was a taste of the bull-hide whip and thus much to be feared. From this came the verb to bulldoze, meaning to override someone or something by brute force. From this root we now have the word bulldozer to describe massive machines that use sheer power to knock down buildings or scoop up the earth.

bullshit. Nonsense; pretentious talk. As a verb, it means to talk nonsense.

bullet, to bite the. To put up with something painful or difficult. It has been suggested that the expression was derived from the practice of giving an injured soldier a bullet to bite on while he bore the pain of an operation without the benefit of an anaesthetic.

bum. Since medieval days an expression meaning 'buttocks' or, less commonly, 'a drunk'. It has been considered vulgar since the 19th century but shows encouraging signs of making a comeback in England, at least in its primary sense. In America bum means a drunkard, a vagrant or a generally no-good person. From it we get the verb to bum, meaning to beg or ask a favour and the phrase bum around, meaning to hang around doing nothing.

bum steer. Originally American underworld slang of the early 1900s, this phrase means erroneous or misleading information or guidance.

bummer or **bum trip.** *See* BAD TRIP.

bum's rush, the. Throwing or pushing someone out by force, particularly from a restaurant or other public place – i.e. the sort of treatment meted out to a BUM (tramp). The phrase has come to signify, more generally, any abrupt dismissal.

bumf. Originally public school and services slang for lavatory paper, derived from the expression 'bum fodder'. The expression came to be applied disparagingly to any unnecessary documentation, publicity material, official correspondence, etc, all of which could be put to the same use.

bunch. The world's major supplier of commercial computer systems is IBM (International Business Machines). The next most important, but some way behind, is Digital Equipment Corporation. After these two come a number of computer manufacturers who are known collectively as the BUNCH. This is an acronym, formed from the initial letters of the companies concerned: Burroughs, Univac, NCR, Control Data and Honeywell. Burroughs and Univac have merged since the acronym was coined to form a company called Unisys, but the acronym is still in use although, strictly speaking, it should now be 'unch', which is not quite so meaningful.

bungalow. A small single-storey house. Originally it was a European residence in India – a building usually, though not always, of one storey with a thatched roof and a verandah all round it. The name comes from the native word *bangla*, meaning 'Bengali'.

bunk or **bunkum.** Bombastic oratory; nonsense; humbug; CLAPTRAP. This expression dates from about 1850. An American Congressman when censured for making a pointless and time-wasting speech retorted that he was not making the speech for the House but for Buncombe – Buncombe in North Carolina being the place where he was elected.

bureaucratese. *See* GOBBLEDY-GOOK.

burger. *See under* HAMBURGER.

burn – to burn one's fingers. This expression is an allusion to taking roast chestnuts from the fire and most authorities simply say that it means to suffer a loss. However, the image evoked by the phrase – of someone impatiently seizing a chestnut before it has time to cool – implies that those who get their fingers burned have only their own foolishness or impatience to blame. *See also* HOT CHESTNUT.

burn rubber, to. To leave in a hurry. The phrase derives from the scorching of tyres when a car accelerates very quickly.

burn the candle at both ends, to. This phrase has been traced back to the early 1600s, when it was an accusation of wastefulness. The meaning has gradually changed and today is someone guilty of trying to do too much and in danger of exhausting themselves as a result. The expression could typically be applied to someone who is juggling both a day and a night job, or whose late-night party-going is in conflict with their day-time occupation.

burn your boats, to. When Roman generals led an invasion they would sometimes order the boats in which the soldiers had travelled to be burned. This was done to impress on the troops the fact that they had no means of retreat; they had to conquer or die. **To burn your bridges behind you** is probably a more modern phrase, but likely to have the same military origin. Today we use both phrases to describe an irrevocable decision, one from which there can be no turning back.

burnout. Total exhaustion; the incapacity to carry on. It is a problem that occurs mainly to people in occupations involving a high degree of pressure, intellectual activity or emotional commitment – particularly those occupations in which a high degree of success is achieved at a young age but cannot be sustained.

Among those most likely to be affected are financial whizz-kids, brilliant mathematicians and young computer geniuses. Nurses, social workers and teachers can find themselves suffering from emotional burnout.

Burton, gone for a. A euphemism for dead or missing. It was coined in the Royal Air Force during the Second World War and is widely believed to have originated with this 1930s advertising slogan for Burton's beer: 'Where's Charlie? Gone for a Burton.' The link between the advert and the euphemistic explanation for someone's disappearance is obvious. The phrase can also refer to the disappearance of things other than people: 'My chances of getting that job have gone for a Burton.'

bury the hatchet. To settle differences and make peace; to let bygones be bygones. This expression, which a been recorded as early as the 18th century, refers to the customs of North American Indians. Hatchets, axes or tomahawks were among their principal weapons, and when peace was made between two tribes that had previously been at war, this was symbolised by burying the weapons of the two chiefs. Longfellow referred to this custom in the *Song of Hiawatha* in 1855:

Buried was the bloody hatchet;
Buried was the dreadful war club;
Buried were all warlike weapons,
And the war-cry was forgotten.
There was peace among the nations.

busboy. In American restaurants, an assistant waiter who clears tables and performs other chores. The expression comes from the 'bus' which was a sort of trolley used in restaurants for carrying dishes.

bush. Wild, uncultivated and sparsely populated country. This expression, which is widely used in Australia and in the USA, was imported from South Africa early in the

19th century, and is derived from the Dutch word *bosch*. In turn it gave rise to the Australian expression 'bushed,' meaning lost or confused.

Bush league. In the USA a baseball minor league of semi-professional teams – so called because they were out in the bush, not in the cities where the major professional teams played. The phrase later came to be used of anything amateur, mediocre or second-rate.

bush telegraph. An informant or chain of informants who warned outlaws of the movements of the police in the days when BUSHRANGERS were hunted through the Australian outback by the authorities. The expression now refers to the means by which rumours, gossip and information not officially disclosed is spread by word of mouth. To say that one heard something over the bush telegraph means to have heard it rumoured. *See also* GRAPEVINE.

bushranger. In the 19th century an escaped convict who lived in the wilds to evade capture by the police and survived by robbery. In modern use a bushranger is a criminal or someone who exploits and takes advantage of others. *See also* BUSH TELEGRAPH.

busman's holiday. Leisure time spent doing the same sort of work that one is engaged in as one's regular occupation. The first use of this expression in print was in 1921 when *The Times* referred to it as a proverbial expression. It is believed to derive from the days of horse-drawn buses, when some London drivers became so fond of their horses that on their days off they would ride as passengers to ensure that the drivers replacing them for the day took good care of the beasts.

butter-fingers. A clumsy person who drops things so often that it is suspected their fingers are greasy with butter. *See also* BREAD.

butter up, to. To flatter and cajole a person with the intention of winning them over. It may be an allusion to the way in which butter could be used to lubricate something, a lock or hinge perhaps, and make it work more easily.

butter wouldn't melt in her mouth. A phrase used to describe a woman so cool and serene that if a piece of butter was to be placed in her mouth it wouldn't melt. It was perhaps once a compliment, but today it is often used in a negative sense, as in 'She may look as if butter wouldn't melt in her mouth but . . .'.

button-down or **buttoned-down.** In American slang, the phrase means well-groomed, conservatively dressed, conventional, respectable. It derives from a style of shirt with buttoned-down collars that was once fashionable among business executives. In business jargon the phrase is also used to describe any formal bureaucratic style of organisation.

buttonhole. To buttonhole someone means to grab them actually or figuratively and hold on to them while one tries to tell or sell them something. The phrase started life as 'button-holding' because it was a button of a man's coat which was usually seized; more specifically, it was the button on the lapel of his coat, which enabled the lapels to be fastened across the neck in cold weather. At some time in the 19th century the fashion for lapel buttons faded and tailors left them off. They continued, however, to create the corresponding buttonhole. Thus to button-hold someone became to buttonhole them.

buzzword or **buzzphrase.** A fashionable word or phrase of jargon that a person uses to make himself seem up-to-date, informed or sophisticated. 1960s buzzwords included 'fab', 'hip' and 'groovy'. Buzz-phrases of the 80s might include 'power dressing', 'doing lunch' and 'streetwise'.

by and large means generally speaking; on the whole. This was originally a nautical expression, dating from the 17th century. In nautical speech, 'by' meant 'in the direction of' and 'large' meant 'before the wind'. By and large was a command given to the helmsman to steer slightly off the wind.

by-law. Local British law. The expression is derived from the Danish word *by*, meaning town. Such places as Whit*by* and Sel*by* were originally Danish settlements.

byte. A unit of storage or of information in a computer. A byte consists of eight BITS. The origin of the term is not known, but it is probably just an arbitrary variation of BIT.

C

cab. A shortened form of the word 'cabriolet' which was a light two-wheeled carriage drawn by a single horse. The word 'cabriolet' comes from the Italian *capriola*, meaning 'the playful leaping of a goat', the name deriving from the lightness and speed of the cabriolet compared to the types of vehicle that it superseded. The first cabs were licensed in London in 1823. *See also* TAXI.

cabal. A group of conspirators. The most famous cabal in history was a group of five ministers in the reign of Charles II. Among their other actions they secretly signed a treaty of alliance with France in 1672, without obtaining the approval of Parliament, and thus drew England into a war with Holland. The initial letters of the names of these five ministers – Clifford, Ashley, Buckingham, Arlington and Lauderdale – in fact spelled the word cabal. There is a popular misconception that this was the origin of the word. The fact is that this matter of the initials was a pure coincidence, though it did have the effect of giving the word a wide currency. In fact the word derives from the medieval Latin *cabbala*, which in turn comes from the Hebrew *qabbalah* – a traditional secret lore with theological, metaphysical and magical aspects based on supposed hidden meanings in the Bible.

cabbage. A word that has been used in the garment-cutting industry since around 1660 to describe the extra fabric left over after an order has been cut. A manufacturer might order a particular number of garments and buy a certain length of cloth to be used for the purpose. The garment-cutter will use his skill to cut the garments required out of a shorter length, thus leaving himself with enough spare fabric to cut out and make up extra garments that can be sold cheaply in street markets.

Cabinet. Members of a ruling council or government, derived from the Italian word *gabinetto* meaning a small room. A small private room was eminently suitable for such groups to hold their private discussions and it didn't take long for the members to become known by the name given to the place where they gathered.

caboodle. 'The whole caboodle' means 'the whole lot', 'the entire collection'. The phrase originated in the USA in the 1840s and is perhaps a corruption of 'the whole kit and boodle' – the word 'boodle' being derived from the Dutch word *boedel*, meaning 'household goods, possessions, property'.

cad. *See under* CADGE.

cadge. To beg or scrounge something. The verb derives from medieval pedlars' baskets, known as a cadges, in which they carried goods from door to door, wheedling, scrounging and begging as they went. From this we may get the word **cad**, meaning a thoroughly nasty and dishonest man – which is a good enough description of a cadger. Brewer, however, points to 'cadet' as the most likely derivation for cad.

Caesarean section. Most sources date this back to the birth of the Roman emperor Julius Caesar who, according to legend, was born by the method to which he gave his name, i.e. extracted from the womb via an incision through the abdominal wall. This is extremely unlikely. Before the advent of modern medicine such an operation would almost certainly have been fatal for the mother, and it was usually carried out only on dead or dying women. We know that Caesar's mother, Julia, survived into old age. Fascinating as this explanation may be, it is more probable that Caesarean section has its origin in the latin word *caesus*, past participle of the verb *caedere*, meaning 'to cut'.

cafeteria. A coffee house or small restaurant, especially a self-service restaurant. The term originated in America in the 19th century, and is of Spanish origin.

cahoots. In cahoots with someone means to be in partnership with them. The word is derived from the French *cahute*, meaning a small hut. Perhaps people in cahoots together shared the same *cahute*. Another derivation traces the source of the word back to cohort. A cohort was originally a body of Roman infantry between 300 and 600 strong, but by the 15th century the word meant 'a band of warriors' and later simply 'a band or group'.

Cajun. A member of a group of descendants of French Canadians who settled in Louisiana. It is used to describe their style of music and cooking. The word is a corruption of 'Acadian', Acadie being the French name for Nova Scotia. When the Cajuns were driven from their homes by the British in the 18th century, they moved south to Louisiana where they formed self-contained settlements and tended to keep themselves apart from other settlers in the area. Cajun music is a foot-tapping form of dance music, often with French vocals, the principal instruments employed being steel guitar, fiddle and accordion. Cajun food is distinguished by its spicy aromatic sauces.

cake, let them eat. This phrase was around long before Marie Antoinette was credited with using it in her reference to the starving Parisian proletariat, who could not afford to buy bread. In French the phrase is '*Qu'ils mangeant de la brioche*', which some experts translate as meaning that the peasants should eat the stale outer crust of the loaf as well as soft interior. Whatever the translation it was certainly a tactless remark, which is why others have claimed that it was part of a 'dirty tricks campaign' designed to discredit the queen and rouse feeling against her. The truth will probably never be known, but we have been left with the phrase 'let them eat cake' as a kind of flippant, unsympathetic observation to someone in trouble.

cake, that takes the. This expression alludes to the cakewalk, a competition popular among black slaves on Southern US plantations. Competitors vied with each other to walk in the most graceful or most eye-catching way, often making up their own complex steps and practically dancing their way around a cake that was, at the end of the event, given away to the winners. From this we get the phrase 'that takes the cake,' meaning 'that takes the prize', though today the expression is sometimes used with the implication that something is unbelievable, too much to be true.

cakes, to sell like hot. The smell of hot bread and cakes fresh from the baker's oven is bound to attract eager customers and this, probably, is the origin of 'to sell like hot cakes', i.e. to be extremely popular, in demand. American sources suggest that the phrase refers to pancakes and griddle scones, cooked in lard and sold while still hot at fairs and bazaars and snapped up by eager consumers.

call one's shots, to. To announce or explain what one is about to do. This American expression derives from the sport of target-shooting.

call the shots, to. Another American expression, not to be confused with the preceding. This expression means 'to be in charge'.

camp. As an adjective this may mean homosexual, effeminate or acting or speaking with exaggerated and flamboyant mannerisms. As a noun, it may mean homosexual or effeminate behaviour. In the arts it describes something that is so highly stylised, artificial or affected as to be laughable. As a verb, to camp or to 'camp it up' means to act ostentatiously and flamboyantly in any of the above senses.

can of worms. A situation that is full of difficulties and is impossible to control. This expression originated in the USA in the 1950s and became current in the UK in the late 1970s.

canary, to sing like a. *See under* SING.

cancel. When a medieval scribe made an error in the manuscript he was writing he would cross out the mistake by drawing short diagonal lines through the words concerned. These marks were known as *cancelli*, meaning 'lattices' because that was what they resembled. Eventually the word was shortened to become 'cancel'.

candid camera. A hidden camera which is used to take photographs of unsuspecting subjects going about their normal activities. The term is also used adjectivally to describe this style of photography or the resulting shots. The term became widely known in the 1960s when it was used as the title of a popular TV series, in which unsuspecting members of the public were set up in ludicrous situations in front of a hidden TV camera.

candidate. A person who seeks or is proposed for any office or appointment. The expression derives from the Latin word *candidatus*, meaning 'clothed in white'. In ancient Rome citizens who sought any high office – consul, questor, praetor, etc. – wore white togas to symbolise purity, fidelity and humility.

candle – to be unable to hold a candle to someone. Before the days of gas or electric lights, theatres employed boys to guide patrons round the auditorium with a candle. Out in the streets, too, servants were paid to light their masters' way through the darkness. This apparently simple job proved to be beyond the capabilities of some people; they got lost and caused so much inconvenience that it was said of them that they could not hold a candle to anyone. Today we still use the phrase to describe someone who is inferior to or less capable than another.

candle – to burn the candle at both ends. *See under* BURN.

candy. A slang term from the 1960s meaning variously cocaine or hashish, a sugar cube soaked with LSD, or any barbiturate drug.

canned laughter. A term, originating in the USA, for recorded laughter that is superimposed on the soundtrack of a TV comedy programme that has not itself been recorded in front of a live audience. *See also* ELECTRONIC SWEETENER.

canned music. The reproduction of recorded music, as opposed to the playing of live music, particularly when used in public or semi-public places such as restaurants, lifts, offices, etc. *See also* MUZAK.

cannon fodder. A phrase originating in the 1930s for men, especially young soldiers with little training, regarded by military commanders merely as material to be expended in war.

canter. Pilgrims travelling through the Kent countryside on their way to Canterbury Cathedral were supposed, according to tradition, to ride at a pace between a trot and a gallop. This pace became known as the Canterbury pace or the Canterbury gallop, and the phrase was eventually shortened to canter.

canvass. To canvass means to question people about their opinions and ideas. Canvassers are most evident during election campaigns, when their task is to discover the way in which people plan to vote so that the political parties can assess the popularity of their policies. The word originally meant a meticulous examination of details, deriving from the old French verb *canabasser*, meaning 'to sift through canvas'.

cap, to put on one's thinking. According to Brewer, this phrase refers to a judge's official cap which he wore while considering the appropriate sentence to impose on an offender. Other suggestions include the speculation that a thinking cap was the kind of square cap worn by lawyers, scholars and members of the clergy, all of whom were considered intelligent and thoughtful. Whatever the origin, to put on one's thinking cap today means to apply oneself to thinking out the solution to a problem.

cap, to set one's. This phrase originated in the days when ladies wore caps or hats – perhaps the ribbon-trimmed caps worn in the 18th century. To catch the eye of a young man in whom she was interested a girl would wear her best cap, perhaps arranging it at a jaunty angle. On seeing this an observer might comment that she was setting her cap at the young man, i.e. aiming to make him her husband. The phrase is still used in this way.

capital punishment. Capital is a word that dates back to the 15th century, a time when those sentenced to death were beheaded. It is taken from the Latin word *caput*, meaning 'head', and it is from this that the phrase capital punishment is derived.

cappuccino. Espresso coffee topped with frothed hot milk or cream, and often flavoured with cinnamon. *Cappuccino* is the Italian word for a Capuchin monk, and the coffee is so called because its colour resembles that of a Capuchin's habit.

car. Motorists may be intrigued to know that the word car was in use to describe a wheeled vehicle around the year 1300. It was derived from the Latin word *carra*, meaning chariot. As chariots gave way to something more sophisticated, 'car' became 'carriage', and with the advent of the engine the carriage gave way to the 'horseless carriage'. Finally, only six hundred years or so after it had been introduced to the language, 'car' was back in use to describe a wheeled vehicle.

card-carrying means authentic, genuine, committed. The phrase derives from the practice of carrying a membership card to show that one belongs to an organisation. The phrase 'card-carrying Communist' became a cliché in the 1930s and 1940s, and was used to distinguish those who were truly committed, as opposed to those who merely paid lip-service to the cause. The phrase is now used figuratively, e.g. 'a card-carrying sceptic'.

cards – it's on the cards. *See under* TRUMPS.

cards, to be given one's or **to ask for one's cards** mean, respectively, to be fired or to resign. This is a relatively modern phrase which alludes to the fact that when an employee leaves a job he is given his National Insurance cards and other paperwork by his employer. **To get the boot**, the SACK or the **elbow**, **to be given the push** or **take the high jump** are all euphemisms for being given one's cards, each implying a degree of rejection. A clever new invention is the American euphemism **to let someone go**, which manages to imply that the employer is doing the employee a favour by sacking him. *See also* OUTPLACEMENT.

card – to keep a card up one's sleeve. To have something to fall back on in case things go wrong. It may be another plan, an argument or a solution to the problem that he can call on if it is needed. The phrase obviously comes from the card table, where it describes a cheat who holds a card in reserve. The modern usage carries no overtones of cheating – indeed, someone who keeps a card up their sleeve is to be admired for their forethought and inventiveness.

cardigan. James Thomas Brudenell, seventh Earl of Cardigan, often wore a knitted woollen waistcoat of his own design as a means of keeping warm. This garment became known as a cardigan jacket and was worn by British soldiers to help keep out the cold during the Crimean war. It is unlikely that Lord Cardigan would recognise the modern long-sleeved version of his famous invention. It was he, incidentally, who led the Charge of the Light Brigade during the Battle of Balaclava in 1854. It was from this battle that the knitted wool helmet we know today as a **balaclava** took its name.

caring professions, the. Throughout history there have always been carers, usually women, whose responsibility it was to look after the young, sick and elderly or those unable to look after themselves. In the last century many of these functions have been formally recognised and taken over by the State, which employs the caring professions to do what was once carried out on a haphazard basis by individuals. Nursing and social work are two of the main caring professions.

carnival. A period of uninhibited revelry, merriment or amusement; a public show or entertainment. The expression originally referred to (and still does in some Roman Catholic countries) Shrovetide – the period immediately preceding Lent and ending on Shrove Tuesday (MARDI GRAS in French). Since Lent was a time of austerity, fasting and abstinence, people liked to let rip beforehand, while they had the opportunity. The expression derives from the Latin *carnem levare*, meaning 'to put away flesh' referring to the Lenten fast.

carpet, to be on the, or **carpeted** means to be reprimanded. It is often used to mean a ticking-off at work. One suggestion is that the phrase describes the posture that someone in this situation should adopt – on their knees on the carpet, asking for forgiveness. Another suggestion is that it derives from the practice in the Civil Service and other large institutions of giving employees a carpet for their office when they reach a certain rank. An official reprimand or demotion could result in the employee losing the carpet.

carpetbagger. After the end of the American Civil War in 1865, many political adventurers swarmed from the North into the defeated Southern states to exploit the newly enfranchised Negroes and the impoverished former slave-owners. They were given the name carpetbaggers – the carpet-bag, with sides made of carpeting, being the common type of travelling-bag at that time.

carry coals to Newcastle. To take something to where it is already most abundant; to perform any super-fluous action. This has long been a proverbial expression. Newcastle-upon-Tyne has been a major coal port and the centre of a coal-mining area for centuries – since it received a royal charter from Henry III for the digging of coal in 1239. The French have a corresponding expression *porter de l'eau à la rivière*, meaning 'to carry water to the river'.

carry the torch. An American slang expression meaning to have a pas-sion, usually unrequited, for a per-son. The derivation of the phrase is unclear, but it is believed to have been coined by a Broadway night-club singer called Tommy Lyman in the 1930s.

cart – to put the cart before the horse. This is an ancient saying, already proverbial by the time of the Romans and still in use in several European languages. It is applied to someone who gets their priorities or plans in the wrong order and is often interchangeable with phrases such as IT'S NO GOOD LOCKING THE STABLE DOOR AFTER THE HORSE HAS BOLTED and 'first things first'.

carte blanche. Absolute freedom of action; full discretionary power. In French, it means simply 'a blank piece of paper'. The expression was first used in English in 1707, and was originally a military term refer-ring to unconditional surrender – a blank sheet of paper to be signed by the vanquished and on which the victor could then choose to write whatever terms he chose to impose.

cartoon. Originally a preliminary sketch for a painting or some other work of art. The word is derived from the Latin *charta* meaning 'a paper' and *cartone*, meaning 'a large piece of paper.' There was no humorous content in the first car-toons, as anyone who has seen Leonardo da Vinci's famous draw-ings can confirm. The modern sense of a cartoon being an amusing illus-tration in fact dates back only to around 1840, when the magazine *Punch* published some satirical draw-ings based on designs for the new Houses of Parliament. Still later car-toon took on its meaning of a film consisting of animated drawings.

Casanova. A man who is described as a Casanova is one with a reputation for womanising. Giovanni Jacopo Casanova (1725–98) established his own formidable reputation through the publication of his *Memoires*, which told the story of his life as he roamed the capitals of Europe posing in turn as an alchemist, gambler, philosopher, preacher, diplomat, spy, raconteur and so on. To modern readers his sexual adventures are rather tame, but in his own time they were enough to establish him as one of the world's greatest lovers.

case-hardened. An expression de-rived from the process of hardening steel by carbonising the surface. The phrase is figuratively used to describe anyone whose attitude is hardened by experience. It may be applied to a hardened criminal, one who feels no regret or shame for what he has done; it might equally well be applied to a doctor, who sees so many patients in distress that he becomes hardened to it.

cash and carry. A wholesale supplier that sells goods only to retailers, suppliers and others in small businesses.

cash cow. Business jargon, originat-ing in America, for any reliable source of revenue that needs very little attention or effort – for example, a product which continues to sell regularly without any marketing effort. *See also* BACKLIST.

cash on the nail. To ask for cash on the nail in Britain means to ask for immediate payment for something. In America the phrase **cash on the barrelhead** means the same thing. It has been suggested that in days when drapers' shops had nails hammered into the counter at intervals to enable cloth to be measured out against them, cash on the nail simply meant that the draper wanted to see the money on the counter before he handed over the goods. The phrase cash on the barrelhead originated, so it's surmised, in some primitive bar on the Western frontier where the barrel served both as the counter and the container for the alcohol being dispensed. Thus the barman would demand to see the customer's cash on the barrel before he would pour a drink.

Shop practice has also given us the phrase **to nail to the counter** (in the USA **to nail a lie to the counter**) meaning 'to expose something false'. Some traders nailed counterfeit coins and bills that they had unwittingly accepted to the counter, both as a warning to anyone tempted to try to pass such 'false' money and also as a reference for shop assistants.

cast about in one's mind for ideas, to. To think things over or look for a solution. The expression is derived from a hunting phrase. When hounds have lost the scent of their prey they cast about, i.e. spread out over a wide area sniffing for a sign of it.

castle in the air. This evocative phrase means to have an extravagant day-dream. Castles in the air can be any fondly-imagined plans or hopes that distract the dreamer from the realities of life. Sometimes the expression **castles in Spain** is used to

mean the same thing. This phrase is a direct translation of the French *Chateaux en Espagne*.

casual. In Britain a young person, usually male, who dresses in expensive designer 'casual' wear. Casuals have been described as the new breed of British football hooligans; outwardly smart and apparently respectable, they are said to be responsible for many of the premeditated acts of violence that have become a feature of football matches. They are, according to some observers, the successors of PUNK. *See also* BEATNIK, LAGER LOUT.

cat, no room to swing a. This expression is used to describe a very small room or space. There have been several explanations of its origin, one of them, animal-lovers will be horrified to hear, from the practice of swinging a cat by its tail for use as a target. More likely, however, is the allusion to the CAT-O'-NINE-TAILS, a vicious whip used to instil discipline on board a ship. The phrase probably arose by analogy to the difficulties of swinging the whip in the confined space of a ship.

cat on hot bricks, a. This phrase is used to describe someone who feels uncomfortable, jumpy and ill at ease – as a cat picking its way across a pile of hot bricks would feel. In America, presumably as a reflection of the different types of house construction, the phrase became **a cat on a hot tin roof**.

cat-o'-nine-tails. A whip used to scourge criminals. It has been suggested that its name derives from the fact that in ancient Egypt whips were made from cat hide, or that its nine thongs left marks like the scratches of a cat's paws. The cat, as it was known, came into use in Britain around 1670 and was not abolished as a civil punishment for violent crimes until 1948. According to superstition it had nine tails because nine was a special number, a 'trinity of trinities', and the whip would therefore be more effective.

cat, there's more than one way to kill a. This phrase means simply that there is more than one way of accomplishing a task. The expression is a shortened version of an older one, 'There are more ways of killing a cat than choking it with cream'. 'There's more than one way to kill a cat' is often used as a critical response when someone suggests a tortuous and unnecessarily difficult method of doing something.

cat, to bell the. This interesting old expression dates back to William Langland's *The Vision Concerning Piers Plowman*, a 14th century poem which includes the tale of how a group of mice decide to hang a bell around the neck of a marauding cat so as to warn them of his presence. All of the assembled mice agree that this is a good idea until the wisest of them asks, 'But who is to bell the cat?' Since that time, anyone volunteering to bell the cat has offered to put his own life at risk in an attempt to help others.

cat, to grin like a Cheshire. Although this simile was popularised by Lewis Carroll in *Alice in Wonderland*, its origins go back further in time. It is said that in the dim past Cheshire cheeses were shaped like cats and that each had a grin on its face. This was apparently because Cheshire was a County Palatine, a county granted at around the time of the Norman Conquest to an earl who had almost 'royal' command of it. County Palatines also enjoyed certain tax privileges – reason enough, perhaps, to explain why the Cheshire cats were smiling so broadly and why they have given their name to anyone who wears an extremely broad grin.

cat – to let the cat out of the bag. To reveal a secret, sometimes without intending to do so. The phrase is said to have originated with the practice of selling piglets in sacks. Some unscrupulous dealers would put one creature on display and tie up the others in sacks to be taken away. Unwary buyers who failed to check the contents of their sacks would sometimes find that they had purchased a cat instead of a pig. Although we must presume that this deception often worked, occasionally something would go wrong, the sack would be opened and the cat would be let out of the bag.

This practice is also the origin of two other phrases. One, **a pig in a poke**, describes a bargain bought without inspection of the goods. The poke was a small bag in which the piglet was kept. **To be sold a pup** means to be swindled and refers to the con-trick described above, with a small dog or puppy substituted for the pig in a poke.

cat – when the cat's away the mice will play. This is an old proverb, found in several languages. It simply means that when the person in authority is absent, their underlings will take advantage of the situation to do what they want.

cat's cradle. A children's game or pastime in which a string is looped around the fingers and passed back and forth between two players so as to form a variety of symmetrical figures. The first recorded use of the expression dates from 1768, but its derivation is not known for certain. It has been surmised that the name is a corruption of 'cratch-cradle', 'cratch' being an old English word for a crib or manger, and that it refers to the manger cradle in which the infant Jesus was laid.

cat's whiskers, the. Something that is excellent or first-rate. In the USA the phrase the **cat's pyjamas** was introduced around 1900 and meant the same thing. In the early days of radio, a cat's whisker was a very fine wire that made contact with the crystal in the first wireless sets.

catamaran. A two-hulled boat derived from the Tamil word *katta-maran*, meaning 'tied-log'. The Tamil word originally applied to three logs tied together to make a primitive raft but was also used to describe two boats that were lashed together with a gap left between them – and from this, the modern usage arose.

catch as catch can. This expression, meaning to get something by whatever means is available, is derived from a form of NO HOLDS BARRED wrestling in which the contestants get a grip in whatever way they can.

Catch 22. A condition or requirement that is impossible to fulfil because of its paradoxical nature. For example, someone who cannot get a job because he lacks experience, and can only obtain the required experience by getting a job, might be described as being in a Catch 22 situation. This expression comes from the blackly humorous novel of the same name by American author Joseph Heller. The novel concerns Captain Yossarian, a US Air Force bombardier in World War II whose aim is to avoid flying any more dangerous missions. He is told that he can only be grounded if he is insane – but the fact that he wants to stop flying proves that he is not insane. There is no way out. As Heller describes it:

There was only one catch and that was Catch 22. All an aircrew member had to do was ask, and as soon as he did he would no longer be crazy . . . If he flew more missions he was crazy and didn't have to, but if he didn't want to he was sane and had to.

Heller originally intended to call his novel *Catch 18*, and only changed his mind at the last moment in order to avoid confusion with another novel – *Mila 18* by Leon Uris – which was published just before. Had it not been for this change of mind, the expression that entered the language would have been Catch 18 and not Catch 22.

caught – to be caught on the horns of a dilemma. Someone who is unable to make up their mind between two equally pressing needs or arguments. Dilemma is derived from the Greek words *di*, meaning two, and *lemma*, meaning something that is taken for granted. Trying to decide between two things that have been taken for granted is a recipe for indecision and head-scratching.

caught out, to be. To be caught in an act of deception or a lie. It comes from the game of cricket, where a batsman may be 'caught' by a fielder and is therefore 'out'.

Catherine wheel. A firework that is attached to an upright with a nail so that it can spin round freely. It is named after St Catherine of Alexandria who was sentenced to be martyred on a spiked wheel by the Emperor Maximus after she had protested at his persecution of the Christians. When the time came to carry out the sentence, Catherine touched the wheel and it miraculously broke. She was later beheaded and, according to the story, her body was taken to Mount Sinai by angels. Four hundred years later it was found there and a monastery built to her. Despite this fame, in 1969 the Church withdrew its official recognition of St Catherine because of doubts about her existence.

caucus. The American term for a political meeting called to discuss the claims of candidates for party office. It comes from the Red Indian word meaning 'adviser'.

cause célèbre. A 'celebrated cause' in

French referring to an individual or situation which attracts great public attention, often because of scandal or outraged reaction. A good example might be that of author Salman Rushdie, whose case became a *cause célèbre* when Islamic leaders called for his murder because of a blasphemy against Islam published in his book *The Satanic Verses*.

Celsius. The temperature scale measured in centigrade, invented by Swedish astronomer Anders Celsius around 1742, as an improvement on the Fahrenheit scale. Celsius's scale is in many ways a more obvious means of grading temperature, with 0 degrees representing the freezing point of water and 100 degrees its boiling point.

cemetery. The word is derived from the Greek word for a dormitory – a place where a number of people sleep. It is a euphemism coined in the 14th century to replace the starker 'burial ground'.

cha or **char.** A colloquial term for tea, in fact derived from the Chinese word for tea – *ch'a*.

chain letter. A letter, usually anonymous, which the recipient is asked to copy and send on to one or more other people. There is often a promise of good luck if the recipient follows the instructions or a curse if he does not. Often there is a financial inducement: the letter contains a list of names and addresses. The recipient has to send a sum of money to the person whose name is at the top of the list, and then send on several copies of the letter with the name at the top of the list removed and his own name and address added to the end of the list. By doing this the recipient is assured that he will eventually receive a very large sum of money when the letter has passed on down the chain and his name reaches the top of the list.

chain reaction. The concept of a single action that precipitates an indefinite number of linked reactions is said to have occurred to Hungarian physicist Leo Szilard while he was waiting for a traffic light to change in a London street in 1934. Scientists working in the field of atomic energy were quick to appreciate the concept; if an atom could be split into two parts by a neutron, the subsequent explosion might continue the sequence of reactions. The phrase is not, however, confined to the world of nuclear physics. It is more generally used to describe the sometimes unexpected results of an apparently insignificant event.

chair. A vogue word of the 1980s, the acceptable, non-sexist version of **chairman**, **chairwoman** and **chairperson**. Some people have regretted the passing of these words and blame their disappearance on a feminist/socialist plot. They may perhaps prefer to use the title madam chairman, turning a blind eye to the obvious contradiction, or they may refuse to acknowledge that the word chairman has any sexist overtones at all – as a High Court Judge observed when refusing to accept chairperson as a valid word: 'chairman has no gender. It is like testator or executor and is merely a description of a human being occupying the office of chairman.' What Mr Justice Harman does not mention is that there are two excellent words to describe a female testator or executor, both with long and honourable pedigrees. Those words are 'testatrix', which the OED dates to 1591, and 'executrix', first used, according to the OED, in 1502.

chance one's arm. Take a risk in the hope of accomplishing something. According to tradition, the phrase originated with an incident that occurred at St Patrick's Cathedral,

Dublin in 1492. Two great Irish families, the Ormonds and the Kildares, were engaged in a bitter feud and the Earl of Ormond and his men took refuge in the chapter house of St Patrick's Cathedral. Gerald Fitzgerald, Earl of Kildare, besieged the place but soon began to regret the conflict. Through the locked and barred door of the chapter house he assured the Earl of Ormond that he could come out and that he 'undertooke on his honour that he should receive no villanie'. Those inside were quite understandably reluctant to do so. At this, Kildare smashed a hole in the door and, daringly, thrust his hand through to the other side – where it was warmly grasped by an equally repentant Ormond.

changes, to ring the. To repeat the same thing in different ways, usually to avoid boredom. For example, someone who regularly makes the journey from A to B may ring the changes by varying the route each time. This expression comes from bell ringing, where a 'change' is the order in which the bells are rung. Theoretically a peal of six bells can ring 720 changes without repeating a ringing order. Eight bells give a total of 40,320 changes and twelve bells would require an incredible 479,001,600 changes before a repeat. The challenge of achieving these theoretical projections has proved irresistible and at least one bell-ringing team has rung the eight-bell changes in a non-stop session.

chap. In Britain a chap is simply a jovial word for a good or useful man. The word is derived from the medieval English 'chap-man', a tradesman or merchant who would try to oblige his customers. In the USA 'chaps' are leather leggings worn over trousers to protect the legs. The word is derived from the Spanish *chaparejos*, meaning leather breeches.

chapel. (1) This word is derived from the medieval Latin word *capella*, meaning a little cloak. The name was first applied to a shrine in which the cloak of St Martin was kept by the Frankish kings as a sacred relic. Thence the word came to be applied to any sanctuary or private place of worship other than a parish church or cathedral. It was later applied to places of worship used by nonconformist denominations such as the Baptists and Methodists. (2) The word can also mean a printing office, or an association of print workers or a branch of a printer's trade union. How this usage originated is not clear. It possibly derives from the fact that the earliest printing presses were set up in chapels attached to abbeys. For example, Caxton's press was set up in the precincts of Westminster Abbey. There is also a theory, however, that the word is in some way connected with the French word *chapellerie*, meaning a hatter's workshop.

chaperone. Originally a hood or cowl worn by, among others, ladies-in-waiting or female companions. It was the job of these women to accompany young unmarried girls in public and to protect them generally from unsuitable advances. Gradually these female guardians came to be known by their characteristic headgear. Since the end of the 18th century chaperone has also been used as a verb to describe the act of accompanying and protecting someone.

char. A common abbreviation of 'charwoman', a woman who does house-cleaning and other domestic tasks. The 'char' in 'charwoman' is simply a variation of the word 'chore'.

character part. Any part in a play, film or television drama that is not a lead role. Such a part is often a stereotyped character – a wicked

55

uncle, worried mother, prostitute or bumbling elderly gentleman, for example.

chase the dragon. To smoke heroin on a piece of aluminium foil is known as chasing the dragon. The expression is obviously an allusion to the mystic eastern origin of the drug, and also to the act of smoking. During the process the heated heroin, the dragon, turns to liquid and runs along the foil. It has to be 'chased' using another tinfoil tube which is used to suck up the smoke.

chauffeur is from the French word meaning 'to heat'. In the days of steam engines a chauffeur was employed as a stoker or fireman, his job being to keep the engine fuelled and ensure sufficient heat to produce the steam. His job might sometimes include driving the vehicle, and when steam gave way to internal combustion a chauffeur became the way of describing a professional driver.

chauvinist. An unquestioning and unthinking patriot, one who is extravagantly attached to any place, group, party or cause. More recently, the word has been taken up by the women's liberation movement in the phrase MALE CHAUVINIST or MALE CHAUVINIST PIG, which is used of men who stubbornly refuse to acknowledge the fact of female equality. The word dates from the time of the first French Republic and Empire. Nicolas Chauvin was a soldier in Napoleon's army and was notorious for his fanatical devotion to Napoleon. He was wounded many times and Napoleon eventually rewarded him with a ceremonial sabre, a red ribbon and a pension of 200 francs. Chauvin was introduced as a character representing extravagant patriotism in several plays – Scribe's *Le Soldat Laboureur*, Cogniard's *La Cocarde Tricolore* and Charet's *Conscrit Chauvin* – and in Baroness Orczy's *The Scarlet Pimpernel*. His name thus passed into both the French and English languages. *See also* JINGOISM.

cheers. *See under* BOTTOMS UP.

cheesecake. No one is absolutely certain how sexy pictures of beautiful women came to be called cheesecake, but one explanation cites a photographer who worked at New York's ocean-liner docks in the early years of this century. He used to take photos of the latest famous arrivals and would pose the women so as to show off their legs to advantage. The results, he swore, were 'better than cheesecake'. The word quickly became synonymous for photos of sexy women. More recently, women have demanded some **beefcake** for themselves; glamour pictures of attractive men wearing little or nothing.

cheque-book journalism. This phrase first became widely used in the mid-1960s. It describes the practice of some newspapers of paying large sums of money – often to criminals or people of some notoriety – in order to obtain exclusive rights to stories. *See also* GUTTER PRESS.

cherry farm. An American slang expression for a penal institution – a form of open prison – in which there is very little security and where the inmates are provided with agricultural work.

Cheshire cat – to grin like a. *See under* CAT.

chestnut. *See under* OLD CHESTNUT.

chew (up) the scenery. To overact; to act over-emotionally in an inappropriate situation; to engage in histrionics. This expression, which was at first show business slang but is now used more widely, originated in a 1930 theatrical review by critic Dorothy Parker: 'More glutton than artist . . . he commences to chew up the scenery'.

chew someone's ear off, to. To talk

at them or lecture them for an over-long time. The speaker may simply be boring or he may be scolding the listener for some misdemeanour. The derivation of this graphic phrase has yet to be traced.

chew the fat, to or **to chew the rag.** Both mean to enjoy a long, gossipy conversation. One American source states that both expressions were army slang and first came into use at around the time of the American Civil War, but another points to a more sedate origin among ladies' sewing circles. As they sat sewing their 'rags', women would chew over local goings-on at length – hence the suggested origin of chewing the rag. Chewing the fat possibly alludes to the juicy bits of gossip which they exchanged and digested at such get-togethers.

chicken-and-egg. Derived from the old riddle 'Which came first: the chicken or the egg?', this phrase is used to describe any dilemma of cause and effect or of priority.

chicken feed. Chickens have traditionally been fed with the poorest-quality grain that is no use for any other purpose. This grain is very small, and when gamblers arrived in American towns with the idea of fleecing the locals of their small savings they contemptuously called their winnings chicken feed. Today the phrase is still used to describe a paltry or insignificant amount of money.

chicken switch. An expression originally used by American test pilots for an emergency eject button, which would enable them to parachute to safety if their aircraft was about to crash. The expression was later adopted by astronauts in the space programme. The term came to be used figuratively in phrases like 'to pull the chicken switch' which means to react to danger in a panicky or hysterical manner or to push the **panic button**.

chickens – Don't count your chickens before they've hatched. This phrase is a warning not to rely on something – particularly profit or pleasure – until you have it in your hand. One of Aesop's fables tells the story of a woman who takes a basket of eggs to sell at market, boasting of the items she will purchase from the profits. On the way there she drops the basket and breaks the eggs and all her plans are ruined. This may, or may not, be the origin of the phrase.

Chiltern Hundreds. To apply for the Chiltern Hundreds means to resign from the House of Commons. A Hundred has, since before the time of the Norman Conquest, been a division of an English county or shire. Historians put the area covered by a Hundred at around 600 to 1,200 acres of land. In medieval times a steward was appointed to administer the Hundreds of Stoke, Desborough and Burnham, Buckinghamshire and to apprehend the robbers who lurked among the wooded Chiltern hills of the area, attacking travellers. Although it is many years since these robbers ceased to be a problem, the position of steward of the Chiltern Hundreds is still in existence and has proved extremely useful to Members of Parliament who wish to resign from the House of Commons. Since 1701 any MP who accepts a paid, non-political position offered by the Crown has had to resign from the House. However, MPs who wish to resign for other reasons are not permitted to do so directly. In a nice example of archaic double-think, this tricky situation can be sorted out if the MP who wishes to resign applies to become steward of the Chiltern Hundreds; in doing so he or she accepts a paid, non-political Crown appointment and automatically relinquishes membership of the House.

57

chin – to stick one's chin out. This expression comes from the boxing ring, where a fighter who 'leads with his chin' sticks it out instead of protecting it and therefore risks a knockout blow to the jaw. Sticking one's chin out has come to mean taking a risk; someone accused by another of sticking his chin out is accused of rash behaviour.

chin, to take it on the. A boxer who can take a blow to the jaw without being knocked out is said to take it on the chin. A boxer who isn't able to take it on the chin is described as having a 'glass jaw'. Used figuratively ('When he heard the bad news he took it on the chin'), the phrase describes someone who takes a metaphorical blow without flinching. We also use the expression in a shortened version – 'to take it'. Someone described as being able 'to take it' is a person who can cope with adversity.

China syndrome. A theoretical model for a nuclear catastrophe in which the cooling system of a nuclear reactor breaks down. If such an event occurred it would cause a meltdown in which the core would collapse. According to this concept the heat generated by such a disaster would make a hole right through the planet, all the way to China. Such an event formed the basis of a film called *The China Syndrome* in 1980. At the time the incidents portrayed in the movie were dismissed by the pro-nuclear lobby, but the Chernobyl disaster in 1986 proved that it was impossible to discount the chance of a similar catastrophe.

chin chin. *See under* BOTTOMS UP.

Chinese fire drill. American businessmen's slang for a confused and confusing situation.

Chinese wall. Within a single major bank or finance house, one department may be selling a company's shares while another buys them for an investment fund and a third is planning that company's takeover. Chinese walls have been erected in an attempt to ensure that each of these departments is kept separate and that insider information from one is not used to influence the deals of another, which is illegal. The Chinese walls are invisible security precautions designed to prevent communication between the various departments concerned.

chinless wonder. A term of abuse aimed at young upper-class men, chinless or not, who have no responsibilities, plenty of money and enjoy a wild and irresponsible social life. The phrase was coined in the 1960s and alludes to the common belief that individuals with weak chins also have weak personalities. Chinless wonders may also be known as **upper-class twits**. *See also* HOORAY HENRY and YOUNG FOGEY.

chip off the old block, a. When a child shows the same characteristics, looks or temperament as one of its parents, it is said to be a chip off the old block, i.e. made of the same stuff as its parent. The image is obviously that of a wood block or log from which a chip or splinter has been cut.

chip on the shoulder. A grudge or grievance; an unprovoked display of defiance; aptness to take offence. The expression originated in the USA in the early 19th century. At that time many backyards would have an area for chopping firewood and there would be quantities of wood chips lying around. It was a custom for an uncouth young fellow who wished to provoke a fight to place a chip on his shoulder and dare another youth to knock it off.

chips are down, the. *See under* BLUE CHIP.

chips, to cash in one's. *See under* BLUE CHIP.

chivalry. The word dates back to the time of the medieval knights, when it was an elaborate code of conduct they were expected to follow. It derives from the French word *cheval*, meaning horse, the implication being that a man wealthy enough to ride a horse was also capable of superior conduct. This conduct was known as **courtesy**, a politeness and civility of behaviour practised by those who attended court.

chockablock. Used since the 1800s to describe anything that is crammed or crowded. The word was originally nautical slang to describe the position of the two blocks of a block and tackle when the device was fully tightened, i.e. block to block. From this came the rhyming word chockablock.

chocoholic. *See* SPENDAHOLIC.

chop chop, meaning 'quick, quick', is a term coined by 19th century traders who saw how speedily the Chinese could eat with their chopsticks and invented the term to chivvy people along.

chop suey. A Chinese-style dish of quick-fried meat and vegetables with rice. The name of the dish is an English rendering of the Chinese Cantonese dialect *tsap sui*, which means 'mixed bits'. *See also* CHOW MEIN.

chow mein. A Chinese dish of various meats and vegetables with beansprouts and fried noodles. The name of the dish in Chinese means 'fried flour'. *See also* CHOP SUEY.

chowder. A fish stew, the best known variety being clam chowder. The name of this American dish derives from the French word *chaudière*, meaning a cauldron.

chubby. The chub is a plump, rounded freshwater fish found in Britain and much of northern Europe, and from its shape we get the word 'chubby' to describe a fat person. 'Anti-chub' is a phrase used to describe methods or programmes for losing weight and a 'chubby-chaser' is a person who is sexually attracted to fat people. We tend to forget that although we live in an age where thin is thought to be attractive, other eras have celebrated the charms of the full-figured woman. Less than a century ago, **a fine figure of a woman/man** was an individual we would now consider overweight. A wide range of euphemisms have been employed to describe a woman with an ample figure, from the classical Junoesque, Rubensesque and statuesque to well-built and well-endowed – all of them carefully avoiding any link with the word 'fat', which has been an insult since the Middle Ages.

chunder means to vomit. It has been suggested that it has a nautical origin in the phrase 'watch under', shouted from the upper decks to warn those below that someone was about to be sick over the side. Others speculate that it was originally rhyming slang chunder loo, for 'spew'. The verb was popularised in Britain and America by Barry Humphries, creator of that archetypal Australian Barry McKenzie. American 'preppies' prefer the verb **to buick** or refer to being sick as 'losing one's lunch' or 'spreading a technicolor rainbow'.

chutzpah. Brashness; effrontery; arrogant presumption. This Yiddish expression was adopted first into American English and thence into British English.

ciao. An idiomatic Italian word used as a greeting or as a farewell. The word has been used by English-speakers since about the mid-1960s. The literal meaning in Italian is 'I am your slave'.

clam up. When someone clams up they refuse to say anything. The phrase alludes to the fact that the shell of a clam, an oyster-type mollusc, is extremely difficult to open.

clap. A euphemism for veneral disease in general and gonorrhea in particular. It was introduced in the 16th century and is a shortened version of the French word *clapoire*, meaning a venereal sore.

claptrap. This word, coined in the 1720s, was originally a theatrical term meaning any trick, device or language introduced into a theatrical performance to win applause – literally a trap to catch a clap. Nowadays it is used merely to mean 'nonsense' or 'rubbish'.

classism. To discriminate against an individual because of their social class. Its first use has not definitely been traced, but it was in use in Britain by the mid-1980s. *See also* AGEISM and SEXISM.

clean as a whistle, as. There are a number of theories about the derivation of this expression. Some authorities suggest that it was originally 'as clean as a whittle', a phrase describing the smoothness and whiteness of a piece of wood after the bark has been whittled away. Another ascribes it to the clean, piercing noise made by a whistle, while yet another suggests that it originally described the whistling sound of a sword swishing through the air – and perhaps the clean cuts and slashes inflicted by a whistling sword.

clean bill of health, a. A document signed by the relevant authorities and given to the captain of a ship to certify that when the vessel left port there was no sign of infectious disease among those on board. This proved that the ship was 'clean' and thus the expression 'a clean bill of health' arose. Today we use the expression to describe someone who is in good health. There was also, at one time, 'a foul bill of health' – an expression no longer generally used.

clean – to make a clean sweep. This expression, derived from the idea of sweeping a place clean and getting rid of all the rubbish, is used generally these days to describe the complete reform of anything. In institutions, someone who is appointed to a new position of authority and decides to revolutionise the place, dispensing with staff and changing methods of working makes a clean sweep of it and may be known as the **new broom**. This is derived from the saying **a new broom sweeps cleanest**, meaning that a new person in power makes the most radical and far-reaching changes.

clear as mud. As an ironic description of anything that is obscure or anything but clear, this modern-sounding expression was in use as early as the 1820s.

clear the decks. Originally a nautical order, issued aboard a battleship before it went into action. It meant exactly what it says; the seamen were required to clear the decks of everything not required for the battle. Today, in general use, it means much the same thing – tidying and clearing away unnecessary clutter.

Clerihew. Edmund Clerihew Bentley achieved fame as the inventor of the Clerihew, a humorous, rhyming four-line poem which does not scan. This is one of his best-known rhymes:

> Sir Christopher Wren
> Said, 'I am going to dine with some
>   men.
> If anyone calls,
> Say I am designing St Paul's.'

cliffdweller. An American slang term for a resident of a high-rise apartment building.

cliffhanger. A story, film, book or situation that keeps people in suspense. The word is said to have originated in the 1910s when actress Pearl White, known as the Queen of the Silent Serials, starred in *The Perils of Pauline*. Some episodes concluded with her dangling from cliffs above the Hudson River, leaving audiences to wait a week in suspense before they could discover if she managed to escape. These were described as cliffhanger endings.

clinging vine. An American term for a woman who is overly dependent on a man and who needs constant reassurance of his affection.

clip-joint. A nightclub, bar or other place of entertainment where the customers are tricked out of their money, 'clip' meaning 'con'.

clock watcher. A person who takes care that he never works any longer than he has to, and who quits work immediately it is time to do so.

clogs, to pop one's, is a euphemism for death. To 'pop' something meant originally to take it to the pawnbrokers (from this source we get the song 'Pop Goes the Weasel'). When someone died and had no further use for their shoes, they would be taken to the pawnshop and exchanged for cash. *See also* CURTAINS, FLATLINE etc.

clone. (1) In the scientific world, to clone something means to make an asexual reproduction of it. Biological and genetic engineering advances have made it possible to take cells from a living creature and reproduce them so as to create an exact copy of the creature – more perfect than any identical twin could be. Cloning has been successfully carried out on mice and has been in use in the orchid-growing industry for many years. Used in its slang form a clone is someone who mindlessly imitates someone else. Young girls who dress like their pop-star idols or women who slavishly follow a fashion style pioneered by someone else are known as clones. (2) Clone is also used in the business world to describe a microcomputer that can use software designed for another manufacturer's computer, especially an IBM computer.

closed shop. A union practice, not as common today as it was ten or twenty years ago, of requiring employers to take on only union members.

closet queen. A latent or covert homosexual. *See also* COME OUT.

clotheshorse. In the fashion world, a person who wears expensive, fashionable clothes and models them beautifully, but has no other talents. This derogatory term invites comparison between the fashion model and the wooden clotheshorse on which clothing is dried and aired. *See also* FASHION VICTIM.

cloud-cuckoo-land. An imaginary place of fanciful notions; a crazy or impractical scheme. This is the English translation of a Greek word *nephelococcygia*, which occurs in the play *The Birds* by Aristophanes of about 400 BC. In the play it is the name of an imaginary city built in the air by the birds to separate the gods from mankind. *See also* CASTLES IN THE AIR.

cloud nine, to be on. To be exceptionally high or happy. In the USA the phrase is sometimes 'on cloud seven'. According to meteorologists, the highest clouds are around eight miles high. To be on cloud nine, therefore, means to be so happy that you're floating even higher. *See also* CLOUD-CUCKOO-LAND.

clover, to be in. A clover meadow is the best kind of pasture on which cows can be grazed and therefore a cow in clover is a very happy animal – which is why someone who is content with their lot and enjoying life is said to be in clover.

cluck and grunt. An American slang expression for the common restaurant dish of ham and eggs.

clue. In Old English, a skein of wool or a ball of thread. It gained its second meaning when the story of Theseus and the Minotaur became popular. In this tale Theseus finds his way through the great labyrinth of Crete unravelling a ball of thread as he goes, so that he can find his way out once he has killed the Minotaur. The story showed how useful a clue could be when it came to solving mysteries and this meaning gradually superseded the original one.

coals, to be hauled over the. *See under* HAUL.

coast is clear, the. This phrase was originally used by smugglers to confirm that there were no coast-guards in sight and that it was safe to bring contraband ashore. We now use it to describe a situation which is safe from the interference of a person in authority.

cobber. An Australian word meaning 'friend' or 'companion', cobber may be derived from an old Suffolk verb, to cob, meaning to make friends with someone.

COBOL. A computer programming language, invented in the 1950s by Commander Grace Hopper of the US Navy, and still widely used in commercial data processing. The word is an acronym for Common Business Oriented Language.

cock and bull story. There has been some dispute over the origin of this phrase, meaning a long and unbelievable story. It may derive from old fables in which farmyard animals conversed together, but an altogether more intriguing explanation points to the Buckinghamshire village of Stony Stratford which had two inns, the Cock and the Bull. In the days when people travelled around by stage coach, the Birmingham coach stopped to change horses at the Cock and the London coach stopped at the Bull. The cock and bull story is said to have originated because of the tales swapped by the passengers as they waited for their coaches to leave.

cock a snook, to. To cock a snook one should, technically, place one's thumb to one's nose and spread wide the fingers of the hand to make a contemptuous gesture. Among the other expressions for describing this particular form of insult are 'making Queen Anne's fan' and 'the five-finger salute.' In modern use the phrase can be applied to any kind of contemptuous gesture against authority, whether it involves actually cocking a snook or not.

Cockney. A native of London. Tradition has it that only those born within the sound of Bow Bells (the bells of the church of St Mary-le-Bow) are entitled to the name. The original meaning was 'cock's egg' and was the name given in the Middle Ages to a small mis-shapen egg occasionally laid by a young hen. Hence the term was applied figuratively to a foolish or spoilt child or to a simpleton. It later came to be used by country people as a contemptuous term for any town-dweller. The use of the word to specify a Londoner dates from the 17th century.

cockroach. A type of beetle. The word is an English rendering of the Spanish name for this insect – *cucaracha*.

cocktail. There have been several theories to explain the origin of this word, none of them more exotic than the legend of Aztec princess Xochitl, who is said to have given a drink concocted from spirits and fruit juice to the king she loved. It is more likely, though less romantic, to have derived from a mixed drink known as a *coquetel*, which was drunk in the French wine-growing region of the Gironde.

codswallop. Nonsense or drivel put forward as if it were serious information. According to the editors of the *Oxford English Dictionary*, the origin of this word is unknown. But some people propound the theory that it dates from around 1870 when one

Hiram Codd started selling bottled lemonade. This apparently came to be known as Codd's wallop, wallop being the current slang term for beer. Either because of its gassy nature or because it was regarded as an unsatisfying substitute for the real thing, codswallop came to have its present meaning.

coffin nail. A cigarette. Surprisingly, this slang term, which originated in the USA, has been in use since at least the 1880s – long before there was medical evidence of the link between smoking and lung cancer.

coke. Slang for cocaine. It is also one of the registered trademarks of the Coca-Cola Company, though for many years they tried to avoid the association. The flavouring for Coca-Cola and the drug cocaine are derived from the same source, the coca plant, and until 1909 the drink contained minute quantities of cocaine.

Cola wars. Used to describe the marketing tussle around the world between Pepsi and Coca-Cola to win a larger section of the vast soft drinks market. There have also been burger wars between McDonald's and Burger King and computer wars between IBM and Apple.

cold, to catch a. This phrase is used in the theatre to describe a disastrous tour of the provinces. It is also used more generally to describe the nervous reaction of investors when a financial venture does badly: 'Investors caught a cold and the share price fell rapidly . . .'

cold feet. In the 17th century, to have cold feet was to be penniless – unable to afford shoes. Quite how the phrase came to have the meaning of being nervous or frightened is obscure, but the connection may simply be that cold is one of the symptoms of fear. These days we use the phrase less to describe terror than as a means of expressing doubts or second thoughts about something to which we have already committed ourselves.

cold shoulder. Someone who receives the cold shoulder from another is rejected by them. The phrase is said to have derived from the social custom of serving a hot joint of meat to welcome guests but bringing out a cold shoulder of mutton or lamb to unwanted visitors. Thus, anyone who receives the cold shoulder knows that they are not welcome.

cold turkey. (1) The plain unvarnished truth; straightforwardly, abruptly. This expression is often used in the phrase 'to talk cold turkey' which is an intensified form of the phrase 'to talk turkey'. (2) A form of treatment for drug addicts, involving sudden and complete withdrawal of the drug, as distinct from gradual withdrawal. This meaning obviously derives from the sense outlined above, but it is older than most people realise. The *Supplement to the Oxford English Dictionary* quotes an example of the expression being used in reference to drug addicts in a Canadian newspaper in 1921.

colours, to go under false. According to the law of the sea, ships are required to show their true flags so that they can be identified by others. Pirates exploited this law by sailing under a neutral or friendly flag and then, when their quarry sailed trustingly close, taking it down and hoisting the skull and crossbones instead. When we use the phrase today we refer to someone who is not what they seem to be; someone who is a WOLF IN SHEEP'S CLOTHING.

come apart at the seams, to. Someone who comes apart at the seams loses their customary composure when pressure is put on them. There is an obvious allusion here to a badly-made garment which falls apart when it receives any rough treatment.

come out, to. Until relatively recently the only people who 'came out' were debutantes, young women from noble and wealthy families, who were presented at Court and participated in a season of parties and social events with their fellow debutantes. 'Coming out' signified that the girls were on the marriage market and the main purpose of the debutantes' balls and other events of the social season seem to have been aimed at finding them suitable husbands. Debs are no longer presented at Court and the social side of coming out has also waned. In current usage, coming out is what homosexuals do when they publicly declare their sexual orientation. It is also known as **coming out of the closet**, i.e. coming out into the open. *See also* CLOSET QUEEN.

come up and see me some time. This phrase, described by Eric Partridge as a 'humorously euphemistic sexual invitation', was made famous by the American actress Mae West and became one of her stock catchphrases. The phrase was first used by Miss West in the play *Diamond Lil*, which was first performed on 9 April 1928 and had a long run. She spoke the phrase to Cary Grant in the 1933 film *She Done Him Wrong*, but in a slightly reworded form: 'Why don't you come up some time and see me?' In the 1939 film *My Little Chickadee* she issued the invitation, as originally worded, to W. C. Fields.

come up to scratch. To reach an expected standard. In the days of bare-knuckle prize-fighting a line was scratched on the ground between the two contestants, and at the start of each round each had to come up to this line and place his left foot on it. A fighter who was incapable of continuing the bout did not come up to scratch and thus forfeited the match.

common-law marriage. Legally speaking there is no such thing, and the expression is in fact a euphemism for what was once called **living in sin** and is now often described as a long-term or live-in relationship, i.e. a relationship in which a man and a woman choose to live as husband and wife without marrying. The term 'common-law wife' is therefore a euphemism or courtesy title for a mistress. In America couples living together outside marriage are sometimes known as **de facto couples**, i.e. are married in fact, if not in law.

community charge. *See* POLL TAX.

commuter. This expression derives from 'commutation ticket', the American name for what the British term a 'season ticket'. In the USA the word has been in use since the 1880s to describe someone who travels to and from work in a town or city centre, but the word was not adopted by the British until the 1950s.

concert party. *See* FAN CLUB.

condom is said to derive from the name of one Colonel Condum, an English Guards' officer, who attempted to protect his men from disease on their French campaigns. Although the details of Colonel Condum's invention have been lost, they may have been made from animal intestines, dried and oiled to give them flexibility. They were a great success and were soon widely available – indeed, Casanova bought a dozen which he tied on with pink ribbons. In English-speaking countries condoms are known as French letters; in France they are called English letters. The condom's popularity waned after the 1960s when new forms of contraception, most notably the Pill, were introduced. In the mid 1980s, however, they have staged a spectacular comeback as a form of protection against AIDS and, thanks to unabashed media coverage, the condom has achieved a new respectability. In 1988 news was released that scientists are testing the efficacy of a female condom which works on the same barrier principle as the male version. Whether this will achieve the same popularity as the original condom remains to be seen.

con-man. Men have been swindling each other for thousands of years, but it was not until the 19th century that the expression 'con-man' was coined. In America in the 1870s a favourite trick was to fool investors into putting their money into non-existent gold mines. Most would-be investors insisted on seeing the mine before they staked their money, and the swindler would ask for a small deposit 'as a gesture of confidence.' Those people who paid it became victims of the 'confidence' game and never saw their cash or the con-man again.

contact magazine. A publication in which people seeking a particular sexual experience advertise to find others willing to supply it.

convenience. Sometimes known in the USA as **convenience merchandise**, convenience goods include groceries, snacks, alcoholic drinks, tobacco, over-the-counter medicines and cosmetics. Among the groceries in a convenience store, a shop which stays open long hours for its customers' convenience, there will probably be a wide selection of convenience food – pre-packed, pre-cooked and ready to be eaten with only the minimum of preparation. Convenience is also a euphemism for a toilet.

conventional. This word has acquired a new meaning since the 1950s. As applied to weapons, warfare or sources of energy, it means 'other than atomic'.

conversation piece. The name given to an unusual, tasteless or downright bizarre piece of furniture, art, decoration or addition to a room. Owners of such items justify them by calling them 'conversation pieces' on the grounds that, if nothing else, they promote conversation.

cook the books. To prepare a set of falsified accounts. *See also* CREATIVE ACCOUNTING.

cool as a cucumber has been used for around three hundred years to describe someone who is exceptionally composed and self-possessed. Only in this century has it been shown that the saying is scientifically accurate. On a warm day the centre of a cucumber is significantly cooler than the air surrounding it.

cop a plea. An American police and criminal slang expression. It means to plead guilty to a charge in the expectation of getting a lenient sentence for doing so, or to plead guilty to a lesser charge in order to avoid being tried for a more serious offence.

cop out. A slang expression that originated in the USA meaning to refuse to commit oneself in a situation in which commitment would present one with problems.

copper-bottomed. Genuine, authentic; sound, especially financially. The expression derives from the practice of covering the bottom of a ship with copper plates in order to protect it from ship-worm.

copy. Originally citizen's band radio jargon, but now used more generally, to copy means to receive a message or information.

copy the mail. Citizen's band radio jargon, meaning to listen in on a CB radio but to do little or no talking.

cordon bleu. This French phrase, meaning 'blue ribbon', originally referred to an order of chivalry. Knights of the Order of the St Esprit (or Holy Ghost) were so called because their insignia were worn on a blue ribbon. Meetings of the order became noted for their excellent meals, and thus the term came to be applied to very fine meals or very fine chefs.

cordon vert (*vert* is French for 'green') was originally conceived by skilled vegetarian cooks as an amusing alternative to cordon bleu, but with the recent boom in the popularity of vegetarian food it has become a recognised mark of distinction, awarded in Britain by the Vegetarian Society.

corduroy. A tough cotton fabric said by some authorities to be derived from the French phrase *corde du roy*, meaning 'cord of the king'. In the days when the fabric was used to make hunting clothes for monarchs, corduroy was woven from silk. That at least is the theory – though the fact that the French refer to corduroy as *velours côtelé* has prompted others to speculate that the phrase is in fact an English invention, coined by a cloth merchant anxious to impress his customers with the fabric's provenance. Trousers made of this material are commonly known as corduroys or cords.

corn ball. An American colloquial term for a person who is boringly and embarrassingly sentimental.

corny. According to one source, corny, meaning something sentimental or old-fashioned, dates from the days when comedians toured the mid-west states of the USA, known as the Corn Belt. There they encountered what were known as 'corn-fed' audiences, unsophisticated people who preferred reliable old jokes and traditional routines to anything new. The performers began referring to this type of material as 'corn-fed humour', which was in time contracted to corny and applied to anything simple or clichéd – like corny jokes.

corporate advertising. A term from the business world, corporate advertising promotes not an individual product, or brand name, but the manufacturing company and, in some cases, the corporation that owns the company. Corporate advertising is sometimes used when a company is under threat of being taken over, or there is a war between two giants – as in, for example, the Guinness takeover bid for Distillers, in which it was the company rather than its components or products that were advertised.

corporate raider. A company or an individual who buys a significant stake in another company, with the intention of taking it over or making a fast profit by forcing share prices up. *See also* GOLDEN PARACHUTES, GREENMAIL.

corpse. When an actor corpses he gets a fit of the giggles or forgets what he is supposed to be saying or doing. This may lead to another actor 'drying' – forgetting his lines.

cosa nostra. Another name for the Italian criminal organisation, the MAFIA. In Italian 'cosa nostra' means 'our thing'.

cot death. The sudden death of an infant in apparently good health due to unknown causes, usually occurring before the age of one year.

cotton on to, to. To be attracted to someone or something and want to stick with them. This expression originated among English cotton weavers and refers to the way in which bits of cotton clung to their clothing as they worked. Someone who suddenly catches on to an idea or line of thought is also said to have cottoned on to it, i.e. grasped it.

couch potato. A term of abuse used to describe those who sit around watching too much television and are in danger of becoming mindless vegetables as a result. The couch potato has a short attention span and demands constant thrills and entertainment. He is thus blamed by thinking TV viewers for the mediocrity of much programming. *See also* KIDULT.

cough up. In modern usage to cough

up means to pay up, but traditionally it meant to reveal or disclose something. It has been suggested that the change of meaning occurred when criminals who were caught and invited to cough up responded with bribes instead of information.

countdown. The word, used to describe the backward count for timing rocket launches, was coined by German film director Fritz Lang in the 1920s – many years before the first rocket was launched at Cape Canaveral. Lang invented the word to add suspense to a scene in the science fiction film *Frau im Mond* in which a rocket was shown taking off. It was adopted by German scientists who later went to America to work on the first rocket programmes.

counter, under the. This phrase arose in Britain during World War II, describing the dishonest practices of shopkeepers who sold rationed goods under the counter at inflated prices to those who could afford them. Thus in modern use an under the counter deal, for example, is an illegal or dubious one conducted in secrecy.

counter intuitive. A fine example of GOBBLEDYGOOK or bureaucratese. It is a phrase first spotted in America where it was used by the Pentagon to describe a proposed policy. Though the Pentagon refused to define what they meant by 'counter intuitive', a *New York Times* journalist revealed its meaning as 'likely to be thought crazy by ordinary people'. That is, something described as 'counter intuitive' runs counter to the intuitive understanding of ordinary people. A counter intuitive policy is thus one that sounds ridiculous to most of us.

courtesy. *See under* CHIVALRY.

Coventry, to send someone to. To refuse to communicate with someone – to ostracise them. This expression dates from the time of the English Civil War when Royalist prisoners who were captured by Cromwell's Roundheads were sent to Coventry, a Parliamentarian stronghold where they would find no sympathy or aid.

cover one's ass or **cover one's tail.** To prepare excuses in advance in order to avoid blame. This phrase originated as US military slang in Vietnam in the 1960s, and passed into general use in the 1970s.

cover the waterfront. To discuss all aspects of a topic; to give a full account of something. This American expression derives from the title of a book written by journalist Max Miller in 1932, exposing crime and corruption on the waterfront.

cowboy. In addition to its traditional usage cowboy is a term applied in both Britain and the USA to describe a workman. There the similarity ends. In the USA a cowboy is a workman who undercuts the going union rate for the job. In Britain the cowboy is a plumber, builder, electrician etc. who might appear to offer a cheap service but whose work is unreliable and not up to standard; he is a CON-MAN.

cowlick. A tuft of hair that will not lie flat on the head, no matter how often it is brushed down. Though no definitive origin has been traced, the phrase probably dates from a time when a despairing mother told her shock-headed child that its hair looked as if a cow had licked it. Another source, however, points out that cows have whorls and tufts of hair on their bodies at places where the direction of the hair changes, and that it may have been thought that these were caused by licking. A child with unruly hair might therefore be described as having a cowlick.

cows – till the cows come home. Left to their own devices, cows don't come home until the discomfort of a full udder forces them to seek the milking parlour. Today's cows give milk all year round, but we must presume that when this expression was coined things were managed rather more naturally and cows were allowed to have a dry period. For this reason 'till the cows come home' means a long, long time – though modern cows would probably be banging on the milking parlour door and begging to be let in after only a day away.

crack has a number of different meanings. It can mean to break, or to break into something, as in 'safe-cracking', or to solve a problem or mystery. It can also mean an attempt to do something, as in, 'I'll take a crack at it.' When someone 'cracks up' they suffer an emotional breakdown; if they are crazy or disturbed, they may be described as 'cracked' or 'crackpot'. In the 1980s crack has become the name for a very pure form of cocaine that can be smoked and provides an immediate high. In Ireland, however, good crack is not to be confused with drugs; it means excellent conversation. On such an occasion cracking open a bottle may lubricate the flow of cracks – funny or witty remarks – and maybe, at the end of the day, lead to the conclusion that nothing is what it's cracked up to be.

cracker-barrel. An American adjective used to describe an unsophisticated outlook or point of view, or persons holding such views. The expression, which dates from around 1930, derives from the familiar image of discussions among plain unsophisticated people sitting on or around the cracker-barrel, which was a common feature of the general store in rural areas and small towns.

cracking, to get. This expression, meaning to get to work on something quickly, originated in the RAF during World War II. It describes the series of fast, skilful manoeuvres to change the direction of an aircraft rapidly when it is under fire. **To get weaving** means the same thing.

crap. There has been some dispute over the origin of the word crap, meaning 'excrement'. One of the most obvious and much-quoted stories concerns Thomas Crapper, the sanitary engineer who invented the first flush lavatory to be widely installed in England. Crapper's Valveless Water Waste Preventor is supposed by many sources to have given us not simply the word 'crap' but other much-censored phrases such as 'a load of crap' meaning 'a load of rubbish' or 'to be crapped on from a great height', a public humiliation. But Crapper's name is, according to others, just an amusing coincidence. They point to the Dutch word for 'scraps', *krappe*, which had been shortened to crap and used to mean 'excrement' for many years before the advent of the flush toilet. Whether this is right or wrong, one cannot help thinking that Crapper's name deserves to live on, linked for ever with his gift to mankind.

Craps. A game of chance played with dice, originating in the USA where it is very popular. There is a theory that the name of the game derives from Johnny Crapaud, the nickname of a Creole whose real name was Bernard Marigny and who is said to have introduced dice-playing from France in about 1800. It is much more likely, however, that the name is simply derived from the word 'crab', which was the term for the lowest throw, 1, in the earlier popular dice game of Hazard.

crash. In computer terminology a crash is what happens when a surge of power or a power cut makes a computer stop abruptly. When this happens the data being processed at the time of the surge can be lost.

crazy like a fox. Apparently crazy but really cunning or calculating. The expression originated in the USA in the 1930s, or possibly somewhat earlier, and was used in 1945 by the American humorist S. J. Perelman as the title of one of his books.

cream, the. Anything that is considered to be the best of its type can be said to be 'the cream', as in, for example, 'the cream of the crop'. This use of the word derives from the fact that when milk is left to stand the cream rises to the top. Figuratively speaking, therefore, anything or anyone that rises above the rest is 'the cream'.

creative accounting. A euphemism for fraudulent book-keeping or falsified accounts – though sometimes a creative accountant can find genuine loopholes or manoeuvres that enable his client to evade payment. *See also* COOK THE BOOKS.

credibility gap. The perceived disparity between what is claimed as fact, particularly by governments or their spokesmen, and what is actually true; a disinclination to believe or take on trust statements made by those in authority. The phrase was coined in 1966 by Gerald Ford, then a US Congressman, with reference to the growing involvement of the USA in the Vietnam War, which the Johnson administration denied was happening.

creek – up the creek without a paddle. This phrase, often abbreviated to 'up the creek' or, in times of extreme difficulty, 'up shit creek', originated in America in the second half of the last century. It first appeared as 'up salt creek', a salt creek being a creek leading through swamps and marshland. To be lost up one in a canoe without a paddle would certainly lead to trouble with no obvious way out – which is what we mean when we use the expression figuratively today.

creep-up calls. These have been employed in different forms for many years, but it was not until the mid-1980s that they were named. The practice originated among council workmen who were paid for each call they made to tenants' homes to carry out routine repairs and maintenance. They adopted the habit of creeping silently up to the front door, knocking quietly and immediately slipping a note through the letter box saying that they had called while the occupant was out. They would then race back to their vehicles, able to claim a payment for having made an abortive call without the necessity of doing any work. The term 'creep-up caller' is a term applied more generally to any person – deliverymen, meter readers or workmen – who mysteriously claim to have called and got no reply at a time when the occupant was at home.

crepe hanger. American slang for someone who constantly takes a gloomy view or talks about the troubles and miseries of life.

croak. To croak means to die. It is probably derived from the death rattle or laboured breathing of someone on their deathbed. *See also* CURTAINS, FLATLINE and TO KICK THE BUCKET.

crocodile tears. False or insincere tears; a hypocritical show of sorrow. There was for a long time a belief that a crocodile would moan and sob like a person in distress in order to lure people within its reach and would continue to shed tears as it devoured its victims. This belief finds expression in ancient Greek and Latin literature and in English literature down to the end of the 16th century.

crop up. This expression began as a mining term describing the way a strata of rock rises to the surface at intervals, appearing, perhaps, as outcrops. It is applied to the occasional recurrence of a problem or a subject in discussion as in, for example, 'The problem of what to do about the lack of parking space cropped up again.'

crossing the Rubicon commits one irreversibly to something. The phrase dates from 49 BC when Julius Caesar, governor of Gaul, crossed the Rubicon, a river that marked the boundary between Gaul and the Roman republic. This act signified the invasion of Italy proper, from which there was no going back.

cross my heart (and hope to die). A solemn or mock-solemn declaration that one is telling the truth. This catchphrase, which could be regarded as a vulgar and superstitious parody of a religious oath, seems to have originated in the mid-19th century and is still very common today.

crow – as the crow flies. Whether it is true or not, the crow has traditionally been believed to fly in straight lines. This gave rise to the saying 'as the crow flies', meaning a direct distance between two points, not allowing for any diversions or obstacles.

crow Jim. Strong prejudice among blacks against white people – the opposite of Jim Crow.

crow's feet. Lines at the outer corners of the eyes, shaped like the splayed claws of a crow's foot. They are the natural result of years of laughter, anxiety and squinting into bright light. The expression has been in use for hundreds of years and was first recorded in 1372 when Chaucer referred to it in his poem, *Troilus and Criseyde*. For those for whom it is too brutal a description of the effects of age, there is a modern euphemism – **laughter lines**.

crow's nest. The lookout perch situated at the top of old sailing ships' masts and probably named because of its visual similarity to a nest high up in the branches of a tree. However, according to one source its name is derived from the early days of navigation when a cage of land birds, among them crows, were kept up there. If the lookout lost sight of the shore one of these birds was released and instinctively flew towards the land, guiding the ship back to safety. Though this makes a charming story, there is no evidence that it is accurate.

crucial. Every generation seems to need to coin its own words to describe what it regards as excellent or admirable. Thus we get a long series of synonyms – from 'spiffing', 'super' and 'wizard' to FAB and BRILL. Crucial is one such word belonging to the late 1980s, originating among black teenagers, and popularised by its use on television by the comedian Lenny Henry. *See also* BAD.

crud. The word is derived from the crust of curds that forms on top of curdled milk. It probably came from the mispronunciation of the word curdled. Today 'crud' is specifically applied to a disgusting layer of filth or muck, but it is also more generally used to describe anything rubbishy, dirty or worthless.

cry all the way to the bank. A phrase originated by the flamboyant popular pianist Liberace, who was derided by the critics and by anyone who took music seriously, but who made a fortune from his performances. When asked how he felt about the hostility of the critics, he is said to have replied, 'I cried all the way to the bank'.

crying – it's no use crying over spilt milk. According to an American source, this phrase is first found in written form in *The Clockmaker; or the Sayings and Doings of Samuel Slick of Slickville* by Thomas Haliburton, published in 1836. It means simply that there is no point in getting upset about things that have happened and can't be remedied.

cul-de-sac. Literally translated from the French, it means 'bottom of the bag'. Quite how this phrase came to be applied to a blind alley or dead-end road is unclear, but like something trapped at the bottom of a bag, someone in a cul-de-sac has only one available exit.

cultural cringe. A phrase coined by writer Arthur Phillips in 1950 to describe a common characteristic he discerned among Australians – a tendency to disparage their own culture and an attitude of subservience to the culture of other countries, particularly Britain.

culture shock. The expression used to describe the alienation and distress felt by some travellers when they are exposed to a culture and lifestyle that is quite unlike their own. For example, wealthy western tourists holidaying in India may be shocked by the scale of the poverty they see, or businessmen transferred to Japan or the Middle East may feel that there is no sense or logic in the way that business is done in the 'new' country.

culture vulture. A voracious devotee of the arts and intellectual pursuits, particularly an ostentatious or pretentious one. An early use of the expression was in Dylan Thomas's *Quite Early One Morning*, published in 1954.

cupboard love. Love, or a pretence of love, inspired by considerations of self-interest or material gain. The allusion is to the love of children for an indulgent adult who might repay their love by giving them something nice from the cupboard.

curate's egg. The November 1895 issue of *Punch* carried a humorous story and illustration of a nervous young curate seated at the breakfast table with his bishop. The curate is eating an egg and when the bishop asks if it is to his liking he is too timid to say that it is bad. Instead he stammers, 'Parts of it are excellent!' This proved extremely popular and the phrase 'Good in parts, like the curate's egg' caught on quickly. It is still heard today, though in modern use it is often abbreviated to 'the curate's egg', describing something that is good only in part.

curfew. Originally an ancient safety precaution adopted in response to the number of devastating blazes caused by domestic fires left to smoulder all night. Laws were passed requiring everyone to extinguish or cover their fires when the church bell was tolled each evening. In France the phrase for 'cover fire' was *couvrefeu*, and this passed into English as 'curfew'. In England the first curfew was instituted in 1068 by William the Conqueror, who decreed that the bell should be rung at 8 pm. Although the original curfew laws have long since been lifted, we still used the word to describe the laws made by an invading army or a government at a time of civil disorder, requiring people to stay indoors between certain hours.

currant. Dried raisins are known as currants because they were originally imported from Corinth, Greece. The commonly-used name for Corinth at the time was Corauntz and from this came 'currants'.

curry favour. To flatter and ingratiate oneself with someone for one's own benefit. The expression derives from a 14th century French play entitled *Fauvel*, about a cunning centaur who symbolises all that is bestial and greedy in man. In the play characters come to 'curry' or groom Fauvel (or Favel) and persuade him to help them in their plans. Thus, in Middle English to 'curry fauvel' was to seek to further one's own ends by flattery, sweet talk and persuasion. The phrase was later corrupted to become the still widely-used 'curry favour'.

curse. A woman who has 'the curse' is

menstruating. This expression alludes to the biblical curse of Eve and the connection between eating the apple and sex. Throughout English-speaking history there have been dozens, perhaps hundreds, of euphemisms to describe a woman's 'time of the month'. In the 19th century she was merely 'indisposed' or 'unwell', though she perhaps had 'visitors', who might have included her 'country cousin', her 'little friend', or maybe her 'aunt had come to stay'. In Australia since the 1930s women have lamented that 'it looks like a wet weekend', while in the USA they have announced that 'the red flag is up', their 'red-haired friend has come to stay' or that they 'have the painters in'. It is interesting to note how many of the older phrases carry an overtone of handicap or infirmity, while in their defiance and graphic quality the modern expressions show the growing influence of feminism.

curtains. One of a number of euphemisms for death. It is said to have originated in Death Row in American prisons, where curtains were drawn around the cell of a prisoner when he was taken away for execution. Whether this is entirely accurate has been a cause of some speculation, for it has long been traditional in Britain to draw the curtains of neighbours' houses on the day of a funeral and this habit may well have been the origin of 'curtains'.

Other euphemisms for death include some reassuring ones: 'to be in Abraham's bosom', 'to go to a better place', 'to be at rest' and 'to be at peace' being just a few. Others are more robust. A cowboy, for example, makes 'the big jump' or attends 'the last roundup', a gambler 'cashes in his chips' and a bank manager 'settles his account', while jockeys may be said to have 'jumped the final hurdle', soldiers make 'the ultimate sacrifice' and members of the air force are 'grounded for good'. Others have less noble ends and are simply 'snuffed out' like candles, 'kick the bucket', 'croak' or 'pop their clogs'. Whatever happens, they usually 'go home in a box' to 'push up daisies'. Romantics and the more refined might 'pay the debt of nature', a phrase that comes from a 13th century guide for female hermits; they might also receive 'the final summons', 'go west', 'lay down their life' or 'go the way of all flesh'. In American hospitals death takes on an altogether more clinical guise; patients who die are said to have 'checked out', despite 'the remains' which offer proof to the contrary, and death is described as 'negative patient care outcome'. In the obituaries death from cancer is often euphemistically described as 'after a long illness' while suicide goes under the heading 'after a short illness'. And of course, whether the illness was long or short, it is to be hoped that the deceased had the wisdom to make 'a pre-need memorial estate', or in plain English, purchase their own grave plot.

cushy. This British slang word, meaning easy or comfortable, does not derive, as one might think, from the word 'cushion'. The word was originally army slang, from World War I, and derives from the Hindustani word *khush* which means 'pleasant'.

cut, to. To cut an acquaintance, in the figurative sense, is to ignore them. The phrase alludes to the pain the victim feels when their friendship is spurned, usually in public. From this idea has come the expression **to cut someone dead**, to inflict silent humiliation on them by ignoring them. In the 18th century, when 'cutting' people was an art, there were four acknowledged kinds of cut. The 'cut direct' was to stare fully at an acquaintance and then pretend not to know them; the 'cut indirect' involved looking away and simply pretending not to see them; the 'cut sublime' necessitated staring at the clouds, the architecture or some other lofty subject until they passed; and the 'cut infernal' involved bending down to inspect one's boots until the acquaintance had gone. *See also* TO BE AT DAGGERS DRAWN *under* DAGGER.

cut and dried. Something that has been planned and prepared beforehand. It may be used, for example, ti describe a Parliamentary debate in which the outcome is a foregone conclusion and plans have already been made to implement the decision. The expression is said to allude to the cutting and drying of timber so that it is ready for immediate use, though an American source claims that it refers to the cut and dried herbs that were popular in the 17th century.

cut and run. To escape in a hurry; to quit. This was originally a naval expression. In the old days of sailing ships, the anchor cable was made of hempen rope. If a ship at anchor needed to escape quickly from an enemy, there was no time to haul up the anchor and instead the anchor cable would be cut.

cut down to size. *See* TALL POPPY SYNDROME.

D

D.J. *See* DISC JOCKEY.

dab – to be a dab hand. A person who shows exceptional skill at something. The word derives from the Latin *adeptus*, meaning 'one who has attained skill'. However, to dab at something – particularly in the boxing ring – comes from the Old Dutch word *dubben*, meaning 'to hit'. Thus, when a man is knighted his sovereign **dubs** him on the shoulder with a sword. As well as this, dub has other more modern meanings. As a verb, 'to dub' describes the practice of recording a new soundtrack over the original film sound, perhaps in a different language. Dub is also a form of reggae music characterised by unexpected sounds and discontinuous beats.

daffodil. *See under* FRESH AS A DAISY.

daggers drawn, to be at. To be at daggers drawn with someone is to be in fierce and dangerous opposition to them. This phrase obviously alludes to that point in a disagreement when words ceased to be enough and the protagonists reached for their weapons. Likewise 'to look daggers' at somebody is to look at them with such hostility as to wound them figuratively – a glance that might be described as a 'killing look'. *See also* CUT.

dagwood. In the USA, a big thick sandwich with a variety of fillings. The expression derives from the name of Dagwood Bumstead, a comic-strip character who was fond of such sandwiches.

dahlia. *See under* FRESH AS A DAISY.

daisy chain. A group sex experience in which there is simultaneous sexual activity throughout a chain of participants.

dancehall. An American slang expression for an execution chamber, or the cells adjoining which house condemned prisoners. The expression comes from the obsolete criminal slang 'to dance', meaning to die by hanging. *See also* DEATH ROW.

Darby and Joan. A couple who have been long and happily married are sometimes described as Darby and Joan. The phrase was coined by Henry Woodfall, who used it in a ballad published in the *Gentleman's Magazine* in 1735. It referred to Woodfall's one-time employer, a printer called John Darby and his wife Joan. Woodfall was obviously fond of them and celebrated their long relationship in his ballad. In modern use Darby and Joan is often applied indiscriminately to any elderly couple.

darkest hour comes before dawn, the. There is no scientific evidence to prove that this saying is true, but in its figurative sense it must be, for it means that when things have reached their very worst they must start to get better – an excellent example of tautology. Other expressions about darkness include **to keep things**

dark, i.e. to keep them hidden or secret, while **to take a leap in the dark** means to act or make a decision blindly, without seeing all the details or consequences. Someone who is an unwelcome visitor may also be warned **don't darken my door again**, referring to the way the door is darkened by the shadow of an approaching visitor.

dark horse. A person whose capabilities are not known; a candidate or contender about whom little is known but who possibly has a good chance of winning. This was originally a racing term for a horse whose 'form' had been kept secret until it appeared on the racetrack. Benjamin Disraeli used the expression in 1831 in *The Young Duke*: 'A dark horse which had never been thought of . . . rushed past the grand stand in sweeping triumph'.

Davy Jones's locker. The name given by sailors to the evil spirit of the sea. Someone who visits 'Davy Jones's locker' is drowned at sea. The origin of these phrases, in use for around two hundred years, is obscure. Some sources suggest that they derive from the West Indian word 'duppy', meaning devil, and the name Jonah – Jonah being the biblical character who was considered so unlucky by his shipmates that he was thrown overboard and swallowed by a whale. Other authorities suggest that Davy Jones was a pirate who was drowned with his locker, probably a seaman's chest.

dawn raid. Business jargon for an attempt at a company takeover, without forewarning, by aggressive buying of shares as soon as the market opens.

day-glo. Gaudy; cheap and flashy. The expression derives from the brand name of a type of luminous paint.

dead as a dodo. The dodo was a cumbersome, flightless and dim-witted bird found exclusively on the islands of Mauritius and Réunion. It also tasted delicious, as the islands' colonists discovered, and this, combined with the fact that it was virtually a sitting target, swiftly brought about its extinction. The name dodo comes from the Portuguese word *dondo*, meaning silly, and is used to describe an exceptionally stupid person. Dead as a dodo is used to describe someone or, more regularly, something, that is completely dead and without hope of life – perhaps a piece of machinery or a car.

dead as a doornail. In the days before electric doorbells, door-knockers used to strike against a nail or stud embedded in the door. It is this nail that is referred to in the phrase 'dead as a doornail'. Being knocked on the head so hard and so frequently, there was no chance of any life being left in it.

dead-cat bounce. A phrase used in the financial world to describe the way in which share prices inevitably make a small, temporary recovery immediately after a major crash, then fall back to a lower level. Plotted on a graph, the line shows a steep descent followed by a brief bounce back. An as-yet untraced wit working in the financial industry decided that a cat thrown off a high building would behave in much the same way as share prices; fall, bounce up slightly and then hit the ground again, dead. Thus the dead-cat bounce got its name.

dead duck. Something that is no further use or something that is worthless for its purpose. *See also* DEAD AS A DODO.

dead from the neck up. Stupid; dull.

dead in the water. Business jargon used to describe a company that is drifting, with no sense of direction, and is ripe for a takeover.

dead man's hand. A poker hand containing a pair of aces and a pair of eights. The tradition is that Wild Bill Hickock, the wild west hero, was holding such a hand when he was shot in the back in Deadwood, South Dakota, in 1876.

dead man's handle. A safety-device used on board trains to ensure that if the driver becomes ill or incapacitated the train will stop. It usually takes the form of a handle which the driver holds; when he releases pressure the current is cut off and the vehicle slows down. Officially the dead man's handle is today known as a Driver's Safety Device, but the original name has stuck.

deadheading. A term used in the transport business to describe the practice of getting planes, trains, trucks and buses to places they are required and, in doing so, giving employees a free trip. 'Deadheads' are employees who use the company's transport for leisure purposes and without paying.

deadline. A final date by which a job must be finished. The concept of a strict limit which must not be overstepped derives from the deadline drawn around American military prison camps during the American Civil War. The deadline was a line marked around seventeen feet from main camp. Any prisoner who ventured beyond the deadline was immediately shot. One camp in particular, Andersonville, was notorious for its strictness. Fortunately modern deadlines are rather more flexible than the original.

deaf as a post. Someone who is so completely deaf that one might as well try conversing with a gatepost.

Dear John. A letter or other communication from a wife, fiancée or girl-friend informing the recipient that the relationship is at an end. The expression originated in the armed forces during World War II.

Death Row. An American expression for that part of a prison housing prisoners who are condemned to be executed. Because of the slowness and complexity of the American legal system it is not unusual for prisoners to spend many years in Death Row. *See also* DANCEHALL.

debrief. To interrogate a returning soldier, spy, astronaut, etc. on the completion of a mission, in order to obtain useful information or intelligence. The expression originated in World War II.

deccie. A person who is obsessed with the interior decoration and design of his or her home. So intent are deccies on keeping up with the latest styles that their houses are more often than not a shambles, the walls and furniture being constantly stripped in preparation for the latest paint finish or look. Deccies tend to be yuppies, with plenty of money to spend on rag-rolling, stencilling, colour-washing or whatever the latest trend happens to be. They also move house compulsively, constantly looking for new interiors to transform. *See also* YUPPIE, FOODIE etc.

decimate. Literally to kill one person in ten. The phrase derives from the practice in the Roman army of punishing mutineers or cowardice by selecting one man in ten at random to be executed by his fellow soldiers. Today we use the term as a synonym for mass destruction, whether it involves a tenth of the population or not.

deed poll. Legal term for a deed made by one party, so called because it was originally written on parchment that had a 'polled' or straight edge, as opposed to an 'indenture' that had an indented or wavy edge.

deejay. *See* DISC JOCKEY.

deep cover. A term used in the world

of espionage to describe an agent who assumes a cover story and a role for a long period and with such intensity that to all intents and purposes they become the character they are pretending to be. Such agents are also known as **sleepers** or **moles**; people who are put in place in the knowledge that it may take them years before they can be of any use, but on the assumption that one day they will attain powerful positions. Interestingly the word 'mole' is one that seems to have started in fiction and been popularised in the works of John Le Carré and other spy writers, before coming into popular factual use.

def, short for 'definitive' and meaning 'brilliant', is a late 1980s youth coinage along the lines of BAD, WICKED and CRUCIAL. It started among Hip Hop *aficionados* and is now in general use among the young. The fact that the BBC has called one of its teenage slots *DEF II* is probably an indication that the word is already on its way out.

de facto couples. *See under* COMMON-LAW MARRIAGE.

defensive medicine. In the USA doctors practise defensive medicine in an attempt to protect themselves from being sued for malpractice. It is reported that they are increasingly ordering a barrage of expensive tests and second opinions in order to cover themselves against charges of negligence. The American enthusiasm for litigation is such that some obstetricians have stopped practising because of the danger of being sued by parents of handicapped or less than perfect babies. Other practitioners have refused to treat people with high-risk conditions in case their relatives decide to sue if the patient dies.

dehiring. An American term to describe the practice and methods of getting rid of an unwanted employee without firing them, thus avoiding having to pay redundancy money or compensation. Generally dehiring means making life so difficult and unpleasant for the employee that he or she finds themself another job. *See also* TO BE GIVEN ONE'S CARDS *under* CARD.

déjà vu. Translated from the French, it means simply 'already seen'. It describes a particular psychological phenomenon in which an individual sees or experiences something for the first time in their lives, yet has a strong feeling that they have seen or experienced it before. It may happen when people visit strange cities and get the feeling they have already been there. Such experiences can sometimes be explained by reference to television and movies, which give us impressions of strange places which we later forget. When we go to those places, the latent memories are revived. It's worth noting, however, that déjà vu and other similar psychological phenomena were identified before the advent of television.

dekko. A slang expression, meaning 'a look'. This started out as army slang, originating in the late 19th century, and comes from the Hindustani word *dekho*, the imperative of the verb *dekhna*, meaning 'to look'.

Delhi belly. *See* AZTEC TWO-STEP.

deliver the goods. Used in its figurative sense, someone or something who delivers the goods succeeds in doing what was expected of them.

demi-veg. A shortened form of demi-vegetarian, describing a diet that is mainly vegetarian but includes poultry and fish. This diet is said to have been adopted by increasing numbers of people in the last few years. Medical experts see this trend towards healthy eating as an encouraging indication that warnings against red meat, fat and salt have been heeded. The meat trade is reported to be less than pleased about it.

demo tape. In the music business slang, a record or tape made by aspiring musicians to demonstrate their skills and the quality of their material. A 'demo' may also be a demonstration of protest against an issue, usually involving large crowds, banners and marching through the streets. In the computer world a 'demo disk' is a disk designed for use by the sales force to give a demonstration of the abilities of a particular computer or software program.

demographics. A phrase used in the worlds of marketing and social science to describe the variables by which a market or population is divided. Some of the most common variables are age, sex, race, occupation, education, religion, income, size of family, family lifestyle, location of home, nationality and social class. By dividing a market or population into these segments for study, businessmen can target their resources more accurately and social scientists can chart demographic changes.

denastify. *See under* NASTY.

denim. This coarse cotton cloth, used today for making JEANS, was known originally as *serge de Nîmes* after the French town where it was woven. Casual blue denim trousers are called jeans because the cloth from which they are made was once called 'jene fustian'. This phrase is in turn derived from Genoa, the Italian city where the fustian was produced. Many other textiles take their names from their place of origin. They include damask, from Damascus, and the woollen cloth known since the 13th century as worsted, which takes its name from the village of Worsted, once a major centre of the wool trade, near Norwich in Norfolk. *See also* BLANKET and CORDUROY.

deserts, to get one's just. To get one's comeuppance; to get the punishment one deserves. The word deserts derives from the French verb *deservir*, meaning to serve or do someone a bad turn.

designer. Used as an adjective, designer is one of the vogue words of the 1980s. The trend began when a few enterprising fashion designers whose names were well-known to the public cashed in on this familiarity by launching perfumes and other items for the mass market under their own names. Thus was 'designer perfume' created, being followed swiftly by 'designer jeans' and all manner of goods from luggage and shoes to underwear. As one pair of jeans or knickers looks very much like another, designers made a point of adding distinctive labels and logos to their products, thus starting the mass market obsession with 'designer labels'. This modern form of snobbishness dictates that the style or quality of an item matters less than the label inside it. The word designer is also loosely applied to anything that is highly fashionable and expensive, and therefore exclusive. Thus, Perrier water is known as 'designer water' and nouvelle cuisine as 'designer food'. There are even 'designer drugs', artificial drugs that simulate the effects of heroin and cocaine and whose formula can be varied to suit the user's individual tastes and requirements. *See also* CASUAL and FASHION VICTIM.

desk jockey. An office worker; a bureaucrat. The expression is a punning variation of 'disc jockey'.

Desmond. A lower second-class degree from a university or polytechnic; a 2:2. This British slang expression dates from 1986 and is a pun on the name of Desmond Tutu, the Archbishop of Cape Town, prominent in the news for his opposition to the South African regime.

devil's advocate. One who criticises or argues against a proposition, particularly one who does so for the sake of argument and not from conviction. In the Roman Catholic Church the *Advocatus Diaboli* (Devil's advocate) is a person appointed to argue the case against the claims of a candidate for canonisation.

die is cast, the. Julius Caesar is said to have uttered the Latin version of this phrase when he CROSSED THE RUBICON. The die is cast means that a gamble has been taken or an irreversible decision has been made; it alludes to the gambling game in which a die or a number of dice are thrown.

die like a dog, to. *See under* DOG.

die with one's boots on, to. This phrase was originally applied to people who were killed or hanged or came to other violent ends rather than dying quietly in bed. In modern usage, however, to die with one's boots on often means to die while still active. Someone who dies while working at their usual job may be said to have 'died in harness', a reference to the way in which overworked horses sometimes died as they worked.

diesel dyke. An aggressively masculine or 'butch' lesbian. *See also* DYKE.

different strokes for different folks. Each to his own taste. This expression was originally exclusively Black American, but was in general use by the 1970s.

dig. Although a vogue word among HIPPIES in the 1960s, the verb 'to dig', meaning to understand, in fact originated around 1935 and may have been in use for considerably

longer. There are two possible sources. One is the Celtic word *twig*, which is still in use in phrases such as, 'It didn't take him long to twig it.' More likely, perhaps, is the African word *degu*, meaning to understand.

digs. The word, meaning lodgings, is said to be a contraction of diggings, used to describe the dug-out homes made for themselves either by lead miners or prospectors in the Californian gold rush.

dike. *See* DYKE.

dingbat. In American slang, a word used for any object of which one has forgotten the name – a 'whatsit' or 'thingummy'. Dingus is an alternative form. The origin of the expression is unknown. Bartlett's *Dictionary of Americanisms* of 1877 says that it derives from a 'bat' (a piece of wood or metal) that could be 'dinged' (thrown), but this theory appears to be neither credible nor useful.

dingbats. In Australian slang, 'crazy'. To have the dingbats means to be in an irrational state or, more specifically, to be suffering from delirium tremens.

dinkum. Honest, authentic, genuine, sincere. Often used in the phrase **'fair dinkum'**, meaning 'on the level' or 'fair and square'. This Australian expression dates from the late 19th century, but the origin is not known.

dipping. Among its other meanings dipping is used in the airline business to describe the way in which stewards decant alcohol from the free bottles offered to first class passengers into miniatures. These are then sold to other passengers at the set price and the steward pockets the cash.

dirty old man. A dismissive phrase used to describe a lecherous, usually (though not always) elderly man. Such an individual might be a 'flasher' or a member of the 'dirty mac brigade' – a person who frequents striptease or sex shows or attends cinemas showing pornographic films. The phrase is said to date from the time when dark-coloured overcoats and mackintoshes were commonly worn, these garments providing an anonymous-looking disguise for anyone wanting to attend such diversions. In addition, the macs had slit pockets designed to enable a man to reach into his jacket or trouser pockets without the inconvenience of undoing the coat. This fact enabled men attending pornographic shows or movies to masturbate beneath their raincoats or to flash – expose themselves to passers-by, usually women.

dirty pool. Any activity that is unethical or of dubious morality. This American expression might be used of some activity that an Englishman might consider to be **not cricket**. *See also* DIRTY TRICKS.

dirty tricks. The phrases 'dirty tricks', 'dirty tricks campaign' and 'dirty tricks department' were three of a number of expressions coined to describe the activities of President Richard Nixon and his colleagues at the time of the Watergate scandal, which resulted in Nixon's resignation in 1974. Dirty tricks are dishonest, underhand and dubious practices used in politics and diplomacy to discredit the opposition. *See also* DISINFORMATION.

disc jockey/D.J./deejay. A performer who plays records and talks about music and other topical and, usually, light-hearted matters on radio shows. The phrase is also applied to one who plays records and supplies a commentary at a DISCOTHEQUE.

disco and **discotheque.** A type of nightclub where the patrons dance to recorded music, often with garish lighting effects. 'Disco' can also refer to the equipment used for playing records or to a particular style of music or style of dancing. The word discotheque was coined in France about 1950. It was modelled on the word *bibliothèque*, meaning a library, and originally a discotheque meant a record library. By 1954 it had acquired its present meaning, but still only in France. It was not until the 1960s that the word was adopted into English, and it was then soon over-shadowed by the abbreviated form 'disco'.

dish the dirt. An American slang expression, meaning to gossip or to spread rumours about others.

disinformation. Coined originally in the USSR but now in use the world over, disinformation is distorted, dishonest and inaccurate information disseminated to the Press and other media by governments or other 'official' sources. *See also* DIRTY TRICKS.

Disneyland daddy. The American term for a divorced or separated father who sees his children rarely but, when he does, takes them for special treats – to Disneyland for example.

distaff. An implement from which flax was drawn for spinning; spinning was women's work, and thus distaff became a way of referring to women, the female line of descent and women's work. From the same source we get the word spinster, to mean an unmarried woman who, one supposes, dedicated most of her time to spinning. Distaff had fallen largely out of common use until it was given a new lease of life by the women's movement. It is now used by feminists to refer to women's lives, work, thought, culture and so on.

ditto means 'the same again'. It is derived from the Latin word *dictum*, meaning 'that which has been said before'. Dictum is still in use to mean an accepted practice or rule.

Dixie or **Dixieland.** The southern United States (roughly identifiable with the former Confederate states). Dixieland is also used to describe the style of jazz originally played by street bands in New Orleans round about 1910. The name Dixie was popularised by Daniel D. Emmett's song *Dixie's Land*, published in 1859, which included the words 'away down South in Dixie'. There are two theories as to the origin of the name. One theory is that it derives from the American slang word 'dix', meaning a ten-dollar bill, which in turn derives from the French word *dix*, meaning ten, that was printed on ten-dollar bills once issued in New Orleans. Another theory is that it derives from the Mason-Dixon line which, before the Civil War, divided the southern slave states from the free northern states.

do a slow burn. An American slang expression, meaning to progress slowly and gradually from annoyance to extreme anger.

do-gooder. A derogatory term, originating in the USA, for a philanthropist or reformer who may be well meaning but whose efforts are ineffectual or unwelcome, or for someone who is pretentiously or ostentatiously right-minded.

do it. A euphemism or double-entendre meaning 'perform the sexual act'. It formed part of numerous slogans popularly used, originally as bumper-stickers in the USA and later as car-window stickers in Britain. For example, 'Surf-boarders do it standing up'.

do one's own thing. A HIPPIE catchphrase of the 1960s, meaning 'follow one's own inclinations'.

Do you come here often? A hackneyed conversational gambit with which a young man might attempt to initiate a conversation with a young woman in a disco or other public place of entertainment. The phrase probably originated in the 1920s. It is such a cliché that nowadays it is used only in a joky way.

doch-an-doris. Scottish term for a stirrup-cup or a final drink before departure. It comes from the Gaelic phrase *deoch an doruis*, literally 'a drink at the door'. The expression was made familiar by a song by Sir Harry Lauder.

Dockny. The redevelopment of London's dockland areas has created a new breed of East Ender, the Dockny. Docknies are, typically, wealthy, YUPPYISH young people who can afford to live in the newly-smart areas once inhabited by cockneys. *See also* DECCIE, FOODIE, YUPPIE etc.

Dr Livingstone, I presume? These words were spoken in 1871 by Henry Morton Stanley, a *New York Herald* journalist, when at long last he met Dr David Livingstone, the Scottish explorer and missionary who was thought to be lost in Central Africa. The phrase had a certain understated humour; not only had Stanley been struggling through the jungle for weeks, but there was absolutely no mistaking Dr Livingstone, who was the only white man in the area. By 1885 'Dr Livingstone, I presume?' had caught on as a catch-phrase and was in use both as a humorous greeting when friends bumped into each other unexpectedly and between strangers meeting for the first time.

Does a bear shit in the woods? An American catchphrase that is used as a response to what is considered a stupid question. It is probably the most common of a number of catchphrases that might be used in the same situation, e.g. 'Do chickens have lips?', 'Can snakes do push-ups?', 'Do frogs have water-tight ass-holes?', 'Does a wooden horse have a hickory dick?', 'Does Howdy

Doody have wooden balls?'. *See also* IS THE POPE CATHOLIC?

Does your mother know you're out? A sarcastic or derisive catchphrase addressed to someone displaying exceptional simplicity, to a conceited or presumptuous young person, or to a young person unsuccessfully trying to appear mature and sophisticated. The expression dates from the 1830s.

dog. In modern use the word dog is usually applied to something that is ugly, unwanted or worthless. An unattractive woman or a temperamental car could both be described as dogs. A handsome dog, however, is a sexually attractive but untrustworthy man. A dirty dog is someone with disgusting physical or moral habits. There are dozens of other phrases that refer to dogs. Many of them allude to the dog's persistent nature and to the fact that it has historically been despised – and still is in many parts of the modern world. Among such sayings are **to lead a dog's life** meaning to be beaten and yelled at and never left in peace. Interestingly enough, because of the way in which many of today's pet dogs are pampered, this phrase is sometimes used ironically or inaccurately to mean a luxurious and worry-free existence. **Let sleeping dogs lie** advises against stirring up trouble while **to go to the dogs** means to go into a miserable and squalid decline and **to die like a dog** describes a shameful end. It's sometimes said that we live in a **dog eats dog** world, i.e. a cutthroat, competitive world in which there is no sympathy for losers. Someone who is depressed by this might be said to be 'dogged' (meaning followed) by a black dog of depression, while others continue doggedly (meaning persistently) in the belief that **every dog will have his**

day i.e. that although they are downtrodden at the moment, their chance will come in the future. **A dog in the manger** is a mean person who has something he doesn't need but won't let others have the benefit of it. It is also generally used to describe a spoilsport – a person who ruins the enjoyment of others, even if he gains nothing by doing so. The saying relates to an old fable about a dog who made his bed in the hay- manger and would not allow the ox to eat from it, even though he could not eat the hay himself.

dog, to put on the. To put on airs; to show off; to dress flashily. This expression originated among American college students, especially at Yale, in the 1860s, and derives from the fact that they had to wear stiff high collars which were known colloquially as 'dog-collars'.

dog, to see a man about a. This is a euphemism, often used as an excuse when someone needs to go to the 'loo' or when they don't want to reveal their true destination. The phrase is American in origin and dates from around the turn of the century when it was often used as an euphemism for going to meet a BOOTLEGGER.

dog days. The hottest and most sultry days of the year that, in the northern hemisphere, occur in July and August. The Romans called this period *caniculares dies*. At this time the Dog Star, Sirius, in the constellation of Canis Major, rises in conjunction with the sun. The Romans believed that it was the combined heat of these two heavenly bodies that was responsible for the hot weather.

dog tags. US armed forces slang, dating from World War I, for the metal identification discs or tags worn around the neck by members of the armed forces.

doggie bag or **doggy bag.** A bag that is provided for taking home leftover food, especially meat, from a meal eaten in a restaurant, the original assumption being that such leftovers were intended for the diner's dog. The practice of providing doggie bags is much more common in the United States than elsewhere.

dolce vita. A life of indolence, self-indulgence and luxury. Literally, in Italian, 'sweet life'.

dollar. The word is said to have originated in the town of Sankt Joachimsthal in Bohemia in the 16th century. The silver from a nearby mine was turned into coins that were known as 'joachimstaler', which was in time shortened to '*taler*'. In Dutch these coins were known as '*daler*' and the Spanish knew them as dollars. The strong trading links between Spain and the USA established the dollar as a major currency, and so it was that in 1785 Congress 'Resolved that the money unit of the United States of America be one dollar.' *See also* ALMIGHTY DOLLAR.

dollar, to bet one's bottom. An American expression which comes from the game of poker and the habit of stacking gambling chips in a column. As play progresses the player takes chips from the top of the column to make his bet. If he is unlucky the column decreases so that eventually he bets his bottom dollar – he stakes everything he has left.

dollar diplomacy. Diplomacy dictated by financial interest; diplomacy in the field of foreign relations involving government support for commercial interests abroad, to further political and economic aims. The phrase became popular among critics of the Taft administration in the USA from 1909 to 1913, which pursued such policies in Latin America and the Far East.

domino theory. Originally the name given to a theory prevalent in the Pentagon and White House, that if one nation in south-east Asia became Communist-controlled, the neighbouring countries would 'topple' in a similar manner. Now used more generally of any situation where one event will precipitate a number of similar events.

Don Juan. A notorious womaniser is often called a Don Juan after the legendary 14th-century lover, scion of a noble Seville family and infamous libertine. According to *Don Giovanni*, Mozart's opera about his life, he had no fewer than 2,594 conquests. His last was young Donna Anna, daughter of Seville's commandant, who was killed when he surprised the great lover in the act. This was one outrage too many and the local Franciscan monks lured Don Juan to their monastery and murdered him. In Mozart's opera the legendary lover is reprimanded by a statue of the father and carried away to hell for his misdeeds. This has a basis in fact for, to conceal the murder, the monks claimed that Don Juan had been spirited to hell by the commandant's statue.

donkey's years. A very long time. This expression is not based on the fact that donkeys are particularly long-lived, but the fact that they have long ears! The original simile was 'as long as donkey's ears', but slurred pronunciation or association of ideas gave the expression its modern form.

don't all speak at once! An ironic catchphrase used by someone who has asked a question or made an offer or suggestion that has been greeted with a total lack of response. The phrase has been current both in Britain and the USA since at least the 1880s.

Don't call us, we'll call you. This phrase originated, around 1945, in the American entertainment business as a dismissal of someone attending an audition. It soon became a cliché, signifying rejection of someone applying for any sort of job or position.

Don't do anything I wouldn't do. A popular catchphrase, usually addressed to someone from whom one is parting. It originated in the first decade of this century. A common rejoinder is 'That leaves me plenty of scope'.

Don't get mad, get even. A sardonic modern proverb, implying that revenge is preferable to futile rage. It originated in the USA in the mid-1960s.

doom and gloom merchant. A person who thrives on bad news. It may be a journalist, whose profession it is to report such stuff, or simply a naturally gloomy individual whose main topics of conversation are death, disaster, the imminent destruction of the universe and the impossibility of escaping it. *See also* MERCHANTS OF DEATH.

Doomsday clock. Each issue of the Bulletin of the Atomic Scientists, a group founded in 1945, includes the representation of a clock whose hands point to the time left before the nuclear doomsday. In 1945 it was set at 11.52 and now stands at 11.58.

doorstepping. To doorstep someone in the non-derogatory sense is to call at their home to canvass their opinions. This kind of doorstepping normally occurs around election time. In its derogatory sense doorstepping describes intrusive tactics used by journalists, particularly those from the tabloids, in their attempts to get a story. This may include besieging someone's house and pestering them for information.

dope. This word, meaning drugs, derives from the Dutch word *doop*,

meaning 'sauce'. In the early 1800s *doop* was used to refer to anything that contained an unknown substance. Later, presumably because they were mysterious substances, it was applied to drugs. Around the turn of the century people made slow-witted by the use of drugs were called dopes and after that time the phrase was used to describe any stupid person, drugged or not. Dope is also used to mean 'the lowdown' or information. There is no agreed derivation of this word, but it may be that one had to search and enquire for such information in much the same way as one had to go looking for dope.

dormitory town. Found in the suburbs surrounding a major city, they are inhabited mainly by commuters who work in the city but cannot afford to or don't want to live there. The name arose because of the way in which a large proportion of the population leaves the area in the morning and returns at night to sleep. Modern planners are addressing this problem by making provision for 'urban villages'; small, self-contained enclaves in which people can both live and work without the necessity of commuting.

dot the i's and cross the t's. While other letters of the alphabet can be written flowing smoothly into one another, without the necessity of lifting the pen from the paper, i and t both require a separate stroke or dot. In the past some slapdash people have tried to economise on ink or time by omitting these dots and strokes, but those who are meticulous always dot the i's and cross the t's. The phrase is generally applied to anyone who takes great care and precision in what they do.

double Dutch. *See under* DUTCH.

double-O. To scrutinise or examine

carefully; to give someone or something the 'once-over' – from the initials of which this American expression is derived.

double talk. Verbal expression that is worded, either by accident or design, so that it is capable of being understood in two or more different ways; talk that sounds to the purpose but in reality amounts to nothing; speech that is deliberately unintelligible or a mixture of real and invented words.

doublespeak. *See under* GOBBLEDY-GOOK.

doublethink. The ability to accept as equally valid two contradictory opinions or beliefs. This expression was coined by George Orwell in his novel *Nineteen Eighty-Four,* published in 1949:

His mind slid away into the labyrinthine world of doublethink. To know and not to know, to be conscious of complete truthfulness while telling carefully constructed lies, to hold simultaneously two opinions which cancelled out, knowing them to be contradictory and believing in both of them, to use logic against logic, to repudiate morality while laying claim to it, to believe that democracy was impossible and that the Party was the guardian of democracy

Doubting Thomas. A person who refuses to believe something until they have seen it for themselves. The expression alludes to St Thomas, one of the twelve apostles, who refused to believe in Christ's Resurrection; 'Except that I shall see in his hands the print of the nails, and put my finger into the print of the nails, and thrust my hand into his side, I will not believe.' Christ later appeared to him and only after Thomas had touched his wounds did his faith return.

down home. An American, especially Black American, expression that means in or pertaining to the Southern USA or DIXIE; simple and folksy.

down in the dumps. Someone who is suffering from a brief period of depression or disappointment. Tempting as it is to make a connection between these feelings and the rubbish dump, the phrase is actually derived from the German word *dumpf,* meaning heavy, gloomy and dull.

down the drain. Wasted; lost.

down the hatch. A common toast, usually proposed before swallowing a drink in one draught.

down under. At the antipodes; in Australia, New Zealand, etc. The expression, which dates from the end of the 19th century, is common in Britain and North America, but is rarely used by Australians or New Zealanders.

downbeat. Pessimistic, depressing, gloomy, sombre; relaxed, unemphatic. This expression, which originated in the USA in the early 1950s, is derived from the musical term 'down-beat', literally a downward beat.

downside. Business jargon for the amount one stands to lose if a financial or commercial venture should fail.

downtime. Originally an American term applied in business to describe the periods when no work is done because of breakdowns in equipment, power failures, absenteeism and holidays, downtime is now applied to any unplanned non-productive time. Thus, someone who has an accident and finds themselves confined to a hospital bed may be asked whether they are enjoying their downtime.

draconian. Harsh rules or laws are often described as draconian. The word commemorates Athenian law-maker Draco, who in 621 BC set down a codified system of law for Athens. Until that date the law had not been officially recorded and those who administered it had interpreted it loosely. Draco's laws were exceptionally severe, making laziness and urinating in public capital offences, and because they were written down it was difficult to avoid imposing them. Most of Draco's code was repealed after his death, but the memory of it remains.

drag has a wide range of idiomatic meanings. It may mean an inhalation of smoke (from a cigarette) or, in the USA, power and influence. A man or transvestite who indulges his interest in women's clothing dresses in drag. A boring task or dull person may be said to be a drag, the same phrase that is used to describe a street (for example, the main drag). It is also, in the USA, a term applied to a slow kind of dance or a dance party.

drag someone kicking and screaming into the twentieth century. To force someone, especially someone with reactionary or old-fashioned views or attitudes, to adapt to change or to modern conditions.

dragon lady. A powerful and intimidating woman. This expression originated in the USA and was based on a character in the comic strip *Terry And The Pirates*, first published in the 1930s. More recently, it has taken on a more specialised meaning as a woman who wields great personal power by virtue of her position as the wife of a ruler – the outstanding examples being Mme Michele Duvalier (wife of Jean-Claude 'Baby Doc' Duvalier who ruled Haiti) and Imelda Marcos (wife of Ferdinand Marcos who ruled the Philippines).

draw a blank, to, has several different shades of meaning. It is used to describe an effort that fails to achieve anything, a negative result or the act of unsuccessfully trying to remember something; the allusion is to a lottery

in which numbered tickets win prizes but blank ones win nothing.

draw the line, to. Someone who draws the line establishes a metaphorical barrier beyond which they are not prepared to go. Several theories purport to have established the 'line' of the phrase. It has been suggested that in medieval England, when fields were divided into strips or smaller areas, a farmer would draw a line with his plough, marking out the boundary of his section. According to another source the expression has its origins in the 15th century, during the early days of tennis. At this time there was no established size for a court and the players would draw their own lines on the playing surface, agreeing that a ball that fell beyond the line was out.

drawing-board, back to the. This expression, used when plans go wrong and meaning, 'Now we'll have to start all over again', is ascribed to a cartoon published during the Second World War in America which showed an aircraft exploding in the background while in the foreground a designer, with his technical drawings under one arm, remarks 'Ah well, back to the old drawing-board.' The phrase can also be used more generally to mean, 'Time to get back to work again.'

drawing room. Until comparatively recently it was the custom for the women at a formal dinner to retire to the withdrawing room at the end of a meal, leaving the men to enjoy their cigars, port and stories together. When this practice came to an end and there was no need to withdraw there any more, the withdrawing room became the drawing room.

dream ticket. A supposedly ideal combination of two political candidates seeking office together, particularly candidates for the American presidency and vice-presidency. The concept usually depends on the fact that the two candidates appeal to different sections within the electorate, so together they can be more successful than either could individually. According to William Safire, in *The New Language of Politics*, the expression was first used in 1967: 'the Reagan and Brooke dream ticket'.

dreck or **drek.** An American term of disgust. Garbage, or something dirty and nasty, perhaps even something that is merely dull and uninspired, is known as dreck.

dressed to the nines. This expression, used to describe someone who is well and showily dressed, has two possible explanations. According to Brewer the phrase was originally 'dressed to the eyne', i.e. dressed to the eyes. Another source suggests that nine was a mysterious number consisting of a trinity of trinities and that therefore someone dressed to the nines was very special indeed. However, an American authority suggests that the phrase alludes to way in which men rate women's looks on a scale from one to ten. A woman who scores a nine is about as near to perfection as it is possible to get. As the phrase seems to have originated before this scoring system was invented, Brewer's derivation seems the most likely.

dressing down, a good. A strong telling-off; a tongue-lashing. The phrase comes from the abattoir and the butcher's shop, where to dress down a carcass is to cut it up. Like the beast hanging from the butcher's hook, anyone who is on the receiving end of a good dressing down ends up figuratively cut about.

drink like a fish, to. Many fish swim along with their mouths open, giving the appearance that they are drinking vast quantities of water. This is not true, of course – the water passes through their gills and supplies them with oxygen – but the image has given rise to the expression 'to drink like a fish', meaning to drink an excessive amount of alcohol.

drongo. A stupid, clumsy or worthless person. This Australian expression derives from the name of a racehorse in the 1920s, that was consistently and notoriously unsuccessful. Drongo foaled in 1921 and retired in 1925, having failed to win any of the thirty-seven races in which it was entered.

drop a brick. To commit a faux pas; to blunder.

drop a bundle. To lose a large amount of money, especially by gambling.

Droppies. An acronym (following the YUPPIES pattern) for Disillusioned Relatively Ordinary Professionals Preferring Independent Employment Situations. That is, people who abandon full-time careers in search of a freer self-employed way of life.

dry. Used in political circles to describe hard-line Conservative politicians who hold uncompromising monetarist policies and loyally support the policies advocated by Margaret Thatcher. The WETS are moderate Conservatives who cannot stomach the more extreme policies of the government.

dub. *See under* DAB.

duck or **duck's egg.** A score of no runs in the game of cricket. In modern usage 'duck' is the more common form, and this is a contraction of 'duck's egg', deriving from the resemblance between the figure 0 and the shape of a duck's egg. The corresponding expression in the USA is 'goose egg'.

duck, to score a. *See* TO LAY AN EGG *under* EGG.

duck and dive, to. In this phrase 'dive' is in fact unnecessary, because 'duck' comes from the Old English word *ducan*, meaning to dive – which is what one should do when one hears someone yell 'Duck!' We use the phrase ducking and diving to describe avoiding or evasive action, much in the way that a boxer ducks and dives to avoid his opponent's punches.

duck soup. An easy task. The origin of this American expression is not known, though it is probably connected with the expression 'sitting duck'.

dud. A match that refuses to light or a firework that fails to go off may be called a dud. The word derives from the Dutch word *dood*, meaning dead.

dunce. A dull-witted or stupid person. The word has an interesting origin, deriving as it does from the name of John Duns Scotus, a 13th-century Scottish theologian. He and his followers, known as Scotists or Dunsers, tried to defend the old style of theology against the influence of the new learning of their time. They failed and their leader's name became synonymous with ignorance and opposition to learning. Dunce is not much in use these days and anyone who is slow-witted at school is more likely to be defined as having 'learning difficulties' or labelled a 'slow learner' or 'low achiever'. In the USA a dunce might be described by his teachers as a 'deliberate abstractor'. In this extraordinary euphemism 'deliberate' is used in its sense of slowness and 'abstract' is used to mean 'to take something out of', therefore to learn.

Dutch. At the time of the Anglo-Dutch wars of the 17th century the word 'Dutch' came to be used in a number of English phrases in a derogatory sense. In most of them Dutch is a synonym for something strange and distinctly inferior. For example, the phrase **double Dutch**, meaning 'gibberish' or incomprehensible language uses 'Dutch' to mean 'foreign'. The expression reflects the traditional English scorn for foreigners who 'talk funny', and the Dutch were thought to be particularly worthy of scorn.

Other derogatory applications include a **Dutch treat**, the term applied when people going out or dining in a restaurant together agree to share the expenses equally. As treats go, **going Dutch** is a distinctly inferior kind – in fact not really a treat at all. The same could be said of **Dutch courage** which, far from being the real thing, is sham bravery inspired by alcohol. We use the phrase **Dutch comfort** to mean 'cold comfort' when things go very badly and the only consolation is that they could have been even worse. **A Dutch auction** is, to the English at least, an unusual 'foreign' affair at which the auctioneer starts at a high price and moves slowly down the scale until someone places a bid. This is the reverse of the usual kind of auction, in which bidders force the price of an item up. **A Dutch wife** is the term given to a bolster-type pillow, a fact that requires little explanation, while a **Dutch wind** inevitably blows from the wrong direction. **If . . . I'm a Dutchman** is a refutation of something the speaker strongly believes to be untrue or inaccurate. For example, 'If this fish is fresh, I'm a Dutchman', asserts that the fish is not fresh. In the 17th century, when the Dutch symbolised all that was despicable, this was a term with considerable force. The unfortunate Dutch were also seen as strict and humourless moralisers, which gave rise to the expression **to talk like a Dutch uncle**, i.e. to offer unwanted and unhelpful advice. Finally, **my old Dutch**, a term used by some men to describe their wives, has nothing to do with the Netherlands. In this phrase 'Dutch' is a contraction of 'duchess' from the Cockney phrase 'Duchess of Fife', rhyming with 'wife'.

dyed in the wool. Through and through; 100 per cent. The expression originated in the medieval textile industry. When cloth was dyed in the wool – that is, dyed in the raw state, before being spun and woven – the dye penetrated more thoroughly and was longer lasting than when it was 'dyed in the piece' – that is, as a finished article. The expression was being used figuratively as early as the 16th century.

dyke or **dike.** (1) A lavatory, especially one for communal use as in a school or army camp. This is a British and Australian slang expression. (2) A lesbian, a female homosexual. The origin of this term is unclear, but it has been conjectured that it is from 'morphodyke', an illiterate rendering of 'hermaphrodite'.

dystopia. An imaginary place in which everything is as wretched as possible. This word, formed by combining the negative prefix 'dys-' with UTOPIA, was coined by John Stuart Mill in 1868.

E

E numbers. In the 1980s, as part of a Common Market scheme for harmonising food control regulations in the member countries, food additives such as colourings, flavourings and preservatives were given numbers prefixed by the letter E (E, standing for European) and had to be listed on the packaging of food products containing them. The expression E numbers quickly came into common use as a synonym for food additives.

eager beaver. Someone who is enthusiastic, earnest or over-zealous in his work or in pursuit of a goal; a glutton for work. The expression normally implies censure rather than praise. The expression 'to work like a beaver' is over two hundred years old, but 'eager beaver' is more recent – it originated in the USA in the 1940s.

ear to the ground. To be in close touch with what's happening around one; alert to the latest trends and information. American Indians were said to put their ears to the ground to listen for the distant noise of horses pursuing them, though according to some sources this is just a myth popularised by Western writers and films.

earmark. In modern use to earmark something is to set it aside for a specific purpose. The expression dates from the time when farmers notched the ears of their sheep so that they could identify them and to discourage theft. Later the word came into more general use to describe any identifying mark and was figuratively applied to something, often money, that has been reserved for a particular reason.

earth, to run to. To discover someone in their hiding place. The phrase was originally a fox-hunting term referring to the way in which a fox runs to its lair, known as an earth, when pursued. The hounds follow the scent to the earth where the fox is dug out.

earwig. There is dispute about the origin of this word. Some sources declare that the name derives from the popular belief that the earwig likes to crawl into the human ear and from there penetrate the brain. They cite the Old English word *ear-wicga*, meaning ear beetle, as its derivation. Other sources suggest that earwig is more likely to have developed from the Old English phrase *eor*, meaning 'bud', and *wic* meaning 'hiding place', an undeveloped bud being the favourite hiding place of the insect. There is no dispute, however, that 'to earwig' someone is to attempt to talk one's way into the confidence of someone by flattery and insinuation.

easy. Especially as used in the colloquial phrase 'I'm easy', this may mean 'ready to comply with whatever is proposed; not having any preference for one course of action rather than another'. According to

Eric Partridge, this originated as RAF slang in about 1938.

Easy Street. Anyone who lives in Easy Street enjoys a comfortable existence with no financial cares. The phrase made its first appearance around the turn of the century but may refer to an earlier expression, 'an easy road', meaning one that is easy to travel along.

eat crow. To be forced to climb down or do something humiliating or extremely distasteful. The expression is said to have originated in the USA with a colourful incident that occurred during the 1812–14 war with England. During an armistice an American out hunting shot down a crow, unaware that he had crossed the British lines in doing so. An unarmed British officer spotted this trespasser and approached him, complimenting him on his marksmanship and asking if he could have a look at the man's gun. No sooner had the hunter handed it over than the officer turned it on him and forced him to take a bite out of the crow. When, with extreme reluctance, he did so, the officer handed him back his gun – at which point the hunter turned the tables and forced the officer to cat what was left of the crow.

eat humble pie. To acknowledge an error; to submit to humiliation. This expression dates from around 1830, but is a punning reference to a much earlier practice. From the 15th century, the word 'umbles' or 'humbles' was used to refer to the heart, liver and entrails of a deer. When a deer was killed on a lord's estate, the lord and his family would dine on venison, while his more menial retainers would partake of the umbles, served in the form of a pie.

eat your heart out. A show business catch-phrase, used by someone who has demonstrated some skill of which he is proud, and mockingly addressed to someone famous for that particular skill. A dancer, for example, having performed a clever dance routine, might express his self-satisfaction by saying 'Eat your heart out, Fred Astaire'. This catch-phrase was popularised in the late 1960s by the American TV comedy series *Rowan and Martin's Laugh-In*. According to Leo Rosten in his book *Hooray For Yiddish!*, eat your heart out is a direct translation of the Yiddish expression *es dir oys s'harts*.

eavesdrop. To listen secretly to other people's private conversation. The 'eavesdrop' used to be the name given to the space of ground on which water dropped from the eaves of a house, and the term 'eavesdropper' came to be applied, at the beginning of the 17th century, to someone who stood in the eavesdrop in order to hear what was being said inside the house. Eavesdrop, used as a verb, was a later back-formation from 'eavesdropper'.

eccentric. Correctly used, the word means 'off-centre' and is applied scientifically to planetary orbits. However, it is more often used figuratively to describe a person whose behaviour is off-centre or mildly unbalanced.

ecofreak. A 1980s word to describe someone who is passionately concerned about ecology. Ecology is derived from the Greek meaning 'a study of organisms in their surroundings' and is basically concerned with the study of our environment and creating a harmonious balance between man and nature. Ecofreaks, or econuts as they are sometimes known, can be characterised by their interest in recycling paper, glass and other materials and their ecologically-sound modes of transport, including bicycles and the Citroen 2CV car. They may choose to live in 'ecological architecture', (i.e. energy-efficient houses), generate their own electricity with wind-pumps and other devices and turn their gardens over to wilderness in which wildlife can thrive. They are also likely to be vegetarian and keen on organic methods of food production. They are deeply concerned about whales, pollution, the ozone layer and the destruction of the Amazonian rainforests among many other worthy causes. Though still a source of amusement in some quarters, **Green politics** seem set to become a major influence for the future; one test of the Greens' success will be the length of time it takes before the derogatory terms 'ecofreak' and 'econut' disappear from the language.

economic refugee. The phrase was first recorded in 1986, when it was used to describe people from third-world countries who attempt to find asylum in the west with the aim of obtaining a higher standard of living.

economical with the truth. This phrase became widely quoted in 1986 when it was used by the British Cabinet Secretary, Sir Robert Armstrong. Sir Robert, representing the British government in its attempt to prevent publication of Peter Wright's book *Spycatcher*, admitted under cross-examination in the Supreme Court of New South Wales that he might have been 'economical with the truth'. The expression, however, did not originate with Sir Robert Armstrong. It appears that it has long been a humorously intended piece of Civil Service jargon, similar to Churchill's phrase TERMINOLOGICAL INEXACTITUDE. Mark Twain is quoted as having said 'Truth is a valuable commodity, we need to be economical with it', and even earlier Edmund Burke had used the phrase 'economy of the truth'.

economy-class syndrome describes the tendency of those who travel in cramped economy-class airline seats to develop blood clots which may in turn lead to a heart attack. Passengers travelling in first class, with more leg-room, do not run the same risks.

ecstasy is derived from the Greek *ek*, meaning 'out', and *stasis*, meaning 'a standing', and used correctly describes a state in which the mind becomes separated from the body – literally an 'out of this world' experience. Ecstasy is also the name of an amphetamine-based drug that has been closely associated with the ACID House phenomenon.

ECU. Much used in international finance, Ecu is an acronym standing for European Currency Unit. It is an artificial currency unit based on the value of a number of Common Market currencies and was invented at a meeting between Helmut Schmidt, the Chancellor of West Germany, and Giscard d'Estaing, the President of France, in 1978. Centuries before the Common Market was thought of, an *écu* was a silver coin used in France, the equivalent of the English crown. The name came from the Latin *scutum*, meaning a shield, this being the symbol that was stamped on the coin.

effing and blinding. A euphemism for swearing. The 'effing' stands for 'fucking', the 'blinding' for 'bloody'. Someone who habitually peppers their conversation with these words may be accused of effing and blinding.

egg, to lay an. This expression is used by comedians and other entertainers to describe a situation in which their act totally fails to work. It has its origins on the cricket field, where the phrase 'a duck's egg' meant a score of zero because of the resemblance in shape of a duck's egg and the figure 0.

At a later date this was abbreviated and today a cricketer who walks back to the pavilion without scoring a run is described as having scored **a duck**. Entertainers on the early vaudeville stage adopted the phrase 'to lay a duck's egg' to describe the experience of failing to get a single laugh out of an audience. This was eventually shortened to 'laying an egg'.

egg on. To egg on a person is to encourage or urge them. In use since the 16th century, this phrase has nothing to do with eggs. Egg as used here is a variant on the old English verb 'to edge', meaning to push, incite or provoke someone nearer the edge. Someone who is being egged on is being 'edged' towards some goal.

egg on one's face, to have. To find oneself in an embarrassing situation as a result of a blunder; to make a fool of oneself. The expression originated in the United States in the mid-1960s. By 1972 the expression was sufficiently familiar in Britain to be used by Lord Chalfont in an article in *The Times*:

There is something reassuringly changeless about the capacity of the highest military authorities for getting egg on their face.

eggs, as sure as eggs is. The origin of this phrase, meaning 100% certain, is found in the world of mathematics. Most sources agree that it derives from the mathematical statement 'As sure as x is x.'

eggs, don't teach your grandmother to suck. An admonition used when a youngster tries to tell an older, more experienced person how to do something. The phrase first appeared in the writings of Jonathan Swift but no satisfactory derivation has yet been found for it. Before Swift's time there were other similar expressions meaning the same thing, notably 'to teach our dame to spin' and 'to teach his grandame to grope ducks'.

eggs Benedict. A typically American dish, consisting of toasted 'English muffins' topped with a thin slice of ham, poached eggs and hollandaise sauce. The name is said to derive from the fact that the dish was created by the chef of Delmonico's Restaurant in New York City especially for a couple of regular guests – a Mr and Mrs Legrand Benedict.

egghead. An intellectual or HIGH-BROW. The expression obviously derives from the popular image of an intellectual having a high dome-shaped head. It originated in either Canada or the United States in the early years of the 20th century, and was used in a letter by Carl Sandburg in about 1918. But the expression really came into popular use when it was used disparagingly by commentators on the 1952 US presidential campaign to describe candidate Adlai Stevenson and his associates.

ego trip. Something that is done entirely to indulge one's own interests or self-esteem or to display to others how splendid one is. The expression originated in the popular music industry in the late 1960s.

el cheapo. An American mock-Spanish expression, this is an adjective used to describe any cheap and inferior product.

elbow, to get the. *See* TO BE GIVEN ONE'S CARDS *under* CARD.

elbow grease. Muscular effort or physical exertion as applied when polishing, scrubbing, etc. The expression has been in use since the 17th century.

elbow room. To give someone enough space to move or to carry out whatever it is they are doing. The expression dates from the 1700s and probably refers to the space required at a table so that diners could eat without jabbing their elbows into each other.

93

electronic mail. *See* TELECOMMU-TER.

electronic sweetener. A euphemism for CANNED LAUGHTER, i.e. taped laughter that is added to a TV show or radio programme with the intention of persuading the audience that what they are watching or seeing really *is* funny.

electronic virus. Used by malicious computer hackers and disgruntled operators to destroy software programs. The virus is in fact a small program which the saboteur inserts into a computer's memory. When the computer is switched on this immediately 'infects' the disk, sometimes ruining it immediately, sometimes initiating a long destruction process. Electronic viruses inserted by employees with a grudge are said to have caused havoc in some fully-computerised companies.

elephants, to see pink. to suffer from a hallucination brought on by an excess of alcohol. The origin of the phrase has not been fully researched but it may be associated with the expression 'seeing the elephant', used by soldiers in the American Civil War to describe their terrifying first experience of battle. This in turn was derived from the awe with which people emerged from the tent of a travelling circus, having seen an elephant for the first time in their lives. Certainly someone who sees pink elephants is likely to find the experience awesome!

elevator music. Bland, instantly forgettable music of the kind played in lifts and other public places. *See also* MUZAK.

Elginism. This word went on record for the first time in 1986 to describe the practice of stealing antique fittings – fireplaces in particular – from old houses. This euphemism is derived from the activities of Thomas Bruce, 7th Earl of Elgin, famous for his collection of ancient Greek artefacts, including sections from the Parthenon frieze, which are now kept in the British Museum. The Greek government has been fighting for many years to have the Elgin Marbles, as they are known, returned. They accuse Elgin of being little more than an opportunistic thief. The British government prefers to take the view that Elgin saved the artefacts from destruction and refuses to return them to their place of origin. Whichever side of the argument one comes down on, the word Elginism to describe the theft of antique architectural fittings is an inspired one.

embuggerance. The journalist John Silverlight drew the attention of his readers to this word in his *Observer* column in 1984. It was apparently used commonly by members of the Royal Engineers in the Falklands to describe an awkward and frustrating problem, caused either by natural difficulties or administrative foul-ups. Subsequent correspondents pointed out that the word had been in use among engineering workers for about 20 years. Presumably the expression is a portmanteau word, combining 'bugger' and 'encumbrance'.

Emerald Isle, The. Ireland, so called because of its lush green verdure. The epithet was coined by Dr E. J. Drennan (1754–1820) in his poem, *Erin*:

Arm of Erin! Prove strong, but be gentle as brave
And uplifted to strike, still be ready to save,
Nor one feeling of vengeance presume to defile
The cause or the men of the Emerald Isle.

emergent nations. Countries which, a few years ago, were known as underdeveloped nations or developing nations.

empty nester. In American colloquial usage, a parent whose children have grown up and left home.

end – to be at the end of one's tether. To have run out of patience. It alludes to a horse or goat which runs out of grass once it has reached the end of the rope to which it is tethered. In America and sometimes in Britain the phrase 'to be at the end of one's rope' is also used to mean the same thing.

end, to the bitter. To go as far as possible, perhaps in some difficult task or journey, until one has either seen it through or been defeated by it. Some sources trace it back to the biblical phrase, 'Her end is bitter as wormwood', to mean death, but it is more likely to have a nautical origin. In early sailing vessels the anchor rope of a ship was attached to an oak pillar called a 'bitt' and the length of rope nearest this pillar was known as the 'bitter end'. If the anchor was lowered and all the rope paid out, one came to the bitter end, which was as far as it was possible to go.

endorsement. This word has recently taken on a new meaning in the world of commerce and advertising. It now means an arrangement whereby a famous person is paid a large fee in return for allowing his name to be associated with a product.

enfant terrible. A French phrase literally meaning 'an embarrassing child'. It is used to describe a talented but wayward newcomer to a field; someone who has no time for the normal conventions or niceties of their situation.

English as she is spoke. A jocular reference to the broken English spoken by some foreigners or to the misuse of English by native speakers. The phrase comes from the title of a Portuguese-English phrasebook produced by a Portuguese gentleman by the name of A. W. Tuer at the end of the 19th century. This phrasebook became the butt of many a joke because of its inept handling of English phraseology. Tuer, it seems, did not speak any English although he did speak French, and he produced his phrasebook with the aid of a Portuguese–French dictionary and a French–English dictionary.

English caps. *See under* FRENCH LETTER.

English culture. Used in CONTACT MAGAZINES, 'English culture' describes sexual activity involving whipping, caning and other physical punishments. This particular sexual predilection has been known as **The English Disease** since the early 1800s and perhaps reflects the influence of the English public school system. Other related phrases include **French culture** (fellatio and cunnilingus), **Greek culture** (heterosexual anal intercourse) and **Roman culture** (group sex and orgies).

English sickness. This phrase was coined in Germany after the Second World War to describe the industrial stagnation caused by a combination of inflation and rampant trade unionism at a time when the Fatherland was rebuilding itself. Not to be confused with THE ENGLISH DISEASE (*see* ENGLISH CULTURE).

enter the lists. Someone who joins in a rivalry or competition. The phrase derives from the 14th and 15th centuries when chivalry was the order of the day and knights met to contest against each other at jousting tournaments. Challengers entered the arena through the lists; in modern figurative terms, anyone entering the lists is prepared for a fight.

enterprise zone. In 1980s business-speak, this is an urban area to which businesses are attracted by means of tax concessions and other financial inducements offered by the government or governmental agencies.

environmental cleaner. *See under* FLIGHT ATTENDANT.

equal opportunity employer. A phrase that has been appearing in advertisements of job vacancies in the British press since the mid-1980s. It is used, mainly by local authorities and other public bodies, who apparently need to state explicitly that their selection of employees will not be prejudiced by AGEISM, racism or SEXISM.

Ernie. Since 1956, when Premium Bonds were introduced in the United Kingdom, the name Ernie has been applied to the machinery that selects the prize-winners. The name is an acronym, standing for Electronic Random Number Indicator Equipment.

Eskimo. The literal meaning is 'eater of raw flesh', a term rejected by the Innuit people. Innuit simply means 'the People' or 'the human beings'.

Eskimo Nell. The central character in a long, bawdy ballad, popular since the late 19th century among drunken lecherous men, especially rugby club members and medical students.

esky. Australian slang in use since the late 1960s, an esky is a portable cooler for drink, particularly for cans of lager. The word is derived from 'Eskimo'.

esoteric. The Greek mathematician Pythagoras gave us the word esoteric, meaning something secret or rarefied, only for the initiated. The term came from his practice of lecturing to his students from behind a curtain. The students who were allowed to listen but not to see him were known as 'exoteric' disciples, members of an outer circle. The privileged ones who were allowed to go behind the curtain and see him as he lectured were known as his 'esoteric' followers.

etiquette. A French word meaning 'ticket'; it is in fact the origin of the English word 'ticket'. It came into English use to describe a code of social conduct because at one time guests at formal functions were issued with a ticket-style slip, known as an etiquette, telling them the correct dress for the occasion and detailing the procedures that were to be followed.

Eve with the lid on. An apple pie. This American lunch-counter slang expression derives from the association of Eve with an apple in the Bible story of the Garden of Eden.

even break. This phrase, meaning to give someone a fair chance, comes from the sport of coursing. In one version of this bloodsport two greyhounds are released to catch a hare. According to the rules the dogs must be released simultaneously from the leash; they must receive an even break.

even Steven. Something that is divided or shared out equally, or a confrontation that is resolved fairly can be described as 'even Steven'. The expression comes from Jonathan Swift's *Journal to Stella*, in which he told the tale of a man named Steven who hit his wife six times for every blow she delivered, declaring that this made him even with her. Why such an obviously unfair contest should have given us a phrase meaning 'an equal outcome' is a mystery that has yet to be solved.

Everest syndrome. When Sir Edmund Hillary was asked why he had climbed Everest he replied, 'Because it is there.' His answer has given us the 'Everest syndrome', used in scientific and academic circles, to describe the tendency of researchers to study obscure theoretical subjects 'because they are there' rather than concentrating on useful and practical projects.

Every dog will have his day. *See under* DOG.

Everyman. The eponymous central character of a famous 16th-century morality play. He is the plain, ordinary man who, in this allegorical tale, makes his journey through life and encounters the characters of Death, Beauty, Knowledge and Goods (among others) on the way. None of them will accompany him on his journey except Good Deeds, who sees him through to the end. Today we used the phrase to mean the average person, the MAN ON THE STREET.

ex. A former wife or husband, boyfriend or girlfriend, etc. This expression is not as modern as one might suppose. The Oxford English Dictionary has an illustrative quotation dating from 1929:

'Phil was your first husband, was he?' 'Yes; he's my ex,' she said.

exchequer. Hundreds of years ago, taxes paid into the king's treasury were counted out on the squares of a chequered tablecloth, the cloth serving as a primitive calculator. From this device the department of royal, and then government, finance became known as the exchequer. The name is still used today despite the fact that more sophisticated (though not necessarily more accurate) equipment has been introduced to aid the calculations.

excrementum cerebellum vincit. A facetious Latin rendering, originating among British army officers during World War II, of their contemporary slang expression 'bullshit baffles brains'. *See also* ILLEGITIMIS NON CARBORUNDUM.

expletive deleted. This phrase originated in 1974 when transcripts of President Nixon's White House tapes were issued as part of an investigation into the Watergate scandal. The tapes contained a lot of strong language which, for public consumption, was cut out and the words 'expletive deleted' inserted. The phrase cropped up so many times and became such a joke that expletive deleted was adopted as a common euphemism for swearing.

extraterrestrial. H. G. Wells is given the credit for inventing the term to describe something from beyond the limits of the Earth. In 1939 it was used for the first time as a noun to describe a being from outer space. The word and its abbreviation, E.T., came into widespread use after the success of the film of the same name in the early 1980s.

eye – to have an eye to the main chance. This phrase means 'to be on the lookout for opportunities'. It is widely believed to have originated with a dice game called 'hazard' in which players threw the dice twice. The first throw was known as 'the main' and the second as 'the chance'. Quite how the two married together to give us an eye to the main chance has not been discovered.

eye-opener. Originally a drink or cocktail taken as a pick-me-up or cure for drowsiness. The expression is now applied to an event or revelation that takes people by surprise and wakes them from a metaphorical slumber.

F

fab. An in-word of the 1960s, used to describe anything that was BRILL, wonderful or amazing. For many people it will always be linked with the Beatles, widely known as the 'Fab Four'. Fab is an abbreviation of fabulous, a word originally applied only to wondrous events and creatures described in fables, but now used to describe more mundane matters. The words incredible and terrific have suffered the same change of meaning. In modern use they are synonyms for wonderful, brilliant, amazing and so on, but applied correctly incredible describes something that cannot be believed and terrific something that inspires terror. *See also* FANTASTIC.

façadism. This expression is the property developer's term for the practice of preserving the façade of a listed or landmark building while demolishing and rebuilding what lies behind it.

face, to laugh on the other side of one's. *See under* LAUGH.

face, to lose. To lose one's dignity in public. It is a literal translation of the Chinese phrase meaning the same thing and came into use in English in the 19th century. Needing something to express the opposite, the English invented **to save face**, meaning to retain or regain one's dignity.

face the music, to. To confront a difficult situation, a hostile reception, etc.; to accept whatever punishment is due. The source of this expression is held by some to be theatrical, referring to an actor on stage who must face the judgement not only of the theatre audience but also of the musicians in the orchestra pit below the footlights. It seems more probable, however, that the phrase is of military origin. When a soldier was dishonourably dismissed from the service, he would literally be 'drummed out' in a formal ceremony.

facility. The word is derived from the Latin *facilitas* and describes easiness or aptitude. A person who has a facility for foreign languages, for example, is someone who finds them easy to learn. In modern use facility has become a euphemism for an institution or a centre, often one that deals with something unpleasant. Thus a prison may be known as a 'correctional facility', a rubbish dump as a 'waste disposal facility' and a town's high street as a 'shopping facility'. Inherent in all these phrases is an idea of modernity, increased efficiency and easiness of use. In the language of politics and government, a 'facility trip' is a trip made by politicians to explore local conditions and facilities. But someone who asks if they may **utilise the facilities** is not requesting to visit the prison, rubbish dump or shopping centre – this is a long-established euphemism for a trip to the lavatory.

faction. An old-established word meaning a contentious party in a state or society. In the 1980s, however, it began to be used in a new and completely unrelated sense, as a portmanteau word referring to books, films, TV programmes, etc. that mingle 'fact' and 'fiction'.

fad. A short-life fashion; something that is all the rage one day, forgotten the next. It probably derives from an English dialect verb fad, meaning, according to the *Oxford English Dictionary*, 'to busy oneself with trifles.' From there fad came to mean the trifles themselves. Another derivation, however, suggests that the word comes from the phrase 'for a day' – the length of time a fad was supposed to last.

fag. The words 'fag' to mean a cigarette and 'fag end' to mean the stub have their origins in the textile industry where the fag was a coarse piece of cloth at the end of a length. The phrases started in mill towns and spread into general use. In the USA a fag is slang for a homosexual. The word is an abbreviation of faggot but there is some debate about which came first; it has been suggested that faggot is a later euphemism for fag. Where the word got this meaning is uncertain but American dictionaries suggest that it is derived from the English public school system: In public schools a fag was a young pupil who was assigned as a kind of servant to an older boy. The avowed aim of this set-up was to teach pupils how to treat servants fairly and responsibly in later life, each boy learning from his experience of being first lackey, then master. Despite such noble aims many fags were sexually exploited. We also use the word fag to describe a boring chore. This also has its origin in public schools, where it was fags who were expected to do such jobs.

fag hag. A woman who enjoys and seeks out the company of homosexual men. *See* FAG.

Fahrenheit. This scale for measuring temperature was invented by Gabriel Daniel Fahrenheit (1686–1736), a meteorologist working in Amsterdam. The scale identifies the freezing point of water as 32 degrees and its boiling point at 212 degrees. Though still in wide use, particularly in the USA, it is being gradually overtaken by the more logical CELSIUS scale.

fail-safe. A system or mechanism designed to prevent a dangerous situation developing through mechanical failures or human error. The original fail-safe system was intended to prevent nuclear war and was developed in the 1950s by the US Air Force. The fail-safe procedure required a bomber to return to base without dropping its nuclear bombs if it failed to receive a specific order to drop them. With this system in operation, failure to receive a radio signal would not accidentally trigger a nuclear conflict. The expression is now used to describe any safety system with built-in checks and precautions. *See also* DEAD MAN'S HANDLE.

fair dinkum. *See* DINKUM.

fairy. A male homosexual, especially an effeminate one. In the Oxford English Dictionary the first quotation illustrating the use of fairy in this sense dates from 1895, referring to a secret organisation of homosexuals, The Fairies of New York.

fake it. To make a pretence of having knowledge, skill, etc. that in fact one does not possess; to bluff. This originated as a slang expression among American jazz musicians in the early 1900s, and meant 'to improvise'.

Falklands factor refers specifically to the phenomenon that followed the Falklands War in 1982, when the unpopular Conservative government experienced a complete turnaround in opinion after the British victory over Argentina in the Falkland Isles. The phrase is also used generally to describe any unpredictable event that radically changes the popularity of a political party.

fall. The word 'fall' to describe autumn is now used exclusively in the USA, but it's not an American invention. It was originally an English term that was taken to America by the settlers and has been preserved there. Autumn was the Latin word for this season of the year; it came into use in the 13th century. Fall started out as 'leaf fall' in the 15th century.

fall guy originated around the end of the last century when professional wrestling became a popular spectator sport. Many of the bouts were rigged, one wrestler promising to 'take a fall' if the other agreed to treat him gently in the ring. It is reasonable to assume that because of this the 'loser' would be known as the 'fall guy'. In the heat of the match the wrestler rigged to win the bout would often forget his promise and do the loser some real damage, and from this we get the modern meaning of a fall guy as a man who is duped or dogged by bad luck.

fall off the wagon. To begin drinking alcohol again after a period of abstinence. Also, by extension, to default from any other self-imposed abstinence or moderation. *See also* ON THE WAGON.

fall-out. In the sense of the radioactive refuse from a nuclear explosion, the term fall-out was introduced in the late 1940s. By the mid-1950s it was being used also in an extended sense, to mean the unintended effects of an action.

fan. An enthusiastic supporter or devotee. Fan, in this sense, is a contraction of 'fanatic' and was first used in the USA in the 1880s, originally being applied to baseball supporters. The word 'fanatic' is itself derived from the Latin word *fanum*, meaning a temple, and the literal meaning is someone inspired or frenzied by religious rites.

fan club. Used in the world of finance and business, a fan club consists of a number of people who, independently and without conspiring with each other, decide to buy significant numbers of shares in a company. A fan club is legal; a **concert party**, which is defined as two or more people who agree 'in concert' to buy or sell a company's shares in an attempt to influence the price, is not legal. The distinction between a fan club and a concert party is often difficult to judge, as some people have found to their cost.

fanny is a word to be used with some care. Though it is most commonly used as a euphemism for 'buttocks' it can also refer to the female genitals. It is probably derived from the eponymous heroine of John Cleland's early pornographic novel *Fanny Hill*.

Fanny – Sweet Fanny Adams or **Sweet F.A.** means 'nothing at all'. It has a gruesome derivation in the tale of eight-year-old Fanny Adams, who in 1867 was murdered and her dismembered body thrown into the river at Alton, in Hampshire. At the same time the Royal Navy was issued with its first rations of tinned mutton and by morbid association the meat became known as Sweet Fanny Adams. Eventually the phrase came to be used for anything that was cheap and worthless and, in its latest evolution, for nothing at all.

fanny-dipper. American surfers' slang term for a swimmer as opposed to a surfer.

fantastic. Today we use the word to describe something that is brilliant, wonderful or excellent, but in its original sense it was used to denote something imaginary, emanating from the world of *fantasy*. This is just one example of a group of words, including incredible, terrific and fabulous, which in modern use are synonymous with each other but which have quite separate and specific original meanings. *See also* FAB.

fanzine. A portmanteau word formed by running together the words 'fan magazine'. The expression was first used by science fiction enthusiasts in the late 1940s in the USA for their amateur fan magazines. The use of this expression in fields other than science fiction – fields such as pop music, home computers, etc. – is comparatively recent.

fascist. The fascists were an Italian political movement who took their name from the *fasces*, bundles of rods with an axe protruding from them, which were used as a symbol of authority by ancient Roman magistrates. The movement was founded in 1919 by Benito Mussolini, who became Prime Minister of Italy in 1922 and in 1925 declared himself Dictator, and the fascists were right-wing totalitarian nationalists who outlawed socialism and other radical left-wing politics. They controlled Italy until they were overthrown in 1943. Once established in Italy, the expression fascism was soon being applied to other totalitarian movements. Hitler's Nazi regime was christened 'fascist'; more modern pundits have used the term to describe the actions of the South African government. In recent years phrases such as 'style fascist' – a person who upholds a single style of dressing, architecture, interior decor etc. and criticises those who do not conform to it – have emerged. Fascist is always used as a term of insult, implying a totalitarian desire to control others.

fashion victim. A term coined in the mid-1980s to describe those people, mainly women, who follow fashion without real understanding or judgment. According to *Vogue*, a fashion victim might slavishly copy the latest trend regardless of whether it suits her, or buy an expensive total 'look' in which she then appears unnatural and unspontaneous. By definition the fashion victim lacks personal style and flair.

fast food. Food that can be prepared and served quickly. Today the phrase almost invariably invokes the image of a hamburger and fries, served in one of the huge multinational catering chains such as Macdonald's. Fast food is not a modern invention – *see* BISTRO for an earlier example. *See also* JUNK FOOD.

fast track. A business whizzkid travels to the top of his career in the fast track, leaving his less go-getting colleagues behind him. The methods he employs to move upwards at such speed are known as 'fast-tracking'.

fat cat. A privileged, wealthy, comfortable and often complacent person; someone who doesn't have to worry too much about their own welfare. This phrase, coined in the 1920s, is an obvious reference to a pampered pet. Fat-catting is a more modern American term to describe the way in which people who reach the top try to make their position all the more comfortable by awarding themselves new perks and privileges.

fate worse than death. This is a euphemism for rape. In the days when sexual purity was the most highly-prized of female virtues, a woman who was raped suffered not only the violence of the act but was also dishonoured in the eyes of the community. She was likely to lose her family, friends, home, livelihood and the chance of marriage – which must certainly have seemed a fate worse than death.

fathom is derived from the Old English word *faethm*, meaning 'embracing arms'. The fathom is a nautical measure of six feet, which is roughly the span of a man's arms. Indeed the fathom was once defined as 'the length of a man's arms around the object of his affection.'

feather in one's cap, a. When American Indians of certain tribes killed an enemy they would add a feather to their headdress to show their bravery. Brewer points out that this custom is followed in other societies too. A feather in one's cap therefore means a significant achievement or honour.

feather one's nest, to. When building nests, some birds use their downy breast feathers to make a soft lining for the eggs. This habit has given us the expression to feather one's nest, meaning to make financial provision for oneself and therefore to be in a comfortable position. It is often used disapprovingly of people who take care of their own interests at the expense of others.

featherbed, to. The action of making comfortable by favourable, especially economic or financial, treatment. This expression has been in use since the 1920s and has almost always been used in either of two contexts: trade unions being allowed by employers to create or retain unnecessary jobs; or the generous treatment by governments of the farming industry.

feet – to go out feet first. To die. Presumably it refers to the traditional way of carrying a body out of a house.

feet of clay. This phrase comes from a biblical story, Daniel 2: 31–32, in which Nebuchadnezzar has a dream about an idol made entirely of metal except for its feet, which are made of clay. The dream is interpreted as meaning that, however mighty the idol, its clay feet make it vulnerable. Today when we speak of someone having feet of clay we mean that no matter how much they are admired or idolised, they are bound to have weaknesses or character flaws that make them less than perfect.

feisty. This American word is used to describe someone full of energy and fight. It derives from the tendency of such a person to use their fists.

fellow traveller. Someone who sympathises with the aims of the Communist Party without actually being a member. An early use of this expression was in the American magazine *The Nation* in 1936:

> The new phenomenon is the fellow-traveller. The term has a Russian background and means someone who does not accept all your aims but has enough in common with you to accompany you in a comradely fashion part of the way.

Fellow traveller is a direct translation of the equivalent Russian expression *poputchik*, coined by Leon Trotsky. Interestingly, the Russians have another word meaning fellow traveller – that is, *sputnik*, the name used for the first artificial satellite.

fence. A slang word for someone who receives and trades in stolen goods.

fence, to sit on the. Refusing to commit oneself to something. When people 'come down off the fence' they commit themselves to standing on one side or other.

fender-bender. In the USA, a minor motoring accident. (The American word 'fender' is the equivalent of the British 'bumper'.)

Ferris wheel. A popular fairground ride, consisting of a huge revolving wheel with carriages attached. The first Ferris wheel was seen at the Columbian Exposition (the 'World's Fair') at Chicago in 1893. The wheel was 250 feet in diameter and carried 36 cars, each capable of taking

40 passengers. It was named after its designer – George Washington Gale Ferris, an engineer from Galesburg, Ohio.

fiasco. A total failure. It derives from the Italian word for 'bottle' and was used by Venetian glassblowers to describe bad workmanship, perhaps on the grounds that a badly-made bottle bursts on use.

fiddle while Rome burns. To be absorbed in something minor while a major emergency is in progress. This phrase is derived from the story that the Emperor Nero set fire to Rome in 64 AD, then sat and watched the blaze while playing his fiddle – or harp. Historians of the period say that in fact he was nowhere near Rome when the city burned.

field – have a field day. A military term for a day when troops perform manoeuvres in front of visitors. It is therefore a special day, and it is in this sense that it has passed into common use to describe a triumphant or important occasion.

field, to play the. In the 19th century this phrase was used by the racing fraternity to mean a betting system which involved placing a bet on every horse in a race except the favourite. Some of that original sense of scattering one's resources widely still remains, for today someone referred to as playing the field would stand accused of having many affairs and romances but showing no sign of a serious attachment.

Fifth – to plead the Fifth Amendment. This American expression refers to the Fifth Amendment of the US Constitution which states that no one should be required to give self-incriminating evidence. Thus in American courts anyone can refuse to give evidence by pleading the Fifth Amendment. The phrase is also used jokily by those who want to get out of something or who don't want to answer a question, make a choice, etc.

fifth column. Traitors, infiltrators or subversives; those within a country who are working for the enemy. The expression originated during the Spanish Civil War. The Nationalist general Emilio Mola had four columns of troops besieging the city of Madrid, which was held by the Republicans. When asked in a radio interview if four columns were sufficient, he replied that he had a fifth column – the people within the city who were on his side and were waiting to assist in its overthrow. The expression was popularised in the English-speaking world when Ernest Hemingway wrote a play entitled *The Fifth Column*.

fifth generation. A term applied in all areas of technology and computers to describe the machines that will be in use in the 1990s. They will be easier to use and more sophisticated than anything currently available, many of them involving ARTIFICIAL INTELLIGENCE. *See also* FIRST GENERATION.

fifth man. When two British Foreign Office officials, Guy Burgess and Donald Maclean, defected to the USSR in 1951 the event sparked a major security hunt to identify the third, fourth and fifth men who had been involved with them. Kim Philby was soon identified as the third man in 1963, but it was not until 1979 that the fourth man was revealed to be the Queen's art adviser, Anthony Blunt. The fifth man has not yet been identified, though there has been no shortage of guesses.

fig, not worth a. When one describes something as not worth a fig or says 'I don't care a fig', one is not referring to the fruit but to an ancient gesture known as the Spanish fig or *fico*. The *fico* was made by thrusting the thumb upwards between the first and second fingers. Why this gesture should be known as a 'fig' is uncertain, but one source tells the story of Emperor Frederick I whose wife was insulted by two Italians. As punishment for this the men were required to remove a fig inserted in the anus of an ass using only their teeth. The Spanish fig may be a reference to this unpleasant incident, and the gesture may mean the ancient equivalent of 'Kiss my ass (or arse).'

filth. This English slang word for the police has, according to Eric Partridge, been in use since around 1950.

filthy lucre. The word filthy in this phrase is redundant; lucre derives from the Latin *lucrum*, meaning 'gain' or 'booty'. Thus lucre on its own means ill-gotten gains and technically there is no need for the qualifying filthy. However, as most people use lucre as a simple synonym for money, when filthy is added it takes on the meaning 'dirty money'.

finagle. To contrive or bring about by dishonest, devious or dubious means; to wangle, fiddle, scheme. This colloquialism originated in the USA, but derives from an English dialect word: 'fainague', meaning 'to cheat'.

finagle factor. The mathematical constant by which a wrong answer needs to be multiplied in order to produce the correct answer.

fine – to be in fine fettle. A *fettle* or *fetel* was a kind of belt worn by ancient English warriors when they went into battle. When their *fettles* were in place they were on good form, ready to go off to the fray. To be in fine fettle today means pretty much the same thing – to be in excellent shape or condition.

fine figure of a woman. *See under* CHUBBY.

fine kettle of fish. According to Brewer, to go to eat a 'kettle of fish' was a description of a riverside picnic where a fresh-caught salmon was boiled and eaten. The discomfort and inconvenience of such a gathering may have led to the phrase a fine kettle of fish or a pretty kettle of fish, meaning a muddle or a mess. Another source traces the origin of the phrase to the *kiddle*, a basket-style trap designed to fit a dam sluice. These devices could only legally be used by royal officials, but they were often raided by poachers who destroyed the baskets when they removed the fish. It has been suggested that on discovering a ruined trap the anguished cry might have gone up, 'Here's a fine kiddle of fish!', meaning 'Here's a fine mess!'

finger-lickin' good. Devised as an advertising slogan for Kentucky Fried Chicken in the mid-1970s, this expression immediately passed into general colloquial use. As a term of approval it is applied usually, but not exclusively, to food.

fingers, to burn one's. *See under* BURN.

fink. A despised person. When it was first coined the word was applied to strikebreakers or company spies, and it has been suggested that it is a reference to the famous Pinkerton detective agency which supplied men to break strikes. Perhaps fink was originally 'pink'. In the 1960s fink developed into 'rat fink', a general phrase to describe any disgusting or contemptible person.

fire, to fight fire with. To respond to a forceful situation with an equal degree of force. The phrase originates from the practice of limiting forest fires by burning an area of woodland to create a firebreak. This could be a dangerous measure, for unless the secondary fires were closely controlled they could get out of hand.

First Australians. A euphemism for Aborigines, the Australian equivalent of 'native Americans', meaning American Indians.

first generation. A term used in all areas of technology to describe the earliest, and therefore the most crude and primitive, models of a specific machine or piece of equipment – computer, plane, video camera etc. *See also* FIFTH GENERATION.

first rate. From the 17th to the 19th century British warships were rated by the weight and number of guns they carried. A first rate ship was the best-armed and the expression was used generally to describe something of the finest quality. From this practice we also get the phrase 'second rate', meaning something inferior or shoddy. *See also* A1.

fish – plenty more fish in the sea. This phrase is usually trotted out to someone who has just been ditched by their boy or girlfriend. It means that there are plenty of other partners waiting to be 'hooked'. The expression **plenty more pebbles on the beach** means the same thing.

fish, to drink like a. *See under* DRINK.

fisherman's tale. Many an angler, returning from long hours by the riverbank with a paltry catch, has entertained anyone who'll listen to him with a story about 'the one that got away.' This fish is inevitably enormous and tends to grow in size as the story progresses. It is from this habit that we get the phrase 'a fisherman's tale' to describe a grossly exaggerated or downright untrue story.

five-finger discount. An American slang term, used mainly by teenagers, and meaning 'shop-lifting'.

five mile high club. A 'club' whose membership is open to anyone who has made love in an aircraft cruising at a height of five miles.

fixed link. A permanent construction – a bridge or tunnel – between two pieces of land separated by a stretch of sea. The expression was coined, and soon became a journalistic cliché, in the mid-1980s, in the context of renewed plans for building a Channel tunnel linking England and France.

flabbergasted. Someone who is taken completely by surprise or totally confused. It was coined around 1770 and is perhaps a simple combination of 'flabby' and 'aghast'. In current British use is the word **gobsmacked**, also describing a state of shocked surprise. Its derivation is obvious; such a surprise is like receiving a smack round the GOB.

flag down. In the days when railway lines ran past dozens of little-used country stations, trains only stopped if there was someone on the platform waving or displaying a flag. This practice was later used to stop other vehicles. Although today we don't wave a flag when we want to hail a taxi, we still flag it down by waving a hand or an umbrella.

flagpole, to run it up the. To try out, or test the reaction to, an idea or concept. This phrase – sometimes used with the addition of 'and see if anyone salutes' – originated in the USA in the 1960s, and is attributed to the advertising industry of MADISON AVENUE.

flak. Serious criticism or blame. This word, now used in a metaphorical sense, was first used during World War II for anti-aircraft fire. It is an abbreviation of the German word *fliegerabwehrkanone*, which means literally 'pilot defence gun'.

flaky or **flakey.** Someone whose mental state is unstable or whose behaviour is ECCENTRIC. The word has been in use in the USA for around fifteen years but only came to Britain when President Reagan used it to describe the Libyan leader

Colonel Gadafy. The origins of the expression are vague, but as 'flake' is a slang term for cocaine it may well allude to the state of mind induced by the drug.

flannel, a load of. A way of describing verbal waffle, flattery or excuses. It probably originates from the time when flannel cloth was used for paddling out winter clothing. Someone who wore a padded coat might look well-built but underneath it was 'all flannel', i.e. lacking in any substance. An alternative suggestion cites the fact that during the reign of Charles II there was a law specifying that shrouds and coffin-linings had to be made of flannel. This move was intended to protect the wool trade, but as wool shrouds were seen as distinctly inferior to linen ones many people broke the law. It may be from this sense of flannel being something inferior, not the proper thing, that we get the phrase a load of flannel.

flap, to be in a. When someone is alarmed or anxious about something they may be described as being in a flap. The phrase allude to the fluttering and flapping of a frightened bird.

flash and **flashy.** In Britain 'flash' means slick, cool or showy. It is often used as term of approval, while 'flashy' tends to be used in a derogatory sense to describe ostenatious style or behaviour. Flashy may be derived from a band of vagabonds and thieves who lived in the Derbyshire village of Flash. They dressed conspicuously and travelled around the county fairs looking for rich pickings. A 'flash man' came to mean a thief and someone who was flashy was not to be trusted.

flash in the pan, a. This phrase owes its origin to the development of the flintlock gun. When the trigger of one of these is pulled it generates a spark which ignites a small amount of powder in the gun's 'pan'. This in turn sets off the main charge of gunpowder which explodes and propels the ball down the barrel. If the powder got wet or the gun was dirty, pulling the trigger might create an instant flash in the pan but no bigger explosion of the main charge. By analogy, a flash in the pan is a spectacular but minor incident that in the long run doesn't amount to much.

flatline. To die, the verb deriving from the flattening of the line on a monitor screen when a patient's heart ceases to beat. *See also* TO KICK THE BUCKET.

flavour of the month. Someone who is described as such is a person who, for a short while at least, is very popular. The phrase can be applied to objects as well as people. The expression probably derives from the way in which American ice-cream parlours promoted a different flavour ice-cream each month, thus guaranteeing each a short-lived popularity. 'Flavour of the week' denotes an even shorter period of fame.

flea in one's ear, to have a. To be annoyed by something that is unwelcome and irritating, in the same way that a dog is irritated by a flea in its ear. To send someone away with a flea in their ear means to give them a ticking off, thus making them annoyed and irritated. The phrase dates from the 15th century at least and may be a direct translation of the same phrase in French, known to have been in use for even longer.

flea market. It's tempting to suggest that flea markets get their name from the insects found in the secondhand bargains on sale at such places, but the expression is apparently derived from a specific market, known as the Vallie Market, established by early colonists in Manhattan. It was known originally as the Vallie Market but this became pronounced 'vlie' and finally 'flea'.

flexitime or **flextime.** Derived from flexible time, this is a system that enables workers to choose what time they start and finish work, so long as the number of hours they put in each week remains constant. The flexibility of this system may be limited in other ways, including the provision of a 'core' period of the day when all staff must be present.

flight attendant. The modern term for an air steward or stewardess This change of title is part of the trend for objectifying job descriptions, a trend which has seen dustmen become **municipal cleansing operatives** and road-sweepers transformed into **environmental cleaners**.

flirtyfishing. The term used by the religious sect The Children of God in the mid-1980s for a method of recruitment by which attractive young female members of the sect would use their sexuality to entice susceptible males into joining the sect. The word is a combination of the words 'flirt' and 'fishing' – fishing being a common metaphor for Christian evangelism, as in Christ's words:

Follow me and I will make you fishers of men (Mark 5:19).

flogging a dead horse. Trying to revive interest in a worn-out subject; attempting a task that is completely hopeless. This expression was coined in the 1860s by the British parliamentarian John Bright. When Lord John Russell attempted to introduce a new reform bill into Parliament, Bright recognised that Parliament had at that time no interest in the matter and said that to rouse Parliament from its apathy was like flogging a dead horse. The French have an equivalent expression: *chercher à resusciter un mort* – literally, to seek to revive a corpse.

FLOPS. When a computer expert uses the word 'flops' he is not referring to failures. Flops is a measure of computer performance, and is an acronym derived from 'floating-point operations per second'. *See also* MIPS.

flotsam and jetsam. Wreckage found in the sea or washed up on shore; figuratively, odds and ends, items of little worth. Both words derive from English maritime law. Flotsam refers to goods lost by shipwreck and found floating in the sea; jetsam refers to things that are thrown overboard for whatever reason.

flower power. The revolutionary 'philosophy' of the HIPPIES from 1967, summed up by the slogan 'Make Love Not War'.

fluffing out. An American phrase describing the changes a female executive makes to her style of dress when she gets to the top of her career ladder. According to observers, once women reach the top they can afford to relax the sober standards of POWER DRESSING and go for the frivolous and feminine.

fly a kite, to. In business use means to try out something new and see what the public reaction is to it. The command **go and fly a kite** is something else entirely; it means 'Get lost'.

fly-by-night. Debtor or swindler who takes others' money and does A MOONLIGHT FLIT with it, i.e. disappears overnight. Before it took on this meaning 'fly-by-night' was a euphemism for 'witch', referring to the belief that witches flew around at night on broomsticks.

fly by the seat of one's pants, to. This phrase was coined in the RAF during the 1930s to describe the sensation of flying a plane by feel and instinct rather than by instruments. Today we use it to refer to a situation without formal guidelines where improvisation, instinct and creativity are called for. Flying by the seat of one's pants is a risky business, but implicit in the phrase is the sense that when it goes well it is an exhilarating experience.

fly in the ointment. A minor problem that ends up spoiling everything; a small defect that causes major annoyance. The expression comes from Ecclesiastes x:1:

Dead flies cause the ointment of the apothecary to send forth a stinking savour: so doth a little folly him that is in reputation for wisdom and honour.

fly off the handle, to. To lose one's temper and start shouting. The phrase refers to the way in which a hammer or axe head can work its way loose from the handle and fly off uncontrollably. This may also be the source of the phrase **to lose one's head**, meaning to lose control of oneself.

fob someone off, to. The verb 'to fob' is derived from the German *foppen*, meaning to deceive or hoax. Thus a person who supplies excuses instead of an explanation, or a trader who sells shoddy goods, can be accused of fobbing someone off.

foggy bottom. An American epithet for the US Department of State. The expression was first used in 1947 by James Reston, the Washington correspondent of the *New York Times*. It derives from the name of a marshy area of Washington D.C., where the State Department and other government offices are located, but there is also an implied comment on the lack of clearsightedness shown by some of its policies.

foodie. Someone who has an intense interest in food and the pleasures of eating, especially someone who is particularly interested in rare and exotic (and expensive) types of food. The word is obviously modelled on the expression junkie, and the invention of the word has been claimed by Ann Barr and Paul Levy who wrote *The Official Foodie Handbook* which was published in 1984.

foolscap. A standard size of printing paper (measuring 13½ by 17 inches) or of writing paper (measuring 13¼ by 16½ inches), now largely superseded by standard metric sizes such as A3 and A4. The name derives from an old watermark that was applied to this type of paper. The earliest known use of this watermark, showing a fool's head complete with cap and bells, dates from about 1540.

foot – to put one's best foot forward. Since ancient times the right foot has been considered lucky and therefore anyone setting out on a journey or entering a house has been encouraged to put their best foot forward. The Greek mathematician Pythagoras even believed that one should put on the right shoe first each morning. Today people are generally less superstitious about such things and the expression now means to walk quickly, to set off at a decent pace.

foot – to put one's foot in it. To commit a social blunder. The allusion is to putting one's foot in a puddle or something even more unpleasant. From this source we get the expression **putting one's foot in one's mouth**, believed to have been recorded for the first time in the 1770s when it was applied to the Irish politician Sir Boyle Roche. He was famed for his FOOT-IN-MOUTHisms, which included such gems as: 'Half the lies our opponents tell about me are not true!'

foot, to shoot oneself in the. A phrase that originated in America and means to injure oneself through ineptness. It is often applied to politicians and public figures who, given the power to attack others, make mistakes or errors and end up injuring themselves. *See also* TO CUT OFF ONE'S NOSE TO SPITE ONE'S FACE *under* NOSE and TO SCORE AN OWN GOAL.

foot-in-mouth disease. A tendency to say things that are stupid, embarrassing or indiscreet. This cliché dates from the late 1960s, being word play on the expressions 'foot-and-mouth disease' and 'put one's foot in it'. The Duke of Edinburgh latinised the expression as 'dontopedology'.

foot the bill, to. To pay the bill. The expression originates from the practice of signing the foot of a bill as a promise to pay it later. In the days of apprenticeships a newcomer to a trade would be expected to foot the bill for a round of drinks for his associates on his first day. Having done so he would be **on a good footing** with them, meaning that he would have an assured place in their company. We still use the phrase today to describe a good relationship, often at a place of work or a bank.

fork out, to. To fork out for something means to pay for it. Fork was originally a slang word for a finger, so the phrase describes the act of producing and handing over money.

FORTRAN. A mathematically-based computer-programming language, dating from the 1960s and still widely used. The name is an abbreviation of 'formula translation'.

forty winks. From medieval times onwards the number forty was used to indicate an indefinite number in much the same way that today we use the phrase 'X-number'. So the phrase 'forty winks', describing a brief nap, simply means a nap of an indefinite period.

four-flusher. A bluffer, fraud, cheat or swindler. The expression derives from the game of poker, and dates from the early 1900s. In poker, a flush is a possibly winning hand consisting of five cards of the same suit. A four-flush (or busted flush) is a worthless hand consisting of only four cards of the same suit. A four-flusher was a player who tried to cheat by passing off a four-flush as a five-card flush.

Fourth Estate. The press, considered as a powerful force in the state – or, more generally, the communications media, including radio and television as well as the press. Historically, three estates of the realm were recognised; these were the classes of society represented in Parliament – the Lords Spiritual, the Lords Temporal and the Commons. From time to time, other groups within society were referred to as the Fourth Estate. For example, Henry Fielding wrote in the *Covent Garden Journal* in 1756 of

that very large and powerful body which form the fourth estate in this community . . . The Mob.

By the 1820s the phrase was being used commonly to refer to the press. It was used thus by Lord Brougham in a speech in the House of Commons, and by Lord Macaulay in the Edinburgh Review in 1826. It was also used thus by Carlyle in his *Heroes and Hero Worship* of 1841, and he attributed it to the 18th century statesman Edmund Burke.

fox-trot. Originally a fast walking pace made with small steps, named after the characteristic motion of the fox. However, in the 1920s it was the name given to a popular dance that was invented in America. It has been speculated that the name derives from Harry Fox, whose fox-trot-style dance was a big hit in a 1913 Broadway musical. The producers are said to have hired a dancing teacher to adapt the steps and teach it to the public, with the aim of getting publicity for their show.

Franglais was first used to describe the influx of English and American words such as 'hot dog', 'weekend' and 'sex appeal' into the French language. This tendency was and is strenuously opposed by those French speakers anxious to retain the purity of the language. Companies and institutions who use such phrases in published material are still liable to an official reprimand. In more recent times Franglais has come to mean the kind of inept mixture of schoolboy French and English spoken by English tourists on holiday in France. In this form Franglais was popularised by humourist Miles Kingston whose book *Let's Parler Franglais* was a brilliant send-up of the British abroad.

freelance. In the Middle Ages, freelances were French and Italian mercenaries skilled in the use of the lance. They would hire themselves out to whoever paid their wages, regardless of whether it was for a good or bad cause. From this practice we use the word freelance to describe self- employed people who sell their skills to whoever will buy them.

French culture. *See* ENGLISH CULTURE.

French-fried. The term 'French-fried' potatoes is regarded by many people as a more elegant way of referring to what are commonly called chips. The word 'French' here is simply a cookery term meaning 'cut into strips'.

French leave. To depart secretly or without permission. This expression originates in a custom that was common in polite society in France in the late 17th century. It was then held to be acceptable, in France but not in England, for a guest to leave a party early without seeking out and bidding a formal farewell to his host or hostess. Despite this origin, the French equivalent of French leave is

filer à l'anglaise – literally, to depart in the English manner.

French letter. A CONDOM or contraceptive sheath. The term has been employed since the mid-19th century, but since the time of CASANOVA the French have known them as **English caps**.

fresh as a daisy. The daisy gets its name from the Old English phrase 'day's eye', so-called because it folds into eyelash-like petals over its centre at night and opens its 'eye' in the morning light. This period of rest and the clear colours of the flower when it opens probably account for the saying 'as fresh as a daisy', used to describe someone who looks bright and refreshed, perhaps by sleep. Other flowers whose names have interesting derivations include the **daffodil**, which was originally known as an asphodel. It was said by the philosopher Pliny to grow along the banks of the River Acheron where it gave pleasure to the dead who had to cross the water. English mispronunciation caused the plant to become known as an affodil and, eventually, a daffodil. The **dahlia** was discovered in Mexico in 1789 by German naturalist Baron von Humboldt. Instead of being named after him, however, the plant was named after Swedish botanist Linnaeus Anders Dahl.

Freudian slip. Among his many theories Sigmund Freud, father of modern psychoanalysis, taught that people give away their unconscious feelings by slips of the tongue and the pen. A Freudian slip is therefore an accidental remark that reveals much more than the speaker intended. Classic examples might include a husband who accidentally calls his wife 'Mother' or someone who, asked for their address, supplies details of a place they have lived in the past – signifying, according to

Freud, a desire to return to that place and time.

-friendly. The suffix -friendly was first introduced in the phrase 'user-friendly', an expression from the computer world to describe machines that were simple to use, unintimidating and enabled novices to obtain immediate results. Following this example, -friendly was taken up in a number of different spheres. Non-aerosol sprays were described as ozone- or environment-friendly, banks promoted themselves as customer-friendly and publications as reader-friendly.

fringe benefits. Perks and concessions offered to employees on top of their regular salary. They can include free lunches in staff canteens, company cars and pensions and medical insurance provided by the company.

Frisbee. A plastic disc that spins when it is thrown into the air, and is used in a catching game. The word is a registered trade name. The first Frisbees were produced in 1957 by the Wham-O-Manufacturing Company of San Gabriel, California, but the idea originally came from students of Yale University, who first discovered the airworthy properties of the pie plates of the Frisbie Pie Company of Bridgeport, Connecticut.

frobnitz. A word originally used by model railway enthusiasts and now adopted into computer terminology. In both spheres it means a whatsit, thingummyjig, a what-d'you-call-it, a widget; any unspecified and probably nameless object or piece of equipment.

frog in the throat. Someone who attempts to speak and is silenced by an obstruction in the larynx is often described as having a frog in their throat. Today the phrase is used jokingly, but when it was first coined it was no laughing matter. At a time when most people's drinking water came from rivers, wells and springs, there was a general belief that if they swallowed frog spawn, tadpoles or fish eggs these would turn into frogs and fish in their stomach. When someone lost their voice temporarily it was genuinely believed that one of these creatures was trying to make its escape up their windpipe.

from the top. From the beginning. This expression originated among musicians in the USA and probably derives from the musical instruction *da capo*, which literally means 'from the head'.

fruit machine. *See* ONE-ARMED BANDIT.

fuck. This famed four-letter word, describing the act of sexual intercourse, was in fact perfectly acceptable from the 14th to the 17th centuries and only after that time became one of our strongest expletives. It has a straightforward pedigree, being derived from the German word *fucken*, meaning 'to hit or penetrate.' A vast number of other words and euphemisms have been applied to the same activity, from the obvious – balling, action, going all the way, sleeping with – to the more obscure such as UGANDAN DISCUSSIONS or Ugandan relations (a British term originating in the 1970s when a Ugandan diplomat was discovered in a compromising position). Sex in the afternoon may be described as a matinée while Irish Americans may allude to *coitus interruptus* as leaving before the gospel, a reference to leaving Mass before that part of the service. In Britain this may be known as getting off at Gateshead, a phrase which probably gave rise to a similar Australian expression, to get off at Redfern. *See also* LOVE MAKING.

fuddy-duddy. A **stick in the mud**; someone who is conservative, old-fashioned, unbending and censorious. The origin of the expression hasn't been traced and most sources point rather vaguely to a link with the word 'fuddle', meaning to be drunk or stupefied (even though a fuddy-duddy is the last person one might expect to get drunk). One American source, however, suggests an intriguing, though by no means certain, derivation. In the past clergymen were sometimes Doctors of Philosophy as well as Doctors of Divinity, and if this was the case they had the letters Ph.D, D.D. after their names. The theory supposes that one of these clergymen was a particularly rigid and scholarly individual and that his parishioners poked fun at him by nicknaming him a fuddy-duddy, referring to the Ph.D, D.D. after his name. It's a nice idea – and until another derivation can be proved, it will do very well.

Fun City. Any city, but particularly New York City, regarded as a place where one can have a good time. The expression is often used ironically. Fun City originated as a public relations slogan for New York City in the 1960s when John Lindsay was mayor.

funk. To be in a funk means to be in a panic or a state of confusion. The verb to funk or funk out means to fail at something, perhaps through panic. Both phrases have their origin in the Walloon expression '*in de fonk zun*', meaning 'to be in the smoke'. 'In a blue funk' is sometimes used to describe someone who is depressed, blue being the colour of dejection. In musical terms, funk is a style of black music based on jazz and African rhythms, with a heavy bass beat.

Funky has a wide range of meanings. As a term of approval it means much the same as 'cool'; in the USA it is applied to something that's quaint and old-fashioned or to someone who is pleasantly eccentric, or as a euphemism for something highly emotional.

funny bone. The ulnar nerve is exposed at the elbow. It is this, when the elbow receives a knock, that is responsible for the familiar painful tingling sensation that is attributed to the funny bone. Funny bone is a pun on the word *humerus*, which is the Latin name for the bone running from the shoulder to the elbow.

funny peculiar. This expression originated about 1930 in order to distinguish between the two different meanings of the word 'funny': comical (or 'funny ha-ha') and odd (or 'funny peculiar').

future shock. A condition experienced by those who are overwhelmed and disoriented by the ever-increasing pace of social and technological change. The phrase was coined as the title of a book by Alvin Toffler.

fuzz. A slang term for the police. There are a couple of theories as to the origin of this slang expression. One theory has it that it originated among narcotics dealers and users in America in the 1920s and is a corruption of the word 'feds', referring to federal narcotics agents. Another theory is that it is Black American slang of the 1930s, originally referring to white men in general, and thence specifically to policemen, and that it refers to the fuzzy testicles of white men. However, it seems that the term fuzz was used to refer to British policemen in a novel written by Edgar Wallace in 1915, pre-dating both these putative origins. Therefore, we must agree with the Oxford English Dictionary that the origin of the expression is unknown.

G

G.I. An American soldier, especially an enlisted soldier. The expression has been in use since World War II. The initials stand for 'government issue'. As they were supplied with G.I. uniforms, G.I. blankets, etc. the troops naturally adopted the expression to refer to themselves.

G-string. Traditionally worn by female strippers and erotic dancers, the briefest of briefs – a small triangle of cloth held strategically in place with a string round the waist and between the buttocks. G-string was originally applied to the strip of cloth tied round the waist and between the legs, worn by American Indians and many other peoples around the world. The expression is thought to be a humorous allusion to the fact that such items of clothing were not much bigger than the G string of a violin. The modern male equivalent of a G-string is a 'posing pouch'.

gadget. Any small, useful device that makes a task easier to perform. In use by the Navy in the 1860s, it first appeared in print in 1886. The origin of the expression is obscure, but it has been suggested that it might come from the French word *gachette*, described variously as a small metal part from the working of a clock or gun and translated as 'a little mechanical apparatus'.

gag. Today a gag is a joke, but the word seems to have been in existence almost as long as actors have been TREADING THE BOARDS. It was first used to describe an actor's deviation from the script of a play – something guaranteed to gag the other performers on stage with alarm. Shakespeare refers to this habit in *Hamlet*, when Hamlet warns the players to say no more 'than is set down', i.e. not to start improvising. This may reflect the way Shakespeare felt about the liberties actors took with his own texts. Gagging then became the practice of filling in an uncomfortable moment when someone missed a cue or forgot their lines with a few apt words. Perhaps these unrehearsed moments became the highlight of the show, because gag finally came to mean a contrived joke or piece of humorous stage business.

gaga. Senile, dotty. This is a direct borrowing from the French language, in which *gaga* may mean either 'senile' or 'a senile person'. This expression has been in general use in France since 1875, and found its way into English in about 1920. It has been conjectured that the expression is derived from the name of the French artist Paul Gauguin (1848–1903), who did show signs of mental disturbance. But as the expression was used in France when Gauguin was only 27 and long before he was at all well known, this seems beyond the bounds of possibility. Nigel Rees has offered a much more likely explanation – that it is derived from another French expression for a senile person – *un vieux gâteau*.

galah. An Australian slang term for a fool or simpleton. This expression, which originated in the 1940s, is derived from the native name of a type of cockatoo.

galoot. An awkward, boorish, uncouth or stupid man. This American slang expression is often heard in Western films, and dates from around 1866. What few people realise, however, is that it was earlier British nautical slang, meaning 'an inexperienced seaman'. This usage dates from around 1812. According to the Oxford English Dictionary, the origin of the expression is unknown. There is, however, a theory that it derives from the word *galut* in the Creole language Krio of Sierra Leone, where it means 'galley slave', and which itself derives from the Spanish word *galeoto*.

galumph was invented by Lewis Carroll for his nonsense poem *Jabberwocky*. It is derived from two words, gallop and triumphant, and describes an ungraceful, clumping kind of movement.

galvanised into action. The eighteenth-century Italian scientist Luigi Galvani was the man who discovered that a chemical reaction could create a current of electricity. In one of his most famous experiments he gave dead frogs an electric shock which made their legs twitch. From this we get the phrase to be galvanised into action, meaning to be roused from a torpor by a shock of some kind.

game, to be. This expression comes from the cockfighting ring. Cocks bred for fighting were known as gamecocks, 'game' in this case meaning 'sport' or 'contest', and were prized for their courage and aggression. Thus a person who shows a lot of fight and courage may be said to be game.

game is up, the. A phrase much favoured by fictional detectives when they finally track down their man – or woman. Today we use the expression to mean that a plot has been discovered or a scheme has come unstuck; it signifies an end. In its original sense, however, it signified the beginning of a hunt, the moment when the game started from cover and took flight.

game, set and match. A complete and decisive victory – deriving from the use of the phrase in the game of lawn tennis.

gameplan. Anyone who has watched an American football match will have seen players huddling together as they decide on their gameplan – the particular tactical manoeuvre they intend to use for outwitting their opponents. From this origin we get the metaphorical gameplan, a set of tactics or progressive steps implemented with the aim of achieving a particular goal.

gamesmanship first saw the light of day in 1947 as the title of a book by Stephen Potter. It is best defined by quoting the book's subtitle: 'The Art of Winning Games Without Actually Cheating'. *See also* ONE-UPMAN-SHIP.

gander. As used in the phrase 'to take a gander', this means a look or glance. The expression originated in the USA and dates from the end of the 19th century. It derives from the way a gander (or goose) stretches its neck to have a good view. *See also* RUBBERNECK.

gang of four. The original gang of four was a group of four influential members of the Chinese Communist Party, led by Jiang Qing, the widow of Chairman Mao Tse-tung. As a result of infighting within the party, the four were tried for political crimes in the mid-1970s and given the death sentence, which was later ganga

commuted to life imprisonment. This expression, being one of those beloved by journalists, was later applied to the four former members of the British Labour Party who founded the Social Democratic Party in 1981: Roy Jenkins, David Owen, Shirley Williams and William Rogers.

ganga. A type of marijuana obtained from a cultivated strain of Indian hemp. This word, widely used in the West Indies, is of Hindi origin.

gaper's block. American slang for a traffic jam caused by drivers slowing down to take a look at an accident or other incident. A potentially useful phrase with, it would seem, no British equivalent.

garbage in, garbage out. *See* GIGO.

garden – to lead down the garden path. Knowingly to mislead someone. It has been suggested that the expression originally meant to seduce someone, to take them down the garden path to a shady bower which provided cover for a seduction, but this has not been proved. Whatever its origin and early meaning, today we say that we have been led down the garden path if we have been deceived or tricked in a relatively pleasant kind of way, so that we had no idea of what was going on.

gargantuan. In medieval legend, which may have been based on Celtic origins, Gargantua was a giant famed for his huge appetite. His name came from the Spanish word *garganta* for 'gullet'. In 1534 the French writer François Rabelais wrote a satire on gluttony called *Gargantua*, in which Gargantua featured as an insatiable eater, and around 1596 the adjective gargantuan was first recorded. It means gigantic, huge, enormous.

gas. Johannes Baptista van Helmont, who was the first to identify the class of substances known as gas, is said to have named his discovery after the

Greek word 'chaos' – though the German word *geist*, meaning 'spirit' has also been suggested as a source. By the end of the 17th century GOSSIPS and idlers were accused of talking gas, but a hundred or so years later a gas simply meant a good long conversation. More recently 'it's a gas' has become a slang term of approval to describe something amusing, impressive or pleasing.

gate fever. In prisons (or 'correctional facilities') gate fever is the apprehension, excitement and anticipation experienced by an offender in the last few days of his sentence. If the excitement and anticipation outweigh the apprehension the prisoner may be described as 'gate happy'.

gauntlet, to run the. A Swedish military punishment which required the offender to run between two lines of men carrying sticks, each of whom struck him as he raced by. It is derived from the Swedish words *gata*, a passageway, and *lope*, meaning to leap, as well one might in such a situation.

gauntlet, to throw down the. In the Middle Ages knights wore armoured gloves down as gauntlets from the French word for 'glove'. When one knight threw down his gauntlet at the feet of another, he challenged him to combat.

gay. Homosexual. Gay in this sense has been in common use since the late 1960s, but previously had been criminal slang since the 1930s, if not earlier. In the 19th century the word gay was used to describe female prostitutes, and it is likely that the use of the word for 'homosexual' evolved from this.

gayola. Coined along the lines of PAYOLA, gayola is money extorted or blackmailed from homosexuals by those who threaten to reveal their sexual secrets.

gazump. To revoke a verbal agreement to sell a house before the stage at which legally binding contracts are exchanged, with the intention of receiving a better offer from another party. This verb and the practice it describes first came to the attention of the public in the early 1970s when house prices in Britain began to rise dramatically. Gazump, however is merely a modern spelling of an older word, 'gazoomph' (also spelled 'gasumph' or 'gezumph') which merely means 'to swindle'. The Oxford English Dictionary quotes examples from as early as 1928. In 1988 another major boom in house prices came to an end and property fell in value. This allowed buyers, once victims of gazumping, to have their revenge and the new practice of **gazundering** developed. Gazundering works in the opposite way to gazumping. A buyer verbally agrees to buy a property at a certain price but later, before contracts have become binding, drops out of the transaction because they have found another, cheaper property. Or they may use the threat of gazundering to force the vendor to lower the price of the property.

gazunder. *See* GAZUMP.

geezer. A CHAP, fellow or guy. The word is often used semi-affectionately to indicate a slightly eccentric or unusual looking person. It comes from the early dialect word 'giser', meaning someone who puts on a mask or disguise, particularly as part of a mummers show; hence someone who looks quaint or extraordinary.

Geiger counter. An instrument for detecting and measuring radio-activity. Hans Geiger (1882–1945) was a German physicist. He worked with Rutherford at Manchester from 1906 to 1912, and then went on to design an instrument for measuring alpha particles, which formed the basis of what is known today as a Geiger

counter. This was developed in the 1920s in collaboration with another physicist Wilhelm Müller, hence its more formal designation as the Geiger-Müller counter.

gen. Information, facts. This originates as RAF slang in World War II. According to the Oxford English Dictionary, there are three possible explanations of the derivation: it may have been a contraction of the word 'general' in the official phrase 'for the general information of all ranks', or it may be a contraction of 'genuine' or 'intelligence'.

gender bender. One whose appearance or behaviour is sexually ambiguous; a transvestite or bisexual. This expression originated in the mid-1980s and was much used by journalists at that time, particularly in regard to the androgynous pop star Boy George, lead singer with the group Culture Club, and his (male) pop star friend Marilyn.

geneism. After SEXISM, racism and AGEISM, geneism may well be the latest area of discrimination. Breakthroughs in genetic science now enable doctors to show that a person is susceptible to particular diseases, with the consequence that it may be difficult for them to obtain insurance or even jobs – not because they *have* a disease, but because their genes indicate that they may be prone to developing it. Though coined semi-humorously, in the future geneism may prove to be no laughing matter.

gentrification. The process by which houses and flats in an area occupied by poorer people are bought by wealthier people, who thus gradually displace the original residents of the area. The expression came into use in the early 1970s when the process it describes became noticeable in areas such as the dockland areas of London. *See also* YUPPIE.

geodesic dome. A domed structure,

invented and named by Buck-
minster Fuller, that is made of light-
weight but rigid triangulated
elements, and with no interior supporting members. The geodesic
dome was described in an article in
The Times in 1966 as follows:

The geodesic dome combines the structu-
ral advantages of the sphere (which
encloses the most space within the least
surface, and is strongest against internal
pressure) with the tetrahedron (which
encloses least space with most surface,
and has the greatest stiffness against
external pressure).

German. In much the same way as
Dutch, German has been used in a
number of phrases to indicate something unsophisticated or worthless.
The phrase 'German silver' is used to
describe an alloy of copper, zinc and
nickel, which looks silvery while
having none of the value of silver.
And in the past the fingers and thumb
were referred to as 'German comb', it
being believed that the Germans
didn't bother doing their hair except
to run their hands through it.
'German measles', however, were
probably so-named because the
disease was first identified by a
German doctor, Friedrich Hoff-
mann.

gerrymander. To rearrange voting
districts in the interests of a particular party or candidate. The expression derives from the name Elbridge
Gerry (1744–1814) who was
Governor of Massachusetts. In an
attempt to keep power, despite a
drop in popular support, he decided
to redraw the boundaries of the
voting districts so as to enable his
party (the Republicans) to retain
their majority in the forthcoming
elections. A local newspaper editor,
Benjamin Russell, commented on
the fact that one district's boundaries
were so contorted that it resembled a
salamander. Thus, putting together

the words Gerry and salamander, he
coined the word 'gerrymander'.

Gestapo. The secret police of Nazi
Germany. The Gestapo was established by Herman Goering in Prussia
in 1933 and extended to the whole of
Germany the following year. The
name is an acronym, derived from
Geheime Staatspolizei, meaning
secret state police. The expression is
much used nowadays as a term of
political abuse, in phrases like
'Gestapo tactics' by people (particularly those of a left-wing persuasion)
who are critical of police methods.
See also FASCIST, NAZI.

get – to get centred. An expression
from the world of therapy. People
who are centred through such therapies are aware of their inner being
and individuality and use this self-
knowledge as a basis for their new
and improved life.

get one's back up, to. This expression is derived from the way in which
a cat arches its back when it is angry.
Someone whose back is up is
annoyed and ready for a fight.

get one's goat, to. Brewer defines this
expression as 'An old Americanism
for annoying one, making one wild',
but American sources don't seem to
be able to supply any local information about the phrase's origin. The
only developed suggestion is that it
refers to the goats that are sometimes
kept as companions to highly-strung
racehorses. The horse grows fond of
its companion and gets upset when
the goat is taken away and this, it is
speculated, was a fact that some
unscrupulous gamblers once
exploited. They wanted to prevent
the favourite from winning a race so
they stole its goat companion, with
the result that the horse became
upset and lost its chance of coming
home first. Whether this story contains much truth or not, it's certainly
consistent with the fact that to get

someone's goat means to make them wild and frustrated.

get out of the wrong side of the bed, to. When someone is grumpy and difficult in the morning they may explain their behaviour by saying that they got out of the wrong side of the bed, the wrong side being the left side. In Latin the word for left is *sinister*; in English 'sinister' describes something foreboding and ill-omened. For many centuries it was believed that entering a house or leaving a room left-foot first was extremely unlucky and it was the job of the household footman to ensure that guests entered with their right feet forward. For the same superstitious reason it was customary to put on the right shoe first and to get out of the right side of the bed. Anyone who didn't was just asking for trouble.

ghetto blaster. A large portable stereo radio, usually incorporating a cassette player, often carried and played loudly in public places. This expression originated in the USA in the early 1980s and reached Britain in the mid-1980s. The ghetto blaster is a fashion almost exclusively confined to young males, particularly in deprived urban areas. Its function is more to impress one's peers than to provide personal entertainment.

ghosts. In politics, publishing, entertainment and the media 'ghosts' are people who produce work that is passed off as someone else's. They write autobiographies of the famous, blockbuster novels fronted by celebrities and speeches for political leaders; they may also have their voices dubbed onto films and produce jokes and routines for performers who claim them as their own work. By definition such people have to be invisible – hence the word ghost to describe their spectral presence.

gibberish. There is some debate about the origin of this word meaning nonsense. One interesting, though obscure, derivation traces it back to the 11th-century Arab alchemist Jabir ibn Hazyan, known as Geber, who wrote down his theories in a kind of nonsensical code to avoid accusations of dabbling in magic. His name, it has said, gave us 'gibberish'. Unfortunately it is more likely that the word is a simple variant of 'gabble' and 'jabber'.

gift – Don't look a gift horse in the mouth. An injunction to receive presents gracefully, without scrutinising them for flaws or trying to estimate their value. The expression alludes to the fact that it is possible to tell the age, and therefore the value, of a horse by looking into its mouth and checking its teeth. It is an ancient saying first recorded around AD 400, when it was referred to as an established proverb.

gift of the gab. A person said to have the gift of the gab might also be described as having KISSED THE BLARNEY STONE, i.e. they have the gift of persuasive speech or, at the very least, the ability to talk fluently and at length. Gab is derived from the Middle English word *gabbe*, meaning 'idle talk or gossip'. *See also* GOB and GOSSIP.

gigantomania. The sociological term for the obsession, common among leaders of nations, institutions and businesses, with developing ever bigger and more expensive projects and expansions, simply because of their size and with no real concern for their usefulness, cost or effect.

gigo. A catchphrase which originated in the computer industry, this is an acronym (pronounced 'guy-go') derived from the phrase 'garbage in, garbage out' – in other words, the quality of what you get out of the system is dependent on the quality of what you put in. The expression has been used since the early 1960s by computer people, but it did not pass into more widespread general use until the 1980s.

gild the lily. To make a superfluous addition to something that is already fine. The phrase is a corruption of a line in Shakespeare's play *King John*:

To gild refined gold, to paint the lily,
To throw a perfume on the violet,
To smooth the ice, or add another hue
Unto the rainbow, or with taper-light
To seek the beauteous eye of heaven
  to garnish
Is wasteful, and ridiculous excess.

gilt – to take the gilt off the gingerbread. During the 17th and 18th centuries it was traditional on special occasions to decorate gingerbread with gold leaf or some other similar substance. If the gilt, as the gold leaf was known, was knocked off it exposed the ordinary cake beneath. From this custom we get the phrase to take the gilt off the gingerbread, meaning to destroy an illusion – to go beneath the superficial appearance and discover that something is less special or interesting than it seemed at first.

gimlet. A mixed drink of gin and lime juice. The gimlet takes its name from Sir T. O. Gimlette, a British naval surgeon who, in 1890, urged naval officers to drink it as a healthier alternative to straight gin.

gimmick. A tricky or ingenious device, gadget, idea, etc., particularly one adopted for the purpose of attracting attention or publicity. Gimmick was originally slang used by American carnival workers, from about the beginning of this century, and meant a secret device by which the operator of a gambling game such as the Wheel of Fortune could control the mechanism, in order to cheat the players. The word was taken up by conjurors, to mean any small device by which a conjuring trick was effected. In 1930, or thereabouts, the word passed into general usage, and came to mean any clever gadget. There are three theories as to the origin of the word. One is that it is a corruption of 'gimcrack', meaning a showy but useless object – but the fact that this is precisely the opposite of the original meaning must make one doubtful about this theory. The second theory is that it derives from the German word *gemach*, meaning 'a convenience'. The third, and the one I incline to, is that it was originally spelt 'gimac', and as such is an anagram of 'magic'.

girl Friday. Employers advertise for a girl Friday when they require a general assistant willing to tackle a wide variety of tasks. The name is derived from Daniel Defoe's novel *Robinson Crusoe*, in which Crusoe is served faithfully by his native companion Friday.

girl on the Clapham omnibus. *See under* MAN IN THE STREET.

gismo or **gizmo.** An unspecified object; a gadget, gimmick or what-d'you-call-it. The slang term originated in the US armed forces in the 1940s. According to George Yost Jr., writing in the magazine *American Speech*, it comes from the Arabic phrase *shu ismo*, which has the same meaning, and was picked up by American soldiers in Morocco during the North African campaign.

give and take. This phrase originated in horseracing, where a give and take was, according to Brewer, a prize for a race in which runners exceeding a standard height carried more, and those coming short of it less, than the standard weight. Thus, both on and off the racecourse, to give and take means to be fair, to make concessions or allowances.

Glam is an acronym for Greying, Leisured, Affluent and Married. Glams are categorised as being aged between 45–59. They are established, have finished raising their children and have surplus money to spend, which makes them a group much targeted by advertisers. *See also* YUPPIE etc.

glasnost. A Russian word, generally translated as 'openness', used to describe the new freer policy adopted in the Soviet Union under the premiership of Mikhail Gorbachev, from about 1985 onwards. The policy of 'glasnost' involves more public discussion of government policies and a greater readiness of the Soviet government to provide information, both to its own people and to other governments, as was demonstrated in the aftermath of the Chernobyl nuclear reactor accident in 1986. Almost as soon as the word appeared in the English language, it was being used metaphorically in all sorts of contexts. *See also* PERESTROIKA.

glitterati. Famous, fashionable and glamorous people; celebrities and jet-setters. This expression, coined in the mid-1980s, is based on 'literati', an established word for authors and scholars as a social group, combined with 'glitter', implying superficial glamour.

glitz and **glitzy.** Glitz means conspicuous showiness, flashiness, gaudiness. Glitzy is the corresponding adjective. This is an American coinage of the mid-1980s. It has been suggested that it is derived from a combination of the words 'glamour' and 'Ritz', but it is much more probable that it comes from the Yiddish word *glitzen*, meaning 'glitter'.

global village. The world regarded as a community in which ideas and information can be quickly and easily disseminated by means of modern communications media. The term was coined in the late 1960s by the Canadian Marshall McLuhan.

gnomes of Zurich. An uncom-plimentary name given to Swiss bankers and financiers who have a major influence on the flow of international funds. This expression was popularised in Britain in November 1964 by George Brown, then Secretary of State for Economic Affairs, shortly after the Labour government of Harold Wilson had come to power. Britain was in the midst of a sterling crisis, and the gnomes of Zurich were held to blame for precipitating this, and for the authoritative measures which they forced the government to undertake. November 1964 is the date of the earliest use of this expression quoted in the Oxford English Dictionary, but Nigel Rees has pointed out that Harold Wilson himself had used the expression much earlier, in a speech to the House of Commons in 1956, in which he referred to

all the little gnomes in Zurich and other financial centres.

go dutch. *See under* DUTCH.

go no-go. This started out in the 1970s as US astronautical jargon. It refers to the critical last stage in a project or mission at which it is possible to make a decision whether to go ahead or withdraw – that is, the last stage before one is irrevocably committed, and at which one can still choose to go or not to go.

go to the dogs. *See under* DOG.

going nineteen to the dozen. Someone who talks quickly and without interruption over a long period, or a person who keeps up a high-pressure activity for a surprising length of time, may be said to be going nineteen to the dozen. The expression dates from the age of steam and was originally a measurement of the efficiency of James Watts' steam-powered pumps. The figures referred to the ratio between the amount of water a pump could shift and the fuel required to power it. Thus it was recorded of one pump in a Cornish mine, 'This week Wheal Fortune hath gone nineteen to the dozen', i.e. it had raised 19,000 gallons of water for every twelve bushels of coal used to power it.

gob. The Celtic word for mouth was *gab*, which gives us the modern-day gob and such phrases as 'shut your gob'. Punk rock contributed the verb to gob, meaning to spit. From the same Celtic source we also get such words as **gobbet**, originally meaning a mouth-sized morsel of food and now commonly used to describe a short piece of literature or poetry, and **goblet**, a drinking glass.

gobsmacked. *See* FLABBERGASTED.

gobbledygook. Dense, jargon-ridden language, often used by government departments and other bureaucratic organisations, that is unintelligible to the outsider. It is also known as **bureaucratese** and, in the USA, as PENTAGONESE. The word 'gobbledygook' was invented by a US Congressman, Maury Maverick, who objected to the obscurity and exclusivity of such language. Trying to think of a disparaging term for it, he had a vision of a turkey strutting about and gobbling away unintelligibly to itself; gobbledygook was born. Bureaucratese is so rife that it is difficult to isolate specific examples. Much of it is caused by the inability of bureaucrats to render legal jargon into plain English. It also tends to euphemism and verbosity – so, for example, in gobbledygook poor people become 'economically disadvantaged persons' and rich people are defined as 'high net worth individuals'. Too often this kind of language is used simply to make things sound more important; thus a cash shortage becomes a 'liquidity crisis' and any activity becomes an 'ongoing situation'. And at its worst gobbledygook becomes **doublespeak**, language designed to hide rather than reveal the truth. In doublespeak a 'serious and candid discussion' actually means 'a major disagreement' and 'useful and businesslike negotiations' describes a meeting at which nothing constructive occurred.

gods, up in the. There is some dispute about the origin of this phrase, which means to sit in the top tier of a theatre. It's said that the ceiling of the Drury Lane theatre was decorated with paintings of Greek gods, and that theatregoers who sat in the gallery nearest the roof were therefore up with the gods. It has also been suggested that the phrase developed because from their position at the top of the house patrons looked down with the lofty disdain of gods on the performers below.

Godzone. Australia. This expression derives from the phrase 'God's own country' as applied by Australians when referring to Australia. It was coined in 1966 in a series of articles in the *Meanjin Quarterly*.

gofer or gopher. An employee whose main function is to run errands – to 'go fer' coffee, to 'go fer' cigarettes, etc.; more generally, any low-ranking subordinate.

golden handcuffs. A business term to describe a financial inducement offered to a key executive whom a company is anxious to keep. The phrase seems to have originated during the financial boom of the 1980s when valuable personnel were lured away by the promise of higher salaries. To keep them, some companies offered a system of bonuses which could only be paid when the executive had come to the end of his or her contract.

golden handshake. A generous payment (or other advantageous arrangements or benefits) paid to an employee as an inducement to take early retirement, and used to reduce a workforce. This expression originated in the late 1950s.

golden hello. A business term that originated in Silicon Valley in America and describes a package of financial incentives offered to important new personnel. In Britain such an offer is better known as 'relocation expenses'.

golden oldie. A term used in the pop music business and originating in the 1960s for a record, song, etc. that is popular today despite being more than a year old.

golden parachute. In the business world a golden parachute is an employment contract designed to deter company takeover bids and to protect top executives should a takeover occur. Also known as a **silver wheelchair**, such a contract might specify that the person covered is entitled to a massive lump sum if they are fired by the company that has taken over. With such a contract to protect them, fired executives can afford to be wheeled out of the office in their silver wheelchairs or take a metaphorical jump and float to the ground under the protection of their golden parachute.

Goldwynisms. American movie mogul Samuel Goldwyn was famous for his own brand of MALAPROPISMS which became affectionately known as Goldwynisms. Among those ascribed to him – though there's some doubt whether he was responsible for them all – are: 'In two words: im-possible', 'We have all passed a lot of water since then', 'Gentlemen, kindly include me out', 'A verbal contract isn't worth the paper it's written on', 'Anyone who goes to see a psychiatrist should have his head examined' and 'Directors are always biting the hand that lays the golden egg.'

good egg. *See under* EGG.

Good Samaritan. The biblical parable of the Good Samaritan tells how a citizen of Samaria rescues and assists a stranger who has been assaulted, after the stranger's cries for help have been ignored by passing holy men. The description Good Samaritan is therefore applied to any kind person who goes out of their way to assist a stranger in need. The Samaritans is a charitable organisation that exists to provide support and a listening ear for the lonely and depressed.

goody two-shoes. An innocent young woman or someone who behaves in a little-girlish way may be called 'goody two-shoes'. The expression comes from a children's story first published in 1765, which tells the tale of a girl who owned only one shoe until someone gave her a pair, at which she was so pleased with herself she went round saying, 'Two shoes!'

gook. A term of contempt, used by American soldiers, for a native of an area, particularly in South-east Asia or Polynesia. The expression originated among American troops occupying the Philippines in the 1890s, and derives from the Filipino word *gugu*, meaning spirit or demon. It was used of Pacific Islanders during World War II, of the Japanese then and during the later occupation of Japan, of the Koreans in the Korean War of the early 1950s, and of the Vietnamese, Cambodians and Laotians in the 1960s.

goolies. The testicles. This word, originally British army slang, comes from the Hindustani word *goli*, meaning a bullet, ball or pill.

goose, to. In modern use to goose someone (and it is normally women who get goosed) means to touch their buttocks or genitals. In its older form, however, goosing was a much more specific form of sexual contact which is why etymologists trace its origin back to the Cockney rhyming slang, 'to have a goose and duck', i.e. a fuck.

goose, to cook one's. According to legend, when Eric XIV of Sweden besieged a town around the year 1560, the inhabitants hung a goose, symbol of stupidity, over the town wall. He retaliated by vowing to cook their goose, which he proceeded to do by burning the place to the ground. Charming as this story is, the phrase to cook one's goose is not recorded until around 1850, when it appeared in an anti-Catholic street ballad. Today the phrase is used to describe an act that brings about someone's downfall.

goose egg. In the USA, a score of zero. *See also* DUCK.

gopher. *See* GOFER.

Gordian knot. This phrase is derived from the story about an ancient king of Phrygia, Gordius. He tied his sacred wagon to the beam of a temple with such a complicated knot that it was declared that anyone who managed to untie it would be lord of all the East. Alexander the Great became the man to do so when he drew his sword and sliced the knot in two. When someone uses the phrase 'the Gordian knot' they refer to a problem so complex that it seems impossible to solve. If they cut the Gordian knot, they solve it in a single, bold act.

Gordon Bennett! This is a minced oath. Instead of using the expletive 'God!', which might be held to be blasphemous, various substitutes were found – for example, 'Gawd!' 'Gordon Highlanders!' and 'Gordon Bennett!' Gordon Bennett II (1841–1918) was a popular figure at the turn of the century – a colourful, eccentric American millionaire, who lived for some time in France. He sponsored, and provided trophies for, motor races and air races. In Paris there is a street named after him, the *Avenue Gordon-Bennett*. The use of his name as an expletive derives simply from the fact that he was well known and that his forename was Gordon; if he had had any other forename he would not be commemorated in this fashion.

gorilla. The huge, hairy apes we known as gorillas were named after a tribe described in an account of the travels of ancient explorer Hanno. While travelling in Africa he came across a tribe of very hairy people. These people were known to the Greeks as *Gorillai*, which in English became gorilla. In 1847 the word was applied to the ape for the first time. It is also sometimes used to describe a huge, hairy and unrefined-looking man.

gossip. In Anglo Saxon times gossip referred specifically to the relationship between people who stood as godparents at a child's baptism. Because they had the child in common, gossips had plenty to talk to each other about – and it is from this that we used gossip to mean both talk and someone who spreads stories.

Gothic novel. When Horace Walpole wrote *The Castle of Otranto* in 1764 he founded a new genre of English literature. His books, and those of his fellow writers in the genre, specialised in a thrilling mixture of the supernatural, adventure and romance, and most of them were set in the past, often in the medieval period. For this reason they became known as Gothic novels, 'Gothic' in this context meaning merely 'medieval'. They were extremely popular among young female readers who identified strongly with their naïve heroines – a fact which Jane Austen treats with irony in *Northanger Abbey*. Emily Brontë's *Wuthering Heights* is perhaps the most sophisticated and successful of all Gothic novels. Popular until the early years of this century, Gothics went out of fashion for around fifty years before making a comeback in the last decade. They always include a beautiful heroine trapped in a mysterious and sometimes terrifying situation, with plenty of sex and violence before the inevitable rescue by a tall, dark and handsome hero.

gourmet. According to one source, a gourmet was originally a minor servant in a French household whose job included, among many other things, tasting the wine. Though wine tasting became a more specialised and prestigious job, the name stuck and eventually came to refer to anyone who is a connoisseur of food and wine. A **gourmand**, by the way, is quite different from a gourmet. A gourmet is interested in quality; a gourmand is more concerned with quantity.

grade, to make the. This phrase is derived from the word gradient, meaning a slope or hill. From it we get the word grade, meaning a mark of attainment in an examination or test; i.e. a position on the slope, somewhere between the top and bottom. Someone who makes the grade passes the test by rising to the required level.

grain of salt. *See* PINCH OF SALT.

grapevine. An invisible and unofficial means of communication via which gossip and rumour are disseminated at great speed. The expression is said to have originated in America, probably because sagging telegraph wires looked a little like grapevines. Maybe, in areas where the telegraph hadn't been installed, it was jokingly suggested that news travelled along the grapevines instead. *See also* BUSH TELEGRAPH.

grass. A slang term for marijuana that originated in the USA in the 1940s.

grass roots. To get back to grass roots means to get back to basics, to get down to the bottom of things. The allusion is obvious. Politicians use it to mean the majority of a party's supporters or its rank and file members in expressions such as grass roots opinion and grass roots reaction.

grass widow. In India during the last century it was the custom for women to leave their husbands during the hottest season of the year and to go to the hill country where the climate was cooler and where grass grew. While they were there they were known as grass widows. The phrase is sometimes used jokingly today to refer to a woman whose husband spends all his time playing golf. Such a woman is also known as a 'golf widow'.

graveyard shift. The late night/early morning shift at a factory operating a twenty-four-hour production line. Two explanations have been offered for the phrase, which originated during the First World War. The first refers to the higher than average accident rate that occurs during this shift, caused by tiredness and slower reactions. The second points to the fact that the shift sometimes started at midnight, a time when the only other place where anyone was stirring was the graveyard.

gravy train. To climb aboard, or get on, or ride the gravy train means to obtain access to a source of easily earned wealth. This expression originated in the USA, where 'gravy' has long been a slang word for money that is gained with little effort. Gravy train is believed to have been railroad jargon for an easy run requiring little work on the part of the crew. The first use of the expression in print was in 1945 in Benjamin A. Botkin's *Lay My Burden Down*, but it was probably in use for a couple of decades before that.

graze. Grazing was once something done only by animals, but since the mid-1980s the word has been used to describe the habits of (mainly young) people who, instead of eating three meals a day seated at a table with a knife and fork in their hands, consume snack-style food while they are standing up or doing other things. A typical grazer might have six or more 'meals' a day, some of them bought from FAST FOOD outlets and most of them eaten on the hoof as the grazer works, walks or travels. In the retail trade grazing defines a kind of low-level shop-lifting – the practice of some customers of opening and eating a food item as they browse in a supermarket, then failing to pay for it at the check-out.

grease one's palm, to. To offer a bribe to someone. Grease makes most things work more smoothly; thus, by greasing someone's palm one ensures that things go easily.

greasy spoon. A small, cheap restaurant or café named, more than likely, for the poor quality of its washing-up and hygiene.

Great Scott! This expression of surprise originated in the USA in the mid-19th century, when General Winfield Scott became an admired public figure after his success in the Mexican War. It has also been suggested that far from being an expression of admiration, Great Scott! originated as a heavily ironic exclamation by those who disliked his pomposity and swaggering. Take your pick.

great unwashed. This expression dates back at least to the 18th century and was originally an insulting reference to the lower classes. As 'the great unwashed' were unwashed not so much through choice but because of the limited hygiene facilities, the phrase is a profoundly patronising one.

Greek – Beware of Greeks bearing gifts. This expression refers to the Trojan Horse, a massive wooden horse left outside the gates of Troy. The Trojans dragged it into the city unaware that it was full of Greek soldiers, who emerged at night and opened the city gates to allow their army to enter. Ever since that time a Greek gift has been a treacherous or dubious one and the warning 'Beware of Greeks bearing gifts' has urged caution when someone who has previously been an enemy offers what appears to be a gift.

Greek culture. *See* ENGLISH CULTURE.

green fingers. Successful gardeners are said to have green fingers. As most gardeners in reality have brown fingers, we must assume that the phrase refers not to the colour of their skin but to some quality in their hands that encourages plants to grow.

Green politics. *See under* ECOFREAK.

greenhouse effect. A scientific term for the phenomenon by which the sun's heat penetrates through the Earth's atmosphere to create warmth which is then trapped by the carbon dioxide in the atmosphere. The expression was coined because the effect compares with the way in which a greenhouse is warmed. Meteorologists predict that because of pollution and the destruction of the ozone layer, the Earth's temperature will soon rise by a significant degree.

greening. Revival or rebirth. It is used by ECOFREAKS and others concerned for the world's ecology to describe the growing awareness of problems of pollution and destruction and action against them.

greenmail. A form of corporate blackmail that has been particularly prevalent in the USA. It occurs when an individual or company buys a significant number of another company's shares, with the idea of mounting a takeover bid. Such people or companies are known as CORPORATE RAIDERS. The company under real or imagined threat of takeover may then buy off the raider with a large sum of money. This payment is known as greenmail because of the association with greenbacks – the American slang for dollar bills.

gremlin. An imaginary gnome or goblin-type creature which can be jokingly blamed whenever machinery goes wrong. Gremlins were invented by members of the RAF around the time of the First World War to explain mysterious engine failures and mechanical faults. In the intervening years the word lost its visual impact and came merely to describe a minor technical problem; 'Gremlins on the line' or 'a few gremlins that can be ironed out.' In the mid 1980s, however, Steven Spielberg's successful film *Gremlins* brought the creatures to life as funny but frightening little devils and this has gone some way to restoring the original image behind the word.

grim reaper. Death personified. Death with his scythe, stalking the land and mowing people down indiscriminately, was a familiar figure in woodcuts and carvings from medieval times onwards. He was also known as the 'great leveller', this name referring to the fact that no one, neither kings nor beggars, peasants nor popes, could escape him. In this apocalyptic vein he is also personified as the **rider on a pale horse** or **the pale horseman**, this image being derived from Revelations:

And I looked, and behold a pale horse: and his name that sat on him was Death, and Hell followed with him.

More colloquially, in Britain he has been known to huntsmen as 'the great whipper in' since 1860 and to gamblers as 'the great croupier' – forever, one presumes, requesting people to 'cash in their chips'.

grockle. *See under* RUBBERNECK.

groovy. Though groovy is strongly associated with the Swinging Sixties it in fact entered the language around the 1930s, at the time when the sound reproduction of phonographs was improving quickly. The word is derived from the groove of a record and the way in which the new phonograph needles kept to it without jumping around. Groovy originally meant 'functioning smoothly' and later came to mean fashionable, up-to-the minute and exciting. 'To groove' means to enjoy intensely, to approve or to do something well. 'To get in the groove' similarly means to be in the right mood, to enjoy oneself – as Madonna's hit 'Into the Groove' indicates. This is not to be confused with 'getting into a groove', which means to be stuck in a rut – to get trapped in a narrow and boring way of life.

grotty. Distasteful, nasty, dirty, ugly, repellent, bizarre – in fact, a catch-all word that can be used of anything one finds unpleasant. This Merseyside slang word, derived from 'grotesque', was popularised world-wide by the 1960s pop group The Beatles, when they used it in their film *A Hard Day's Night* (1964), of which the screenplay was written by the Liverpudlian playwright Alun Owen. The word 'grotesque' has itself an interesting history. It was originally an architectural term, from the Italian word *grottesco*, meaning 'in the style of a grotto'. Grottos – picturesque artificial caves with fanciful and sometimes outlandish ornamentation, as a feature of a landscaped estate, were fashionable in the 18th century.

groupie. Originally, in the 1960s, a

groupie was a young woman who followed pop groups and sought to attach herself to them by offering sexual favours. Since then, the expression has come to mean simply a FAN or devotee, in fields other than pop music, and is used in expressions like 'political groupie' or 'literary groupie'.

grub. In the last century a person anxious to profit from the gold rush but unable to go and prospect themselves might have put up a 'grub stake', a sum of money to equip a prospector in exchange for a share of his finds. Part of this stake would go on providing food, and for this reason 'grub' came to be a slang term for food.

Grumpie. A word coined in the mid-1980s, based on YUPPIE, and meaning a grown-up mature person – one, presumably, who would look down with some disdain on the pretensions of a yuppie.

guillotine. Named after Dr Joseph Ignace Guillotin, who is sometimes erroneously credited with inventing it. The inventor was in fact Dr Antoine Louis, who adapted the machine from existing versions used in Scotland, Italy and Germany and gave it its original name, the *louisette*. Dr Guillotin became interested in it because it offered such a quick and pain-free method of execution to the lucky members of the aristocracy, for whom it was reserved. Arguing from a humanitarian viewpoint, he suggested that it be used for all executions – a suggestion taken up in 1792. He was appalled when the machine was named after him and spent years trying to disassociate himself from it.

gulag. A prison camp in the Soviet Union. The word was introduced to English-speakers by Alexander Solzhenitsyn's book *The Gulag Archipelago 1918–1956*. Gulag is an acronym formed from the Russian words *Gosudarstvennoye Upravleniye Lagerey*, meaning 'State Directorate of the Camps'.

gunboat diplomacy was first practised in the last century when gunboats were sent to various parts of the British Empire to persuade local rulers to co-operate with British aims. The expression is therefore a euphemism for a threat. *See also* DOUBLESPEAK.

gung ho. Eager; enthusiastic; zealous; totally committed. The expression comes from the Chinese *kung ho*, meaning 'work together'. During the early part of World War II this Chinese phrase, which was in use as a slogan of the Chinese Co-operatives, was adopted as a motto by the US Second Marine Raider Division. This marine division, which was also known as Carlson's Raiders, was led by Lt. Col. Evans F. Carlson, who had previously served as an observer attached to the Chinese army, where he picked up the phrase.

Guppie. This word was coined in 1985 to denote a YUPPIE who is concerned with ECOLOGY. It is a portmanteau word, combining the words 'green' and 'yuppie'.

guru. This Hindi word, meaning a teacher, has now been fully assimilated into the English language. It is still used in its original context to denote a Hindu spiritual teacher or leader of a sect. But since the 1960s it has been used in a wider sense to apply to any leader, expert or authority in some field, especially a charismatic figure who has a devoted following.

gutter press. Whether because most of the stories to be read in the gutter press have been found among the muck in the gutter, or because that's where such newspapers end up, the origin of this phrase is uncertain. The gutter press is the home of BONK

JOURNALISM; the tabloid pages of such newspapers (and it is widely disputed whether they should be called newspapers at all) are full of KISS AND TELL tales about the sexual misdemeanours of minor celebrities and have a limited hard news content.

H

hack. From the 14th century 'hackney' was the name used to distinguish a medium-sized horse used for riding, and the term came to be used specifically for a horse let out for hire. Hence 'hackney carriages' – vehicles for public hire, first introduced in London in 1637 during the reign of Charles I. 'Hackney' in this sense has nothing to do with the London Borough of Hackney but derives from the Old French word *hauenee*, meaning an ambling horse. Hackney came to be shortened to hack, which in turn came to be applied to anyone whose services are for hire, particularly writers and journalists. Today the phrase is used as a semi-affectionate and often modest description of themselves by freelance writers of all kinds.

hack it, to. To do something successfully – not with great style, perhaps, but to get there in the end. American dictionaries define the phrase as jargon used by loggers employed to hack down trees; someone who could hack it made the grade as a logger. This passed into general use in the 1960s. However, it may simply derive from the fact that 'hacking' in its original sense means to ride a horse at a steady pace, often on a journey. Someone who hacks it reaches their desired destination, even if not at a fast pace.

hacker. In the world of computers, hacker is a word with several shades of meaning. It may mean simply someone who spends much of his time writing computer programs. It may mean someone who expends a great deal of effort trying to analyse other people's programs, particularly games programs that are run on a home computer, in order to be able to amend them so as to change their characteristics. But the commonest meaning is someone who seeks to gain unauthorised access to computer systems through telephone links. The archetypal hacker is a teenage boy with a home computer linked through a 'modem' to the telephone network who manages to gain access to commercial, government or military computer systems.

hair – to let one's hair down. Short hair for women is a relatively recent fashion. In the past most women grew their hair long and kept it pinned up in various ways, only letting it down to its full length in the privacy of their own homes. For this reason to let one's hair down means to relax, to enjoy oneself, to feel comfortable and unrestricted.

hair – to make one's hair stand on end. *See under* HAIR-RAISING.

hair-raising. Popular belief has it that this phrase, meaning 'terrifying', is related to the American Indians' habit of taking scalps from their enemies. As the expression only came into use in the first decade of this century it's more likely to be an abbreviated version of the phrase **to make one's hair stand on end**, referring to the way in which at times of extreme fright the hair at the back of the neck stands on end.

hair of the dog (or, in full, a hair of the dog that bit you) refers to an alcoholic drink taken as a supposed cure for a hangover. From ancient Roman times it has been a popular belief that 'like cures like' or, as the Latin medical maxim has it, *similia similibus curantur*. It was, for example, believed that the best cure when one had been bitten by a dog was to apply to the wound some hair taken from the dog that had bitten you. The same reasoning underlies vaccines or the homeopathic approach to medicine – the system of treating disease by minute quantities of drugs that produce symptoms similar to those produced by the disease being treated.

hairs, to split. When this phrase was coined in the 17th century it was believed to be nigh impossible to split a hair entirely in two lengthways and so to split hairs was applied to QUIBBLING, overrefined distinctions, so minute as to be virtually invisible. The advent of the microscope made the literal splitting of hairs an easy task, but the phrase lives on.

hairy. Difficult, complicated; hazardous, dangerous, distressing. This is one of the slang usages of the word hairy – at various times it has also meant: crude, deficient in breeding; old, out-of-date; angry or excited. Hairy has been used to mean 'difficult' since the 19th century in Britain, and in the sense of 'dangerous' seems to have originated in the British armed services in the 1930s, doubtless as a contraction of the expression 'hair-raising'. The expression has had a renaissance since the early 1960s, stemming from its widespread use in the world of motors and motor-racing, as exemplified by this 1968 quotation from the *Sun* newspaper:

A fast driver is a hairy driver.

half-baked. In modern use something foolish, ridiculous or not properly planned. It is said to date back to the 1600s and was probably coined in the bakery to describe loaves that looked fine from the outside but were only half-cooked inside. Similarly a half-baked idea may seem okay on first inspection, but closer scrutiny reveals a serious flaw.

half-seas over. Fairly well inebriated – 'staggering drunk' but not quite 'falling down drunk'. This expression has been in use since at least the 17th century, and the allusion is a nautical one, referring to a sailing ship, heeled over in the wind, with the sea washing over half the slanted deck. It is easy to see why a drunken man, staggering along the street at a similar angle to the perpendicular, might be likened to such a storm-beset ship. For another nautical metaphor for drunkenness, *see* THREE SHEETS IN THE WIND.

hallmark. A mark of excellence, an indication that a thing has passed a certain standard. The hallmark was an official mark stamped on gold and silver articles after they had been tested and passed at the Goldsmiths' Hall, London, from 1300 onwards. Any item that had been stamped was guaranteed to be pure. We now use the term to mean an indication of any kind that something is of a good standard: 'The hallmark of a good hotel is plenty of towels in the bathrooms.'

Halloween. The Christian feast of All Saints or All Hallows has been celebrated on 1 November since the year 834. 31 October, the eve of this feast – All Hallows Eve or Halloween – has long had many superstitions attached to it. Many of them derive from the ancient Celts. In the Celtic calendar 31 October was the last day of the year and then, it was believed, witches and warlocks and 'ghoulies and ghosties and long-leggety beasties' went abroad to torment mankind.

ham. There is much dispute over this term, used to describe a bad actor. Many sources cite the fact that in the 19th century actors used ham fat to remove their makeup, which gives us the word 'hamfatter', meaning an actor. From this, it is said, we get the abbreviated form ham. Others have suggested that ham is derived from the slang 'hamateur', which might itself have been punning comment on an amateurish actor tackling the lead role in *Hamlet*. Perhaps most convincing of all is the theory that the word derives from Hamish McCullough, who led a touring group of actors around the mid-western states of the USA. The company went under the name of Ham's Actors and were, by all reports, pretty bad. Ham's Actors were touring at around the time 'ham' came into use, about 1880, which makes it more than likely that the word derived from their activities. From ham we also get 'hammy' and 'hamming it up', meaning to overdo the theatrical gestures.

hamburger. A flat round cake of minced beef, with spices and flavourings, that is fried or grilled and served in a bun. The original name was 'Hamburg steak' and it was introduced into America by German immigrants in the mid-19th century, since when it has become thoroughly Americanised and re-exported worldwide. The name is often contracted to **burger**, and other prefixes may be added, e.g. 'lunchburger'. Sometimes the contents are varied, as in the 'cheeseburger', 'fishburger' or 'porkburger'. This has led to some confusion and to avoid the impression that a hamburger is made from ham, the term **beefburger** was introduced.

hammer – to go at it hammer and tongs. A blacksmith working away in his forge, bashing the metal with his hammer and thrusting it in the fire with his tongs, made a terrific noise and expended a lot of physical effort. From this source we get the phrase to go at it hammer and tongs, meaning to do something (often arguing) with great vigour and force and possibly a lot of noise.

hand over fist and **hand over hand.** Someone who makes a lot of money easily may be said to be making it hand over fist or hand over hand. This expression refers to the traditional method seamen used to climb up rigging or haul in ropes. They did it hand over hand, rapidly putting one hand in front of the other to ensure a firm grip. In such a way they could haul in ropes or nets with great efficiency, and this is why the phrase is applied to someone who is 'hauling' in money.

hands – to win hands down. A jockey who has the winning post in sight and finds himself well ahead of the field may drop his hands to the horse's neck and let it run on without bothering to urge it forward. From this habit came the phrase to win hands down, meaning to win something with ease, without making a great effort.

hands-on. An adjective used mainly in business and education circles to describe practical work experience as opposed to theoretical study. Implicit in the phrase is the idea of rolling up one's sleeves and getting involved, rather than simply observing or reading about it.

handicap originated from the 17th-century sporting phrase 'hand in cap', referring to the way in which participants in a race would put their hand in a cap and draw lots. This evolved into handicap racing, where horses are allocated specific weights to carry, some of the runners being hampered by heavier weights than others. From this sense came the word handicapped to describe someone whose performance is encumbered by a physical or mental disability, that disability being known as a handicap.

Handsome is as handsome does. This proverb simply means that it is not looks that count but actions – a handsome person is only as handsome as the things they do.

hang loose. This expression, coined in the 1960s, means to be relaxed, nonchalant, uninvolved. It is the exact opposite of being **uptight**, a word which describes someone in a state of stress or depression.

hangdog look. In medieval Europe it was the practice to take animals that had killed or maimed people to court and try them for their crimes. Among the animals successfuly prosecuted and condemned to death in this way were rats, pigs, dogs and even a plague of insects that had ruined crops. In 1595 it was recorded that a dog was hung in the town of Leyden after it had bitten a child's finger, the bite eventually proving fatal. It is probably from this source that we get the phrase a hangdog look, meaning a guilty, shame-faced, sorry expression.

hangnail. In Anglo-Saxon times, a corn on the foot, an *angnaegl* – this word deriving from *ang*, meaning 'pain' and *naegel*, meaning 'nail'. It retained its meaning, though the pronunciation evolved to become the present hangnail, up to the 17th century. No one can be certain why it suddenly shifted meaning and was applied to the tiny but painful tags of skin at the side of the nails, but perhaps it was because the word was such an appropriate description.

hanky-panky. The exact origin has not been traced, but all sources agree that it is probably closely related to HOCUS POCUS. It means mild, usually amusing trickery or game-playing; naughtiness. It is also used as a humorous euphemism for illicit sex.

happy – to be happy as a clam. This American expression, meaning to be deliriously happy, was originally 'happy as a clam at high tide'. This first version was self-explanatory, because at high tide clams are safe from clam-diggers.

happy as a lark. *See under* LARK.

happy hour. In American usage this originally meant the hour after finishing work, spent relaxing in a bar and drinking with one's colleagues. The expression became commercialised when bars used it to denote a time when drinks are sold at less than the usual prices, in order to attract customers when trade would otherwise be slack.

hara-kiri. The classic Japanese method of suicide practised by members of the military and government when they have been seriously disgraced or dishonoured. It comes from the Japanese words *hara*, 'belly' and *kiri*, 'to cut', which, combined, translate as 'belly-cutting', a graphic description of the elaborate disembowelling ritual.

hard act to follow, a. Originally used by vaudeville players unfortunate enough to be billed to come on stage immediately after a star act. Implicit in the saying is the idea that no amount of effort can hope to equal what's gone beforehand.

hard-boiled. Tough and cynical, lacking illusions. There are two suggestions about the derivation of the term. One proposes an analogy between a hard-boiled person and a hard-boiled egg. An American source suggests that the term comes from the practice of boiling shirts, a habit which apparently toughened the cotton.

Hare Krishna. The title of a mantra (or chant) in honour of the Hindu god Vishnu, used by members of a religious cult known as the International Society for Krishna Consciousness. The phrase is also used to refer to this cult or its followers, who are often to be seen in groups in the streets of cities, dressed in orange robes, with shaven heads, chanting to the accompaniment of tinkling oriental instruments. The name is formed from the Hindi words *hare* ('Oh God!') and *Krishna*, the name of an incarnation of the god Vishnu.

hassle. When it was originally coined in the USA in the mid-1800s a hassle was a major disagreement or fight. Today the word is used to describe more minor inconveniences or boring tasks. It may be derived from the French verb *harceler*, meaning to importune or attack constantly, or perhaps from the German verb *hassen*, meaning to hate. It may equally possibly be a combination of two English words, tussle and haggle, which between them describe what a hassle is.

hat, at the drop of a. This term comes from the American frontier practice of waving or dropping a hat as a signal for a fight to start. This gesture was also used to start races or competitions of other kinds. The expression now describes someone who needs no encouragement to do something – who does it instantly, without a moment's delay.

hat trick. This expression derives from the game of cricket, and refers to a bowler taking three wickets with three successive balls. In the early days of the game it was the custom for a bowler who achieved this feat to be rewarded by his club with the prize of a new cap. Nowadays the expression is widely applied to any threefold success or achievement.

hatchet, to bury the. When North American Indians came together to smoke their peace pipes they ritually buried their hatchets, scalping-knives and other weapons so that all signs of hostility and war were out of sight. Longfellow recorded the custom in his poem *The Song of Hiawatha*:

Buried was the bloody hatchet.
Buried was the dreadful war-club;
Buried were all warlike weapons,
And the war-cry was forgotten.
There was peace among the nations.

This has given us the phrase to bury the hatchet, meaning to let bygones be bygones; to forget old scores and come together in peace.

hatchet man. A person brought in from outside to do someone's dirty work for them. It has been suggested that the phrase originated in the USA when Chinese gangs in San Francisco and New York hired killers, armed with hatchets, to assassinate rival gang-members. These days a hatchet man is more likely to be hired by an organisation that wants something vaguely unethical done or is seeking radical reorganisation. The hatchet man carries out the unpleasant tasks of destroying a political rival's reputation or firing a company's established workforce. Then, having taken all the acrimony and bad feeling on himself, he departs for his next job.

hauled – to be hauled over the coals. To be severely reprimanded – an unpleasant experience but not, fortunately, as unpleasant as that from which the phrase derives. In the Middle Ages people suspected of heresy or witchcraft were subjected to trial by fire. Methods varied, but one of them required the accused to be dragged over hot coals. If they survived their burns they were decreed innocent and those who died were deemed to have been guilty.

hay – to make hay while the sun shines. To get on with something while the going is good, to grab an opportunity when it is offered. The best way of making hay is to leave the grass to dry in the sun, and thus it is only sensible that farmers should grab the chance to make hay while the sun shines. The saying was published in 1546 but was probably an established proverb by that time.

haywire. When something goes haywire it breaks down or becomes uncontrollable. There is no agreed derivation of this phrase but there have been a couple of suggestions. The first is that it refers to a breakdown in a piece of machinery that can be fixed using a piece of haywire – wire used for binding bales of hay. The second, and most likely, is that it describes the difficulties of handling a large coil of such wire without getting it tangled or twisted.

head – to bury one's head in the sand. Ostriches were popularly believed to bury their heads in the sand when pursued, apparently under the impression that if they could not see the enemy, the enemy could not see them. Wildlife documentaries have dispelled this illusion, but we still use the phrase to describe someone who, faced with danger, tries to ignore it.

head, to lose one's. *See* TO FLY OFF THE HANDLE.

headhunt, to. When a company requires a senior executive it may employ a recruitment agency, often known as a headhunter, to ferret out candidates who are already successfully holding similar positions in other companies. The chosen person is then approached by the headhun-

ter and persuaded to change jobs, usually with the promise of a better salary. Two explanations have been put forward to explain the word headhunting. The first is that it is usually only the heads of departments who are poached in this manner. The second points to the fact that recruitment agencies are asked to go for specific 'heads', rather than drawing up a general list of candidates. *See also* OUTPLACEMENT

healie-feelie. The American craze for crystals, believed by some to have healing and restorative powers, has not (so far at least) caught on in Britain. Healie-feelies are people who believe that handling mineral crystals such as quartz and tourmaline has a therapeutic effect.

Hear! Hear! An exclamation of approval for what a speaker has said. This phrase was originally 'Hear him! Hear him!', used to call attention to a speaker's words, in the days when public meetings were generally rowdier than they are today and those who disagreed with the speaker's sentiments would often try to drown his words with hissing and booing.

heart, to warm the cockles of one's. In this phrase cockles are not shellfish but the *cochleae cordis*, the ventricles of the heart. Something that is said to warm the cockles of the heart therefore gives pleasure right to the heart. The expression can be used to describe the literal warming effect of good food or wine or, more symbolically, a kind gesture or friendly word that makes one feel good.

heart – to wear one's heart on one's sleeve. When a medieval knight participated in a jousting tournament it was customary for him to carry a token from the lady he loved – a handkerchief or scarf, for example. From this we get the phrase to wear one's heart on one's sleeve, used in these less romantic times to describe someone whose affection for another is plain for everyone to see.

Heath Robinson. A phrase commonly applied to any absurdly elaborate, ingeniously improvised or impracticable device. William Heath Robinson (1872–1944) was an English cartoonist, whose humorous drawings of such eccentric inventions were published in *Punch* and elsewhere.

heavy hitter. In the business world a powerful person – someone with authority to make major decisions or with lots of money or brains. A heavy hitter might also be described as a person with 'clout', both phrases alluding to the power and effectiveness of their actions.

heavy metal. Extremely loud, basic and monotonous rock music – often played over massive banks of speakers to audiences that consist almost exclusively of teenage boys. Led Zeppelin are the archetypal heavy metal band.

heebie-jeebies. The jitters; a feeling of discomfort, unease or distress. Heebie-jeebies originated in the United States in the early 1920s. The expression was coined by Billy de Beck, a comic strip artist who created popular characters such as Barney Google and Snuffy Smith. He also coined the expression HORSE FEATHERS.

heel, to bring to. One of the first things a dog learns at a canine obedience class is to walk at its owner's heel, i.e. just behind and to the side. The dog is required to maintain this subservient position until it is given permission to do otherwise. It is this sense of subservience that is implied in the expression to bring to heel when it is applied to humans. To bring someone to heel is to remind them of their inferior status and obtain obedience from them – if

necessary by the use of restraints to curb their independence.

heightism is discrimination against individuals because of their height. Exceptionally tall and short people have always been aware that their height influences the way others treat them, but recent studies have shown that height plays a significant factor in success at work. Tall people, for example, have a better chance of getting to the top of their chosen profession; so much so that in the latest American presidential election sociologists argued that the height of the two candidates could be an important deciding factor. It has also been shown that short men and tall women experience more difficulties in finding a suitable partner. Heightism therefore joins ABLEISM, AGEISM, ALPHABETISM, SEXISM and all the other discriminatory-isms that beset most of us from time to time.

Heinz 57. A term for a mongrel dog, coined from the Heinz advertising slogan which boasts 57 different varieties and implying a similar number of different breeds in the dog's ancestry. When the slogan was coined in 1892 Heinz in fact offered 60 varieties.

helping the police with their enquiries. This is a classic police euphemism used in countless statements to inform the media that a person or persons have been detained for questioning about a crime. Though some people help the police with their enquiries on a voluntary basis, the phrase is usually applied to those who have been arrested.

henpecked. Anyone who has spent a few minutes watching chickens in a coop will have observed how frequently they peck each other. Studies of this behaviour have shown that there is a definite PECKING ORDER in which hens peck those who are below them in rank and submit to pecking by those higher up the scale. In the 17th century, however, it was believed that the hens had a particular habit of pecking the young cockerels and this was compared with the way some wives dominated their husbands – hence the expression henpecked for a man who is nagged and dominated by his wife.

hep. Aware, well-informed, up-to-date, 'in the know'. This expression originated in the early 1900s, among American jazz musicians. The derivation is obscure, but it has been suggested that as early jazz musicians often marched in parades, the expression, with the original meaning of 'in step', may have derived from the drillmaster's shouted commands '*Hep*, two, three, four. *Hep*, two, three, four'. A number of elaborations of this expression have been in vogue at one time or another: 'hep to the jive', for example, and 'hep cat' or 'hep dude' to describe someone who is hep. For another variation, *see* HIP.

hick. To people who live in the city a hick is a stereotyped, slow-witted country bumpkin. The word originated in the 1600s as a nickname of Richard which was thought to be a country name. Though it is rarely used in Britain these days hick is still in common use in the USA, where 'hick town' or 'hicksville' is used to denote a dull, unsophisticated place.

hide one's light under a bushel. This is a biblical expression:

A city that is set on a hill cannot be hid. Neither do men light a candle and put it under a bushel, but on a candlestick (Matthew 5:15)

In Christ's day a bushel was a solid container and thus anyone hiding a candle under one would completely block the light. From this the phrase means to conceal one's talents or abilities.

hidebound. It has been suggested that this was a term applied from around the 16th century to describe a cow so emaciated that its skin virtually clung to its bones. As a result it had difficulty moving and after the beast's death it was impossible to prise the hide from the skeleton. We use hidebound today to describe people who are figuratively strait-jacketed; those who have rigid and immovable opinions.

highbrow. According to 19th-century phrenologists – 'scientists' who believed that character and intelligence could be determined by the shape and bumps of the skull – a high forehead denoted intelligence. This belief gives us the word highbrow to describe an intellectual person. Anything that requires a high degree of intelligence to comprehend (books or films, for example) may also be described, sometimes disparagingly, as highbrow. From this source we also get 'lowbrow', referring to something that is intellectually undemanding, and 'middlebrow', a coinage of the 1940s, to describe something that falls between the two. Middlebrow is often used as an insult to describe an uneasy compromise between highbrow ideals and lowbrow popularism. *See also* EGGHEAD.

hightail it. This American verb, meaning to get away or flee, was coined by hunters who noticed that rabbits, horses and other animals raised their tails high just before they fled.

hijack. At the time of the American Prohibition, BOOTLEGGERS moving illicit alcohol around the country sometimes fell prey to other criminals. The gunmen raided trucks transporting the booze and instructed drivers to 'Stick 'em high, Jack'. It is from this command that the word hijack is derived.

hip. Aware, well-informed, up-to-date, 'in the know'. Hip is a variant of the word HEP, originating in the same era, at the beginning of the 20th century. It eventually became more widespread, however, particularly in the 1950s when it was a vogue word associated with the subculture of the BEATNIKS, and again in the 1960s with the HIPPIE or HIPPY subculture.

hip hip hooray! The origin of this phrase remains something of a mystery. Hip hip hooray (or variants such as hep hep hoorah) is said to have been the cry of Crusaders as they fought the Turks to win back Jerusalem. Most authorities venture to suggest that hip hip is derived from the initial letters of the expression *Hierosolyma est perdita*, meaning 'Jerusalem is lost', and apparently '*hep hep*' was the shout of German knights when they hunted down Jews. Hooray is said to derive from a Slavonic phrase *hu-raj*, meaning 'to Paradise'. From this is obtained the literal meaning, 'Jerusalem is lost and we are on our way to Paradise', which is probably not what most people have in mind when they use the expression!

hip hop. A style of music, dancing and youth subculture originating among black and Hispanic teenagers in New York in the mid-1980s and now to be found in Britain. Hip hop music is characterised by rap; dancing by 'body-popping' and 'break-dancing'; culture by graffiti art – often seen on the city's subway trains. *See also* RAP MUSIC.

hippie or **hippy.** A participant in the major youth subculture of the latter half of the 1960s, characterised by dreamy idealism ('Love and peace, man!'), FLOWER POWER, exotic dress, interest in oriental religion,

experimentation with drugs such as cannabis and LSD, and PSYCHEDELIC effects. Although the word hippie (or hippy) is very much associated with the 1960s it was in use earlier, meaning someone who was HIP, as in this 1953 quotation from *North Light* by D. Wallop, (quoted in the Oxford English Dictionary):

'I really get a bellyful of these would-be hippies.'

hitch a lift means to beg a free ride in another person's vehicle. It is easy to imagine that this is a relatively new expression, coined since the advent of the internal combustion engine, but in fact the word hitch is, in this context, based on the verb **to hitch-hike** which has far older origins. To hitchhike originally referred to a means of travel involving one horse and two people. One person would ride the horse a decent distance, then dismount, hitch the animal to a convenient tree or post, and hike on by foot. Eventually the second traveller would reach the horse, mount it and ride until he caught up with his friend. This way of getting about was widely used and was generally known as 'riding and tying'. In 1737 Dr Johnson and the actor David Garrick travelled from Lichfield to London using the method, but they were certainly not the first or last to do so.

hobnob. A variation on the old English phrase 'hab-nab', meaning 'have or have not'. It derives from the atmosphere of give and take, or sharing, that characterises a close friendship. To hobnob with someone means to share time with them; to be cronies or buddies.

Hobson's choice. No choice at all. We owe this expression to a certain Thomas Hobson who kept a livery stable at Cambridge in the early 17th century and who was a well-known figure in his day. He had a thriving business hiring out horses to students from the university. To avoid his best and most popular horses being ridden too hard, he insisted that each customer take the horse nearest the stable door. In this way each horse was hired out in turn; the customer, instead of taking his own choice of horse, was forced to take Hobson's choice.

hock, to be in. Two theories have been advanced to explain this expression, meaning to owe money. English authorities trace the phrase back to the ancient festival of Hocktide, observed until the 16th century. At Hocktide it was the custom for the women of a village to intercept men, tie them with ropes and hold them to ransom for a small sum. A day later the men did the same to the women. Passers-by might also find themselves bound and held in hock until they had paid up. The money raised went to the local church. (This practice of kidnapping and holding to ransom to raise money for a good cause is still common among university students during Rag Weeks.) An American source offers a different explanation, pointing in the direction of the card table where, in 19th-century America, the last card taken from the box in a game of faro was called the 'hocketty card'. Anyone who placed a bet on this card was said to be in hock, and as such bets were usually lost the phrase came to mean 'owing money'. Whatever the origins of the phrase, people in hock often resorted to the pawnbrokers to raise money to pay off their debts, with the result that pawnbrokers became known as 'hock shops'.

hocus pocus. Trickery or deception; MUMBO JUMBO. During the reign of James I of England there was a popular conjuror known by the name of Hocus Pocus, his name deriving from the meaningless mock-Latin formula he used while performing each of his tricks: *Hocus pocus, tontus talontus, vade celeriter jubes.* This was copied by other conjurors; hence the association of hocus pocus with trickery and deception. It has often been conjectured that the words were intended as a blasphemous parody of the words of consecration in the Roman Catholic Mass – *Hoc est corpus meum* – but no proof has ever been found of this assertion. What is more certain is that the word 'hoax' is derived from hocus pocus.

hog, go the whole. To go all the way; to stop at nothing; to carry through to completion. One theory has it that the phrase arose from a poem by William Cowper in 1779: *The Love of the World Reproved: or Hypocrisy Detected.* This poem comments on the restrictions of the Muslim faith on eating pork. Muhammad decreed that certain parts of the pig could not be eaten, but left vague which parts were forbidden. Thus his followers were free to exempt from the ban those parts which they particularly enjoyed. As Cowper wrote:

And set their wit at work to find
What joint the prophet had in mind.
Much controversy straight arose,
These choose the back, the belly those;
By some 'tis confidently said
He meant not to forbid the head;
Whilst others at that doctrine rail,
And piously prefer the tail.
Thus, conscience freed from every clog,
Mahometans eat up the hog.

Another theory is that the phrase is based on the slang word 'hog' at one time used for a shilling in England or a ten cent piece in America. Thus, to go the whole hog would mean to spend a whole shilling or dime. If this theory is true, then the phrase is clearly a close relation of the proverbial expression 'In for a penny, in for a pound'.

hoi polloi. The common people; the masses. This is a transliteration of the Greek words meaning 'the many'. Purists often shudder if anyone refers to 'the hoi polloi', pointing out that this is equivalent to saying 'the the many'. But this usage is sanctioned by no less a writer than John Dryden in his *Essay of Dramatic Poesy* (1658):

If by the people you understand the multitude, the hoi polloi, 'tis no matter what they think . . .

hoist – to be hoist with one's own petard. To be beaten by one's own weapons, caught in the trap set for others. A petard was a kind of primitive mine or mortar, filled with gunpowder and attached to the gate or wall that was to be breached. It was lit by a slow-burning fuse which in theory should have given the person who set it time to escape, but this was not always the case and sometimes an engineer was hoisted into the air by the explosion he had caused.

hoity-toity, meaning pretentious or superior, may be derived from the French *haut toit*, meaning 'high roof'. The allusion is to someone looking down disdainfully on others from on high. A more mundane explanation suggests that it is a rhyming construction based on the old word 'hoit', meaning to romp. *See also* TO BE ON ONE'S HIGH HORSE. *under* HORSE.

hold the fort. To assume temporary responsibility during the absence of another. Hold the fort originally meant to defend a position at all costs. The phrase originated as a message signalled by General Sherman to General Corse in 1864 during the American Civil War. The American evangelists Sankey and Moody obviously had this incident in mind when they included in one of their hymns the line:

Hold the fort for I am coming, Jesus signals still.

hole, to be in a. Someone in trouble is said to be in a hole. One source suggests that this expression can be traced back to 19th-century American gambling dens where the proprietor of the place raked off a percentage of the stake money for each game. This money was pushed down a hole in the centre of the table connecting with a locked drawer, to which only the proprietor had access. An unlucky player might find himself with less cash in his pocket than under the table, and hence he would be in a hole. On a less fanciful note, the expression may simply allude to the fact that someone who falls down a hole, or whose vehicle gets stuck in a hole, is in trouble.

holistic. Medicine which aims to treat the individual as a whole, body and mind, instead of just a set of isolated parts or symptoms, is a relatively new development. But the word holistic and the concept behind it goes back to 1926 when it was coined by South African prime minister Jan Smuts. Smuts believed that, 'There is a synthesis which makes elements or parts act as one', and that therefore whole things should not be regarded as simply the sum of their parts.

holocaust. The word derives from the Greek *holokaustos*, meaning 'burnt whole'. It originally referred to burnt offerings made to the gods, but for around three hundred years it has been used to describe a massacre or terrible slaughter. 'The Holocaust' refers to the millions of murders carried out under Hitler's orders, including the extermination of six million Jews.

honcho. The person in charge of any situation; the boss. This comes from the Japanese word *hancho*, meaning 'squad leader'. The expression was picked up by US troops stationed in Japan during the military occupation following World War II, and during the Korean War.

honeymoon. An old Germanic custom dictated that for thirty days following the wedding feast the bride and groom should drink diluted honey to keep their love sweet. This period was dictated by the cycle of the moon. Thus we get the word honeymoon, meaning a period of holiday or celebration following a wedding.

Hong Kong dog. *See* AZTEC TWO-STEP.

honkey, honkie or **honky.** A Black American slang term, used disparagingly, for a white man. The origin is not known for sure, but it may be a variation of another American slang word 'hunky' that was originally applied to immigrants from eastern and central Europe, and is a corruption of 'Hungarian'. The earliest appearance in print identified by the Oxford English Dictionary is dated 1946.

honky-tonk, describing a cheap saloon bar and the kind of piano music played there, may be derived from *hunkie*, a derogatory term applied to the Hungarian labourers who frequented such places. *Hunkie* later became the black word HONKIE, meaning a despised white person.

hooch or **hootch.** (1) Alcoholic liquor, especially when of inferior quality or of illegal provenance. This word comes from the name of a small tribe of Indians in Alaska, the Hoochinoo. These Indians produced their own crudely distilled liquor which became known as 'hoochinoo' – hooch or hootch, for short. In the years of the Klondike gold rush at the end of the 19th century saloonkeepers there also distilled their own liquor, which acquired the same appellation. (2) A Korean or Vietnamese village hut or, by analogy, an army barracks. This was US forces slang used in Korea and Vietnam, and derives from the

Japanese word *uchi*, meaning a house.

hoodlum. A ruffian, a small-time gangster or criminal. This slang term originated in the San Francisco area *c*.1870. The earliest use of the word in print identified by the Oxford English Dictionary is from the *Cincinnati Commercial* of 6 September 1871:

Surely he is far enough away in this hideous wild of a swamp, to escape the bullying of the San Francisco "hoodlums".'

The true derivation of the word is not known, but there are a couple of theories. One is that it was an accidental coinage of a San Francisco reporter, aided by the compositor on his newspaper. Fearing reprisals for an article he was writing about a local gang of ruffians led by someone called Muldoon, the reporter changed the name of the gang-leader by spelling it backwards – 'noodlum'. The compositor misread this word and printed it as 'hoodlum'. Though this is an entertaining story, there is no real evidence to support it. The other theory, advanced by Dr J. T. Krumpelmann in *Modern Language Notes* in 1935, based on the fact that there were a number of German immigrants in San Francisco in the 1860s and 1870s, is that it derives from the Bavarian dialect word *hodalum*, meaning 'a scamp'.

hook, line and sinker. It's likely that this phrase originated among anglers, for it describes the way a greedy fish swallows not just the angler's baited hook but also the sinker (the lead weight used to keep the hook beneath the surface) and some of the fishing line too. Such a fish is well and truly caught. Used metaphorically, the expression is applied to a gullible person who, like the fish, 'swallows' every detail of a story or hoax.

hook or by crook, by. To achieve something by hook or by crook means to achieve it by any means possible, whether rightfully or wrongfully. The expression is said to be derived from medieval laws applying to the gathering of firewood. Peasants who entered a forest to gather wood were only allowed to take the dead branches from the ground and, using a bill-hook, to cut down those they could reach with a shepherd's crook.

hooker. A prostitute. There is a popular misconception in the USA that this word derives from the name of General Joseph Hooker (1814–79) who fought in the Civil War. Hooker's reputation for moral probity was not the highest, and he has been described as a

man of blemished character . . . whose headquarters was a place that no self-respecting man liked to go and no decent woman could go, for it can only be described as a combination of bar-room and brothel.

The area of Washington D.C. in which Hooker had his headquarters became known as Hooker's Division. The word 'hooker', however, is known to have been in use in the USA in the 1840s – before General Hooker acquired his unsavoury reputation. It in fact derives from an area of New York City known as Corlear's Hook, or simply 'the Hook', which was the site of many brothels, frequented especially by seamen.

hooligan. A vandal, a violent young ruffian, a member of a street gang. According to the Oxford English Dictionary, this word first appeared in print in police-court reports of daily newspapers in the summer of 1898. The origin of the word is not known for sure. It has been conjectured that the word is a corruption of 'Hooley's gang', the name of a gang that is supposed to have existed in London. It may have come from a music-hall song of the 1890s about a quarrelsome Irish family with the surname of Hooligan. But Clarence Rook, who wrote a book called *Hooligan Nights* in 1899, maintained that the original was an actual London petty criminal named Patrick Hooligan, a thief who often assaulted his victims.

Hooray Henry. A well-connected, well-educated, probably wealthy young person of either sex who, on his or her own, is well-behaved and polite but who is transformed into an upper-class hooligan when in the company of other 'hoorays'. Throwing food in smart restaurants, taking off their clothes and getting riotously drunk are just a few of the things 'hoorays' enjoy when they are in groups. Young Fogeys, though of similar background, have nothing but contempt for their Hooray Henry counterparts. *See also* CHINLESS WONDER.

hoosegow. This American slang expression, meaning 'jail', has been in use since the early 1900s. It comes from the Mexican word *juzgao*, derived from the Spanish *juzgado*, meaning a court or tribunal.

hop on the bandwagon. This is an American expression meaning to race to join something popular, to try to get a slice of the action. Bandwagons were originally horse-drawn wagons on top of which a brass band played. They were often used to attract crowds and lead them to a circus or other place of entertainment. Politicians later adopted this kind of attention-grabbing tactic and their supporters would sometimes jump up onto the bandwagon to show their enthusiasm – a habit that led to the coinage of the phrase.

horns, to pull in one's. To retreat,

to take defensive action or to moderate one's behaviour. In use since the end of the 16th century, this expression refers to the way in which a snail pulls in its 'horns' when confronted with something that makes it anxious.

horse. This slang term for the drug heroin originated in the USA around 1950 and was in vogue in the early 1950s. It possibly derives from the Greek word *heros*, meaning hero, that is the root of the name heroin itself. The drug was so-named because it has the effect of making the user feel, temporarily at least, like a hero.

horse, to be on one's high. In medieval England the tallest horses were ridden by people of the highest rank who, from their lofty position, looked down on their lesser subjects. From this we get the phrase to be on one's high horse, describing someone who behaves scornfully or assumes superiority over another.

horse, to flog a dead. *See under* FLOGGING.

horse's – straight from the horse's mouth. Experts have long been able to judge the age of a horse by examining its teeth, so an owner who deducted a few years from his animal's age in order to sell it might have the deception exposed when the buyer checked its mouth. From this we get the phrase straight from the horse's mouth, meaning straight from source – the truth as told by the person who really knows about it rather than an intermediary.

horse feathers. Rubbish, nonsense, balderdash. This expression was coined in the early 1920s by comic strip artist Billy de Beck, who also originated the expression HEEBIE-JEEBIES.

horses – to change horses in mid-stream. To make a major change

to one's plans in the middle of a difficult or important activity; to create added difficulties for oneself. The phrase might be used, for example, when a new political leader is elected in the middle of a war or a new company director appointed at a critical period of a company's development. The expression alludes to a person trying to swap from the back of one horse to another as it crosses a stream – making both manoeuvres doubly difficult and greatly increasing the risk of disaster.

horses for courses. This expression comes from the world of horseracing, where it is accepted that some horses always perform best on certain courses. In general use horses for courses is a maxim advising that certain individuals are best-suited to certain types of work or situation.

hot – to blow hot and cold. *See under* BLOW.

hot chestnut. A hot chestnut, straight from the fire, is difficult to hold or eat. A metaphorical hot chestnut is an issue that is so fraught with emotion and difficulties that it is too hot to handle. The implication is that it has to be allowed a cooling-off period before it can be satisfactorily dealt with – otherwise one might be in danger of BURNING ONE'S FINGERS. *See also* HOT POTATO.

hot dog. A frankfurter sausage, grilled and served in a split bread roll, usually with mustard and relish. Its invention, in the year 1900 or thereabouts, is generally attributed to one Harry Stevens, who held the catering concession at the New York sports stadium the Polo Grounds, home ground of the New York Giants. The person who gave this comestible its name, however, was T. A. Dorgan, familiarly known as Tad, who was a renowned sports cartoonist at that time.

hot line. This used to mean a direct, exclusive communications channel between two points, originally and particularly that established in 1963 between the White House and the Kremlin for use in a crisis. It is now generally applied to any emergency telephone line or telephone number.

hot potato. An American phrase meaning something embarrassing or difficult to deal with. The allusion is to handling a potato straight from the oven – a messy and potentially painful business. *See also* TO BURN ONE'S FINGERS and HOT CHESTNUT.

hour, at the eleventh. To do something just in time. Surprisingly it does not derive from the race to complete something on a given day, before the hour of midnight, but from a biblical parable, Matthew XX, 1–16.

house – bring the house down. When an audience rises in rapturous applause so loud and vigorous that it seems to shake the fabric of the theatre, a performer, company or production can be said to have brought the house down. Whether a theatre has ever actually fallen down due to the enthusiasm of an audience is not on record!

house – to go like a house on fire. Americans trace this phrase back to the log cabins erected by Swedish settlers as early as the 16th century. These houses were practical and easily constructed, but they are also reported to have burned down with terrifying speed. Though it's difficult to believe that such solid logs could burn like matchsticks, American authorities report that pioneers compared the speed at which a house burned with that of their horses. A fast horse was said to go like a house on fire. This may well be true, but it seems more

likely that the phrase originated first in Britain. Fires which could destroy an entire city were feared for hundreds of years. That was why, when William the Conqueror invaded Britain in 1066, one of his first acts was to establish the CURFEW, a fire safety precaution which required all domestic fires to be extinguished at a certain time each night. One can imagine that fire would destroy a medieval timber building, its walls made of flimsy wattle and daub and its roof thatched with straw, far more quickly than a solidly-built log cabin. It seems reasonable to assume, therefore, that the phrase originated in Britain and was exported to the USA by settlers.

how the other half lives. Interestingly enough, when this phrase was introduced 'the other half' were the poor. Today we normally use the expression to refer to the lifestyles of the rich and famous. It comes from a book entitled *How the Other Half Lives* by Jacob Riis, published in 1890.

how to win friends and influence people. A catch-phrase, now often used ironically and derisively, popularised by Dale Carnegie (1885–1955), an American who ran a school training people in public speaking and self-improvement, etc. Carnegie used the phrase as the title of a book, published in 1936, which over the following three years sold more than a million copies.

how's your father? This is not really a solicitous enquiry concerning paternal well-being, but a phrase used facetiously to mean 'thingummy' or 'whatsit', and in phrases like 'a bit of how's your father' for sexual innuendo. The use of this phrase originated in the British music-hall, and was popularised by comedian Harry Tate.

hue and cry. A kind of ancient Neighourhood Watch scheme; a legal requirement for local people to attempt to capture a criminal in their midst or pursue him to the boundary of their manor, whence the pursuit was taken up by their neighbours. This practice involved chasing the villain with 'horn and voice', i.e. making a terrific noise as they went. From this we get the modern use of hue and cry, meaning a noisy disturbance or alarm and with the implication that it may all be a fuss about nothing.

hum, to make things. To get them moving. This is an American expression, dating from around the turn of the century. No one knows for sure but it has been suggested that it refers to the humming of machinery in a busy factory, with the implication that to make things hum meant originally to switch on machinery and get everything working.

humongous. A slang expression used to describe something massive. It derives from a combination of 'huge' and 'monstrous'.

hunch, to have a. For hundreds of years it was believed that people with hunchbacks had a special link with the devil which gave them the ability to predict the future. Thus someone who had a lucky premonition might describe themselves as having a hunch.

hunky-dory. Something that is all right, perfectly satisfactory, may be defined as hunky-dory. There is some difference of opinion about the origin of the expression, some sources identifying it as a play on words derived from the Dutch *honk*, meaning a goal or aim and therefore something good. Another source

points in the direction of a breath-freshening product called Hunkidori that was introduced to American stores at about the time hunky-dory came into use. A third suggests that it comes from the name of a street in Yokohama, Japan, a city much-frequented by sailors, where a sea-faring man was guaranteed to find whatever he required to have a good time.

hustler. When Dutch colonists first established themselves in the USA a hustler was the Dutch word for someone who worked fast and efficiently. It later came to mean a confidence trickster or thief, perhaps alluding to the speed at which such people 'work' or disappear. More recently still it has been applied to go-getting people who live on their wits and ability to manipulate others. Hustler is also a euphemism for a prostitute.

hype. This slang word is often used in reference to publicity stunts, especially when they are promoting something essentially worthless, or to any advertising or promotion that is blatant, extravagant or dishonest. It is also used, either as noun or verb, to mean, simply, 'swindle'. In the pop music industry, to hype a record means to get it into the charts by buying large numbers of the record from selected shops whose sales figures are used in compiling the charts. The origin of the word is obscure. It has been conjectured that it derives from the Greek prefix *hyper-*, meaning 'over' or 'in excess', as in 'hyperbole' or 'hypersensitive'. Or that it derives from 'hypodermic' – i.e. something used to administer a stimulant. Or that it derives from 'high-pressure salesmanship'. Each of these putative derivations sounds plausible for some of the contexts in which hype is used. But not for the early usage in the USA in the early 1920s, when it referred simply to a cheat, particularly someone who shortchanged customers.

I

I'm all right, Jack. This is a bowdler-ised version of a catch-phrase that originated in the British navy *c*.1880. The original form was 'Fuck you, Jack, I'm all right', referring to the arrogance shown by many officers towards the common sailor, the Jack Tar. The phrase, with variations, became widespread throughout the armed forces. In 1960 a film entitled *I'm All Right, Jack*, a comedy about trades unions and industrial rela-tions, starred Peter Sellers and Ian Carmichael.

I've started so I'll finish. A jocular catch-phrase used by one who is interrupted while speaking or while performing some other activity. The phrase originates from the long-running BBC Television quiz pro-gramme *Mastermind*, in which it is used by the quizmaster Magnus Magnusson whenever he is inter-rupted by the time signal while posing a question to a contestant.

iconoclast. The first iconoclast in history was the Byzantine Emperor Leo III, so-called because in AD 726 he ordered the destruction of religious icons and images in churches. The word was coined specially by those who opposed him.

identikit. The Identikit was a method of identifying criminals or persons whom the police wished to interview. A composite picture of the required person was built up of individual features – facial shape, hair, eyes, eyebrows, mouth, etc. – as selected by witnesses from a stock of drawings representing all possible varieties of each feature. The method was de-veloped by Hugh C. McDonald and first used by the Los Angeles Police Department in 1959. The word iden-tikit soon came to be used figura-tively, as a noun or adjective, to describe any similar process of pro-ducing a composite portrait of a person or thing. For example, in the 29 September 1967 issue of *The Spec-tator*:

> One at least managed to build up an identikit description of the soul.

if anything can go wrong, it will. *See* MURPHY'S LAW.

if it's Tuesday, this must be Belgium. This was the title of a 1969 Amer-ican comedy film about a very fast package tour of Europe. The phrase perfectly sums up the confused, be-wildered reactions of American tourists attempting to 'do' all the capitals and cultural attractions of Europe in the space of a few weeks. Although still frequently used in this context, the phrase is also more gen-erally applied in the context of any fast travel.

If the mountain won't come to Muhammad, Muhammad must go to the mountain. This expression is derived from the time of the prophet Muhammad, founder of the Muslim religion. The Arabs demanded that he prove his miraculous powers by ordering Mount Safa to come to him. The mountain did not move and Muhammad explained that God had been merciful, for 'Had it obeyed my words, it would have fallen on us to our destruction. I will therefore go to the mountain and thank God that He has had mercy . . .'

Today we use the phrase to describe someone who cannot get their own way and has to submit to the inevitable.

If you can't stand the heat, stay out of the kitchen. Don't undertake a difficult job if you are not prepared to stand the pace and strain associated with it. This has been an American catch-phrase since about 1950. It was coined by the American politician Harry S. Truman who used it frequently, specifically in reference to the US presidency.

ignoramus. Until the 17th century the word was simply the Latin for 'We don't know'. Grand juries would write it on the back of an indictment if they felt there was not enough evidence for a case to be pursued. Those accusers who had their suits flung out for this reason felt, quite naturally, that it was proof of the stupidity of the jury – hence the fact that today we apply it to a stupid or ignorant person.

illegitimis non carborundum. 'Don't let the bastards grind you down'. This mock-Latin catch-phrase originated, according to Eric Partridge, in British Army Intelligence early in World War II. It soon spread to become more widespread Army slang, principally among officers, and was later taken up by the Australian and American forces. There are several variations of the phrase, one of which, *Nil Carborundum*, was used by Henry Livings as the title for a play, which was first performed by the Royal Shakespeare Company in 1962.

imbecile. The origin of the word is the Latin *bacillus*, meaning 'stick', and it was first used to describe someone who was physically weak and required a stick to walk. It was only after the 17th century that it came to be applied to a weakening of the mind rather than the body.

in a holding pattern. In abeyance, in an inactive state. From about 1950 this has been a piece of aeronautical jargon, referring to aircraft flying on a prescribed circular route near an airport while awaiting clearance to land. Hence its use in the metaphorical sense, particularly in business and political contexts, which has been spreading since the mid-1970s.

in like Flynn. This expression, strangely, has two separate origins and usages – the American and Australian. In the American usage it means: in an advantageous position or one of assured success; 'sitting pretty'. The reference is to Ed Flynn, a New York political boss. In the 1940s, his Democratic Party machine wielded absolute political power in the Bronx, New York City. Flynn, and any candidates he backed, were sure to be 'in' whenever they ran for office. In the Australian version, in like Flynn means 'seizing an opportunity that is offered, especially a sexual one'. The reference is to the Australian-born film actor Errol Flynn (1909–59), who was notorious for his sexual exploits.

in spades. Superlatively; to the highest degree. This American expression derives from card games such as bridge, in which spades have a higher value than the other suits.

in the black. *See* IN THE RED.

in the doghouse. In disgrace; out of

favour. The expression originates from J. M. Barrie's *Peter Pan*. Nana, a Newfoundland dog, is the guardian and general favourite of the Darling children, Wendy, John and Michael. Mr Darling, their father, treats Nana badly, thus offending the children who go away. As penance Mr Darling lives in the doghouse until they return. Incidentally, *Peter Pan* is also the origin of Wendy as a girl's name. The name was invented by the author.

in the grip of the grape. This typically colourful Australian catch-phrase, dating from about 1950, means, of course, 'drunk' or INKED.

in the red. To be overdrawn at the bank. This phrase originated because overdrawn accounts were shown in red ink and accounts in credit in black – from which comes the phrase **in the black**, meaning to be in credit.

inauspicious and **auspicious** were both coined by Shakespeare, the former in *Romeo and Juliet*, the latter in *The Tempest*. Auspicious means favourable, well-omened, inauspicious the opposite.

include me out. Leave me out of whatever it is that is being proposed. *See also* GOLDWYNISMS.

indenture. A contract binding two parties in an exchange of services. In the past servants and apprentices often committed themselves to working for another for a specified period of time. The word indenture means 'a document with teeth', being derived from the Latin word *dens* for 'tooth'. At one time indentures and other forms of contract were cut or torn in two in a random serrated pattern, and each party involved in the deal received a piece. If the document needed to be authenticated at a later date this could be done by placing the serrated 'teeth' together and seeing if they fitted.

Indian file. Moving in a single line, one behind another. This expression derives from a custom of American Indians. A group of warriors on the move would walk in a single file, each treading in the footprints of the man in front, and the last man obliterating the footprints as he went. Thus they left no trace of their passage.

Indian giver. One who gives a present and then wants it back again. This American expression stems from the first contacts between whites and American Indians, and mutual misunderstanding between the two cultures. The ceremonial exchange of gifts was a widespread Indian custom, not always understood by whites. An Indian who gave a gift to a white man, and was disappointed in his expectation of the customary gift in return, would demand the return of his original gift, thus giving rise to the disparaging expression.

Indian summer. A period of fine sunny weather in late autumn. This expression comes from the USA, and derives from the fact that such weather conditions were found to be more common in the western areas occupied by Indians than in the eastern states first occupied by white settlers.

inferiority complex. This term is used in psychiatry and is described thus in the Oxford English Dictionary:

Generalized and unrealistic feelings of inadequacy caused by a person's reactions to actual or supposed inferiority in one sphere, sometimes compensated for an aggressive self-assertion.

The expression originated *c.*1920, and was popularised by the psychoanalyst Alfred Adler. It is often used colloquially for an exaggerated feelings of personal inadequacy.

influenza. Today we use the word to refer to a particular kind of illness, but in the 17th century in Italy, where it was coined, it was applied to almost any major outbreak of plague and sickness. It was believed that such diseases were affected by the configuration of the stars, which sometimes cast an evil influenza over the earth. Thus the Italian word was adopted into English to represent the illness known commonly as 'flu.

information technology. An umbrella title covering a wide range of areas and subjects, all of them involving the use of computers, microelectronics and the latest communication techniques to store, produce and disseminate information.

infotainment. Television news that is short on hard facts and long on brilliant camera-work, minimising information and playing up the entertainment value of the story, is defined as infotainment. This kind of programme is popular with COUCH POTATOES, who like to think they know what's going on in the world but don't want too many demands on their concentration or intelligence.

inked. An Australian slang word, meaning 'drunk', that has been in use since the late 19th century – a contraction of the word 'incapacitated'.

insider dealing. This specialist financial term found its way into newspaper headlines and into general usage in the mid-1980s. It describes the use by 'insiders' of confidential company information to gain an advantage in the buying or selling of shares, before the information is made public – for example, in advance of a company take-over. In the wake of several celebrated cases

more extensive legal powers were sought to limit this sort of activity.

inspirational. A word much in use in the publishing world, where it is applied to expensive, glossy, picture-packed LIFESTYLE books that promote an up-market, idealised image of their subject. Inspirational books tend to focus on interior decor, gardens, food and anything else that lends itself to stunning photography and presentation. These books are not intended to be practical or even very informative; they are designed merely to illustrate a lifestyle to which the reader aspires. Publishers also like to think that the books inspire readers to adopt some of the more easily attained facets of the lifestyle and, therefore, call them 'inspirational'.

intelligentsia comes from the Russian word 'intelligentsiya', derived in turn from the Latin *intelligere* meaning 'to perceive or understand'. It describes the intellectual elite, those who perceive and understand most acutely.

intrapreneur. An entrepreneur is someone who initiates or runs a business enterprise. The word 'intrapreneur' was coined to describe someone who fulfils a similar role within an established large corporation. The origin of the word is attributed to Gifford Pinchot III, an American management consultant and author of the book *Intrapreneuring*, which was published in 1985.

Irangate. *See* WATERGATE.

Irish. The English language is full of insulting expressions referring to their traditional enemies, none of whom take a heavier battering than the Irish, who receive even worse treatment than the unfortunate DUTCH. Among the phrases incorporating the word 'Irish' and denoting something contrary or inferior are an 'Irish buggy', meaning a wheelbarrow, and 'Irish confetti', for bricks. An 'Irish grape' is a potato, also known as an 'Irish apple' and an 'Irish lantern' was the moon, while 'Irish draperies' were cobwebs and an 'Irish promotion' is a demotion. 'The Irish Mail' is a sack of potatoes, an 'Irish hurricane' a flat sea and an 'Irishman's feast' is a fast. Fortunately there are many other phrases incorporating the word 'Irish' in a more positive way – including 'Irish coffee', coffee with whiskey in it, 'Irish stew' and a much-prized breed of dog, the 'Irish setter'.

Iron Curtain. Figuratively, any impenetrable barrier – specifically that which divides the Soviet Union and its satellites from the West. The phrase was popularised by Sir Winston Churchill. In a speech given on 5 March 1946 at Fulton, Missouri, where he was being awarded an honorary degree, he said:

From Stettin in the Baltic to Trieste in the Adriatic, an iron curtain has descended across the continent. Behind that line lie all the capitals of the ancient states of central and eastern Europe. Warsaw, Berlin, Prague, Vienna, Budapest, Belgrade, Bucharest and Sofia, all these famous cities and the populations around them lie in what I might call the Soviet sphere, and all are subject, in one form or another, not only to Soviet influence, but to a very high and in some cases increasing measure of control from Moscow.

This, however, was not the first use of the phrase in this context. The *Sunday Empire News*, for example, carried an article on 21 October 1945 with the headline 'An Iron Curtain Across Europe'. But perhaps the person who should really be credited with the origin of the phrase is Joseph Goebbels, the Propaganda Minister of Nazi Germany. In a prophetic editorial in the newspaper *Das Reich* on 23 February 1945 he wrote:

If the German people should lay down their arms, the agreement between Roosevelt, Churchill and Stalin would allow the Soviets to occupy all Eastern and South-Eastern Europe, together with the major parts of the Reich. An iron curtain (*eiserner Vorhang*) would at once descend on this territory, which, including the Soviet Union, would be of tremendous dimension.

Iron Lady. A phrase used to describe a strict or severe woman. In particular the phrase has been much used in reference to Margaret Thatcher, the British Prime Minister, renowned for what some would call her authoritarian style of government and her inflexible views and for what others would call her strength of will and firmness of purpose. Similar designations have formerly been applied to other strong leaders – for example, the Duke of Wellington (the Iron Duke) and Bismarck, founder of the German Empire in 1871 (the Iron Chancellor).

iron lung. An apparatus for providing prolonged artificial respiration mechanically. It consists of a chamber that encloses the patient's chest, the air pressure within the chamber being varied rhythmically so as to force air into and out of the patient's lungs. The expression is American in origin, the first usage quoted by the Oxford English Dictionary being in an article in the *New York Times* of 3 October 1932.

irons – to have irons in the fire. A person with plenty of irons in the fire has choice; they have other opportunities waiting to be exploited if what they are doing at the moment goes wrong. They may also be warned against having too many irons in the fire, the implication being that they will not have enough time to attend to them all. This expression comes from the laundry where, in the days before electric irons, flatirons were heated in the fire. A busy laundress would keep two or three irons warming in reserve, so that when the one she was using cooled down she had a hot one waiting. If she put too many irons to heat in the fire she ran the risk of overheating them and ruining her ironing.

Is the Pope Catholic? An American catch-phrase that is used as a response to what is considered a stupid question. Variations are 'Is the Pope Polish?' (since the accession of John Paul II) or 'Is the Pope Italian?' (before that). *See also* DOES A BEAR SHIT IN THE WOODS?

It takes two to tango. Used with reference to any wrong-doing involving two people – for example, illicit sexual relations or the taking of a bribe – to imply that one partner cannot be guilty without the other being equally so. The phrase dates from around 1930, and stems from the title of a song that was popular at that time.

ivory tower. A place of retreat or refuge from the world and from the harsh realities of life. The expression originated in French as *une tour d'ivoire*, and was coined by the French literary critic Charles-Augustin Sainte-Beuve. In his poem *Pensées d'Août* (*Thoughts of August*) written in 1837 he contrasts two poets, Victor Hugo and Alfred de Vigny. The lines may be translated thus:

Hugo, strong partisan . . . fought in armour, and held high his banner in the midst of tumult; he still holds it; and Vigny, more discreet, as if in his tower of ivory, retired before noon.

Ivy League. The American equivalent of OXBRIDGE. It is the name given to a group of old-established universities in the north-eastern United States: Brown, Columbia, Cornell, Dartmouth, Harvard, the University of Pennsylvania, Princeton and Yale. Like Oxbridge, too, Ivy League is also used adjectivally in reference to the social and academic prestige or other characteristics of these institutions or of their members or former members. The term seems to have originated in 1933, specifically as a disparaging reference to the football teams of these universities, which at that time suffered several embarrassing defeats at the hands of newer and less prestigious universities such as Fordham. Caswell Adams, a sports writer for the *New York Herald Tribune*, claims to have coined the expression, and it was first used in an article by Stanley Woodward, the sports editor of that newspaper.

J

Jack – before you can say Jack Robinson. According to one authority, Jack Robinson was the name of a gentleman who became well known for changing his mind. He was in the habit of calling at his neighbours' homes, then changing his mind and racing off before the servant could announce him. Thus, 'before you can say Jack Robinson' means 'in a flash', 'immediately'. Less credible is the French suggestion that the phrase derives from the combination of 'Jacques', which was a popular name for a servant in France, and 'Robinson', which was the name for a gingham parasol in vogue in the 19th century. Apparently ladies of fashion were so keen to show off this latest accessory that they would order their servant to go and get it with the words, 'Jacques, Robinson.'

Jack of all trades, master of none. When this phrase was first recorded in 1618 it was simply 'Jack of all trades' and was used approvingly to describe someone who could turn their hand to a number of different tasks. A century or so later it had come to be used disparagingly; perhaps by this time the short-comings of the 'Jack of all trades'' work were becoming obvious. In the 19th century 'master of none' was tagged onto the end, entirely changing the meaning of the original phrase. The name Jack is widely used in English to mean 'the common man' or EVERYMAN. Thus we get expressions such as 'every Jack will have his Jill', meaning that every man will get his woman, and 'every man Jack of them', meaning every single one of them. *See also* COWBOY.

Jack Tar. Though used less frequently these days than in the past, a Jack Tar is still a term for a sailor. It dates from the days when a ship's ropes, timbers and canvas were made waterproof with a layer of tar. This process gave us the word **tarpaulin** to describe a heavy-duty waterproof fabric which, it has been suggested, was used to make weatherproof capes and hats for sailors. Whether 'Jack Tar' derived from these outfits or simply from the fact that sailors' clothes were spattered with tar from their work, no one is sure, but the phrase certainly originated from one or other of these sources.

jackpot. A large win in a gambling game; a prize money fund that continues to accumulate until there is a winner. The source of the expression is in the game of draw poker. The 'pot' (consisting of equal stakes from all the players) is allowed to accumulate until won by a player who has drawn a pair of jacks or better.

jacuzzi. Trade name for a form of hot bath, with swirling water, used for relaxation. Candido Jacuzzi (1903–86) was an engineer and inventor, who worked mainly in the aviation industry. He invented a form of portable pump so that his young son could be treated in the bath at home for the rheumatoid arthritis from which he suffered. Later, in 1968, another member of the family, Roy Jacuzzi, saw the commercial possibilities of the device, and went on to become president and managing director of the Jacuzzi Whirlpool Bath Company.

Janus. *See under* TWO-FACED.

Jar Wars. As part of an anti-drugs campaign in 1986, President Reagan ordered all government staff to supply a urine sample for testing. This requirement was known as 'Jar Wars' by analogy with the 'Star Wars' project, which also had Mr Reagan's enthusiastic backing.

jaywalker. A pedestrian who crosses the road without regard to traffic signals or regulations. This expression originated in the USA in the early years of the 20th century. It derives from an earlier slang expression – 'jay', used, like 'rube' and 'hick', by American city-dwellers to refer to a rustic. Hence, a jaywalker was one who behaved like a country-man unused to city traffic.

jazz has for a long time confounded those who try to trace its origins. It has been speculated that it derived from Creole French, where a *chasse beau* was a suitor who chased away all his rivals in love. When minstrel shows became popular the *chasse beau* was transformed into a dancing character known as Jazzbo, and it's said that his shortened name was applied to the improvised music played by black musicians in the show. Another source points to Charles Alexander who became famous in the first decade of this century with the ragtime hit 'Alexander's Ragtime Band.' He was known as Chas and when he and his fellow musicians were improvising they

would be urged on with shouts that turned 'Chas' to 'Jazz'. Other theories trace jazz back to the African word meaning 'hurry', the Hindu word *jaizba*, meaning 'desire', or the Arab word *jazib*, meaning 'one who is alluring'. As none of these derivations has been proved, the origin of jazz must remain something of a mystery.

jeans. Close-fitting trousers, usually made of DENIM. Jean was the name given to a hard-wearing cotton twill cloth, first introduced into Britain as 'jene fustian', taking its name from *Gênes*, the French name for the Italian city of Genoa. Jeans were trousers, usually worn as working clothes, made from this cloth. Those who think of jeans as an essentially modern form of dress might be surprised to come across this sentence in *Handley Cross* by R. S. Surtees, published in 1843:

Septimus arrived flourishin' his cambric, with his white jeans strapped under his chammy leather opera boots.

As the 'uniform' of the young and would-be-young, the wearing of jeans really took off in the late 1950s, when 'jean-ager' was used for a while as a journalistic synonym for 'teenager'. *See also* LEVIS.

jeep. A small sturdy four-wheel-drive military vehicle, first used by US forces during World War II; later, a similar vehicle adapted for civilian use. The jeep derives its name from the letters G.P. (standing for 'general purpose') used by the army as the code designation for this vehicle, and from the name of the character Eugene the Jeep, a tiny creature with amazing powers, who had appeared in the popular *Popeye the Sailor* comic strip of E. C. Segar since 1936.

Jekyll and Hyde. The phrase comes from Robert Louis Stevenson's novel *The Strange Case of Dr Jekyll and Mr Hyde*. This tells the tale of Dr Hyde who undergoes a personality change when he drinks a chemical potion of his own making. Under the influence of the potion his evil side, previously hidden, comes to the fore as the terrible Mr Hyde. These days we use the phrase a Jekyll and Hyde personality to describe someone who reveals an unsuspected and unpleasant side to their normal character.

jerkwater. Insignificant, trivial. This disparaging term was originally US railroad slang, applied to a town that was too small and of insufficient importance to have a station, but where water pans were laid between the tracks so that a locomotive could 'jerk' water into its tender as it passed through.

jeroboam. *See under* JERRY.

Jerry. A slang term for a German which dates back to World War One. At that time German troops wore domed helmets that, to the English eye, resembled chamberpots. The slang for a chamberpot was a 'jerry', derived from **jeroboam**, a very large wine bottle which usually contained at least four standard bottles – perhaps the capacity of some of the larger chamberpots. *See also* LOO.

jerry-built. Constructed insubstantially, of inferior materials. According to the Oxford English Dictionary this expression dates from 1881, but the origin is obscure. Nevertheless, there are several theories. It has been claimed that the expression derives from two brothers by the name of Jerry, who were notoriously bad builders in Liverpool, but there is no evidence to support this theory. It has also been conjectured that there is some connection with the biblical city of Jericho, the walls of which came tumbling down at the sound of Joshua's trumpet. Alternatively, a derivation is conjectured from the name of the prophet Jeremiah, famed for his prolonged lamentations. Another theory is that it derives from the French word *jour*, meaning a day, perhaps because a jerry-built structure might last only a day, or because it is supposed to be built by workers paid by the day, who would therefore take no pride in their work. The most persuasive theory, in my view, is that the expression is a variation of the nautical term 'jury' (as in 'jury-rigged', 'jury-mast', 'jury-rudder', etc.) referring to something temporary and not meant to last.

Jerusalem artichoke. This root vegetable has no connection with the city of Jerusalem. The word 'Jerusalem' here is, in fact, a corruption of the Italian word *girasole*, meaning a sunflower, which this vegetable resembles in its stem and leaves.

jib, to know someone by the cut of their. This phrase does not get much use these days but was popular in the last century. It alludes to the triangular sail that billows at the front of the main mast of a ship and which was often used to identify them. Today when we say we know someone by the cut of their jib we mean that we know what kind of person they are by their appearance and manners.

Jim Crow. A derogatory term for the American black man. The expression later came to symbolise for American blacks all forms of segregation and discrimination imposed on them, and the accompanying laws and practices. Jim Crow schools and Jim Crow cars, for example, were segregated schools and railroad coaches set apart for the use of blacks. The expression derives from the name of a 'nigger minstrel' song first performed in Louisville, Kentucky, in 1828 by a white blackface comedian by the name of Thomas D. Rice. This song, and its accompanying dance, formed part of a revue that was immensely popular and was taken to Washington in 1835 and even to London in 1836. *See also* CROW JIM.

jingoism. 'By jingo' was a euphemism for 'by Jesus', coined in the late 17th century. In 1878 the expression was used in a popular song that urged the British to fight the Russians who had invaded Turkey:

We don't want to fight, but by Jingo, if we do,
We've got the ships, we've got the men, and got the money, too.
We've fought the Bear before, and while we're Britons true,
The Russians shall not have Constantinople.

This kind of aggressive patriotism, initially aimed against the Russians, became known as jingoism. The phrase is still in use to describe any war-mongering and chauvinistic attitude.

jive. It has been suggested that the word jive comes from the African word *jev* meaning 'to talk critically'. Jive first came into use among American blacks in the early 1900s and meant joking, teasing talk or play. In the 1930s and 40s it was applied to fast-moving, jazz-influenced swing music played by the big bands and jiving was the fast, intricate style of dancing which accompanied the music. This gave rise to 'jive talk', a rapid, patter-style way of talking that used catchphrases and rhymes and was accompanied by much finger-snapping and jerky body movements.

Job, the patience of. Great patience. The Old Testament Book of Job tells the story of Job's terrible sufferings through which he loses his fortune, his family, his servants and his health. All this he endures patiently, accepting the injustice of the world with rare stoicism. In his misfortune

he receives visits from three of his friends; their consolation involves reminding him that he has brought these disasters on himself. From this element of the story we get the phrase a **Job's comforter**, describing someone who, while being apparently sympathetic about a problem, actually adds to one's suffering.

Job's comforter. *See* THE PATIENCE OF JOB.

jobsworth. A petty official or narrow-minded bureaucrat who sticks rigidly to the rule book – someone who makes their own life easier by making others' more difficult. When asked to bend the rules such people inevitably preface their refusal with, 'It's more than my job's worth to do that . . .'

John. Being the commonest male forename in English-speaking countries, John has had many slang uses, representing the average or typical man. (1) A slang term for a prostitute's client dating from the early 1900s in the USA. It probably stems from earlier uses of the name to represent a man regarded as a potential victim for a trickster, an easy target for a salesman, etc. (2) A slang term for a lavatory, also originating in the USA. It was originally used in the form 'Cousin John' or 'cuzjohn', and in this form goes back to at least 1735 when this Harvard College regulation was issued: 'No freshman shall mingo against the College wall or go into the fellows' cuzjohn'.

John Bull. A nickname for the typical Englishman, or for Englishmen collectively. The name was invented by Dr John Arbuthnot (1667–1735), a friend of Swift and Pope. He issued in 1712 a series of pamphlets entitled *The History of John Bull*, which were designed to advocate, in the form of humorous allegories, the cessation of the war with France. The various parties concerned were designated under the names of John Bull (England), Nicholas Frog (the Dutch), Lord Strutt (King Philip of Spain) and Lewis Baboon (King Louis of France).

John Doe. *See under* BODY WORKER.

John Hancock. When an American refers to his 'John Hancock' he means his signature. John Hancock (1737–93), a merchant of Boston, Massachusetts, was the first person to sign the American Declaration of Independence in 1776. Not only was his signature the first, it is also much larger and bolder than that of any of the other founding fathers. Reputedly he made his signature large 'so the king of England could read it without spectacles'.

John Henry. Another American term for a signature. This expression originated in the western USA in the early 19th century as a variation of JOHN HANCOCK. Nobody knows who the John Henry referred to might have been – John Henry the folklore hero of railroad fame is of a later date than this expression.

John Thomas. An ancient slang term, dating back to the Middle Ages, for the penis. The expression has been traced by some to one John Thomas, a Wiltshire farmer, who lived around the year 1400 and was the proud possessor of a truly enormous penis. Indeed, so proud of it was he that he liked nothing more than to show it off to people. This proved a very dangerous habit and he was eventually hanged and quartered – whether for 'flashing' or some other crime is not known. After this gruesome fate his monster member was removed and displayed at fairs all over the country, with the result that John Thomas became the by-word for a penis. Wonderful though this story is, it's almost certainly untrue and was probably made up at about the time it was first recorded in 1840. John and Thomas being extremely common names, it's more likely that John Thomas was just an affectionate name given to the penis; other names are 'Dick', 'Peter' and 'Willy'. Other euphemisms for this particular part of the male anatomy include 'Hampton Wick', Cockney rhyming slang for prick, and the more inventive 'Bald-headed hermit' and 'the member for Cockshire'.

jolly hockeysticks. A phrase used adjectivally or as an exclamation to describe a particular type of young lady – games-playing, hearty and enthusiastic – the type of character encouraged in many British girls' public schools. The phrase was coined by comedy actress Beryl Reid and used by her in her role as Monica, the schoolgirl friend of Archie Andrews, in the BBC radio series *Educating Archie* in the early 1950s.

Jonah. A person believed to bring bad luck. The expression comes from the biblical story of Jonah, whom God punished by raising a storm at sea. The crewmen on Jonah's boat decided that he was an evil influence and threw him overboard, at which the storm ceased. Jonah was swallowed by a huge fish and after three days and nights in its stomach, eventually made it back to dry land. In the USA there is even a verb, to jonah, meaning to behave in a way likely to ruin the plans of others.

juggernaut, or Jagganath, is the name of a Hindu god, an incarnation of Vishnu, whose temple is at Puri in Orissa. The name, in Sans Krit, means 'Lord of the World'. The principal annual festival held in worship of the god is commonly known as the 'car festival'. In this festival a great statue of the god is dragged along the road in a car 35 feet square and 45 feet in height. The car has sixteen wheels, each seven feet in diameter. The journey takes several days, and it was believed that fanatical worshippers used to throw themselves under the wheels to be crushed to death, in the belief that such a death would ensure for them eternal bliss. This led to the expression 'car of the juggernaut' being used to describe any relentless destroying force, crushing all those in its path. The word is applied today to any wheeled 'monster', specifically a large heavy lorry.

jukebox. A coin-operated machine that plays selected gramophone records; the successor of the 'juke organ', a coin-operated machine that produced a tune similar to that made by a hurdy-gurdy or barrel organ. The word 'juke' comes from a dialect called Gullah – a Negro dialect of South Carolina, Georgia, and Florida – and means 'disorderly' (as in 'disorderly house'). A 'juke house', or simply 'juke', is a roadhouse or brothel, and it was in such establishments that the first juke organs and jukeboxes were to be found.

jumbo. A familiar name for an elephant. The word is used as a noun to refer to anything very big of its kind, or as an adjective to describe anything huge. The modern commercial use of the word, as in 'jumbo pack' or 'jumboburger', is nothing new – as early as 1897 the Sears, Roebuck mail order catalogue in the USA was advertising 'Jumbo Californian Peaches'. The original jumbo was an exceptionally large African elephant exhibited at London Zoo for seventeen years from 1865. He stood 10 feet 9 inches high at the shoulder, and weighed six and a half tons. In 1882 he was sold to Phineas T. Barnum's circus, the Greatest Show on Earth, and shipped to America. Jumbo died in 1885 after being hit by a freight train. The Oxford English Dictionary suggests that the name was probably derived from MUMBO JUMBO. Dating from the mid-1970s, jumbo was also used as a slang term for cocaine or CRACK.

jump the gun. To act prematurely. This expression comes, of course, from the world of athletics, and the reference is to a contestant leaving his starting mark before the starting-pistol is fired. The expression dates from around 1940, when it replaced an earlier variation 'beat the gun'.

junk. The word, meaning 'rubbish', derives from the Latin word *juncus*, meaning 'rush' – rushes having once been used to make ropes. Sailors called useless old rope ends junk and eventually the word was adopted into more general use. That's one derivation, anyway. A second finds the origin of junk in a small Javanese sailing boat called a *djong*. The nearest English tongues could get to pronouncing it was junk, and this word was also applied to the bits and pieces of rubbish that inevitably piled up on such a boat.

junk bonds. High yielding speculative securities, especially those issued to raise finances for an intended takeover. This type of bond was invented in the late 1970s by the Wall Street investment bank Drexel Burnham Lambert.

junk food. Hamburgers, french fries, fizzy drinks, sugar-coated cereals and sweets are all junk food – bland, highly-processed food full of artificial colours and flavours. Although extremely popular, especially with children, junk food contains little nutritional value. *See also* FAST FOOD.

Juppie. A Japanese Yuppie. *See also* BUPPIE, GLAM, YUPPIE etc.

K

K. In business, computing and general slang a K is a thousand. In business it may be £1,000, so that one could say of a contract that it was 'worth £50K'. In computing it is a measure of the storage capacity of a microchip; thus a computer might boast a 5,000K memory.

kamikaze. This Japanese word means, literally, 'divine wind'. The first kamikaze was a wind that wrecked an invading Mongol fleet off the coast of Japan in 1281. In World War Two the phrase was applied to Japanese bomber pilots who deliberately and suicidally crashed their planes, often loaded with explosives, on enemy ships and other targets. As a result, kamikaze has come to be used figuratively, as a noun or adjective, to refer to something reckless or potentially suicidal.

kanga. An Australian slang word for money.

kangaroo. According to legend, when Captain James Cook was exploring the eastern coast of Australia in 1770 he asked an aborigine to tell him the name of a strange animal he'd seen bounding through the bush. 'Kangaroo,' was the reply, meaning 'I don't know' in the tribal language, and in this way kangaroo came into use to describe Australia's most famous marsupial. Some authorities have cast doubt on this story because they have been unable to trace an aboriginal word like kangaroo and meaning 'I don't know', but as they offer no alternative explanation the Captain Cook story must remain the best explanation.

kangaroo court. An improperly constituted court or tribunal with no legal standing – for example, one held by mutineers or strikers or prison inmates to administer judgement and punishment to those of their fellows who 'break the rules'. This expression originated not in Australia, as one might have expected, but in the USA where it has been in use since the middle of the 19th century. Even today it is more commonly used there and in Britain than it is in Australia. The origin of the expression is obscure. It may be that there is an association of ideas between a court held by prisoners in a jail, as many early kangaroo courts were, and the history of Australia, the home of the kangaroo, as a penal settlement. Or, since the date of origin appears to coincide with the California gold rush of 1849, there may be a humorous reference to the practice of such courts dealing with 'jumpers' who seized the mining claims of other prospectors.

Karaoke. Originally a craze in Japan and introduced to the West in the late 80s, Karaoke is the practice of singing along to a professionally prerecorded backing-tape. Karaoke machines have a large repertoire but the most popular tracks seem to be old favourites such as *My Way*, *Heartbreak Hotel* and *Yesterday*, which offer the singers the chance to emulate their heroes Frank Sinatra, Elvis Presley and Paul McCartney. In Japan there are karaoke bars where normally mild-mannered businessmen relax after a hard day in the office by crooning their favourite songs. The point is not necessarily to sing well; Karaoke entertains either by the passion of the rendition or by its sheer awfulness.

karma is derived from the Sanskrit word meaning work or action. It was originally used by Buddhists to describe the results of a person's work or deeds during their lifetime. This karma would in turn determine the form they would take in their next reincarnation. In modern use karma is a synonym for 'vibes'. A person or place can be said to have a good or bad karma i.e. to emanate a good or bad sensation or atmosphere.

keel-hauled. In modern use we sometimes describe a reprimand or ticking-off as keel-hauling, but this does not reflect the severity of the original punishment. Keel-hauling was introduced by the Dutch navy in the 16th century as a way of disciplining sailors and was later adopted by other navies. Victims were tied to a rope and weighted, then dragged under the ship's keel – a process which often resulted in drowning and terrible lacerations caused by the barnacles that had encrusted the hull. *See also* TO BE HAULED OVER THE COALS.

keep one's eyes peeled, to. To keep a lookout; to be alert. Despite the revolting image it evokes, the phrase alludes simply to keeping one's eyes open, with the lids drawn (or peeled) back.

keep one's pecker up, to. In the late 19th century pecker became a slang word for penis, a fact which has led many people to banish this phrase from their vocabulary under the impression that it is rude. Actually 'to keep one's pecker up' originated earlier than the slang and pecker refers to the mouth or lips, alluding to a bird's beak which it uses for pecking. Someone who is encouraged to keep their pecker up is advised to keep a stiff upper lip or to try to be cheerful.

keeping up with the Joneses. Striving, especially beyond one's means, to keep up socially and financially with others in the same neighbourhood or in the same social circle. The phrase originated as the title of a comic strip invented by Arthur R. ('Pop') Momand, and which appeared in the New York *Globe*, the Chicago *Daily News*, the Philadelphia *Bulletin*, the Boston *Globe* and other newspapers. First appearing in February 1913, it ran for twenty-eight years, and was based on Momand's own experiences in his early married life of living beyond his means and trying to keep up appearances in Cedarhurst, Long Island. He originally intended to call the strip 'Keeping Up With The Smiths', but changed the name to Jones, as being more euphonious.

Kensington Gore. Theatrical slang for fake blood mixed by the bucketful for use on stage and in films. The expression is a pun on 'gore', for blood, and Kensington Gore, a street running south of Hyde Park in West London.

ketchup, meaning a sauce, comes originally from the Chinese word *koe-chiap* meaning 'brine of pickled fish'.

kettle of fish. *See under* FINE.

Kewpie doll. A chubby doll with a curl or topknot on its head, designed in the early years of the 20th century by an American lady, Rose O'Neill (1874–1944). The Kewpie doll had a vogue rivalling that of the TEDDY BEAR. The name derives from a baby-talk version of 'Cupid'.

keynote speech. In politics, an opening address at a convention or rally that sets the theme or tone of the occasion. Though no derivation has been confirmed, it is probably an allusion to the way in which an orchestra is given a note to which to tune their instruments before they begin to play.

khaki. The name of the dull brownish-yellow cloth used for British military uniforms is derived from the Urdu word *khaki* meaning 'dust-coloured'. Khaki uniform was first worn by an irregular corps of Guides (known as the *Khaki Risala* or Khaki Squadron) raised by the British at Meerut during the Indian Mutiny of 1857–9. It did not come into general use until the Boer War of 1899–1902.

kibitz and **kibitzer.** To kibitz is to look on at a game of cards or other activity and to offer gratuitous and intrusive advice. A kibitzer is one who does this; an intrusive meddler. These are Yiddish words which became assimilated into American English in the 1920s. They are derived from the German word *kiebitz* meaning a peewit – a noisy bird!

kibosh – to put the kibosh on. To dispose of finally. The derivation of this phrase, which seems to have originated in Britain in the early 1800s, is obscure. Although it sounds somewhat Yiddish, the likeliest explanation is that it comes from the Irish *cie bais*, meaning 'cap of death'.

kick the bucket, to. To die. Sources trace the origin of the phrase to the practice of hanging a dead pig by its heels once its throat had been slit. The pig's rear legs were tied to a wooden block which was raised by a pulley system onto a frame which supported the carcass. Because this process resembled raising a bucket from a well, the block was known as a 'bucket'. As the pig struggled in its final throes, it kicked the bucket. Equally macabre is the alternative but unproven theory that the phrase refers to a method of committing suicide in which a person stands on a bucket with a noose around his neck and then kicks the bucket away.

kidnap. The verb to kidnap was first in recorded use in the 17th century, when it referred specifically to the crime of stealing children. Some of the kids were held to ransom until their parents paid to have them back while others were sold to sea captains and transported to work in the colonies. The word came into more general use first in America and later in Britain, where it now describes the abduction and holding to ransom of anyone, adult or child, for all kinds of motives.

kidult. A term invented by New York University professor Neil Postman to describe the modern American child. Postman's theory is that traditional childhood innocence is fast becoming obsolete in the USA because of the barrage of information and images that children are subjected to by television. By the time he is eleven, despite his emotional immaturity, the typical kidult will believe he knows all about life. His attitudes and manners will not be significantly different from those of adults and he will expect to be treated like one. His attention span will be short, limited by the ten-second blasts of information he receives from the television, and because of this he will find reading, writing and reasoning difficult. According to the theory, the classic kidult grows up into an adult philistine; uncultured, semi-literate, largely unthinking and obsessed with materialism and gadgetry. *See also* COUCH POTATO.

kill the fatted calf, to. This expression is derived from the biblical tale of the prodigal son, told in Luke, 15:11. It tells of an ungrateful son who demands that his father give him his inheritance and then wastes the money. After much suffering he returns home and repents. His father forgives him and kills the fatted calf to provide a great feast to celebrate his homecoming. To this day to kill the fatted calf means to provide an elaborate and sumptuous banquet to welcome someone.

kill with kindness, to. Someone who overwhelms another through sheer benevolence may be said to kill with kindness. The phrase is said to have originated when Draco, an Athenian law-maker, was killed as a result of his popularity. During a visit to the theatre in Aegina the audience expressed its enthusiasm for Draco's laws by throwing their caps and cloaks in the air. Unfortunately so many landed on him that he was smothered by this display of approval. *See also* DRACONIAN.

Kilroy was here. A common graffito written on walls and elsewhere. It originated in the USA in the 1940s and was spread around the world by US forces (particularly Air Transport Command) wherever they were stationed during World War II. It has been claimed that it originated as the 'trademark' of a certain shipyard inspector at Quincy, Massachusetts, who chalked the phrase on each piece of equipment he had inspected.

kinky. Originally a German word to describe a piece of thread or rope that has twisted back on itself and become tangled. This sense of something twisted and tangled was picked up by psychoanalysts, who earlier this century began to use the word kink to describe a personality quirk. Often such a kink would involve strange sexual desires – which was why in the 1960s kinky evolved to mean any

kind of weird sexual fetish, particularly of the sado-masochistic variety.

Kir. A drink consisting of chilled dry white wine mixed with crème de cassis (which is a sort of alcoholic blackcurrant syrup). Kir has long been a popular aperitif in France. It takes its name from Canon Felix Kir (1876–1968), a French Resistance hero and mayor of Dijon, who did much to popularise it.

kiss-and-tell stories are the bread and butter of BONK JOURNALISM. Kiss-and-tell memoirs are usually sold to the tabloids by discarded partners and friends of the rich and famous. Such stories often involve torrid, much-exaggerated and downright inaccurate accounts of their bedroom capers and the other person's callousness and cruelty. The candid autobiographies of famous figures, concentrating on their sexual exploits, are also classified as kiss-and-tell and as such are extensively serialised in the tabloid press. *See* BONK JOURNALISM.

kiss of death. Something that looks positive and useful but turns out to be lethal. The expression alludes to Judas' betrayal of Christ with a kiss.

kiss something better, to. When a child falls over and grazes its knee its mother may offer to kiss it better. As well as being an act of maternal concern, both phrase and practice may well derive from the custom of sucking poison from wounds.

kiss the Blarney stone, to. *See under* BLARNEY.

kitchen cabinet. An American expression for an unofficial and informal group of advisers to a president, made up of close friends and cronies, and having greater influence than the official cabinet. The expression was first used in reference to such a group advising President Andrew Jackson in 1829.

kith and kin. This ancient phrase,

describing one's family and friends, originated in Old English. *Kith* meant friends and neighbours and *kin* meant family or blood relations.

kitsch. A book or work of art described as kitsch has mass appeal but no aesthetic value. Kitsch is cute, sentimental, intellectually undemanding, lowbrow and popular. The word derives from the German verb *kitschen* meaning to throw together a work of art. *See also* HIGHBROW.

knacker. In the 19th century a knacker was a man who bought old and worn-out horses and slaughtered them for dog meat and leather. From this we get the phrase the 'knacker's yard', meaning any slaughterhouse, and also the expression 'to be knackered', meaning that one is exhausted, half-dead, ready to go to the knacker. In slang usage 'knackers' is sometimes used to refer to the testicles – a use suggested, perhaps, because a long bout of sexual activity might leave one knackered.

knee – to be knee-high to a grasshopper. Someone who is young, inexperienced or short. Before this American phrase became established in the 19th century there were other variations on the same theme; thus a young or short person might be described as being knee-high to a frog or knee-high to a duck.

knee-jerk reaction. An automatic, unthinking response to something. The phrase originated in 1878 when medical experts discovered that by striking the tendon below the kneecap they could obtain a reflex jerk of the leg. The knee-jerk effect is still used today to test the condition of the body's reflexes.

knock on wood. *See* TOUCH WOOD.

knock someone into a cocked hat, to. A cocked hat has three corners; it was the similarity between its triangular shape and the triangular arrangement of pins in the game of ninepins that gave us this phrase, meaning to beat someone easily. A ninepins player who roundly defeated his opponent by knocking over all the pins was said to have knocked him into a cocked hat.

knock the spots off someone, to. To beat them easily in a contest or game of skill. The phrase probably derives from the time when playing cards were used as targets for shooting practice. The best marksmen could knock out the 'spots' at the corners of the card.

knot, to tie the. To marry. The phrase alludes to an ancient and in some countries still-practised part of the marriage ceremony in which the bride and groom tie a knot as a symbol of their new unity.

know the ropes. This phrase, meaning to be informed, to know what one is doing, was originally a nautical term. Someone who knew the ropes on board a sailing ship was an experienced crew-member, one who didn't need to be told what to do.

Knowledge, The. In London anyone who wants to drive one of the famous black taxis has to take stringent tests to ensure their knowledge of the city's streets. This is known as The Knowledge.

kowtow. In China to *k'o-t'ou* meant to kneel down before a superior and knock one's forehead on the floor in a gesture of abasement. Early European explorers to China were required to observe this custom of kowtowing, as they came to know it, and they brought the word back with them. We use it today to describe any form of deferential or obsequious behaviour to a superior.

Ku Klux Klan. An American secret society founded at Pulaski, Tennessee, in 1866 at the end of Civil War, with the aim of protecting white supremacy in the territory of the defeated Confederacy. Its members wore white hoods and robes, suggesting the idea of the ghosts of the Confederate dead, and its terrorist activities led to its being outlawed in 1870, although it continued in existence for some time afterwards. It was revived in 1915 as an anti-Catholic and anti-Jewish as well as anti-Negro organisation, and gained considerable political influence in the Southern states in the 1920s. The name is a corruption of the Greek word *kuklos*, meaning a circle. It has also been suggested that the name is onomatopoeic, representing the sound made by the cocking of a rifle.

L

la-di-da. Dandyish; affectedly refined, especially in speech or bearing. This expression comes from the refrain of a song made popular in the 1880s by the music-hall entertainer Arthur Lloyd:

La-di-da, la-di-da, I'm the pet of all the ladies, / The darlings like to flirt with Captain La-di-da-di-do.

labyrinth. Today we use the word to describe a maze, but originally it referred to a particular maze, that at Knossos in Crete. Its name came from the *labrys* or double-bladed axe that was used around the time the palace of Knossos was built and which is pictured in the frescoes on the walls. Labyrinth means 'house of the axe' and it is widely believed that this refers to the maze of rooms and passages built under the palace. According to legend it was built by Daedalus for King Minos, who kept a fearsome beast called a minotaur there. The Minotaur was eventually killed by Theseus, who marked his route through the maze with a ball of thread, then used it to retrace his steps.

Lady Bountiful. A character in *The Beaux Stratagem*, the last play to be written by George Farquhar who died in 1707. In the play she is a wealthy character who distributes her money to worthy causes, and thus her name is applied to any benevolent woman who gives her money and time to charity or the community. Though originally a positive expression, Lady Bountiful is sometimes used today as an insult. It implies that such a person is rich and idle, with nothing better to do than patronise others in a less fortunate position.

lager louts. The late 1980s saw spates of vandalism and street battles with police in a number of usually quiet market towns around Britain. The young men who caused the trouble were widely described as 'lager louts'; young lager drinkers, many of them with good jobs and from respectable backgrounds, who become violent and disorderly after an evening's drinking. Drunken football fans who fortified themselves with several cans of lager before a match were also declared to be lager louts. Various theories were put forward to explain this new phenomenon.

Some pundits pointed to the LOADSAMONEY effects of the economic boom, which not only enabled young people to afford to get drunk on expensive lager, but which fostered an arrogance and lack of consideration for others. Real ale drinkers attacked the lager louts' tipple, arguing that its innocuous taste encouraged youngsters to drink too much. Others criticised the lager advertisements on television, which seemed designed to appeal to and promote loutish, adolescent behaviour. More cynical observers remembered the seaside riots between Mods and Rockers in the 1950s and 60s and noted that although the location and vocabulary had been changed, nothing much else was new.

lagniappe. A small bonus or free gift, given over and above what is purchased or earned, by way of gratuity or to make good measure; a small bribe. This American colloquialism (pronounced 'lan yap') comes from New Orleans Creole. It derives from the Spanish *la ñapa*, meaning 'the gift', which itself derives from the language of the Quechua, a race of Peruvian Indians.

laid back. Very relaxed in style or character; easy-going. It originated in the 1930s, among black American jazz musicians, when it meant 'lagging behind the main rhythm'. The expression burst into general use, via the pop music industry, *c.*1973.

laissez(r)-faire. Those who support the laissez(r)-faire theory of politics believe that governments should not interfere in business and financial affairs but should leave the markets to regulate themselves. The phrase comes from an 18th-century school of French economists, the Physiocrats, who believed in free trade and the abolition of restrictions. Their motto in the fight against import and export taxes was, '*Laissez faire, laissez passer*', meaning 'Let us alone, let us trade freely.' The British government under Margaret Thatcher has in many respects pursued a laissez(r)-faire policy.

lamb – in two shakes of a lamb's tail. *See under* TWO.

lamb – like a lamb to the slaughter. A lamb is a sweet, innocent, trusting creature, which is why we call a sweet, innocent, easily duped person a lamb. Lambs also trot happily off to the slaughterhouse without suspec-

ting the fate in store for them. Thus like a lamb to the slaughter describes any innocent person who walks unsuspectingly into trouble.

lame duck. An expression that has been used in a number of different contexts. In 18th and 19th century London, it was used to mean a member of the Stock Exchange who 'took a tumble' and was unable to meet his debts. In the USA since about the period of the Civil War, it has been used in reference to an office-holder, particularly a congressman or president, who is approaching the end of his term of office and who is not seeking, or is disqualified from seeking, re-election. His powers are therefore severely curtailed. In British politics, *c.*1970, the expression 'lame duck industries' came to be applied to those industries that were unable to survive without substantial financial support from the government.

lampoon. A satire, a sketch, film, book or other production that ridicules someone or something. The word originated in the 17th century and was probably adapted from the French word *lampons*, meaning 'let us drink', taken from the chorus of a French drinking song that was known in England. The original lampoons were extremely sarcastic and coarse attacks on well-known figures of the day, but modern lampoons tend to have a more healthy respect for the laws of libel.

Land of Nod. The biblical 'land of wandering' where Cain was exiled after he had killed his brother Abel. The story of Cain and Abel is told in Genesis. In 1738 in a work entitled *Polite Conversation*, Jonathan Swift made a pun on the phrase, saying that he was going to the Land of Nod, meaning 'the land of sleep'. It caught on, and to this day many people desiring FORTY WINKS claim that they are off to the Land of Nod. To get there one might have to go **up the wooden hill to Bedfordshire**, another play on words meaning simply 'up the stairs to bed'.

Land of the Midnight Sun. Why this should refer specifically to Norway is something of a mystery, for during the summer months several other areas in the high latitudes above the Arctic Circle also receive light twenty-four hours a day. According to speculation, Norway gets this appellation because it receives most visitors to witness the phenomenon.

landlubber. Back in the 14th century 'lubber' was the Danish word for a yokel or clumsy person. The word was adopted into English and applied to inexperienced sailors who did not KNOW THE ROPES. At a later date the insult was lengthened to become 'landlubber', a person happy on dry land and useless at sea.

lark, to have a, or **to lark about**, has nothing whatsoever to do with the bird known as a lark. It is derived from the medieval term *laik*, meaning to play, which in turn came from the Anglo-Saxon word *lac*, meaning a contest. In some parts of northern England 'laking' still means to play or mess about. In the 19th century to lark about became known as **sky-larking**, presumably just as a play on words and with no direct connection to the bird called a skylark. However the phrase **happy as a lark** *is* a reference to the song of the lark as it hovers in the sky.

last straw. A shortened version of the phrase 'it's the last straw that breaks the camel's back'. This is said to have been coined by Charles Dickens in his novel *Dombey and Son*, and is an exotic variation on a much older one, ''Tis the last feather that breaks the horse's back'. Both phrases refer to someone's breaking point, the last straw in each case being the last small

detail or request that overloads a heavy burden.

lateral thinking is defined thus by the Oxford English Dictionary: 'A way of thinking which seeks the solution to intractable problems through unorthodox methods, or elements which would normally be ignored by logical thinking.' The expression was coined by Dr Edward de Bono, *c.*1965, and the concept was explored in his book *The Uses of Lateral Thinking*, published in 1967, and in subsequent works.

Latin Quarter. The university area of Paris, renowned for its cosmopolitan and bohemian life, is known as the *Quarter Latin* or Latin Quarter. It acquired this name in the Middle Ages when Latin was the common language of the scholars who gathered there from all parts of Europe.

Laugh and the world laughs with you. Authorities agree that this famous line was written by American poet Ella Wheeler Wilcox in her poem *Solitude*, which was published in 1883. However a seed of doubt remains as to whether she was its original author, for she was challenged by one John A. Joyce who claimed to have penned the poem twenty years previously. The indignant Mrs Wilcox offered a $5,000 reward for a copy of his poem but none was ever found. Despite this, Joyce refused to relinquish his claim and on his gravestone he is attributed with writing the two most famous lines of *Solitude*:

Laugh and the world laughs with you;
Weep and you weep alone.

laugh on the other side of one's face, to. When someone laughs at the misfortune of another they may be told that before long they will be laughing on the other side of their face, i.e. that what is so amusing to observe will be painful or disappointing when it happens to them.

laugh up one's sleeve, to. To laugh to oneself; to conceal one's amusement from someone else. The date when this phrase first came into use has not been traced, but all sources agree that it must have been at a time when the sleeves of garments were cut very wide, enabling someone overcome with an inappropriate fit of giggles to conceal their face with their sleeve. There is a degree of nastiness implicit in the phrase; people laugh up their sleeves when they are enjoying a joke at someone else's expense.

laughing all the way to the bank. This phrase was coined by flamboyant entertainer Liberace, who in the early days of his career was criticised for his outrageous costumes and his syrupy style of music. After one particularly harsh attack someone asked him how he could go on, saying, 'The critics are laughing at you.' 'I'm laughing too,' replied Liberace, 'all the way to the bank.' The phrase caught on and is used today by many people to justify a money-making venture that enjoys popular success in the face of criticism.

laughter lines. *See under* CROW'S FEET.

laundering. Causing funds of dubious or illegal origin to appear legitimate by channelling them through a third party, usually abroad, and later recovering them from what appears to be a legitimate source. The usage originated in the USA, as an outcome of the Watergate inquiry in 1973–4.

law of diminishing returns. Used by economists to work out the optimum levels of input and output. Basically the law says that by adding extra units of input to a fixed output, one will eventually get a situation in which output declines per input unit. For example, a farm may be run reasonably efficiently by three men. A fourth man may increase efficiency and boost production. A fifth may have the same effect. But if the farm is then running at peak output, putting in a sixth man will not increase output and will in fact decrease the value of the output because of the costs involved in employing him.

lead – to lead a dog's life. *See under* DOG.

leading article. Most newspapers contain a leading article, written by a leader writer, which gives comment and opinion on the most important issues of the day. These articles got their name because they were intended to lead the opinion of the reader in the direction supported by the paper.

leaf – to take a leaf out of someone's book. To copy something useful or instructive. Several suggestions have been proposed to explain the phrase, the most popular being that it refers to acts of literary plagiarism. It has also been speculated that it refers to schoolchildren copying notes from another child's book or, less dishonestly, to an attempt to improve one's behaviour after reading moral essays or sermons. The phrase seems to have first come into use around the turn of the 19th century, but the crime of plagiarism dates back long before that time.

leaf, to turn over a new. To start again. The phrase refers to turning the page in a blank book or diary so that there is a clean space on which to begin anew. It has also been suggested that the emphasis on reform – turning over a new leaf means trying harder, reforming one's ways – may refer to a lesson in a book of moral essays. Every time one turned over a new leaf there was another improving set of precepts to follow.

learning experience. In the business

169

world, a mistake – from which, it is hoped, those involved will learn something. This process of making mistakes and gaining experience by them is known as the **learning curve**, the theory that when someone starts something new they have a lot to learn and therefore make mistakes. Once they have had some practice they are more efficient but their learning level drops.

leathernecks. A nickname for members of the United States Marine Corps, since *c.*1914, derived from their old custom of facing the stiff neckband of their uniform with leather so as to make it more comfortable to wear.

left-brain thinking. Researchers have discovered that the left side of the brain is responsible for logical and analytical thinking while the right side of the brain seems to give rise to creative thinking and the production of music, literature and art. Thus people can be categorised with left- or right-brain thinking according to the degree of logic or creativity they display.

leg, to pull someone's. The meaning of pulling someone's leg has been diluted by time. Today we use the phrase to refer to a practical joke or good-natured trick, but in Scotland, where it originated more than a century ago, it meant to make a complete fool of someone. One of the best ways of doing this was to trip them up, and thus originally to pull someone's leg meant to pull their leg from beneath them, to make them fall over.

leg – to shake a leg or **to show a leg.** The traditional waking-up calls, yelled each morning to rouse sailors from their hammocks. It has been suggested that it came about during the time when women were allowed to travel below decks with the men and that on the instruction 'show a leg' they had to stick a leg out of the

hammock, proving that they were not crew members and were therefore entitled to sleep in. Sceptics have come up with a less elaborate explanation, namely that it merely meant, 'let's see your legs over the side of the bunk', i.e. 'let's see you getting up.' To shake a leg, often used instead of a show a leg, normally means to hurry, get a move on. It can also mean to dance.

lemmings. Small rodents, allied to voles, and native to Norway. They breed at an amazing rate, and every three or four years, when their territories become over-populated, great numbers of them undertake mass migrations from the hills and mountains to the coast, where they plunge into the sea and are drowned. Since the late 1950s, the term has been used figuratively to denote people bent on a headlong rush, often to their own destruction.

lemon sole. The name of this fish has no connection whatsoever with the fruit of the lemon tree, nor with the colour lemon – it derives solely from the French word for the fish – *limande*.

leopard cannot change its spots, a. This phrase means that a person cannot change their character, however hard they try, just as a leopard cannot change its spots. The expression is stated in the Bible, Jeremiah 13:23:

Can the Ethiopian change his skin or the leopard his spots?

leotard. A close-fitting garment, worn by dancers and acrobats. Jules Léotard (1824–70) was a very famous French acrobat who performed in many countries, including Britain, and who is said to have inspired the song *The Daring Young Man on the Flying Trapeze*. In his memoirs, Léotard wrote:

Do you want to be adored by the ladies? A trapeze is not required, but instead of draping yourself in unflattering clothes, invented by ladies, and which give us the air of ridiculous mannikins, put on more natural garb, which does not hide your best features.

leprechaun. An Irish elf or sprite, usually portrayed as a shoemaker, who helps housewives by mending shoes, grinding meat, etc. The name derives from the Old Irish word *luchorpán*, meaning 'small body'.

lesbian. A female homosexual, so-named because it was on the Aegean island of Lesbos that the poetess Sappho lived and taught the art of poetry to her female followers. Though little is known of the group and only fragments of Sappho's verse remain, legend has it that she and her students engaged in female homosexuality – hence the fact that sapphism, from her name, is a euphemism for lesbianism. Unlike male homosexuality, lesbianism has never been illegal in Britain. This is mainly due to Queen Victoria who, when asked to sign a bill outlawing the practice, refused to believe that such a thing could exist. No one dared enlighten her and thus lesbians have enjoyed a freedom only recently allowed their male counterparts. *See also* DYKE.

lese-majesty. Legally speaking, lese-majesty is treason against the sovereign of a nation. It comes via French from the Latin for 'violated majesty'. The expression is more commonly applied to any form of disrespectful or offensive behaviour directed against a social superior, or an attack against an individual or institution that is supported by a great number of people.

let it all hang out. Be candid, free and uninhibited. This was a popular catch-phrase of the late 1960s and early 1970s, originally black American but mainly associated with HIPPIES and their counter-culture. Almost certainly, the 'it' in the phrase was originally a reference to

the male sexual organ. The expression is still heard today, but almost always as a vague sniggering double-entendre rather than as a genuine expression of an uninhibited attitude to life. *See also* DO ONE'S OWN THING.

Let sleeping dogs lie. *See under.* DOG.

let someone go. *See under* CARD – TO BE GIVEN ONE'S CARDS.

let the cat out of the bag. To disclose something that has been kept secret. At old English country fairs you had to be careful when buying a PIG IN A POKE. If you were dealing with an unscrupulous trader, the bag that you thought contained a pig might in fact contain a cat. Only when you opened it and let the cat out of the bag would the secret be revealed.

level, to be on the. A phrase from the secret world of the Freemasons, a society that has existed for many centuries and is said to be able to trace its roots back to the time of King Solomon. In the Middle Ages Freemasonry was dominated by stonemasons who established secret passwords, signs and tests based on the jargon of their trade. To be on the level is one such phrase that has entered common use. In the stonemason's trade it describes something that is flat, properly aligned, correct; applied to a person it means that they are honest, trustworthy and reliable. A situation or event may also be described as on the level, meaning legal or legitimate.

Leviathan. A legendary sea monster of tremendous size. Its name comes from the Hebrew and it is mentioned several times in the Bible, appearing variously as a crocodile, a whale and a sea serpent. Psalm 104:25:

So is this great and wide sea, wherein are things creeping innumerable, both small and great beasts. There go the ships: there is that leviathan, whom thou hast made to play therein.

Leviathan has therefore come to be applied to any huge sea creature or vessel and, on occasion, any other thing of great size or stature. The great English man of words and letters, Dr Samuel Johnson, is known as the Leviathan of literature.

Levis. DENIM working trousers or JEANS. Levi Strauss was a Bavarian immigrant to California, who in 1850, at the time of the Gold Rush, set up a business making working trousers from jean sailcloth and selling them to miners.

liberation theology links traditional Catholic theology with political theory. It argues that spiritual freedom and freedom from social and economic repression should go hand in hand. In Latin America, where it is most widely practised, this has led to an unlikely association between the Catholic Church and left-wing and Marxist movements. The Vatican, though supporting the work carried out for the poor by liberation theologians, cannot reconcile itself to involvement in left-wing politics and has therefore condemned the movement.

lick – to lick into shape. Until the 16th century people genuinely believed that bearcubs were born as shapeless blobs and had to be literally licked into shape by their parents. This extraordinary idea was fostered by the Arab physican Avicenna, who lived in the 11th century and wrote an encyclopaedia which contained this among other items of misleading information. In 1400 a book entitled *The pylgremage of the sowle* asserted that:

Beres ben brought forth al fowle and transformyd and after that by lyckynge of the fader and moder they ben brought in to theyr kyndely shap.

By the time early naturalists were brave enough to venture into the bear's den and disprove the theory, the expression to lick into shape, meaning to make someone or something look good or presentable, was firmly established and has remained in use ever since.

lido. A bathing-beach or resort, often with sun-bathing facilities and various entertainments; a public open-air swimming pool. The original lido is a sandy spit of land facing the Adriatic, just outside Venice, and famed as a beach resort. The name derives from the Latin *litus*, meaning a shore.

lifestyle. One of the BUZZWORDS of the 1980s. In its purest form it is used by sociologists and the media to describe the ways in which individuals or groups choose to live in society. In this context lifestyle can be broken down into interests, activities, opinions and values. From this has developed the concept of lifestyle merchandising in which retailers aim their merchandise at people with a particular lifestyle.

lig means to get something for free. A ligger is a person who habitually obtains food, drink, entertainment or other services for nothing. The most successful liggers are usually fashionable young people with the gift of the BLARNEY who haunt music, club and PR circuits on the look-out for parties and events that they can talk their way into.

light year. A unit used by physicists and astronomers for measuring stellar distances, a light year is the distance travelled by a beam of light in one year. Since light travels at 186,000 miles per second, a light year is approximately 6,000,000,000,000 miles. The term is often used figuratively to mean any incredibly large distance – and frequently, by the ignorant, to mean an incredibly long time!

Lightning never strikes twice in the same place. When something terrible happens to a person they are often told they needn't fear it happening again because lightning never strikes twice in the same place. Unfortunately the laws of science indicate that such advice is wrong. Lightning strikes the tallest object in the area of the storm. If that object, be it a tree or a building, isn't felled by the first stroke it is quite likely to be hit by another.

like billyo or **like billio.** To do something with great energy and enthusiasm. There are three theories as to the origin of this expression. One is that it comes from the name of a 17th-century clergyman, Joseph Billio, who was ejected from his position as a rector in the Church of England for nonconformity and who founded the Independent Congregation at Maldon in Essex. This theory seems somewhat improbable for two reasons: it is not the sort of phrase one would normally associate with a Puritan divine, however energetic he might have been, and the early date does not square with the fact that the earliest uses of the phrase seem to date from the 19th century. A second theory is that it comes from the name of Nino Biglio, one of Garibaldi's lieutenants, who used to lead his troops into action in a swashbuckling manner with the words 'Follow me, and fight like Biglio!' The third theory is that the phrase comes from the name of George Stephenson's locomotive, 'Puffing Billy'.

Lilliputian. Jonathan Swift's famous satire *Gulliver's Travels* tells the story of Gulliver's capture by the people of the fictional land of Lilliput, where no one grows much more than six inches tall. The inhabitants of this land hold him prisoner by means of thousands of tiny bonds and restrictions and treat him with arrogant pettiness. From this we get the word Lilliputian to mean someone small of

stature and, just as importantly, small of mind and character, too.

lily-livered. Rather as the spleen was once thought to be the source of melancholy and bad temper, the liver was believed to be the source of love and violent passion. Thus a person who constantly fell in love or picked quarrels was described as liverish, a problem ascribed to an excess of blood in the liver. Conversely it was also believed that cowards' livers contained no blood and that therefore they were white as a lily. From this concept came the word lily-livered, meaning cowardly, lacking in passion and courage.

lily, to gild the. *See under* GILD.

limbo. A concept from the Catholic Church to describe the state of inbetween-ness of a child who dies before it is baptised. Being unbaptised it cannot enter heaven and, being innocent, it cannot go to hell. Instead it occupies an area between the two known in Latin as *Limbus puerorum*, *limbus* meaning 'edge' and *puerorum* meaning 'of the children'. In Italian this is known as limbo. Extended to more mundane matters, we use the phrase 'to be in limbo' to describe an 'inbetween' situation in which we are neither one thing nor another, or in which we are powerless to act until someone else has made a decision.

limelight. Someone who is in the limelight is in the full glare of publicity. A limelight was a kind of lamp invented by Thomas Drummond around 1830. It used lime, technically known as calcium oxide, to give off an intense white light. These lamps, known as Drummond lights, were used in lighthouses and as stage spotlights to illuminate the star of the show – hence anyone centre-stage is in the limelight.

limerick. A five-lined humorous or nonsense verse (often bawdy), with the first and second lines rhyming with the fifth, and the third with the fourth. The first instances of this verse form appeared in the anonymous *Anecdotes and Adventures of Fifteen Young Ladies* and *History of Sixteen Wonderful Old Women*, published in 1820. The limerick was subsequently popularised by Edward Lear (1812–88) with his *Book Of Nonsense* of 1846. The name limerick, however, was not used by Edward Lear, and did not come into use until fifty years after his work appeared – the earliest use of the word identified by the Oxford English Dictionary is in a quotation by Aubrey Beardsley in 1896. No-one knows the origin of the name. It has been suggested that it is a corruption of 'Lear-ic', or that it was a popular fad for a group of people to recite limericks, interspersed with the chorus 'We'll all come up, come up to Limerick'. Or – a more likely explanation – that limerick was chosen simply to suggest an Irish origin for the verse form, given the common English habit of attributing nonsense to the Irish.

limey. American and Australian slang term for a British person. The term originated as a derogatory nickname for a British sailor, and derives from the Royal Navy practice, especially in the 18th century, of issuing lime juice to a ship's crew in order to prevent scurvy.

limousine. A large motor car with an enclosed body and a roofed place for the driver, who is separated by a partition from the passengers; loosely, any large, luxurious motor car. The name, which has been in use since 1902, derives from the French word *Limousin*, which is both the name of a province of France and the name of a hooded cloak once worn by natives of that province.

limousine liberal. A person with liberal political views who is very wealthy – by inference, wealthy enough to be chauffeured in a LIMOUSINE. The expression originated in the USA in the late 1960s.

limp wrist. A male homosexual, particularly an effeminate one. This slang expression originated in the USA in the late 1950s, and also gave rise to the adjective 'limp-wristed'.

line, to toe the. To accept and observe regulations or discipline, to fall into line with everyone else. It is derived from the line drawn to mark the start of a race. All competitors have to stand behind this line, their toes on it, before the race can begin. The phrase is often used negatively as in, 'He refused to toe the line', referring to a person who refuses to accept discipline or authority.

line one's pockets, to. George 'Beau' Brummell (1778–1840) was the most exquisite dandy of his time, the arbiter of fashion in London and Bath and a friend of the Prince Regent, later to become George IV. Tailors, wig-makers, hat-makers and glovers were all desperate for his custom, for once Beau Brummell had been seen wearing one of their creations, fashionable society would flock to them for something similar. According to legend one tailor in particular was so anxious to win his favour that he sent him a coat whose pockets were lined with money. Brummell is said to have replied that he approved of the coat and particularly of the pocket lining. It has been suggested that it is from this source that we get the phrase to line one's pockets, meaning to become rich on the proceeds of bribery or corruption. A second story tells of the time Sir Thomas More, acting as a judge at a trial, was sent a gift of a pair of gloves stuffed with money by one of the parties involved. More's principles being higher than Brummell's, he returned the gloves saying that he disliked such linings. Neither story can be proved true but both give an indication of how the expression got its meaning.

lines, to read between the. Today this means to find a concealed meaning, to go beneath the surface and discover something that was not obvious. But when the phrase first came into use it meant, quite literally, reading between the lines. One way of sending a secret message was to write with invisible ink between the lines of a letter, or to compose the letter so that the secret message could be read in alternate lines. This method of sending messages became so well known that by 1865 to read between the lines had taken on its modern, figurative, meaning.

lingua franca. The original (meaning literally 'the Frankish tongue') was a mixture of Italian, French, Greek, Turkish and Arabic that was spoken around the Mediterranean coast and enabled traders from France, Italy, North Africa and so on to communicate with each other. The phrase is also used more generally to describe any language that is composed of a variety of tongues. A prime example would be Pidgin English, which started out as a combination of English and Chinese and is now in use in various different forms throughout the Pacific area. In Pidgin English Her Majesty Queen Elizabeth II is known simply as 'Missus Kwin'.

lion's share. The greater part of something that is shared out. One of Aesop's fables provides the origin of this expression. Four animals – a lion, a heifer, a goat and a sheep – went hunting and caught a stag. The four decided to share the catch equally. The lion did the dividing, and he divided it into four equal portions, taking the tastiest for himself. Then he claimed a second portion, saying that he was entitled to it

by right of being the strongest. The third portion he also claimed, saying it was his by right since he was the most valiant. The fourth portion he said was for the other three animals. 'But,' he added, 'touch it if you dare!'

lit up like a Christmas tree. *See under* BRAHMS AND LISZT.

litterbug. Someone who drops litter in the street or in other public places. The word was coined by some unknown person in the USA, probably around 1945 and probably in connection with a civic anti-litter campaign. It was certainly by means of such campaigns, and the attendant publicity, that the word came into widespread use. The *New York Herald Tribune* used the word (though in inverted commas) in a headline in its edition of 16 February 1947: '47,000 subway 'litterbugs' pay $107,000 in fines in 1946 drive'.

little green men. The archetypal mysterious alien beings associated with 'flying saucers' or UFOs. The phrase seems to have originated in Canada in the 1950s, and was obviously influenced by the garish illustrations to be found on the covers of science fiction magazines. *See also* EXTRATERRESTRIAL.

live in sin. *See under* COMMON LAW MARRIAGE.

Loadsamoney was originally a satirical character created by comedian Harry Enfield to make fun of the breed of newly-rich yobs, beneficiaries of Mrs Thatcher's enterprise culture. The character was a loutish, ill-educated London plasterer who used any excuse to flaunt his cash and yell his catchphrase, 'Loadsamoney'. Unfortunately the irony of this creation was lost on many people. Football fans from southern England adopted loadsamoney as a catchphrase to taunt less well-off northern fans and Loadsamoney became accepted as an amusing and almost lovable rogue. If proof were needed that the satire had backfired, it came when the advertising industry offered its seal of approval by signing Mr Enfield, in the guise of his *enfant terrible*, to make television commercials for watches. Soon after this Mr Enfield announced that he would not be using the character any more, but loadsamoney was already established in the English language. In its simplest form it means conspicuous and extensive wealth. Used ironically, as originally intended, in phrases such as 'loadsamoney attitude' or 'loadsamoney economy', it denotes something vulgar, opportunistic, obsessed with short-term gain. The phrase also spawned the prefix loadsa-, which enjoyed a brief vogue in expressions such as loadsaglasnost, loadsabargains, loadsaprizes and loadsapeople.

lobster shift. Quite why the night shift at a factory or place of work should be known as the 'lobster shift' is not clear. Perhaps it has something to do with the fact that for working such unsocial hours (midnight to eight a.m.) they get a bonus which, should they want it, enables them to afford lobster.

local yokel. Citizens Band Radio jargon in the USA for a City police officer, as distinct from a member of the State Police or Highway Patrol.

lock, stock and barrel. The whole lot. The lock (or firing mechanism), the stock (or handle) and the barrel are the three parts which go together to make up a gun. *See also* HOOK, LINE AND SINKER.

lock the stable door after the horse has bolted, to. To take wise precautions only after a mishap has occurred.

loco. Crazy. This is a Spanish word, which was adopted into English in the American West in the latter part of the 19th century.

log-rolling. Mutual aid among politicians, as, for example, helping one another to get favourite pieces of legislation passed. This American colloquialism, which has been in use since at least the 1830s, carries suggestions of corruption and underhand practice. But in the literal sense it goes back to the earliest days of Western migration and refers to an honourable and neighbourly custom. When a settler had cleared a site for a new dwelling, which was customarily built of logs, his neighbours would pitch in and help to roll the logs into position and erect them.

loganberry. A delicious fruit resembling the blackberry, named after James H. Logan, an American lawyer who developed the fruit in 1881. He did it by crossing wild American blackberries with raspberry bushes and named the resulting fruit after himself.

loggerheads, to be at. The precise origin of this phrase, which means to be in violent dispute with someone, quarrelling with them, hasn't yet been pinpointed. Several theories have been advanced, none of them totally convincing. We know that a loggerhead was originally a stupid person, a blockhead. Later the word was applied to an extremely nasty weapon used in sea battles. It consisted of a long-handled implement topped by a metal ball which could be heated and dipped in boiling tar which was then flicked at and daubed on the enemy. And when they got too close for the tar to be much use, the loggerhead also proved a useful weapon for flailing around and smashing skulls. This may be the origin of the phrase, implying that two people who were at loggerheads with each other were slogging it out in the figurative sense.

logic bomb. A set of instructions secretly programmed into a computer system, as an act of sabotage, that will cause the system to break down when triggered by specific circumstances such as the occurrence of some future date and time. The terminology dates from the mid-1980s, although the concept has existed as long as computers have been used in industry and commerce. There are many instances of logic bombs being set by disgruntled computer staff who have been sacked, and which take effect some time after their departure. There are other instances where logic bombs have been set from motives of pure disinterested mischief, or for the sake of the technical challenge involved.

Lolita. Vladimir Nabokov's novel *Lolita* tells the story of a middle-aged man seduced by his landlady's under-age daughter. The book (and the ensuing film) caused a stir when it was published in 1955 and since that time the word Lolita has been used to describe any sexually precocious adolescent girl.

Lombard. Someone who is rich but stupid. This is an acronym coined in the City of London in 1987, when there was a vogue for such coinages following the pattern of YUPPIE and DINKIE. Lombard is said to stand for 'loads of money but a real dickhead'. The aptness of the acronym lies in the fact that lombard is also an archaic word meaning a banker or money-changer.

long – to be long in the tooth. Someone who is long in the tooth is merely old. One source states that the phrase comes from the fact that as they grow older, horses' gums recede and thus make their teeth appear longer. The same gum problems are experienced by humans in their advancing years, which probably explains why the phrase is applied not simply to old horses but also to old people.

long shot. In the early days when cannon were carried aboard warships they were exceedingly inaccurate and could only be guaranteed to hit their target at a short distance. If a captain decided to fire a long shot he knew that there were high odds against him hitting his target, and thus the phrase long shot came to be applied to anything that had little chance of success. These days the expression is most often used in horseracing, sporting events and political elections to describe a competitor who doesn't have much hope of winning.

long time no see. A Pidgin English phrase, brought back to the English-speaking world by sailors who had heard it on their trips to China and the Far East where Pidgin, a combination of Chinese and English, was used as a LINGUA FRANCA. It is a literal translation of the Chinese phrase *ch'ang chih mei*, which in more elegant translation means 'It's a long time since we last saw each other.' Though heard more rarely than it once was, long time no see is still a popular catchphrase. Another phrase from the same source is 'no can do'.

loo. Lavatory, toilet, water-closet. No-one knows the origin of this expression, though there is certainly no lack of theories. Some would find a derivation in the French word *lieu*, meaning 'place'. It is said that at the time of the French Revolution lavatories were sometimes known as *lieux d'aisance* – 'places of easement'. And it has been pointed out that some hotel lavatories in Paris used to have notices on the lines of '*On est prié de laisser ce lieu aussi propre qu'on le trouve*' – 'Please leave this place as tidy as you find it'. One fact in favour in this theory is that the Germans have a similar expression, *der Locus*. Another proposed derivation is from the French *l'eau*, meaning 'the water'. Or from the traditional Edinburgh cry 'Gardyloo' (which is garbled French, *gardez l'eau*, meaning 'mind the water') which was commonly used when emptying slop pails from tenement windows into the streets. Professor Alan Ross (of *U and Non-U* fame) investigated the matter in a 1974 edition of *Blackwoods Magazine*. His conclusion was that 'loo' derived 'in some way which could not be determined' from the name Waterloo. Support for the theory that this punning derivation is the correct one is provided by James Joyce who wrote in 1922 in *Ulysses*: 'O yes, *mon loup*. Waterloo. Water-closet.' Lord Lichfield, the photographer, was told by the historian Sir Steven Runciman that 'loo' derived from the name of Lord Lichfield's great-great-aunt, Lady Louisa Anson. At a house- party in Ireland, it would appear, in the 1860s, the two young sons of the host, the Duke of Abercorn, played a practical joke by taking the namecard from Lady Louisa's bedroom door and placing it on the door of the guests' W.C. This incident led to the W.C. being known thereafter, in aristocratic circles, as the 'Lady Lou'. Certainly, until the 1960s, loo was a word used almost exclusively by the upper and upper-middle classes.

look at the world through rose-tinted spectacles, to. Pink-tinted glasses give everything a cheerful glow, which is why someone who habitually sees the optimistic, pleasant side of things may be accused of looking at the world through rose-tinted spectacles. The phrase was first recorded in the mid-19th century.

Loony Left. A term used in the 1980s, particularly in the tabloid press, to describe those advocating or implementing extreme (or merely

rather silly) left-wing policies in Britain. As well as minority groups like the Socialist Workers Party, the term Loony Left has been used to refer to a number of Labour MPs and a number of Labour councils, notably in some of the London boroughs. Many of the stories in the tabloid press in the mid-1980s about the Loony Left were totally spurious – as, for example, the one about a London borough which banned the nursery rhyme *Baa Baa Black Sheep* from its schools on the pretext that it was racist. But many had more than a grain of truth. *See also* MILITANT.

loophole. In modern use a clever, often morally dubious, way out of a difficult situation. It is used most often to describe an ambiguity or gap in the law that allows offenders to escape prosecution on a technicality. In the great castles of the Middle Ages, however, a loophole was a narrow slit in a castle wall through which arrows could be fired. From outside it was scarcely visible but inside it widened to allow defenders the space they needed to rain arrows on their attackers. In the 17th century the word developed to describe a narrow way out of something and from this comes the figurative use of a narrow escape we know today.

loose – to be at a loose end. A person is described as being at a loose end if they have nothing to do. Although no origin has been conclusively traced, the phrase may have derived from the practice of letting a horse run loose in a field after a day's work in harness. The horse is at a loose end; untethered and with nothing to do.

lose one's head, to. *See under* FLY OFF THE HANDLE.

lose one's lunch, to. *See under* CHUNDER.

lose one's marbles, to. According to one source, this phrase alludes to an old story about a boy whose marbles were carried off by a monkey. The boy was so upset that he became irrational and foolish. Today when we describe someone as losing their marbles we mean that they are losing their memory or suffering the effects of senility. Elderly people who retain their faculties may be glowingly described as having all their marbles. *See also* TO HAVE A SCREW LOOSE, *under* SCREW.

lotus-eater. According to the Greek poet Homer in his epic the *Odyssey*, the original lotus-eaters lived somewhere on the north African coast and ate the leaves of the lotus plant that grew there. The leaves made them dreamily happy, and travellers who were tempted to taste them forgot all ideas of returning home to their families and wanted only to live a life of idleness and dreams in Lotusland. From this we apply the phrase lotus-eater to any person who lives in a dreamworld and is lost to reality, or to people who have an idle and luxurious lifestyle.

lounge. It has been speculated, though without any evidence to support the theory, that the verb to lounge, meaning to loll or sit about casually, is derived from the Roman centurion Longinus. Tradition has it that it was Longinus who stuck his spear into Christ's side as he suffered on the cross. Longinus later converted to Christianity, a fact which was incorporated into some medieval mystery plays. These portrayed the unredeemed Longinus hanging around at the foot of the cross while other soldiers gambled for Christ's garments. It has been suggested that it is from this image of him that we get the verb to lounge and, later, the noun lounge to describe a room where people relaxed and sat about casually. The O.E.D. points tentatively in the direction of the Old French word *longis*, a dopey, lolling

person, which may in turn derive from Longinus' name.

love. The use of the word 'love' for a score of zero in tennis derives from the French *l'oeuf*, 'the egg', and is based on the resemblance between the shape of an egg and the figure 0. *See also* DUCK, GOOSE EGG.

love child. *See* LOVE NEST.

love making. This is a phrase to be used with care, for it means different things to different generations. To the older generation it is a synonym for 'courting' and describes nothing much stronger than hand-holding and kissing, but to the post-war generation it is a euphemism for sexual intercourse.

love me, love my dog. This proverb was first quoted in the 11th century by St Bernard of Clairvaux. This was not the St Bernard famed for founding a hospice to assist travellers who crossed the Great St Bernard Pass, which was named after him. Nor was he the St Bernard after whom the famous snow-rescue dogs are named; both the pass and the dogs were named for St Bernard of Menthon. These days, when so many of us keep dogs as domestic pets, love me, love my dog seems pretty much a matter of common sense. But when Bernard of Clairvaux used the phrase dogs were despised, dangerous animals that carried disease; in saying love me, love my dog, meaning 'If you love me, you'll have to love everything about me, faults and all', he was asking far more of someone than we do now.

love nest. A salacious phrase beloved of tabloid journalists to describe any house, apartment or room in which illicit lovers enjoy their secret assignations. It dates to around the turn of the century, but **love child**, an equally popular phrase in the scandal sheets and referring to a child born out of wedlock, a BASTARD, is older. Love child has been traced back to the very early 1800s and was probably in use before that. Interesting to note, perhaps, that in these phrases and others (such as love affair), love is associated with sexual misbehaviour or infidelity and not with marriage and convention. It seems rather unfair that a love child cannot, by definition, be born to married parents.

low-level Munchkin. An American slang term for a menial or low-ranking employee or member of an organisation. The Munchkins were the dwarfish helpers in L. Frank Baum's book *The Wizard of Oz*, which was made into a popular movie starring Judy Garland.

LSD. (1) LSD is sometimes used to refer to the British currency prior to decimalisation in 1971. The initials stand for *librae*, *solidi*, *denarii* – the Roman equivalents of pounds, shillings and pence, which were the units of the pre-decimal currency. (2) LSD, also known as ACID, is the best-known of the synthetic hallucinogenic or PSYCHEDELIC drugs. The full name of the drug is lysergic acid diethylamide. There was a vogue for the recreational use of LSD in the late 1960s, especially among the HIPPIES. At this time The Beatles issued their song *Lucy In The Sky With Diamonds*. Because the title includes the initials L, S and D, and because its lyrics are typically PSYCHEDELIC, it has always been believed that it refers to the sensations produced by LSD, although this has consistently been denied by those involved.

Luddite. The original Luddites were textile workers in the north of England who, between 1811 and 1816, organised themselves into bands to smash the new machinery that was being introduced into their industry and which they blamed for their unemployment and distress. They

had a fictitious leader, variously named as 'General Ludd', 'Captain Ludd' and 'King Ludd', who may have been based on folk myths about a certain Ned Lud or Ludlam, living about 1779, who in a fit of rage smashed up two frames belonging to a stockinger (or hosiery framework knitter) in Leicestershire. Today the term Luddite may be applied to anyone who attempts to obstruct technological or industrial changes (not necessarily by breaking machinery) especially when such changes reduce the demand for labour.

lunatic. As early as Roman times and probably long before, people were aware of the phases of the moon and believed that they influenced the mind. In particular they believed that madness was caused or made worse by a full moon. Thus we get the word lunatic to describe a frenzied, crazy person, since it is derived from the Latin *luna*, meaning 'moon'. A lunatic is, literally, a moon-struck person. The word was used for hundreds of years as a medical classification of madness but was dropped more than a century ago. Today someone described as a lunatic is merely reckless or a little crazy, but not clinically insane.

lunatic fringe. A minority group containing the more extreme or eccentric members of a political party or other movement or community. The expression was coined in 1913 by the American president Theodore Roosevelt.

lunch, there's no such thing as a free. Used by cynical businessmen, public relations executives and almost everyone else who has ever done business over lunch, this American phrase is said to have originated in saloon bars of the past, where those who bought a drink were entitled to help themselves to a 'free' lunch served on the counter. There's no such thing as a free lunch meant then as it does now – you can't get something for nothing. *See also* POWER LUNCHING.

lurch, to leave in the. There are two compatible suggestions for the derivation of this phrase, meaning to leave someone in a difficult situation. The first traces it to the game of cribbage, where a player is left in the lurch if his opponent reaches a score of sixty-one before he has scored thirty-one. If this is the case, the player with the lower score cannot win; he is in a helpless situation. The second derivation points in the direction of a 16th-century French game called *lourche* and Anglicised to 'lurch'. In this game, something along the lines of backgammon, a player who suffered a 'lurch' fell so far behind his opponent that it was impossible for him to win. He, like the cribbage player, was left in the lurch. As cribbage was invented some time after *lourche*, it seems likely that the expression started with the older game and was transferred to the newer one.

lush. An alcoholic. Although this expression is more common in the United States than in Britain, it derives from an old English slang term for beer and other intoxicating drinks. This expression is related to the name of a noted London drinking-club for actors, called 'The City of Lushington', which was founded in the 18th century and met at the Harp Tavern in Russell Street. The club itself is said to have derived its name from a London brewer called Lushington.

lynch. There is little doubt that the verb to lynch, denoting a mob killing, is derived from a man named Lynch. The problem is in deciding which of several Lynches is responsible. Colonel William Lynch of Pennsylvania, USA, is one of the prime suspects. He was well-known in the 1780s for the way in which he took the law into his own hands by forming a squad of vigilantes dedicated to meting out summary justice. His method of operation became known as the Lynch Laws and he instituted the practice of hanging a man by placing him on horseback with his hands tied and a noose around his neck, the end of the rope tied to a tree branch above him. Lynch and his men would then ride away, leaving their victim in this state. Sooner or later his horse would move away from the tree, leaving the rider dangling from the rope. Using this method Lynch and his men could swear that when they left the victim he was alive and well. Then there was James Lynch Fitz-Stephens, mayor of Galway, Ireland, who in 1793 hanged his own son from a window in his own house when he was accused of murder. He, too, has been identified as the originator of lynching. And finally we have to take into account Charles Lynch, a Quaker from Virginia, who was fond of tossing people into jail on the flimsiest of excuses. However, there is no evidence that this rough justice resulted in anyone's death. All things considered, Colonel Lynch is by far the most likely candidate for the dubious honour of inventing the lynching gang.

M

macguffin. The concept of the macguffin and its name were invented by film director Alfred Hitchcock, who had a macguffin in all his plots. It was an item that kicked off the action of the plot – a missing object for which the characters were searching, perhaps – but which ultimately turns out to be a red herring and is not relevant to the outcome of the film. With the audience busy looking for the macguffin, Hitchcock could play all kinds of unexpected tricks.

mach number. An expression, devised by the Austrian physicist and philosopher Ernst Mach (1838–1916), used to denote the ratio of the air speed of an aircraft to the velocity of sound. An aircraft travelling at mach 1 is flying at the speed of sound; an aircraft travelling at mach 2 is flying at twice the speed of sound.

Machiavelli. Niccolò Machiavelli (1469–1527) was a celebrated Florentine statesman and political theorist. He wrote several books on history and statecraft, of which the most celebrated is *Il Principe* or *The Prince*. In this book (written in a very turbulent era) he preached that a strong and ruthless leader was necessary to preserve the city state from foreign usurpers. For the acquisition and effective use of power, the ruler would be justified in using unethical methods, including deceit and terrorism, which were not in themselves desirable, since the result would be a peaceful and prosperous state. In other words, he proposed the view that the end justifies the means. Thus the name of Machiavelli, used in phrases like 'Machiavellian cunning', came to be associated with cunning and ruthless statesmanship.

machisma. In modern American slang, the female counterpart of machismo. A machisma woman flaunts her femininity in much the same way as the macho man flaunts his virility.

macho. Aggressively or ostentatiously manly and virile. Macho may also be used as a noun to mean either an aggressively virile man or the quality of aggressive virility – in which latter sense the word *machismo* is also used. Macho is, in origin, a Mexican-Spanish word meaning 'male' and applied to both animals and plants. In the late 1950s it was taken up by a few American writers, such as Norman Mailer in his *Advertisements For Myself*, and soon became a journalistic vogue-word.

mackerel snapper. An American slang insult for a Catholic. It derives from the fact that Catholics traditionally eat fish on a Friday.

mackintosh. In 1823 Charles Mackintosh, a Glaswegian chemist, patented the process for making waterproof fabric by sandwiching a layer of rubber between two layers of cloth. This technique was invented by a surgeon called James Symes, but it took Mackintosh's knowledge of chemistry to perfect it. The new waterproof material quickly caught on and was turned into diving-suits, bags, pillows, hot water bottles and, most importantly, raincoats. Such was the usefulness of a truly waterproof coat that such garments were named mackintoshes in honour of the man who had made them possible.

macrobiotics, derived from the Greek words for 'long life', was being advocated in Europe as long ago as 1797, when Hufeland became one of the first to jump on the BRANWAGON with *Die Makrobiotik*, which propounded the theory that by eating the right combination of foods one could prolong life. Modern followers of macrobiotics refer to the theory as 'large life' and believe that by eating the right kinds of food one can support one's body and help to achieve one's aims. A simple comparison makes the point: a mountaineer climbing in the depths of winter requires certain kinds of food, while an accountant working at his desk requires others. If the two eat the same diet, or the accountant eats filling, energy-giving foods while the mountaineer tries to survive on salads and fruit, neither will achieve their full potential.

Those who follow a macrobiotic diet eat WHOLE FOODS, i.e. foods which have not been processed or deprived of any of their natural goodness. The main elements of the macrobiotic diet are whole cereal grains, fresh fruits and vegetables, fish and seafood, sea vegetables, beans and pulses, soya products and natural seasonings and sweetenings such as malt extract. To decide on the proportions of these items in their diet, followers use the Zen Buddhist principles of Yin (female) and Yang (male). This theory identifies two personality types; the Yin – slow, relaxed, patient, sensitive – and the Yang – impatient, active, angry, dynamic. Foods are also divided into Yin and Yang. Yin foods include fruits, salads, leafy green vegetables and nuts and seeds. Yang foods include fish, cereal grains, root vegetables and salty seasonings. According to macrobiotic principles, by identifying one's personality type and then adapting the Yin and Yang in one's diet accordingly, it is possible to achieve a harmonious balance of the two that will not only improve one's health but will also enhance other aspects of life. *See also* WHOLE-FOOD.

mad as a hatter. Crazy. This phrase has become associated with Lewis Carroll because of the character of the Mad Hatter that he portrayed in *Alice's Adventures in Wonderland* (1865). The phrase, however, predates this work. It was used by Thackeray in *Pendennis* (1850) and before that by Thomas Haliburton in *The Clockmaker* (1837). It appears that compounds of mercury were used in the making of felt hats. People working as hat-makers, exposed to the fumes of these chemicals, could be afflicted with uncontrollable twitching of the muscles. An observer of someone suffering from these symptoms might conclude that he was mad, hence the expression.

mad as a March hare. Crazy. March is the mating season for hares, and at this time their behaviour is unusually skittish and 'hare-brained'. The expression goes back at least to the time of Geoffrey Chaucer (1340–1400) and he alludes to it in *The Friar's Tale*.

Madison Avenue or **Mad Ave.** A generic term used to describe the American advertising business, and the people, behaviour, values, etc. associated with it. The expression originated in 1944 when an article in the magazine *New Republic*, on the contribution made by the advertising industry to the war effort, was signed 'Madison Avenue'. Although at that time many New York advertising agencies did have offices on Madison Avenue, very few do so now – perhaps the pejorative connotations of the expression Madison Avenue have led many to seek a different address.

Mae West. The name, originally used by RAF personnel in World War II, for an inflatable life-jacket. The name derives from that of the popular American movie star, noted for her curvaceous and buxom figure.

maelstrom. The original maelstrom is a whirlpool located off the coast of the Lofoten Islands, off the west coast of Norway. According to legend the whirlpool was created when a ship carrying two magic millstones sank there. The millstones kept on grinding, which is why the area is turbulent and dangerous even today. The term maelstrom was invented as a result of this tale; it is made up from *malen*, meaning 'to grind', and *strom*, meaning 'stream'. The word is now applied to any deep and dangerous whirlpool and is used figuratively to describe other kinds of turmoil. Someone whose thoughts and feelings are confused may describe themselves as being in a psychological maelstrom, for example.

Mafia. A secret criminal society originating in Sicily, the Mafia (or COSA NOSTRA) became increasingly powerful during the 19th century. It was introduced by Sicilian immigrants into the USA and elsewhere. The Mafia controls many illegal activities such as gambling, narcotics, prostitution and pornography in many parts of the world, particularly in the USA where it is especially powerful. In some area it has also used terrorism to take over legitimate trades, as in the garment industry and the trucking industry, and to drive out or eliminate competitors. The name apparently derives from an Arabic word *mafia*, meaning 'a place of refuge', and refers to the Arab conquest of Sicily in the 9th century when many Sicilian families found a refuge in the hills whence they operated as bandits. The word is also used loosely to describe any secret or conspiratorial group believed to control some organisation or institution. There have also been a number of punning variations on the name. Just as 'kosher nostra' refers to a supposed Jewish conspiratorial group, 'taffia' refers to a Welsh one, and 'murphia' to an Irish one.

magazine. For something we take so much for granted, magazine has a strange history. It started out as the Arabic word *makhzon*, meaning a warehouse or storage place, and first came into English as the place where weapons, known as 'pieces', were kept. The word 'pieces' may hold the clue as to why, in 1731, magazine became the word to describe a periodical containing a variety of stories and reports. In its first issue the *Gentleman's Magazine* described itself as 'a Monthly collection to treasure up, as in a magazine, the most remarkable Pieces on the Subjects abovemention'd'. If this is truly the origin of the magazine as we know it today, it seems rather surprising that such a casual mention should stick.

magenta. Napoleon's victorious battle against the Austrians at Magenta in Italy in 1859 was such a bloody affair that when, soon after, a new red dye was invented it was named after the place. Thus we get magenta, a brilliant red-blue colour.

magnum-force. Very powerful. The expression comes from *Magnum*, the trade-name for a powerful revolver, patented in the US by Smith & Wesson Inc. of Springfield, Massachusetts in 1935.

magnum opus. The Latin phrase for 'great work'. It refers to an artist's major dramatic, literary, architectural, artistic or musical achievement.

mah-jong. An old Chinese game for four players, played with 136 or 144 'tiles' which are similar to dominoes and usually made of bamboo or ivory. The game was introduced into America and Europe in the early 1920s. The name derives from the Chinese *ma-ch'iao*, meaning 'sparrows' – from the resemblance between the chattering of sparrows and the clicking noise made by the tiles in the game.

maharishi. A Sanskrit word meaning 'great inspired sage', and an honorific title awarded to a Hindu sage or holy man. In the West, the best known bearer of the title is the Maharishi Mahesh Yogi, a GURU who became a cult figure in the late 1960s and numbered The Beatles among his followers.

mahatma. This Sanskrit word, which means literally 'great soul', is an honorific title bestowed in India on people who have gained a reputation for sanctity and wisdom and who are deemed worthy of reverence. Most people in the West associate this title with the Indian nationalist leader Mohandas Karamchand Gandhi (1869–1948) – to such an extent that most people probably are under the mistaken impression that Mahatma was his forename.

Mai tai. A cocktail made with rum, curaçao, orgeat and fruit juices, and usually garnished with fruit. The name derives from the Tahitian *maitai*, meaning 'good'.

maiden. In a number of commonly used phrases maiden, meaning a young and innocent girl, is a euphemism for 'virgin'. In the horse-racing world, for example, a maiden is a horse that has never won a race. In cricket an over from which no runs are scored is a 'maiden over' (and thus we get the phrase 'bowled a maiden over'), while a maiden castle or fortress is one that has never been taken during an attack. The first voyage of a ship is known as its maiden voyage and a Member of Parliament's first speech in the House of Commons is his maiden speech.

main – to have an eye to the main chance. *See under* EYE.

mainline, to. An expression used among junkies to describe the act of injecting drugs directly into the bloodstream and thus to get an immediate effect.

mainbrace, to splice the. The mainbrace is a heavy rope attached to the main yardarm of a ship and splicing it (that is, adding to it by splitting the end and carefully interweaving the strands with those of a new rope) was a time-consuming and difficult job. Those are the basic facts, according to some authorities, behind this saying. On a day when such a job had to be done an extra tot of rum was handed out to the sailors as reward for their hard work. Thus to splice the mainbrace came to be a naval expression meaning to have a celebratory drink, and it is in that sense that the phrase is in use today.

make (both) ends meet. To balance

one's income and expenditure; to survive without going into debt. The expression in its original form was 'make both ends of the year meet', and in this form it is used in Tobias Smollett's *The Adventures of Roderick Random* (1748). 'Meet' here is an adjective, meaning 'even' or 'quits'.

make do and mend. This phrase has a naval origin, referring as it does to the weekly session of mending that sailors on board ship were allotted each week. During make do and mend they patched up their clothing and kit and 'made it do' for the next week. The expression passed into general use to describe the practice of repairing old items – not just garments but larger things too – and extending their life a little longer.

make my day. In the film *Magnum Force*, Clint Eastwood plays the role of a tough cop who challenges a criminal to attempt to kill him so that he in turn can have the satisfaction of killing the criminal in self-defence. He does this with the words: 'Go ahead, punk. Make my day!' As a result of this film, make my day became a popular catchphrase, implying a challenge to a would-be attacker.

make out like a bandit. To emerge successfully from some enterprise; to win everything. This American expression is based on the Yiddish word *bonditt*, meaning a clever, resourceful fellow.

make the cheese more binding, to. This expression means to make things more difficult or complicated than they already are; to delay or hold up a situation. This is an American pun based on the idea that cheese is 'binding', i.e. is constipating. Someone who makes the cheese more binding makes a tricky situation more difficult to resolve.

make the fur fly, to. A furious fight or argument in which those involved do each other a great deal of physical or verbal injury may be described as making the fur fly. This expression comes from the 'sport' of animal baiting, popular for hundreds of years, in which bears, bulls and other creatures had dogs set against them. In the ensuing fights the fur did, literally, fly.

make waves, to. To make trouble, to make an impact that upsets things. Though it is not necessarily the true derivation of the phrase, it has been suggested that the expression is based on the punchline of a joke about a person who dies and goes straight to hell. On his arrival he hears the sound of beautiful singing which, on later exploration, turns out to be the voices hundreds of other residents, all of them standing in pit of excrement which comes up to their chins and all of them carefully chanting, 'Don't make waves, don't make waves.' That's the story, anyway, and even if it's not the origin it is probably more amusing than the real explanation.

malapropism. Mrs Malaprop is a character who appears in Richard Brinsley Sheridan's comedy *The Rivals*, written in 1775. Her name is based on the French phrase *mal à propos*, meaning something out of place or inappropriate, and Mrs Malaprop's most enduring characteristic is her ability to use unsuitable words without realising what she is saying. Thus, describing the perfect education for a young lady she says,

. . . she should have a supercilious knowledge in accounts; – and as she grew up, I would have her instructed in geometry, that she might know something of the contagious countries . . . and likewise that she might reprehend the true meaning of what she is saying.

Among the other lines she utters are, 'as headstrong as an allegory in the Nile', meaning 'alligator', and 'He is the very pineapple of politeness', meaning 'pinnacle'. These errors, and others like them, have become known as malapropisms.

male chauvinist or **male chauvinist pig.** Sometimes abbreviated to MCP, a man who stubbornly adheres to old-fashioned ideas of male supremacy and female inferiority. The phrase was coined *c.*1970, in the early days of the women's movement and is contemporary with such concepts as feminism and SEXISM. *See also* CHAUVINIST and PIG.

Malley's cow. An Australian colloquial expression referring to someone who has gone away leaving no indication where he may be found. It derives from a piece of Australian folklore about a man named Malley who lost a cow he was supposed to be looking after.

mallie. The shopping-mall phenomenon has yet to hit Britain with full impact, but when it does we should expect to see the development of a new sociological group, the mallies, along American lines. Mallies are young people who hang around shopping malls, window shopping, meeting friends, snacking in the restaurants and generally treating the place as a kind of social club. Also haunting the malls are compulsive shoppers, usually women, who are addicted to spending money. Their slogan is 'Born to Shop'.

Mamba. An acronym for Middle--Aged Middle-Brow Accomplisher; one of the conservative, conformist, reasonably successful, reasonably well-off professional people who get things done without making a great fuss about it. *See also* YUPPIE.

mammon. 'Ye cannot serve God and mammon,' it says in the Bible, (Matthew 6:24). Mammon was originally just the Syriac word for 'riches', but later writers created the character Mammon, the personification of the evils of wealth and greed. We say that someone who is obsessed with acquiring money and personal possessions worships mammon. In *Paradise Lost* Milton wrote:

Mammon, the least erected spirit that fell
From Heaven; for even in Heaven his
  looks and thoughts
Were always downwards bent, admiring
  more
The riches of Heaven's pavement, trodden
  gold,
Than aught divine or holy.

man – one man's meat is another man's poison. This phrase, meaning that what suits one person perfectly may be anathema to another, was coined by the Roman philosopher and poet Lucretius. His greatest work was *De rerum natura* (*The Nature of the Universe*) and in the fourth part of it he wrote,

What to some would be food was to others the deadliest poison.

man bites dog. This is a saying, in the form of a fictitious newspaper headline, which reflects the journalist's idea of what makes a good news story. It derives from a passage in an article in the *New York Sun* in 1882 by the journalist Charles A. Dana (1819–97):

When a dog bites a man that is not news, but when a man bites a dog that is news.

man in the street, the. A cliché to describe the mythical average citizen. The man in the street is forever having conflicting views and opinions ascribed to him by politicians, who might be surprised by what ordinary people really do think if they only stopped to ask them. The female equivalent is **the girl on the Clapham omnibus**, a phrase coined around the turn of the century to describe the kind of ordinary, average woman. The Americans have the phrase 'The man on the cars', referring to streetcars, as a male equivalent.

man of straw. A man without substance or power; someone who is unscrupulous and willing to do anything for money. It is widely believed that the phrase originally referred to men who loitered around the Law Courts offering to stand as a witness and say anything required in exchange for payment. Such men identified themselves by sticking a straw in their shoe and thus became known as men of straw.

man-sized. An adjective used by manufacturers to mean 'large' – for example, man-sized tissues are considerably larger than the standard kind. In the USA man-sized is in general use to mean anything big or abundant – a man-sized meal, for example, or a man-sized beer.

mañana. In Spanish the literal meaning of *mañana* is tomorrow. But in English-speaking countries it has been adapted to mean 'at some unspecified time in the future', and is used to represent the habit of easygoing procrastination, and lack of a sense of urgency, that is said to be common in Spanish-speaking countries. Mañana has been used in this sense since at least the middle of the 19th century.

Manhattan. An American cocktail, named after Manhattan Island in New York City, and consisting of whisky and vermouth with a dash of bitters.

Manhattan eel. An American slang expression for a used condom, derived from the fact that there are so many of them floating with other detritus in New York Harbour.

mantelpiece. No matter how elaborate architects have made mantelpieces in their grandest designs, there is no escaping the fact that they were originally no more than a shelf set into the wall above the fire and supported a number of hooks on which wet mantles could be hung. A mantle is the old-fashioned name for a coat, cloak or other outer garment.

marathon. A race over a distance of 26 miles and 385 yards. The name derives from the legend that after the battle of Marathon of 490 BC, in which the Athenians defeated the Persians, a runner named Pheidippides ran with the news of the victory from Marathon to Athens. When the Olympic Games were revived in Athens in 1896, the marathon was included as one of the events, and was run over 26 miles. The extra 385 yards was a later addition. In the 1970s and 1980s there was increasing interest in this type of race, with events such as the annual London Marathon. There were also less demanding variations such as 'half-marathons' and 'mini-marathons'. The term marathon is also widely used to represent any test of stamina or endurance. New coinages have also been introduced, using the suffix -athon or -thon, to suggest the same idea in different contexts. See, for example, TELETHON.

Mardi Gras. Shrove Tuesday – the day before the beginning of Lent. The phrase is of French origin, and means literally 'fat Tuesday'. In many countries there is an old tradition of celebrating Shrove Tuesday or Mardi Gras with carnival and festivity – probably a survival of the Roman festival of Lupercal, which was held at about the same time of year. In Paris it used to be the custom to parade a fattened ox – *un boeuf gras* – through the streets at the head of a procession of merry-makers.

mare – to find a mare's nest. To come across something new and exciting, only to discover that it's no great thing at all. The origin of this phrase hasn't been traced, but in Britain there are many regional variations which suggest that it goes back a long way. In Scotland, for example, a skate's nest replaces the mare's nest, while in Devon 'a blind mare's nest' means nonsense.

margarine. Many people have found it strange that something as mundane as margarine should be derived from the Latin word *margarita*, meaning 'pearl'. Margarine was in fact originally a product derived from pork fat and was a pearly white colour, hence the origin of its name. Only comparatively recently has yellow dye been added to make it look more like butter.

Marie Celeste. The mystery of the Marie Celeste has never been solved. In 1872 the ship was found drifting among the Azores, her sails set, her one boat, sextant, chronometer, log and crew all missing. Many explanations have been offered for their disappearance but none has ever been proved. The incident might well have been forgotten had it not been incorporated into the language. Thus, more than a century later, we may say of a mysteriously deserted office or shop or other normally bustling place, 'It's just like the Marie Celeste around here.'

Marines, tell that to the. Someone who is told a tall story may reply disbelievingly, 'Tell that to the Marines'. This expression dates back to the 18th century when the Marines were first established as a force of soldier-sailors. They were heartily disliked by the Navy who considered them little more than jumped-up LANDLUBBERS, ignorant of the sea and seafaring customs. As a consequ-ence the Marines became the butt of naval jokes and were generally char-acterised as stupid and gullible. According to an old story, Samuel Pepys was once telling Charles II some stories about life in the Navy when he mentioned flying fish. No one believed this except a Marine officer who said he too had seen such things. The king listened and accep-ted his evidence, saying

From the very nature of their calling no class of our subjects can have so wide a knowledge of seas and lands as the officers and men of Our Loyal Maritime Regi-ment. Henceforward 'ere ever we cast doubts upon a tale that lacks likelihood we will first 'Tell it to the Marines'.

mark, to be up to the. In the past all articles of gold and silver had to be submitted for testing to the Assay Office. Those which reached the standards set by the office were hall-marked. Those which failed to achieve this level were declared not up to the mark.

mark time, to. To keep moving but without progress. It was originally a military term, first used in a manual of 1833, in which marking time is described as 'marching without gain-ing any ground'. Today we apply the phrase to any activity that takes up time but doesn't result in progress.

Mark Twain. When ex-riverboat pilot Samuel Langhorne Clemens was looking for a pen-name under which to publish his stories of Tom Sawyer and Huckleberry Finn, he remembered the cry 'Mark twain' called out by riverboat leadsmen as they sounded the depth of water. Mark twain was an abbreviated ver-sion of the phrase, 'Mark on the twine', referring to the weighted twine they held over the side and against whch the water was mea-sured. Clemens adopted this short-ened version as his pseudonym and thus Mark Twain became one of the best-known and best-loved American writers of all time.

marmalade. The bitter orange jam traditionally eaten at breakfast has two possible origins. The first and most convincing is that it derives from the Latin *milimelum*, meaning 'honey apple', which was a variety of quince grafted onto a quince tree. From this came the Portuguese word *marmelada*, meaning quince jam – marmalade having once been made of quinces rather than the Seville oranges most usually used today. A more intriguing tale tells of the time Mary Queen of Scots was ill and could eat nothing but this kind of jam. It has been suggested that marmalade may derive from the French phrase *'Marie malade'*, meaning 'sick Mary'. There's no evidence to disprove this theory except a gut feeling that sickly-sweet marmalade is one of the last things anyone would want to eat if they were feeling unwell.

martini. A cocktail, also known as a dry martini, consisting of gin and dry vermouth. The proper proportion of vermouth to gin is a subject that is much debated by those who take an interest in such matters. Lemon peel, a dash of orange bitters and a green olive on a stick are optional extras. At least three full-length books have been written on the subject of this one cocktail. Nevertheless, the origin of the name is veiled in obscurity. Some authorities, including the *Oxford English Dictionary*, say that it derives from the name of the firm of Martini and Rossi, the Italian wine-makers who produce a widely popular dry vermouth. Others derive the name from an earlier cocktail, the martinez, though this was apparently a quite dissimilar concoction. The theory which seems most plausible is that the martini was invented *c*.1910 in the fashionable Knickerbocker Hotel in New York City and took its name from the head bartender there, one Signor Martini.

martyr. The word is derived from the Greek for 'witness' and was originally applied only to those who had born witness to their faith by shedding their blood for Christ. As early as the 14th century, however, the word was applied more generally and sometimes ironically to describe people who sacrifice themselves for a cause.

masochism. The name given to a sexual perversion in which gratification is obtained from being dominated, humiliated or treated with cruelty. The word is also nowadays used more generally to describe a condition in which there is enjoyment of pain or humiliation, without there necessarily being any sexual connotation. The term derives from the name of Leopold von Sacher-Masoch (1836–95), an Austrian novelist who both exemplified the perversion in real life and wrote about it in his novels, the most famous of which was *Venus in Furs*.

Mason-Dixon line. The boundary line between the states of Pennsylvania and Maryland. It was fixed at 39° 43' 26" N, and was named after its surveyors, the Englishmen Charles Mason and Jeremiah Dixon, who marked it out between 1763 and 1769. In the years leading up to the Civil War, the term was popularly used to represent the demarcation between the free states of the North and the slave states of the South.

masterpiece. These days the word is generally applied to a fine work of art executed by one who is a master of his or her skill – but originally a masterpiece was a piece of work made by an apprentice. Before any apprentice could join the guild that regulated his craft he had to make a high-quality piece of work that would be worthy of a master. The item was submitted to the guild and if it was judged a masterpiece he would be admitted as a member and become a master himself.

Mata Hari, meaning 'eye of the dawn', was a Dutch spy in the First World War. She was born Margarete Zelle but chose this exotic eastern pseudonym when she became a dancer specialising in Indonesian dances. By flaunting her naked charms she attracted the attention of a number of high-ranking German officials who persuaded her to become a German spy. Subsequently she slept with a number of important Allied officers and reported the military secrets she learned back to the Germans. In 1917 she was exposed as a spy and tried before being executed by the French, according to legend opening her dress to reveal herself naked in front of the firing squad. This and the other revelations of her trial aroused massive public interest, with the result that Mata Hari has passed into the English language to describe any femme fatale or glamorous female agent.

maudlin. Sickly-sentimental. This word, often applied to people who get emotional or tearful when drunk, has a religious origin. It is a variation or corruption of the name Magdalene. St Mary Magdalene was often depicted in Christian art with red swollen eyes as a result of weeping tears of repentance.

mausoleum. A large and elaborate monument or tomb. The first was erected for King Mausolus, king of a region of ancient Greece known as Caria. Before his death in 353 BC Mausolus made plans for a magnificent tomb which was to be of white marble, more than one hundred feet tall and to include statues of himself and his wife. At his death his wife obediently had the tomb erected at Halicarnassus, and such was its beauty and size that it became known as the seventh wonder of the world. It was toppled by earthquakes in the 12th century and was subsequently broken up and used in the construction of other buildings, but in 1846 English explorer Sir Charles Newton brought back to the British Museum the two huge statues of Mausolus and his wife and part of the original mausoleum's frieze.

maverick. An individual who does not conform. Samuel A. Maverick (1803–70) was a Texan rancher who left the calves of his herd unbranded. The term maverick thus came to be applied to any unbranded calves on the open range. From the 1880s onwards the term began to acquire a wider meaning, particularly in the field of American politics where it was used to describe a politician who did not acknowledge any party affiliation.

mayday. An internationally recognised distress call, as described by the International Radio Telegraph Convention of 1927. Mayday is a phonetic rendition of the French imperative infinitive *m'aider*, meaning 'help me'.

mayonnaise. The salad dressing known as mayonnaise is named after Mahon, capital of the Spanish island of Minorca. In 1756 the French staged an attack on the island, which was at that time held by the British, and drove the occupiers out. The French leader was the Duc de Richelieu and according to legend he was so hungry after the battle that his troops threw everything they could find ashore into one pot, blended it and came up with mayonnaise. Another version says that they merely made a blended stew but that on receipt of the news in Paris, the best chefs of the day threw together eggs and olive oil, two of the most common ingredients in the French kitchen, and came up with a mixture which they called mahonnaise to celebrate the victory.

mazel tov, meaning 'good luck', is a Yiddish phrase. Translated absolutely literally it means 'May a good star shine upon you'.

mazuma. An American slang word for money. This Yiddish word, derived from Hebrew (and before that, say some authorities, from Chaldean) migrated into the English language in the early 1900s.

McCarthyism was named for Joseph Raymond McCarthy, an American Republican senator. A virulent anti-communist, in 1948 he was appointed as head of the Subcommittee on Investigations, a committee established to root out communism wherever it existed. This was a job that McCarthy approached with terrifying zeal. He mercilessly hounded writers, Hollywood stars and other prominent figures, many of whom lost their jobs and were ruined even though they were never proved to be communists. Those who refused to give evidence against their friends were implicated and also suffered. Fired by this, McCarthy went further and began to attack the State Department and the Democratic Party, alleging that they were hotbeds of communism. Despite being unable to justify his allegations, and despite being exposed on television by Ed Murrow, it wasn't until he overstepped the mark in 1954 by criticising President Eisenhower that McCarthy was fired and his political witch-hunt condemned. Today we use the word McCarthyism to describe a political investigation that resembles one of these witch-hunts.

McCoy, The Real. There are at least two contenders for this title. The first is Norman McCoy, a boxer who fought under the name of Kid McCoy in the early years of this century. On one occasion McCoy was harangued by a drunk who persisted in challenging him to a fight. The drunk's friends warned him about the identity of the man he was provoking, but he refused to believe them. Eventually McCoy's patience snapped and he knocked the drunk out with a single punch. When the man came round his first words were said to have been, 'You're right, that's The Real McCoy.' Another source suggests, however, that the phrase comes from Scotland where there are two rival branches of the MacKay family. Because of this there was constant contention over who was the true head of the clan, The Real McKay. From this use the phrase was applied to men, whisky and other things that were the best of their kind – the real thing, as one of the world's most famous advertising slogans would have it.

mealy-mouthed, to be. To be called mealy-mouthed is not necessarily the insult that most people think. The expression is derived from the Greek *melimuthos*, meaning 'honey speech' and may originally have been applied simply to people with the BLARNEY. Whatever its first meaning, mealy-mouthed soon came to refer to someone whose sweet words hid their insincerity; a hypocrite or a flatterer.

meaningful. One of the in-words of the 1980s. It is most often used as a prefix to other words such as 'relationship' and 'experience' to denote something special, out of the ordinary or with a deep spiritual dimension. That's the theory, anyway, but in everyday use a meaningful relationship is nothing much more than an ordinary relationship, 1980s-style. *See also* PSYCHOBABBLE.

meat and potatoes. With the rumbling of the BRANWAGON and the increasing popularity of DEMI-VEG and WHOLEFOOD, meat and potatoes are no longer the staple English diet. However, that is what this phrase implies, for a meat and potatoes issue or debate is a basic one, one without frills or finer points.

Mecca. The birthplace of Muhammad in Saudi Arabia, and a place of pilgrimage for Muslims. The word has come to refer to any outstanding place which attracts visitors. St Andrews, for example, might be described as a Mecca for golfers.

media event. An event designed by public relations specialists to attract the attention of press, radio and television. Media events are staged not for their entertainment value but to publicise something else. Thus an attempt to break the world peanut-eating record, for example, may turn out to be just a media event designed to draw media attention to a new brand of salted peanuts.

meerschaum. A fine light whitish clay, used for making tobacco-pipes; a pipe made from this material. The word *meerschaum* is German and means literally 'sea-froth'. The clay, found on the seashore in rounded lumps, was popularly supposed to be petrified sea-foam.

mega-. The prefix mega- (derived from the Greek *megas*, meaning 'great') has been used scientifically since the 19th century. It denotes a million, as in the names of units such as 'megacycle', 'megawat', 'megaton'. In the 1980s the use of mega, either as a prefix or as a separate word, in either case with the sense of 'great' or 'greatly', has become – to coin a word – megapopular. Typical coinages are: megabucks (a large sum of money), megastar (a super-super-star), megabang, megaloan, megablockbuster, megaplan, mega-city, mega-trendy, etc. etc.

megillah. American slang term for a long, involved and tedious story or account. The word, which comes from Hebrew via Yiddish, means literally a scroll or volume, and is used especially of the Book of Esther which is read out aloud in its entirety at the Purim celebration.

Melba toast and **Peach Melba.** Both are named for Dame Nellie Melba, a famed Australian opera singer. According to culinary legend, Melba toast was invented by accident when the diva ordered toast at the Savoy Hotel in London and was served very thin, over-toasted slices that had been made by mistake. Far from being angry, Dame Nellie rather enjoyed this extra-crispy toast and the management were so delighted that they named it Melba toast on the spot. Peach Melba has a more calculated origin, being invented specially for her by the great French chef Escoffier. His concoction combined delicious fresh peaches on a base of vanilla ice-cream, topped with fresh raspberry purée – a far cry from the mass marketed Peach Melba on offer today.

meltdown. Literally, the accidental melting of the core of a nuclear reactor. Figuratively, any economic collapse – for example, of an industry, a currency or of a stock market. The use of this term dates from the mid-1980s, the literal usage being given wide coverage by the Chernobyl nuclear reactor disaster in 1986, and the figurative usage by the world-wide stock market collapse of 1987.

melting pot. Originally a crucible, in which metal could be melted down and blended together to make alloys. Then around the turn of the century a play entitled *The Melting Pot* was staged in which the author, Israel Zangwill, compared the breaking down of racial barriers and the inter-marrying of races as 'the great Melting Pot where all the races of

Europe are melting and re-forming!' The phrase caught on, particularly in America where immigrants of so many different races liked the image of themselves breaking down old barriers and creating something new and 'American'. Today we apply the phrase to many situations in which different ideas, beliefs or races are thrown together in a way that breaks down barriers and leads to something new.

mentor. A wise person who acts as another's guide; someone who provides friendly advice and support. The original mentor appeared in the *Odyssey*, in which Mentor ran Odysseus's household while he was away at war. He also acted as adviser to Telemachus, Odysseus's son, helped in this task by the goddess of wisdom, Athene.

merchants of death. Those who make a living by manufacturing or selling weapons and armaments may be known as merchants of death. The phrase came into use in 1920 when a book with that title was published by H. C. Engelbrecht and F. D. Hanighan. This explores the idea that munitions manufacturers were actively involved in starting World War One. *See also* DOOM AND GLOOM MERCHANT.

mesmerise. Franz Anton Mesmer was an 18th-century CAUSE CÉLÈBRE. He believed that the universe was filled with an invisible magnetic force and he developed a style of 'medicine' that used magnetism as its foundation. He soon developed a cult following for his treatments, which involved mass gatherings at which dim lights, soft music and other effects were used to relax the patients, whom Mesmer would then provoke to a high-pitched state by asking blunt questions about their ailments. These meetings often sent patients into convulsions. Such was

the adulation that Mesmer received that in 1784 Louis XVI of France set up a committee to investigate his activities. Benjamin Franklin was one of those who served on it. He and his fellow committee members came to the conclusion that it was imagination rather than magnetism that was responsible for Mesmer's effects. 'Imagination with magnetism produces convulsions . . . magnetism without imagination produces nothing,' they stated. As a result Mesmer was forced to leave Paris and live the rest of his life in Switzerland, where he died in obscurity in 1815. What neither he nor the investigating committee realised was that by his use of music, mood and light Mesmer was sending his patients into a hypnotic state – which in some cases was beneficial. When this was realised at a later date Mesmer's achievements were commemorated by naming the act of putting someone into a hypnotic trance after him.

Mexican. In exactly the same way that the British remember old scores by using phrases designed as insults against the Dutch and the Irish, so the USA demonstrates its opinion of Mexico with a number of contemptuous expressions aimed at that nation. Among the best examples are a 'Mexican promotion', which in fact describes a rise in rank without a rise in salary, and a 'Mexican breakfast', which consists of a glass of water and a cigarette.

Mexican stand-off. A stalemate situation; deadlock. The origins of the phrase are a mystery, but an American source suggests that the word Mexican may be used to give a sense of danger and suspense, evoking an image of two heavily-armed Mexican bandits holding each other at gunpoint. The same expression is used to describe the actions of a gambler who, having won or lost a small amount at the gambling table, decides to quit. Inherent in both phrases is the idea of being in a no-win situation from which one has to walk away.

Mexican wave. The appearance of a wavelike motion among a crowd of people, as at a sports match, produced by sections of the crowd rising from their seats and sitting down again in sequence in an informally progressive manner. This phenomenon was first brought to the attention of the British public by television coverage of the 1986 World Cup football championship in Mexico, hence the name, and was much imitated thereafter.

mickey, to take the. To make fun of, tease, even humiliate a person. The origin has not been discovered but it has been suggested that it refers to the nickname Mick or Mickey for an Irishman and the racially stereotyped image of Irishmen as stupid. A more modern version of taking the mickey is taking the piss, which, being unacceptable in some circles, has generated a euphemism – 'extracting the urine'.

Mickey Finn (or, elliptically, a Mickey) is a narcotic substance slipped into a person's drink in order to render him unconscious. The original Mickey Finn is said to have been a notorious bar-tender in Chicago (*c.*1896–1906) who was in the habit of adulterating his customers' drinks with chloral hydrate and then robbing them when they passed out.

Mickey Mouse. If something is described as being Mickey Mouse it is regarded as being insignificant, worthless, shoddy or inferior. Why should the name of an extremely popular cartoon character created by Walt Disney (1901–66) have acquired such a pejorative sense? The answer lies not in the cartoon character itself but in the merchan-

dising associated with it. The use of Mickey Mouse as a disparaging description originated in the 1940s when Mickey Mouse wristwatches were introduced. These watches, which had a picture of the cartoon character on the dial with his arms as the hands of the watch, were widely regarded as being gimmicky and shoddy.

Midas touch. Midas was ruler of the ancient kingdom of Phrygia, an area which is now part of Turkey. He is the subject of several tales, but the best-known one tells of the time the gods granted him a single wish in return for a favour he had performed for them. Midas greedily asked that everything he touched should turn to gold. This led to unforeseen complications, for every time he tried to eat or drink something it turned to gold in his hands. Eventually, when he was on the verge of starvation, the gods agreed to lift the spell. From this story we get the phrase the Midas touch, which is applied to any individual who has a seemingly magical gift for making money in everything he does.

Middle America was coined in 1968 by a journalist called Joseph Kraft to describe the people on whom Richard Nixon hoped to rely for his powerbase. Middle America refers to the middle-class, MIDDLE-OF-THE-ROAD Americans who believe in traditional values but whose views are largely overlooked by the opinion-makers and media who almost invariably operate from the two coasts. Middle America is neither smart New York nor laid-back California, but the SILENT MAJORITY of American politics. *See also* THE MAN IN THE STREET.

middle of the road. The origin of this phrase is not known. It has been suggested that it referred originally to cautious people who walked down the middle part of a road to avoid the puddles and possibly the lurking robbers at the edges. One might equally argue that cautious people would not do this because of the danger of being run down by the traffic. Whatever its beginnings, middle of the road is now applied to people who sit firmly between extremes. In politics middle of the road individuals tend neither to the right nor left but take an unerringly central position. The music industry has developed a whole category known as M.O.R. specially for middle of the road people who dislike pop or classical stuff and prefer 'easy listening'. Used as a term of disdain, the phrase has similar connotations to middle-brow. Both expressions imply that something is intellectually undemanding, totally respectable and extremely dull. *See also under* HIGH-BROW.

militant. Since the early 1980s in Britain the word militant has been used particularly to refer to a member of an extreme left-wing organisation known as the Militant Tendency. This group, whose policies include abolition of the House of Lords and of the monarchy, functioned for a time as a separate party within the Labour Party, and managed to take effective control of several constituency parties and local councils, most notably in Liverpool, before steps were taken to exclude militants from Labour Party membership. *See also* LOONY LEFT.

mind mapping. A relatively new training technique aimed at developing an individual's use of the right side of their brain and thus encouraging a creative approach to thinking. *See* HOLISTIC and LEFT-BRAIN THINKING.

mind the store, to. This expression is said to derive from an old joke about a Jewish businessman lying on his deathbed. He looks around the room and sees his children waiting tearfully by the bedside. 'Is that you, Jacob?' he asks. 'Yes, it's me, Poppa,' said Jacob. 'And is that you, Mimi?' 'Yes, I'm here,' sobs Mimi. 'And Benjamin, is that you I see in the corner?' 'Yes, it's me, Poppa.' 'Then,' says the old man, 'who the hell is minding the store?' Minding the store in this case means looking after routine business – keeping the everyday things running.

miniature. Originally a manuscript which contained letters or illustrations made with *minium*, paint made of red lead. The Latin word for 'small' was *minimus* and it has been suggested that at some point in history the two sources were muddled, with the result that the term miniature was erroneously applied to small scale paintings. Other authorities, however, state that miniature was applied to small paintings because they were executed on vellum, just as the original miniature manuscripts had been. Whatever the truth, having been applied to small portraits miniature soon came into general use to describe anything that is a small-scale version of a larger object.

mint, to make a. The word mint, meaning a place where money is made, is derived from the Old English word *mynet*, which is in turn derived from the Latin *moneta* meaning 'money', Someone who makes a mint therefore makes a great deal of money.

MIP and **MIPS.** Mips was originally an acronym, coined *c*.1980, and used in the computer industry as a measure of a computer's processing power. It stands for 'million instructions per second'. Thus a computer might be described as having a 5 Mips processor. However, almost as soon as the term was introduced people tended to forget that it was an acronym, and treated it as a plural noun. Now the 'singular' form Mip is often encountered.

Miss/Mistress/Mrs. Those traditionalists who spurn such new-fangled modes of address as Ms, used by women who do not wish their title to indicate their marital status, and prefer to stick to the clearcut Mrs and Miss may be surprised to learn that the distinctions are not as clear as they may appear. Well into the 18th century many single women were known as Mrs and it was traditional in the 19th century for cooks and other senior female domestic staff to be styled Mrs, regardless of whether they were married or not. Likewise, in the 17th century Miss was a title often applied to courtesans – and definitely not implying sexual innocence. Feminist Ms-es looking for ammunition against those who wish to categorise them may like to point out that Miss used to be spelled Mis and may well have been pronounced Miz. Indeed, some authorities trace Ms, coined in the USA in the 1950s, to the American title Miz, widely used in the southern states for a hundred years or more. Ms, Miss and Mrs all derive from the same source, Mistress, which in the 17th and 18th centuries was applied to both married and unmarried women. Now, of course, a mistress is the kind of woman once known as Miss and a line such as 'O mistress mine, where are you roaming' (from Shakespeare's *Twelfth Night*) has a quite unintended connotation.

miss is as good as a mile, a. In its original form this expression was 'An inch in a miss is as good as an ell', an ell being a measure of around eighteen inches. This older version (meaning that it doesn't matter how close you come to hitting something, if you miss it, you miss it) makes far more sense than the modern, up-dated version which, if one bothers to analyse it, is nonsense. Some sources lay the blame for this at the feet of Sir Walter Scott, who changed the 'ell' to the more modern 'mile' and may also have pruned the phrase to the point where it lost its meaning.

missionary position. A coital position in which the female lies on her back and the male lies on top of her, between her spread legs. The name may derive from the belief that Christian missionaries among primitive peoples insisted that this position, sanctioned by tradition in the West, was the only permissible one, or possibly to the belief that missionaries were in the habit of having sex with native women in this position.

moaning minnie is applied to anyone who constantly moans and grumbles. Such people are named after the original moaning minnie, a six-barrelled German mortar used during the Second World War which gave out an ear-piercing shriek as each mortar was launched. Air raid warning sirens were also known as moaning minnies because of their high-pitched wail.

mob. The humble mob began life in the 17th century as the rather grand *mobile vulgus*, Latin for 'fickle crowd'. The phrase was introduced to the English language by Latin scholars but it was too much of a mouthful for everyday use and was consequently abbreviated to *mobile*, and thence to the plain and simple mob. This radical pruning upset some people including the writer Richard Steele, who protested,

I have done my utmost for some years past to stop the progress of 'mob', but I have been plainly borne down by numbers, and betrayed by all those who promised to assist me.

mole. *See* DEEP COVER.

mollycoddle. The Latin *mollis*

meaning soft, may be the source of this old expression; certainly a weak or effeminate man was known in the 18th century as a 'Molly'. Add this to 'coddle' meaning to pamper or look after someone with extreme care and one gets mollycoddle, meaning to pamper someone as if they are weak and helpless.

Molotov cocktail. A home-made incendiary device, consisting of a bottle filled with petrol or some other inflammable liquid and plugged with a saturated rag. The rag is ignited and the bottle is thrown at the target, whereon the bottle bursts, spreading flames all over the target. The first Molotov cocktails were used – as anti-tank weapons – by the Finns in the winter of 1939–40 when their country was invaded by the Russians. The devices were so called because the Soviet foreign minister at the time was Vyacheslav Mikhailovitch Molotov (1890–1986) and to the Finns he represented the Russian aggressor.

moment. Today we use the word moment to indicate a brief length of time (perhaps not so brief if one takes into account the number of times 'I'll just be a moment' has heralded a considerable delay). However, the length of a moment has varied throughout history and culture. In medieval times it lasted one fortieth or one fiftieth of a minute. In the 18th century it stood for a second. Today a moment is, 'specifically', a minute. According to Hebrew calculations it is one 1/1.080th of an hour. No wonder that when we say 'It will take a moment' we are so vague.

moment – at this moment in time. *See* ON-GOING.

money for old rope. Old rope is worthless rubbish that would normally be thrown away, and in the time when this phrase originated there would probably have been plenty of it lying around the dockside or the streets. Therefore anyone who offered money for old rope was paying for something that could very easily be collected. Today we use the expression to describe profitable work – tasks that can be done quickly and effortlessly.

money talks. This phrase, meaning that money gives one power and opens doors that would otherwise be shut, is first recorded in J. D. Salinger's most famous book *Catcher in the Rye*, published in 1950. It was in oral use well before that, however.

monitor. The word derives from the Latin word *monere*, meaning 'one who keeps discipline or one who teaches'. The original monitors were what we today would call nursery school teachers, while families had a house monitor to wake them up each morning and generally run the household, and young soldiers were LICKED INTO SHAPE by military monitors. In British schools today monitors are capable children selected to assist the staff. Monitor has also become a verb, meaning to study or keep an eye on something, and this in turn has given us monitor in the sense of an instrument used for checking something – a radar monitor, perhaps.

monkey business. Someone who is up to mischief, playing frivolous jokes. The phrase first appeared in the early years of the 19th century and probably reflected the growing popularity of zoos, where people could go and see the primates monkeying around for themselves.

monkey suit. Someone who feels uncomfortable dressed in a dinner jacket, TUXEDO or other formal style of dress may describe such outfits as monkey suits. According to some source this phrase dates back to the 19th century when organ grinders kept small monkeys that were trained to dance to the music and play tricks. These monkeys were often dressed in outfits that made them look quite ridiculous. We must presume that one day a man who was feeling uncomfortable in a formal jacket and trousers compared it to a monkey suit – and the name stuck. Another source disputes this theory and suggests that monkey suits are so called because they have tails - like monkeys. Interestingly enough, what sailors call a monkey jacket is a short jacket that has no tail at all.

monkey wrench. A wrench or spanner with an adjustable jaw. The first known reference in print to this useful tool occurs in Simmonds' *Dictionary of Trade Products* of 1858. How it got its name is not known for sure, but there is a general consensus that it is a humorous corruption of the name of its inventor. Opinion is divided as to whether the inventor was an engineer named Monk in Springfield, Massachusetts, or a London blacksmith named Charles Moncke.

monokini. A pair of very brief pants – a topless BIKINI.

Montezuma's revenge. *See* AZTEC TWO-STEP.

moon, over the. This phrase, much favoured by British football managers when their team wins a match, means thrilled or delighted, flying high with success. When their teams lose the same managers are likely to declare themselves **sick as a parrot**. The origin of this phrase is unknown. Both over the moon and sick as a parrot are now used as self-conscious clichés.

mooning. Exposing one's buttocks to someone, usually as an insult or a protest. The expression originated in the USA in the 1950s. The act, however, is an old custom among the Maoris. It received a great deal of publicity when the Queen, on more than one occasion, was exposed to such a display during a Royal Visit to New Zealand in 1986. Incidentally, the word 'moon' as a euphemism for 'buttocks' was not uncommon in England in the mid-18th century.

moonlight – to do a moonlight flit. To up and disappear overnight without warning, leaving debts and responsibilities behind. *See also* FLY-BY-NIGHT.

moonlighting has had, in the past century or so, a number of different meanings – but all concerned with illicit or underhand activities carried out at night. In Ireland in the 1880s it referred to acts of agrarian outrage such as the burning of hayricks or the killing of farm stock, carried out at night by discontented peasants in protest against their British landlords. In the early 1900s it referred to doing a 'moonlight flit' – that is, leaving a place of residence secretly and at night, leaving rent unpaid. From the 1950s onwards, moonlighting has meant having a second job to supplement the income from one's main employment – a fact which is often concealed both from the primary employer and from the taxman.

moonshine. In the USA the colloquial name, dating from about the turn of the century, for illicitly distilled liquor. The name derives from the fact that the distillers often worked at night to avoid the attention of revenue agents. At the end of the 18th century moonshine was the name given to brandy smuggled into England from France. Again the name refers to the operation being carried on mainly at night. *See also* POTEEN.

moot point. An issue that merits serious debate. The phrase derives from the Anglo-Saxon word *mot*, meaning 'to meet', a *gemot* being a meeting at which matters of public concern were settled by debate – a precursor of Parliament in some ways. In the 16th century moot courts were established at the Inns of Court in London. At these student lawyers had the opportunity to practise debating and public speaking on important subjects of the day. From these origins we get the phrase a moot point, meaning a serious issue which requires discussion before it is settled.

moron. A mentally deficient person. The word was coined as recently as 1910 and had originally a very precise meaning. It was proposed by Dr Henry H. Goddard to the American Association for the Study of the Feeble-minded as the official term for an adult with a mental age of between eight and twelve years, as distinct from one with a lower mental age who was graded either as an imbecile or an idiot. Dr Goddard coined the term from the Greek word *moros*, meaning 'stupid'.

morris dance. A traditional form of dance in England, that became widely popular in the 15th century when it was especially associated with May Day festivities. The name derives from the fact that it was originally a 'Moorish' or 'Morisco' dance, introduced into England from Spain in the reign of Edward III. It soon became thoroughly naturalised, with characters from the Robin Hood legends being represented in the dance.

mosey along. There are two explanations for this American phrase but only one acknowledged meaning; to stroll aimlessly, to wander slowly. Theory number one has the expression deriving from the nickname Moses which during the last century was applied to male Jews (rather as the name Jock is applied to Scotsmen) and in particular to Jewish street vendors. The way they slouched along under the weight of their goods came, it is said, to be known as moseying. Theory number two traces moseying to a corruption of the Spanish injunction *vamos*, meaning 'let's go'. Both explanations are plausible and neither, as far as we are aware, has been proved conclusively true or false.

motel. An hotel catering principally for motorists, and usually consisting of a number of self-contained accommodation units with adjacent parking space. The word is, of course, a combination of 'motor' and 'hotel' and is of American origin. The first use of the word in print, identified by the *Supplement to the Oxford English Dictionary*, is from the American *Hotel Monthly* of March 1925:

The Milestone Interstate Corporation . . . propose to build and operate a chain of motor hotels between San Diego and Seattle, the hotels to have the name 'Motel'.

Mother Carey's chickens. BIRDERS and 'tickers' will be aware that Mother Carey's chickens is the name given by sailors to the petrel, a common seabird. A number of authorities put forward the theory that the name derives from the Latin phrase *Mater Cara*, meaning 'dear mother' and referring to the Virgin Mary – though why petrels should be called this is not so easily explained. Other sources are reduced to vague speculation that it is an anglicised version of a foreign phrase – though which, remains a mystery.

Motown. During the late 60s and 70s Motown music was scarcely ever out of the pop music charts. Motown is a nickname for Detroit, one of the great car-manufacturing centres of the USA, being an abbreviation of motor town. The Motown record label, established by Berry Gordy, featured such stars as the Jackson Five, the Supremes and Stevie Wonder.

mountain – to make a mountain out of a molehill. To make a major issue out of something insignificant. The expression is recorded for the first time in Foxe's *Booke of Martyrs*, published in 1570. It is widely thought that the phrase was a variation on a much older one, 'to make an elephant out of a fly', (in Latin *arcem ex cloaca facere*). In French and German this original phrase is still used.

mouse. An input device connected by a lead to a microcomputer. It consists of a small box with buttons on the top. When the mouse is moved across the desk it causes a cursor to move on the computer screen. The name of the device derives from the supposed resemblance to the rodent of the same name.

mouse milking. An American business phrase applied to any difficult and time-consuming project that gives only a small return. The allusion is obvious.

mouseburger. A word apparently coined by Helen Gurley Brown, editor of American *Cosmopolitan*, to describe women who are

not prepossessing, not pretty, don't have a particularly high IQ, a decent education, good family background, or other noticeable assets,

but are still ambitious. Mouseburgers tend to adopt a policy of hard work and comformity and get to the top by climbing established ladders rung by rung.

mud – here's mud in your eye. Two theories have been put forward to explain the origins of this toast. According to one, it originated during the First World War when it was better to get mud in one's eye than something more deadly. Here's mud in your eye meant 'Here's hoping that mud is the only thing you get in your eye.' Theory number two speculates that the expression comes from the racecourse and that the person who proposes it is actually drinking a toast to himself and not the others present – for in this case here's mud in your eye refers to the way in which horses throw up clods of mud as they race. According to this theory the phrase means, 'Here's hoping my horse comes in first and throws mud up in the eyes of your horses.'

muesli-belt malnutrition. In 1986 this phenomenon was reported by Professor Vincent Marks of Surrey University. He found that some children brought up on a high-fibre, low-fat, low-sugar diet by health-conscious parents were seriously undernourished. It was suggested that it took these children so long to chew their way through a few mouthfuls of muesli, raw vegetables or wholemeal bread that they simply weren't eating enough to sustain their growth and energy levels. The news upset the BRANWAGON for diet-conscious parents, while those whose children were brought up on chips and chocolate rejoiced.

mufti. To wear mufti means to wear civilian clothes rather than a uniform. A mufti is a doctor in Muslim law and it has been speculated that on some occasion an English officer stationed abroad donned the robes of a mufti – for what purpose no one can say, but perhaps to pass unnoticed among civilians. From that time onwards, it is suggested, mufti was used to describe a military officer in plain clothes.

mugging. Robbery with violence, usually in a public thoroughfare. Mugging originated as a 19th-century criminal slang term in Britain. The expression had a revival in the USA in the 1960s, which spread to Britain *c*.1970.

mugwump. An Americanism based on the Algonquin Indian word for 'chief' and used to mean a boss or leader. In modern use it is also applied to those members of a political party who cannot be relied upon one hundred per cent to follow the party line.

multiunit organisation is what was once known as a chain store. This latter expression had, according to one business expert, unfortunate echoes of 'chainsaw', 'chain letter' and 'chain gang'. Leaving aside the issue of whether or not this is true, there's no doubt that 'chain store' trips off the tongue rather more easily than multiunit organisation. In fact a cynical observer might suspect that there will still be chain stores around long after multiunit organisations have been forgotten.

mumbo jumbo. Meaningless incantation or ritual; an object of superstitious awe or reverence. Mumbo jumbo derives from the African language of Mandingo. Mungo Park, the explorer of the Niger, describers it in his *Travels in the Interior of Africa* (1795–7). It was a fictitious spirit invoked by the men of a village to keep their women in subjection. Whenever a woman became quarrelsome or unruly, the husband or one of his friends would come to the village at nightfall in the guise of mumbo jumbo, making hideous noises. To the accompaniment of ritual songs and dances, the erring woman would be stripped naked, tied to a post and whipped by the 'spirit' before the assembled villagers. *See also* HOCUS POCUS.

mummerset. The name given to fake west-country accents adopted by actors when they play rural peasants. The word is an amalgamation of Somerset and 'mummer', a contemptuous name for an actor. 'Mummer' comes from the time when groups of country people toured their local area each Christmas 'mumming',

i.e. putting on a short play in each house they stopped at, in dumb-show.

mum's the word. This phrase, used to caution people to say nothing, derives from a line in Shakespeare's *King Henry VI Part II*:

Seal up your lips, and give no words but – mum.

The allusion is to the inarticulate sound 'Mmmmm' which is all one can manage (unless one is a ventriloquist!) with tightly-closed lips.

municipal cleansing operative. *See* FLIGHT ATTENDANT.

Muppie. A middle-aged urban professional – what a YUPPIE becomes as he grows older.

murphia. *See* MAFIA.

Murphy's Law (sometimes known as Sod's Law) in its briefest form states: 'If anything can go wrong, it will'. According to the *Concise Oxford Dictionary of Proverbs*, it was the invention of one George Nichols, who worked for Northrop, the Californian aviation company, and who in 1949 developed the idea, based on a remark by a colleague, a Captain E. Murphy of the Wright Field-Aircraft Laboratory. Murphy's Law was, however, expounded much earlier, in a slightly different form, by Benjamin Disraeli (1804–81) when he wrote:

What we anticipate seldom occurs, what we least expect generally happens.

Murphy's Law has given rise to several variations. According to some, there are in fact three laws: (1) Nothing is as easy as it looks. (2) Everything will take longer than you think. (3) If anything can go wrong, it will.

museum. The first place to go on record as a museum was the university founded at Alexandria, Egypt, by Ptolemy around the year 300 BC. This university was a 'temple of the muses', for that indeed is the literal translation of the word museum.

mustard, to cut the. Someone who can cut the mustard is capable of succeeding at whatever task or job he has been set. This phrase is American in origin and derives from the time when 'mustard' was slang for 'the real thing' or 'the genuine article'. Quite how the expression developed from these roots remains a mystery.

Mutt and Jeff. Two friends or a couple who are described as looking like Mutt and Jeff look about as dissimilar to each other as it is possible to be. This American expression originated with the 'Mutt and Jeff' comic strip drawn by Bud Fisher in the early years of this century. In it Mutt was a tall, lanky, chinless character and his great friend Jeff was small and round.

muzak. Background music played in shops, restaurants and public places with the aim of making people feel more relaxed and at ease. It arouses the wrath of music-lovers, who object to the way that perfectly good tunes are emasculated and rearranged for soaring strings and bland electronic effects. *See also* ELEVATOR MUSIC.

N

nabob. Originally, in the 18th century, a man who had made a fortune in India; more generally, any wealthy and powerful person. The term is a corruption of the Hindi word *nawab*, meaning in general a rich man, and in particular the governor or ruler of a province under the Mogul empire.

Nadsat. Anthony Burgess' novel *A Clockwork Orange* was published in 1962, and in 1972 Stanley Kubrick made it into a film which aroused a great deal of controversy. The story concerns Alex, a teenage hoodlum, in the 'not-too-distant future', who is jailed and subjected to an experimental form of mind control known as 'Lodovico's Technique'. Most of the story is told in a synthetic teenage argot called Nadsat, described in the book as

Odd bits of rhyming slang . . . A bit of gipsy talk, too. But most of the roots are Slav.

The name Nadsat is derived from the Russian *pyatnadsat*, meaning 'fifteen'. Here is an example:

Our pockets were full of deng, so there was no real need from the point of view of crasting any more pretty polly to tolchock some old veck in an alley and viddy him swim in his blood . . . nor to do the ultra-violent on some shivering starry grey-haired ptitsa in a shop and go smecking off with the till's guts.

naff and **naff off.** Naff was described in the *Daily Express* of 17 September 1982 as the 'newest four-letter word'. As an adjective it may be used to refer to something considered wrong, worthless, flashy, shoddy or unfashionable. The expression naff off is simply a euphemism for the phrase 'Fuck off'. It sprang into prominence in April 1982 when it was widely reported that Princess Anne had used this expression to a group of press photographers. But before that Ronnie Barker had popularised it in the TV series *Porridge*, which was scripted by Dick Clement and Ian La Frenais, and first shown in 1974. These writers had picked up the phrase from Keith Waterhouse's novel *Billy Liar* (published in 1959) which they had adapted for the stage. Keith Waterhouse in turn remembered it from his RAF service *c*.1950. It seems almost certain that naff and naff off originated as armed forces slang and derive from the word NAAFI (the acronym for the Navy, Army and Air Force Institutes) which has provided shop and canteen facilities for servicemen since 1921 and has often been the target of derogatory remarks by servicemen.

nail, to pay on the. To pay promptly. In some medieval markets the 'nail' was a flat-topped waist-high pillar. Bargains struck in the market were concluded by payment in cash 'on the nail'. Such a 'nail' can still be seen today outside the Corn Exchange at Bristol.

nail one's colours to the mast, to. To fight to the bitter end. In a naval battle an intention to surrender was indicated by hauling down one's colours – that is, one's flag. Thus, nailing one's colours to the mast, literally or figuratively, means that one will fight on with no possibility of surrender.

nail to the counter. *See under* CASH ON THE NAIL.

naked truth. An old fable tells of how Truth and Falsehood went to bathe together in a river. Falsehood climbed out of the water first and put on Truth's garments. Rather than put on Falsehood's clothing, Truth preferred to remain naked. Whether this tale is the origin of the phrase the naked truth, or whether it was devised to explain the expression, is not entirely clear. What *is* clear is the moral of the story; falsehood comes in many guises but truth never pretends to be other than what it is.

namby-pamby. A word coined for Ambrose Philips, a minor 18th-century poet who specialised in pretty but wimpish pastoral verse. After a particularly wet poem penned for the children of Lord Carteret, one of his critics, a writer named Henry Carey, invented the nickname Namby-Pamby for him. The name stuck and was immediately adopted by other of Philips' critics. Today we still use the term to describe someone or something that is weak, watery or terribly sentimental.

name – his name is mud. This phrase is named for Dr Samuel Mudd, an unfortunate American doctor who spent years in jail for a crime he didn't commit. Mudd was at home one night when a man arrived with a broken leg and requested treatment. Mudd complied, not realising that his patient was John Wilkes Booth, the man who had earlier that evening assassinated President Lincoln at the theatre. Booth had broken his leg as he fled the scene of the crime but had escaped the police nonetheless. When, next day, Mudd and his wife heard the news of the president's murder they contacted the authorities and told them about their strange visitor. The authorities promptly brought charges of conspiracy against Mudd and he was sentenced to life imprisonment. Public feeling against the assassination was running so high that poor Dr Mudd's name came to be used as a kind of swear-word; the phrase 'his name is mud' came into use to describe someone who is despised because of his actions. That's one story, anyway. Another traces the first uses of 'his name is mud' back to the early 1800s, long before Lincoln's assassination, and suggests that 'mud' was a dialect word meaning 'fool'. It also seems feasible that 'mud' was chosen because it is mucky, messy, generally despised stuff. What better way of defaming the reputation of someone who is heartily disliked than by comparing them with mud?

napalm. Strictly speaking, a thickening agent consisting of aluminium naphthenate (hence the derivation of the name) and the fatty acids of coconut oil. But the name is more generally used of the mixture of this thickening agent with petrol, forming a gel which is used in flame-throwers and incendiary bombs. Napalm was made familiar to millions world-wide by TV reports from the US-Vietnam war in the late 1960s, though in fact the material dates from the 1940s.

Naples – see Naples and die. There is much dispute over this phrase. Various sources suggest that the expression derives from a mistranslation of *vedi Napoli e poi Mori*, (see Naples and then Mori), Mori being confused with *morire*, meaning 'die'.

Others credit the same confusion but say that it was a deliberate pun. It has also been suggested that the phrase implies that there is nothing more beautiful than Naples to be seen on earth; having seen it, it only remains to die. Another authority wonders whether it has anything to do with the nearby volcano Vesuvius, which occasionally erupts spectacularly and might therefore be considered a risk. And yet another asserts that in the 18th century Naples was a synonym for syphilis, a disease picked up by many a young aristocrat when he made the Grand Tour of Europe. He would almost inevitably stop off at Naples, and having contracted syphilis he would be likely to die from it.

napoo. Nothing; no more; good for nothing; dead. Soldiers' slang from World War I, napoo is a mangled form of the French phrase *il n'y en a plus* – 'there is no more'. It occurs in a popular song of the period:

'Bonsoir, old thing, cheerio, chin-chin, / Napoo, toodle-oo, goodby-ee.'

Narcissus. In Greek myth Narcissus was a good-looking youth who refused the advances of the nymph Echo. Her revenge was to wish that he would fall in love with himself and suffer in the same way as she did. When one day he caught sight of his own reflection in a pool he was so attracted by it that he drowned as he leant over the water, studying his own face. From this fable we get the word 'narcissist' to describe a person who is in love with themselves. We also get the pretty spring flower known as the narcissus, which was said to have been fashioned by the gods after the death of the original Narcissus.

nark. A police informer, sometimes known as a copper's nark. Nark derives from the Romany word *nak* meaning 'nose', probably refers to the way in which the nark pokes his nose into others' business.

narrowcasting. Planning a television programme for a small specialised audience rather than for mass consumption. This American TV jargon is an obvious back-formation from 'broadcasting'.

nasty. Though the history of 'nasty' has not been conclusively traced, it is widely believed that it was originally 'nesty' and referred to the unpleasant way in which birds fouled their own nests. This word was applied to anything that was disgusting or unpleasantly dirty. At some time in the 1400s 'nesty' became 'nasty'. In 1984–5 a new word, **denastify**, emerged. It meant to make something less unpleasant and was applied in particular to the crackdown on English soccer hooligans which had denastified football crowds. Hot on its heels in 1986 came 'nastify', meaning to make something *more* unpleasant. This too was applied to the phenomenon of football violence. Whether these two words are permanent additions to the English language remains to be seen.

nation of shopkeepers. A phrase attributed to Napoleon Bonaparte to describe England: '*L'Angleterre est une nation de boutiquiers*'. The phrase had, however, been used earlier by Adam Smith (1723–90) in his *Wealth Of Nations* (1776):

To found a great empire for the sole purpose of raising up a people of customers, may at first sight appear a project fit only for a nation of shopkeepers. It is, however, a project altogether unfit for a nation of shopkeepers; but extremely fit for a nation that is governed by shopkeepers.

naughty. Today we use naughty to describe a badly behaved child, but it once meant something far stronger than that. It derives from the Anglo-Saxon phrase *na whit*, meaning 'nothing'; from the same origin we still have the word 'nowt', meaning 'nothing'. Naughty was therefore first used to describe someone who was totally worthless, beneath contempt. From the Middle Ages to the time of Shakespeare it meant 'evil', which is why in *The Merchant of Venice* Portia talks about 'a good deed in a naughty world.' Since that time naughty has been steadily drained of its strength so that now it is a word applied only to mischievous children.

navvy. In the 18th century 'canal mania' overtook Britain and thousands of labourers were employed in the excavations. The canals were known as 'navigations' and the men who worked on them became known as navvies. Though other means of transport have replaced the canals, we still remember the remarkable work carried out by such men in the phrase 'to work like a navvy', meaning to do hard, heavy and unpleasant work.

Nazi. The name given to the German party of which Adolf Hitler became leader. It is a shortened form of *National sozialist*.

Neanderthal. A palaeolithic species of human inhabiting Europe before the last Ice Age, *c*.40,000 BC. Also used figuratively, in political and social contexts, as a term of abuse for people, institutions, ideas, etc. thought to be hopelessly old-fashioned and out-of-date. Neanderthal is the name of a valley, between Dusseldorf and Elberfeld, where a skull of this species of prehistoric man was first discovered in 1856.

nebbish. A nobody, a nonentity; an ineffectual, luckless, hapless person; a WIMP. This word became naturalised American English *c*.1960. It is derived from the Yiddish *nebech*, which is used as an interjection and means 'poor thing'. It is Slav in origin, and is allied to the Polish

nieboze meaning 'poor creature' and the Czech 'neboh' meaning 'wretched'.

neck – to stick one's neck out. To take a risk or to expose oneself to danger unnecessarily. One theory is that the phrase alludes to the way in which chickens sometimes stretch out their necks on the chopping block, assisting their executioner to cut off their heads.

necklace killing. A method of LYNCHING victims peculiar to the black townships of South Africa. The expression gets its name from the way in which people who are thought to have betrayed the black cause have a rubber tyre (sometimes filled with petrol) placed round their necks like a necklace and set alight. Mrs Winnie Mandela, the now discredited leader of the black movement in Soweto, is reported to have said in May 1986, 'With our matches and our necklaces we will liberate this country.'

need-to-know. Governments and large organisations may decide to use a need-to-know system of disseminating information about their activities, plans and so on. This concept has as its basis the idea that only those who need to know a specific item of information to perform their job properly are given that information. In this way government and organisations can argue that the public or the media do not need to know information about their activities and that therefore they are not obliged to supply it.

Needle Park. Any public place in which addicts gather for the purpose of buying drugs from pushers and injecting the drugs they purchase.

Neighbourhood Watch schemes are either a crime-busting boon or a charter for NOSY PARKERS, depending on one's experience of them. They are schemes by which the residents of an area form a voluntary group which, in co-operation with the police, attempts to prevent crime by keeping a watchful eye on the district. Members of the scheme keep a look out for suspicious strangers, check each others' property when someone goes away and generally try to be alert to any potentially criminal activity. In some cases these measures have resulted in a marked drop in the crime rate. In others, however, it has simply given nosy people the licence to snoop on their neighbours.

nepotism. Someone who takes advantage of their authority to install members of their family in powerful positions, regardless of whether those family members are suited for the job, may be accused of nepotism. This kind of corruption has probably been going on since the beginning of civilisation, but the ruler whose actions gave us the word to describe it was the 15th-century Pope Alexander VI. He packed the highest Church offices with his relatives, but the appointment that really caused criticism was when he made his young nephew Giovanni a cardinal. In Latin the word for 'nephew' is *nepos*; so it was that the word nepotism was coined. It means not merely to place a nephew but any close relative in an unmerited position.

nerd. 1970s American slang, originating among surfers and hot-rodders, and meaning a tedious, contemptible or conventional person, or someone who is not HIP. In other words, someone who would have been described by an earlier generation as a 'square'.

nest-egg. An amount of money put away in reserve. Probably for as long as men have kept poultry it has been customary to place an egg in a hen's nest to encourage her to add to it by laying her own eggs there. Hence nest-egg came to mean a small amount of money that one sets aside

with the idea of inducing oneself to increase the amount.

net player. In the movie world, a person who gets a percentage of the receipts of a film once all the costs have been deducted, i.e. a percentage of the final profits. A net player is not, therefore, a major force in the deal – unlike the 'gross player', a person (perhaps the film's BANK-ABLE star) who is contracted to receive a percentage of the gross profit from the film. The gross player's percentage is deducted from box-office takings *before* the expenses have been accounted for, and therefore he or she has a significant stake of the profits. From this origin the phrases 'net' and 'gross' player have moved into more general business use to describe individuals of minor or major significance in a deal.

networking. As a concept networking made its appearance in the 1970s; it is a means of climbing a career ladder by building up and using contacts to obtain information, jobs, advice, entrées and so on. In the USA and Britain attempts were made to establish networks of professional women who were all willing to provide support for their fellow networkers. Whether this has turned out to be the solution that was hoped at the time is a debatable point. Men, of course, already have their own networking channels through which they obtain news, jobs, etc. including the OLD BOY SYSTEM, gentlemen's clubs, the Masons, Rotary Clubs and other male-dominated organisations where professional men regularly gather and discuss business. Any man who joins one of these organisations finds himself automatically plugged into the informal male network.

never-never. A pay-by-instalments or hire purchase agreement. It gets its name because it feels as if one has to go on paying for an item for ever, perhaps with the suspicion that one will never own it.

never-never land. Peter Pan is probably the most famous inhabitant of never-never land, the imaginary land where children never grow up. It was the idea of J. M. Barrie, Peter Pan's creator. Today we might describe someone who lives in a dream world of their own or who has unrealistic expectations as 'living in never-never land'. It is also Australian slang for a deserted, remote area. It was in fact once applied to most of Australia and is now sometimes used in reference to central Australia or the western outback. It has been speculated that these areas got the name because people going out there said they were never, never returning; or perhaps because their more cautious friends warned them that they would never, never come back.

New Age. The term applied to the new spirituality and philosophies of the 1980s, which embrace Eastern religion, mysticism, personal growth therapies, alternative medicine etc. Many leading New Agers are middle-aged hippies looking for a modern equivalent of the counter-culture of the 1960s. New Age music, often performed by musicians who were famous in the 60s, is sophisticated and non pop-orientated, intended to enhance mood and meditation.

New Brutalism. An architectural school of thought in the 1950s. Briefly, the New Brutalists' theory was that modern materials such as concrete and glass should be used in modern ways. Their aim was to establish an 'honest' relationship between the fabric of the building and its design. In practice New Brutalism turned out to be the vast concrete towers and blocks that mushroomed in the 1960s, often to the distress of the people who were forced to live in them – and also to Prince Charles,

who has described this kind of architecture as being like 'monstrous carbuncles'. Twenty years after they were built many New Brutalist buildings are being torn down and replaced by others that take account of human needs rather than aesthetic theory.

New Man. Said by some to have been dreamed up by the advertising industry, and conspicuous by his absence in public, the New Man is a gentle, caring, anti-SEXIST creature, in touch with his feelings, able to express his emotions and free of the usual MACHO values. New Men are willing to stay at home and look after their children, do the washing and shopping and generally break out of stereotyped male roles. *See also* NEW WOMAN.

new wave. A literal translation of the French *nouvelle vague*, used to refer to any new movement or trend – originally used to refer to one in film-making in France in the late 1950s.

New Woman. The phrase New Woman first appeared in the nineteenth century where it was applied to the new breed of emancipated women who espoused female independence, precursors of the modern women's liberation movement. Today it is applied to what is called the 'post-feminist' woman. In theory a New Woman is a woman who enjoys and exploits the benefits brought about by the women's movement but is also comfortable with her own femininity. She, according to the new magazines aimed at her, may wear a tailored suit in the boardroom but dons stockings and suspenders in the bedroom. Unlike the bra-burning, man-hating separatists of the 60s and 70s, the 80s New Woman participates in the male-dominated 'system' and seeks to change it from within; she diets and exercises because she takes care of her body for herself, not for her man; she cooks, sews, knits and has babies when she wants to and because she enjoys doing it, not out of duty; she expects her partner to shoulder his share of the domestic work and also expects him to be free of traditional MACHO attitudes and prejudices. Cynics, observing that the New Woman's interests are pretty much the same as the 'old woman's' – fashion, romance, diet, exercise, children, cookery – have suggested that the New Woman is just a figment of the advertising industry's imagination. *See also* NEW MAN.

news. Several sources give credence to the theory that the word 'news' was devised from the initial letters of the four points of the compass; information came streaming in, we're told, from North, East, West, South and thus news was coined. Other sources are more cynical and suggest that it is a much older word derived from the Old English *newes*, meaning 'new', which was applied to new information. Though this has not been proved beyond all doubt, it is certainly true that the word news was in existence long before the first newspaper was printed.

newspeak. The name of the artificial language used for official communications in George Orwell's novel *Nineteen Eighty-Four* (1949), a language 'designed to diminish the range of thought'. Generally used of any official language or propaganda that is used to obscure the truth and to impose an official point of view. *See also* GOBBLEDYGOOK.

newzak is to news what MUZAK is to music. That, at least, was the theory behind this new word, coined in Britain in 1986 to describe the media's coverage of the American *Challenger* disaster in which seven astronauts were killed. The first time the film of the spacecraft exploding was shown it had a great impact. This impact remained for the second and third showings but after being played over and over again it became, as one commentator put it, 'a puff of pretty white smoke.' Like muzak, newzak is a debased form of the real thing; the viewer becomes accustomed by dint of constant repetition, so that the events shown lose their power to shock and become merely background decoration.

nice. In the six hundred years or so since it first came into use 'nice' has changed its meaning completely. It started out as the Latin word *nescius*, meaning ignorant or unknowing. It retained this meaning when it came into use in the English language in the 14th century and for a couple of hundred years it described something silly or foolish, gradually also coming to mean wanton and lascivious. By the end of the 15th century, however, it had come to be applied to those who dressed too ostentatiously, and in fairly rapid succession it came to have the meanings 'strange', 'lazy', 'delicate', 'over-sumptuous' and 'accurate', (today we still use the phrase 'a nice distinction', meaning a very fine, accurate distinction). Around the 1800s nice came to mean something pleasant in much the way that it is used today. However, it is such an over-used word that now many people employ it with conscious irony, describing as nice something that is prettily bland but not very impressive. Who knows – nice may soon have evolved a new meaning altogether.

nice guys finish last. An American catchphrase coined in the 1940s and attributed to Brooklyn Dodgers team manager Leo Durocher, who described a rival manager as 'so nice his team will finish last for him'. Honed to 'nice guys finish last', the expression caught on among baseball fans and then the general public. Its meaning is obvious and cynical; people who play fair can't expect to win. Durocher would doubtless be surprised to know that in recent years feminists have found a new meaning for his saying. Nice guys finish last is now, among women at least, a term of approval describing a man who allows his partner to reach a sexual climax before he does so himself.

nick – to be in the nick of time. Before the advent of clocks, time was recorded by means of a series of nicks in a piece of wood. From this we get the phrase to be in the nick of time, meaning just in time, not a moment too soon. *See also* TALLY.

nickname. This word, meaning a familiar or slang name, was originally *ekename*, an Old English word meaning 'an also-name' – an extra name. In the five hundred or so years that have passed since it was first used, *ekename* has evolved into the modern nickname.

nicotine. The French diplomat Jean Nicot is the man responsible for giving us the word nicotine. Nicot was introduced to tobacco when he went as ambassador to Portugal in 1560. When he returned to Paris he took with him a number of tobacco plants which were later named Nicotiana in his honour. At around the time he was inspiring a fashion for tobacco in France, Sir Walter Raleigh was introducing it in England.

nifty. A nifty little word to describe something that is clever, ingenious or smart – a nifty little gadget or nifty little outfit. The only explanation that has been offered for it is that it is an Americanism derived from the word 'magnificent'.

nightmare. During the Dark Ages (and since that time, too) people were obsessed with fears of demons and witches. One of the most feared was the incubus, a male demon who appeared at night and had intercourse with women while they slept. When a woman woke terrified, sweating and with a sensation of having been suffocated or crushed in her sleep, she knew that she had been visited by an incubus. Men were preyed on in the same way by a female demon known as a succubus. The word nightmare is commonly supposed to have something to do with horses but in fact, the 'mare' of nightmare is the Latin word *mare*, meaning 'incubus'. Thus a nightmare was a night-time visit from an incubus.

-nik. The suffix -nik is Russian in origin and can be traced through Yiddish into the American language and from there into British English. Among -nik words that are familiar today are SPUTNIK, the first Russian space satellite, launched in 1957, BEATNIK, and refusenik, describing people who wish to emigrate from Russia but have been refused permission to leave. In the USA -nik became a gimmick in the 60s, with the result that psychoanalysts were called 'Freudniks', homosexual men became 'gayniks', peace campaigners were known as 'peaceniks' – and on, and on.

Nimby. An acronym for Not In My Back Yard. It was coined in Britain in 1986 to describe those people who support issues such as nuclear power or the building of new housing estates, but who strenuously object if they find a power station or building development planned near their own home. When it comes to such issues a Nimby might find himself in opposition to a Namby – who believes Not in Anyone's Back Yard.

nincompoop. This word has

flummoxed many authorities including the great Dr Johnson, who suggested that it is based on the phrase *non compos mentis*, meaning 'not in possession of the mind'. However, early versions of the word were spelled in a number of different ways (including *nickumpoo*) which suggest that it is probably just a nonsense word, an individual's personal invention which wriggled its way into the language.

nine days' wonder. Any fad, fashion or event that causes great excitement for a few days but is likely to have been forgotten within a fortnight. Various theories have been put forward to explain the expression. One identifies the Catholic devotion known as a *novena*, which lasts for nine days in succession, as the source. A *novena* may attract attention for the nine days it is observed, but after that a new one supersedes it and the old one is largely forgotten. Certainly Chaucer makes a reference to this in *Troilus and Criseyde*. Another theory has it that puppies and kittens were the original nine days' wonder because, having been born with their eyes closed, on the ninth day or thereabouts they suddenly opened them.

nineteenth hole. American golfers coined the phrase to describe the clubhouse, and more particularly the clubhouse bar. A standard golf course has eighteen holes and a player who has no luck at any of them may at least drown his sorrows at the nineteenth. The expression was first used in the 1920s and quickly caught on.

ninety days' wonder. A term sometimes applied to graduates of the ninety-day officer training courses offered at military colleages. The expression has been in use since the First World War and is a punning construction on the phrase NINE DAYS' WONDER.

ninny. An insulting term applied to someone who is habitually stupid. Its first recorded use was in 1592 and it has been suggested that it is derived from the word 'innocent'. But why should someone who is stupid be described as innocent? The question is probably explained by the fact that simpletons (people who would today be described as having 'learning difficulties') were often known as innocents because they were innocent of the ways of the world.

nip in the bud, to. A gardening term meaning to nip off excess flower or fruit buds at an early stage of development so that a plant or tree can concentrate its energy on forming a few, larger, flowers or fruits. From Elizabethan times the phrase has been used figuratively to describe the act of halting dubious plans or bad behaviour before they become full-grown problems.

nipper. London slang for a child, particularly a young boy. In the 19th century young boys were employed by costermongers to 'nip' around running errands, and so the name nipper came to be applied first to children employed in this work and later to any child.

Nissen hut. A semi-cylindrical corrugated-iron hut with a cement floor. Originally used during World War I, it is named after its inventor, Lt-Col. Peter Norman Nissen (1871–1930). *See also* QUONSET HUT.

nitpick. Someone described as a nitpicker is a pedant, a fusspot, one who is obsessed with DOTTING THE I'S AND CROSSING THE T'S. Nitpickers were, however, originally people whose nimble fingers and sharp eyes enabled them to pick the lice from others' hair. In the 19th century and probably long before that time, too, anyone who habitually combed through another's work looking for tiny mistakes became known for their nitpicking.

nitty-gritty. The realities or basic facts of a problem or situation. This expression originated as Black American slang in the early 1960s. According to the *Supplement to the Oxford English Dictionary* the etymology is unknown, but almost certainly it derives from the idea of nits (the eggs of lice infesting the hair and scalp) and 'grits' (a slang term for granules of excrement adhering to the hairs of the anus), both being basic and unpleasant facts of life for some people living in deprived circumstances.

nitwit. Two theories have been ventured to explain the origins of this word, describing someone without much sense. The first suggests that it comes from the Dutch phrase *Ik niet wiet*, meaning 'I don't know', which is just the kind of response one might anticipate from a nitwit. The second suggests that it is a compound of the German *nicht*, meaning 'not', and the English word 'wit', the two together meaning 'no wits'.

nix. This American word means to cancel, forbid or refuse, but is more frequently used as an interjection, with the sense of 'no!' or 'stop it!'. Strangely, unlike many other American colloquialisms, it has never caught on in Britain. It derives from the German *nichts*, meaning 'nothing'.

no can do. I am unable or unwilling to do that. This phrase, originally Pidgin English, was adapted and spread by seamen, and was popularised in the 1940s as the title of a song.

no great shakes. Someone who is described as no great shakes is nothing extraordinary or special. This expression is widely believed to derive from the gambling table where dice were thrown. A mediocre gambler – one who inevitably threw low numbers when it was his turn with the dice – would be described as no great shakes. An alternative suggestion, offered in 1867 by Admiral Smyth in the *Sailor's Word Book*, is that the staves of a wooden cask were known as shakes. When the cask was dismantled the 'shakes' were worth very little and thus no great shakes was used to describe people and things that were of little value.

no holds barred. To go at something no holds barred means to approach it without inhibitions or restrictions. The phrase comes originally from the boxing or fighting ring, where a no holds barred fight was one in which all kinds of tactics, from hair-pulling to kicking, were allowed. A no holds barred contest, whether it involves real or metaphorical fisticuffs, is therefore one in which there are no rules and the dirtiest, toughest fighter wins.

No Man's Land. We use this phrase to describe a deserted area of wasteland or a desolate, abandoned place. The phrase was used from around the 14th century to describe the area of land outside the city walls of London where criminals were taken to be hung or suffer other more alarming fates. The sight of their gibbets and rotting carcasses deterred anyone from claiming the land for themselves and thus it became known as No Man's Land. The phrase was later applied to any similar desolate spot but had particular force during the First World War, when it described the stretch of land between the trenches of opposing forces. Churned up by mortar fire, littered with dead bodies and barbed wire, it was a bleak, nightmarish place. Today No Man's Land is also applied to areas of cities blighted by urban decay; places that were once thriving and bustling and are now abandoned and left to waste.

no-win situation. A situation in which whatever you do or whatever happens there is no way for you to gain anything or avoid loss. The phrase comes from the theory of war-gaming and dates from the early 1960s. *See also* MEXICAN STAND-OFF.

nob. When lists of Oxford and Cambridge students were drawn up the letters NOB, short for 'nobility', were placed after the names of the more aristocratic and high-born undergraduates. From this practice we get the word nob, in general use these days to refer to the upper classes and not simply to the nobility.

noblesse oblige is French for 'nobility is obliged'. It is an adage, sometimes a motto, meaning that people of a high social status have a responsibility to behave in a generous and noble fashion to others worse off than themselves. In these days of free enterprise and every man out for himself it seems a rather quaint concept.

nom de guerre. An assumed name. Literally 'a name of war', this phrase derives from the once customary practice of all French soldiers adopting an assumed name when they entered military service.

nom de plume. A 'pen-name' – that is, an assumed name used by a writer who does not wish to publish under his own name. Whoever coined this phrase probably had the parallel with NOM DE GUERRE in mind.

non-paper. A relatively new adjective to describe a transaction carried out on screen by a computer. In the past transactions involved paperwork and processing but today, thanks to modern technology, it can all be done automatically.

Non-U. *See* U AND NON-U.

nookie. Sexual intercourse; a woman, regarded as a sexual object. Nookie was established as American slang in the 1920s, but was not widely used in Britain until the 1970s. In Britain it is regarded, oddly, as an inoffensive, even affectionate, term. The derivation is from 'nook' used as a euphemism for the vagina.

nose, it's no skin off my. Someone who habitually sticks their nose into another's business may find sooner or later that their interference gets them into trouble. Maybe the expression was coined when a NOSY PARKER was punched in the nose by someone they annoyed with their snooping. Or perhaps they got their nose stuck in a keyhole through which they were peeping. Either way, a nosy person might sooner or later expect to graze their nose. From this idea we get the phrase 'It's no skin off my nose', meaning 'It's nothing to do with me' or 'It's not my concern at all' – i.e. 'I'm not going to go grazing my nose over this.'

nose, on the. On the nose means 'exactly on time'. We use it in expressions such as 'cash on the nose', describing a prompt payment in cash. The phrase originated in American television studios where the producer would signal to the presenters that the show was running on time by putting his finger to his nose.

nose – to cut off one's nose to spite one's face. The derivation has yet to be traced, but the meaning is clear – the action of someone whose anger results only in injury to himself. *See also* TO SCORE AN OWN GOAL and TO SHOOT ONESELF IN THE FOOT *under* FOOT.

nose, to follow one's. To go straight ahead, taking an undeviating course, or to follow one's instincts. The first meaning is based on the idea that the nose precedes the rest of the body;

one has only to point one's nose in the right direction and the rest of one's body will follow. The expression's alternative nuance is derived from the fact that dogs follow their noses when tracking a scent. A person may likewise track a scent using their nose ('How did you find the kitchen?' 'I just followed my nose') or, by association, following their other senses and instincts.

nose – to have a nose that glows in the dark. *See under* BRAHMS AND LISZT.

nose – to have a nose to light candles at. *See under* BRAHMS AND LISZT.

nose – to keep one's nose to the grindstone. Chisels, scythes and other tools that need to be sharp to work efficiently have to be regularly whetted on a grindstone. The painful-sounding phrase 'to keep one's nose to the grindstone', meaning to keep working hard, employs an analogy between the nose and one of these instruments. The implication is that like a chisel or a scythe one's nose has to be kept sharp on the grindstone.

nose, to lead by the. No one knows when man first discovered that by putting a ring through an animal's nose he could lead and dominate it, but this method of controlling a creature is the origin of the phrase to lead by the nose. Even huge and dangerous beasts such as bears and bulls can be disciplined by this means. Today we use the phrase figuratively to describe someone who holds another in submission or under domination. Someone who is led by the nose obediently and unquestioningly does what they are told without thinking for themselves.

nose, to look down one's. When someone holds their chin in the air and half-closes their eyes in an expression of disdain and disapproval, they appear to be looking down their nose. For this reason we use the phrase to describe someone who is arrogant, condescending or disapproving – regardless of whether they actually make the necessary facial gesture or not.

nose, to pay through the. When someone is forced to pay an exorbitant price for something it's often said that they had to pay through the nose. It has been suggested that this expression is an elaborate play on words based on the fact that in the 17th century money was known as 'rhino'. The Greek word for 'nose' was *rhinos*. Someone who was forced to pay out a lot of money was described at the time as being bled – like a nose. From this group of vague associations came the idea of paying through the nose. Another source suggests that the phrase is based on memories of a tax levied on the Irish by the Danes in the 9th century. Those who did not pay it had their noses slit – they might be said to have opted to pay through the nose.

nosy parker. The original Nosy Parker was a 16th-century Archbishop of Canterbury – Dr Matthew Parker, who became Archbishop in 1559. He was a fanatically religious Protestant who made a habit of investigating all areas of the Church's business and weeding out corruption and mismanagement. Though in many ways he was a good man whose reforms were well overdue, his long nose and his habit of prying into other people's affairs earned him the derogatory nickname Nosy Parker. This, anyway, is the most popular explanation. Many sources put forward this as their prime theory and then point out the less entertaining fact that for centuries the word nose has meant an informer and 'pauk' is a dialect word describing someone who is inquisitive. It is quite possible that nosy parker started life as nosy pauker. A third theory is advanced by an American source which identifies Richard Parker, leader of a rebellion known as the Sheerness Mutiny in 1797, as the source of the phrase. He was eventually hanged for prying into military affairs. Whatever the derivation, we still use the phrase today to describe someone who is forever sticking their nose into other people's business.

nosh. This Yiddish word, from the German *naschen*, meaning 'to nibble or eat on the sly', may be used as noun or verb, but its precise meaning differs on opposite sides of the Atlantic. In Britain it is generally used simply to mean 'food' or 'to eat'. In the USA, however, it is generally used more precisely to mean 'a snack or titbit eaten between meals' or 'to nibble such a snack or titbit'.

not – it's not what it's cracked up to be. To crack has as one of its many meanings the sense of boasting, story-telling, bragging. Something that is cracked up is boasted about and made to sound much better than it really is. Advertising is a prime example of an industry geared to cracking things up. When the disappointed consumer discovers that the new miracle soap-powder or orange juice falls short of the glowing descriptions of the adverts, they may express their disappointment with the phrase 'It's not what it's cracked up to be.'

not cricket. *See under* DIRTY POOL.

not to be sneezed at. No one is entirely certain why something impressive is described as not to be sneezed at. We know that at the beginning of the 19th century an associated expression 'to sneeze at' meant to find something dull or pedestrian, but why this was so remains something of a mystery. Perhaps when they went to a play or

social gathering they found boring, snuff-takers would pass the time by making themselves sneeze – sneezing being thought to be an exhilarating, exciting experience (it is not for nothing that women, asked to describe the sensations of an orgasm, often compare it to a big sneeze!). Or it may be that one way of showing contempt for something or someone was to sneeze all over them. Whatever the origin of to sneeze at, its opposite phrase came into use and remains so today.

not tonight, Josephine. A catch-phrase since the late 19th century, used by, or referring to, a man declining sexual intercourse with a female partner. The phrase is attributed to Napoleon Bonaparte in reference to the Empress Josephine, but there is no authority for this attribution.

not worth a dam(n). Worthless. There are two schools of thought as to the derivation of this expression – sometimes elaborated to 'not worth a tinker's dam(n)'. Hence the variation in spelling between 'dam' and 'damn'. One theory is that a 'dam' was a temporary plug of clay used by a tinker to block a hole in a pot or pan that he was mending. Once the solder had been poured into the hole and had set, the 'dam' had no further use and was discarded. The other theory is that it merely refers to the fact that tinkers were often drunken blackguards, renowned for their blasphemy. A tinker's 'damn' would be so common as to be worthless.

not worth a rap. Worthless. A 'rap' was a counterfeit halfpenny, commonly found in Ireland in the 18th century.

notting. A useful new word, coined in 1986 by Dr Tony Lake to describe the practice of not doing something, even though one knows it needs to be done. Notting describes the behaviour of someone who, for example, knows they should spend their morning sorting out a problem in the office but instead decides that this is the perfect opportunity for turning out their desk drawers.

nous. Liverpudlians and others who use the word 'nous' to describe common sense or intelligence may be surprised to learn that the word is a Greek one, meaning exactly the same as its modern usage.

nudge nudge, wink wink. This phrase was most famously used in a sketch included in the cult television comedy series *Monty Python's Flying Circus*. One of the characters in the scene followed everything that was said with the words 'nudge nudge, wink wink', indicating that there was something sexually suggestive in what had just been expressed – and regardless of whether it was merited or not. Nudge nudge, wink wink (which, if memory serves, went on 'Say no more, squire, say no more . . .') caught on immediately and became, for a short while at least, a widely used catchphrase. It is still used as a kind of verbal finger-pointing to indicate sexual innuendo: for example, 'When the car broke down they had to spend the night in a hotel you know, nudge nudge, wink wink . . .'

number cruncher. The term is used to describe a person who is skilled at manipulating numbers. The expression can be used admiringly of someone who is truly 'creative' with numbers (*see* CREATIVE ACCOUNTING) or disparagingly of an individual who, though good at working out the figures, has no idea what to do with the results.

number-fudging describes the manipulation of figures to give a required result. Fudging in this sense may refer to the soft, sticky sweet; when added to an unacceptable set of figures, fudge softens and sweetens them, making them easier to digest. Alternatively it may derive from the old word fadge, meaning to patch something up, make it temporarily acceptable.

numerati. Coined along the lines of 'literati' and GLITTERATI, numerati are financial whizz-kids, wheeler-dealers whose success rises and falls on their ability to interpret statistics and predict future financial trends.

nuts in May. This phrase, from a children's rhyme, may appear to be nonsense when one considers that Autumn, not May, is the time when nuts are available to be gathered. The phrase, however, is a corruption of 'knots of May', referring to the old May-Day custom of gathering knots or posies of flowers, including may or hawthorn blossom.

O

O.K. All correct; all right. There have been numerous conflicting attempts to explain the derivation of this common American expression which is now understood and used all over the world. The most widely accepted explanation until quite recently used to be that it originated in 1840 as an abbreviation of, and was used as a slogan by, the Old Kinderhook Club, a political organisation supporting the presidential candidate Martin Van Buren who was born in Old Kinderhook in New York State. However, it is now known there are at least five instances of O.K. being used in American newspapers a year earlier in 1839 with the implied or stated meaning of 'orl korrect' – a humorous mis-spelling of 'all correct'. This is almost certainly the true derivation – and it is likely that Van Buren's supporters made use of an expression that was already popular. But no-one has yet been able to explain why this mis-spelling of 'all correct' was used in the first place or why it was so popular. Other attempted explanations of the derivation can be discounted. President Woodrow Wilson insisted that it was a Choctaw Indian word that should properly be spelled 'okeh'. The linguist Charles Berlitz believed that it came from Aux Cayes, the name of a port in Haiti, of high repute among sailors for the quality of its rum, and hence used as a general expression of approval. Others have claimed that it derives from a word meaning 'good' in one of a number of West African languages spoken by slaves transported to America or that it comes from the Greek words *ola kala*, meaning 'all is good'.

O.T.T. *See* OVER THE TOP.

oar – to put one's oar in. This phrase was originally 'to put an oar into someone else's boat', which was in use in the 16th century. Though the origin of the expression has not been traced, both original and modern versions share the same meaning, i.e. to meddle in someone else's affairs.

oater. American slang for a 'horse opera' – a Western. It refers to the oats fed to the horses required for such movies.

oats, to sow one's wild. There is some disagreement about the origin of this expression, which is an indulgent description of the sexual promiscuity of young men. Indeed, the phrase often carries an overtone of approval, for a young man who sows his wild oats leaves no doubt about his masculinity. One authority notes that a horse fed on oats becomes frisky and easily sexually aroused and links this with the dissipations of youth. Other authorities offer a more convincing explanation, pointing out that wild oats are just a variety of weed and are virtually useless. Only cultivated oats yield a useful crop. This fact has been known at least since Roman times, when the first reference to sowing one's wild oats was used by Plautus. The phrase alludes to the way in which young men sow their seed unproductively; they sow useless weeds instead of a good, productive crop.

obscene. The origin of the word obscene, meaning disgusting, foul etc., have yet to be fully traced. However, one theory suggests that the word comes from the ancient Greek theatre where it may have meant simply 'off stage' (being derived from *ob*, 'against', and *scaena*, 'stage'). Greek drama had many conventions, one of them being that violence was not shown on stage. Thus many violent incidents (for example, the murder of Agamemnon in *The Oresteia*) occurred off-stage and were reported by messengers, the chorus or other characters. It seems probable that the Romans took the Greek word and created the Latin *obscenus*, meaning something terrible and offensive, which was in turn adopted into the French language. By the late 16th century obscene had been absorbed into English to describe violent, despicable deeds, and a hundred years or so later had taken on its modern meaning of something sexually offensive, pornographic.

ocker. In Britain ocker is slang for an Australian. In Australia it is more specifically applied to the uncultivated, beer-swilling male Australian of the kind played by Paul Hogan in *Crocodile Dundee*. Female ockers are known as 'ockerinas' and the whole phenomenon of Australian boorishness is known as ockerism.

of that ilk. Ilk comes from the Old English word *ilca*, meaning 'the same'. The phrase 'of that ilk' is correctly applied when the surname of a person is the same as the name of their estate.

ofay. In Black American usage, an offensive term for a white person. It has been conjectured that ofay is pig Latin for 'foe'. The *Supplement to the Oxford English Dictionary* rejects this conjecture and says that 'the balance of probabilities is that it is a word of African origin'.

off the cuff. This phrase may have derived originally from the habit of waiters, barmen and others of jotting down orders and accounts on their shirtcuffs. Around the turn of the century, when this expression first came into use, it was common for men to wear celluloid cuffs that could be wiped clean after use; they therefore made excellent notepads. So much for the origin of the phrase. Quite how it got its meaning is less easy to explain. An American source points the finger at Hollywood film directors who made notes on their cuffs as they watched actors playing difficult scenes. These off the cuff observations were later incorporated into the scene. Another authority suggests that the expression derives from the way in which after-dinner speakers jot down ideas that occur to them during the meal and incorporate them, unrehearsed, into their speech. Either way, an off the cuff remark or speech is one that is unrehearsed and unprepared.

off the wall. Crazy, irrational, odd or eccentric. This expression which originated in the USA (probably derived from the way in which a ball bounces off a wall in a game such as squash) is one of a number of similar expressions – for example, 'off one's rocker', 'off the rails', **out of one's pram, out of one's tree, out to lunch**.

oggi-oggi-oggi, oi-oi-oi has been used as a chant at Rugby Union matches, particularly by Welsh supporters, since the mid-1970s. It was at the same time popularised by the Welsh comedian Max Boyce, who incorporated it into his stage performances. Despite its strong Welsh connections, this rallying cry probably originated in Cornwall. An 'oggy' is the local nickname for a Cornish pasty, and the nickname 'Oggy-land' has been used for Cornwall itself.

oil – to pour oil on troubled waters. The origin of this phrase lies in the ancient belief that a stormy sea could be calmed by pouring oil onto it. Plutarch and Pliny mentioned it in their writings and the Venerable Bede tells of how a priest who had been given the task of escorting King Oswy's bride across the water was equipped with a flask of holy oil to pour on the waves if a storm blew up. Much later Benjamin Franklin is said to have demonstrated the effect of oil on water on a pond in one of London's royal parks. Today we use the phrase figuratively to describe someone who uses diplomatic words or actions to soothe a difficult situation.

Old Bill. The police, particularly London's Metropolitan police. It has been suggested that this name derives from a train of thought connecting the song *Won't You Come Home, Bill Bailey* and the Old Bailey (London's Central Criminal Court). I find this rather unlikely. It is much more probable that the name originated in the years after World War I when many London policemen would have been ex-soldiers, and some of them may have had walrus moustaches like Bruce Bairnsfather's famous cartoon character, Old Bill, a soldier in the trenches whose well-known phrase was 'Well, if you knows of a better 'ole, go to it.'

old boy network. An old boy is a term describing an ex-pupil of a school. Every school has its old boys, but in the phrase 'old boy network' or 'old boy system' it usually alludes to an ex-pupil of one of the more influential public schools. When pupils leave these establishments they have access to a network of contacts who can be relied on for assistance, thus giving them important social and business advantages. *See also* NETWORKING and OLD SCHOOL TIE.

old chestnut. A stale joke. This phrase originated in an old stage melodrama entitled *The Broken Sword*, which contains a character who tells the same old jokes time and time again with only minor variations. In one exchange in the play, this character starts to tell a story about his exploits with a cork tree. Another character interrupts with the words, 'Not a cork tree – a chestnut. I have heard you tell the joke twenty-seven times, and I am sure it was a chestnut.' From this developed the expression 'an old chestnut' referring to a stale joke, an old story or a worn-out excuse.

old guard. The phrase describes the most stalwart, traditional members of a political party or movement. The original old guard were the four elite veteran regiments chosen to be Napoleon's Imperial Guard. Their experience and loyalty were unquestionable and they received better treatment than the regular army. They were also known for their opposition to any attempts at military reform, which is why today old guard describes someone reliable, reactionary and wedded to old-fashioned ways.

old hat. We use the phrase to describe something old-fashioned or out of date perhaps because, in the days when everyone wore hats, fashions in headgear went very quickly out of style. However, according to Grose's *Classical Dictionary of the Vulgar Tongue*, published in 1785, old hat was a punning name for a woman's genitals – because, like an old hat, they were frequently felt.

Old Lady of Threadneedle Street. A nickname for the Bank of England which is situated in Threadneedle Street in the City of London. It was first used at the end of the 18th century and alludes to the cautious way in which the Bank operated – much as an elderly lady might manage her savings.

Old Nick. When 17th-century English poet Samuel Butler penned these words in his epic satirical poem *Hudibras* (1663–78), he created a myth that lives on to this day:

Nick Machiavel had ne'er a trick
(Though he gives his name to our Old Nick)
But was below the least of these.

As a result of that bit of poetic invention, it has been suggested that the phrase Old Nick, meaning the devil, was named for the Italian statesman Niccolò Machiavelli. At the time Butler wrote his lines Machiavelli was despised for his cynical work of political philosophy, *The Prince*, in which he expounded his theory that the end justifies the means – even if the means include lies, cunning and treachery. By using poetic licence to suggest that he was the original Old Nick, Butler was merely reflecting the popular image of Machiavelli as the epitome of evil. This error gained currency largely because no other firm derivation has been found. It has been suggested that there is a link with St Nicholas or perhaps with the German word *nickel*, meaning a goblin, but so far nothing more concrete has been established.

Old school tie. These are worn by OLD BOYS of the most famous English public and grammar schools as a way of identifying themselves to each other. Those who didn't go to such schools and disapprove of the social and business 'advantages' an old school tie is supposed to bring may refer to the people who wear these as the 'old school tie brigade' – the implication being that the wearers have got where they are by influence and not by merit. *See also* OLD BOY NETWORK.

olive – to hold out the olive branch. The olive branch has, since ancient times, been the symbol of peace. It was an olive branch that the dove brought to Noah's Ark to indicate that the Flood was subsiding and God's wrath was appeased. And in ancient Greek myth when Pallas Athene named the city of Athens, she presented it with an olive branch as a sign of peace. From these traditions we derive the phrase 'to hold out the olive branch', meaning to make a peaceful gesture, to offer to end hostilities.

omelette – You can't make an omelette without breaking eggs. This phrase is attributed to the Russian leader Lenin. By it he meant that it is impossible to achieve any desirable end (the omelette) without doing some damage on the way (breaking the eggs). Lenin had social revolution in mind when he used the expression but it is used today to justify the upheavals and difficulties caused by change of almost any sort.

on, it's not. This phrase, meaning that something is impossible, derives from the game of snooker. A shot is described as 'not on' when the angle is too difficult to play or another ball is in the way.

on-going. A much-despised and much-used little phrase which was coined in the late 1800s but failed to achieve popularity until the 1970s. On-going simply means that something is continuing to happen; that it is in action, progressing. Hence, negotiations between heads of state came to be described as 'on-going negotiations' – or, even worse, an 'on-going negotiation situation'. This pairing of on-going and situation has become such a cliché that it is often used to construct jokey euphemisms. Thus, a birthday party might be known as an 'on-going celebration situation' or sex an 'on-going fornication situation'. To make matters worse, the heyday of on-going coincided with the popularity of another despised phrase, **at this moment in time** – meaning simply 'now'. This latter expression was particularly popular with politicians, perhaps because it gave them an extra second or two in which to think up their answers. Put together, the two phrases lent themselves to such tortuous statements as, 'At this moment in time we have an on-going precipitation situation' – meaning, 'It's raining.' *See also* GOBBLEDY-GOOK.

on hold. In a state of abeyance; postponed. This American expression derives from the button marked Hold on a telephone, used to suspend a connection temporarily.

on ice. To put something on hold, keep it in reserve. The expression refers to the way in which food or perishable goods can be preserved by chilling or freezing. Something that has been kept on ice can be taken out of its metaphorical cold storage and used at a later date.

on one's Pat. This is the Australian equivalent of ON ONE'S TOD, and is similar rhyming slang. In this case, Pat is Pat Malone, but the identity of the eponymous Pat Malone remains a mystery.

on one's Tod. This is rhyming slang. On one's Tod = on one's Tod Sloan = on one's own. Tod Sloan (1874–1933) was a famous American jockey.

on stream. This phrase started as oil industry jargon describing the mo-

ment when oil began to flow freely. It is now used generally to describe the time when almost anything – perhaps a new computer system or an updated set of information – comes into force or begins operating.

on the ball. This phrase, meaning to be quick-witted, clever, adept at what one is doing, probably comes from the game of football. A football player who is skilled at dribbling and manoeuvring is often described as on the ball.

on the carpet. Before the days of mass manufacturing carpets were extremely expensive and could be afforded only by the rich. In a large house they were used to cover the floors of the master or mistresses' rooms but the servants had to make do with bare boards, home-made rugs or linoleum. A servant whose job kept him or her 'below stairs' would only stand on the carpet when they were called up by their master or mistress for a reprimand. From this came the phrase 'on the carpet', meaning to be disciplined or ticked off by a superior.

on the house. Something given away on the house is free, a gift. It is most often applied to a free drink in a pub or bar, which is where the expression originated a couple of centuries or more ago. It was the custom in those days to offer a free drink for every three bought. Today, when a free drink or meal or coffee is used as a kind of marketing tool to encourage free-spending customers, one usually has to buy rather more than three drinks before getting one on the house.

on the QT. This 19th-century phrase is still occasionally used to describe something that is done secretly. QT stands for 'quiet', hence on the QT means something that is carried out quietly, without fuss.

on the rocks. A business or a marriage that is in trouble is sometimes described as being on the rocks. The comparison here is with the plight of a ship caught on rocks and in danger of being torn apart by the waves. From this source we also get the word rocky to describe a difficult, potentially disastrous, situation. When someone orders a drink on the rocks in a bar, they mean that they want the drink served with chunks of ice.

on the wagon. This expression, meaning to be TEETOTAL, originated in the late 19th century in the USA where water carts were used to damp down dusty roads. People who had signed the pledge and sworn to give up alcohol would describe themselves as being 'on the water cart', meaning that they would rather drink water from the cart than swallow the demon alcohol. The phrase gradually evolved to today's familiar 'on the wagon'.

once in a blue moon. Just occasionally, on a clear night, the moon takes on a blue tinge. As this doesn't happen very often we have the phrase 'once in a blue moon' to mean hardly ever, almost never. It is interesting to note that the expression 'Till a blue moon' originally came into use in the 19th century, when it meant 'never'. Presumably someone then noticed that the moon *did* occasionally take on a blueish hue and so both the expression and meaning underwent a change.

one – to go one better. In a game of poker a player who wishes to continue betting has to keep raising the stake. This was known as going one better. In general use it means to improve upon the performance of another person, to better them.

one-armed bandit. Coin-operated gambling machine which is played by pulling a handle or lever at one side. They got their name because of this arm-like handle and because, like bandits, they tend to rob players of their money. They are also known as **fruit machines** because many of them involve a game in which players must attempt to line up a matching row of fruits.

one degree under. This phrase alludes to the fact that a person whose temperature is one degree below the normal body temperature of 36.8° C (98.6° F) is likely to feel mildly unwell. We describe ourselves as one degree under when we lack vitality and energy or feel **under the weather**. The origin of this latter phrase has not been traced, but it may refer to the feelings of lethargy and exhaustion experienced during a hot, humid spell of weather.

one-night stand. Originally an American show-business expression, meaning an engagement for a single evening performance by a touring theatre company, a band, etc. Now often used metaphorically to describe a casual sexual liaison.

one over the eight. According to an old superstition, drinkers stay sober for the first eight drinks – but one more after that makes them drunk. From this belief we get the phrase one over the eight, referring to someone who is drunk.

One swallow does not make a summer. Each spring swallows make the journey from Africa, where they spend the winter, to Europe, where they nest and spend the summer months. Their annual migration has been observed since ancient times and it was the Greek philosopher Aristotle who first wrote, 'One swallow does not make a spring' in his *Nicomachaean Ethics*. His meaning is clear; just because you have seen a swallow it does not necessarily mean that spring is here. The expression is also applied figuratively, meaning that it is a mistake to imagine that all the troubles in one's life are over just because one has overcome one problem.

one-upmanship. The art or practice of getting ahead of, or gaining a psychological advantage over, another person. The expression was coined by the British humorist Stephen Potter, who also gave us GAMESMANSHIP.

open-collared. An American business term used to describe a relaxed managerial style. An open-collared business organisation is one where, figuratively at least, no one wears a tie.

Open Sesame! The password used by Ali Baba to open the door of the robbers' cave in the tale of *The Forty Thieves* from the *Arabian Nights*. It is now used to describe something that has an apparently magical effect; for example, someone with what seems to be an insoluble problems may only have to have a few words with the right person and Open Sesame! the problem is solved. At least one source speculates that it was originally a pun; sesame seeds are, apparently, renowned for their laxative effect!

opium of the people. It was Karl Marx who first described religion as the opium of the people in *On Hegel's Philosophy of Law*. His belief was that while poor and oppressed people were 'drugged' by religion and its emphasis on the hereafter, not the here and now, they would not band together to change the systems and institutions that oppressed them.

oralism, coined along the same lines as SEXISM, AGEISM etc, is prejudice in favour of oral communication. Oralists discriminate against the deaf and mute by refusing to accept the usefulness of sign language and insisting they learn oral speech. Increasingly militant sections of the hearing-impaired community are now questioning this approach, which they say is one of the main reasons why deaf people consistently under-achieve in education. Attempting to make profoundly deaf people 'hear' and 'speak' rather than encouraging them to communicate fluently in sign language is, they argue, a form of prejudice. *See also* ABLEISM.

orange goods. In the retail business orange goods are items (clothes, for example) which have a moderate rate of turnover and therefore usually have a decent profit margin. *See also* BROWN GOODS and WHITE GOODS.

oreo. A term of abuse used by American blacks of other blacks, an oreo is an AFRO-SAXON or UNCLE TOM – that is, a black regarded as 'playing the white man's game' or adopting white values, behaviour, etc. The term comes from the brand name of a chocolate cookie which has a white cream filling.

organisation man is known in Britain as 'company man'. Both phrases describe an individual who totally accepts the values and goals of the organisation he works for and is unquestioningly loyal to it. Both expressions tend to be applied insultingly, implying that a company man hasn't the individualism or imagination to hold his own independent views.

orgy. Followers of the ancient Greek and Roman god Dionysus (Bacchus, as he was known to the Romans) used to indulge in secret night-time feasts and celebrations. These were known as *orgeia* and were famous for their drunken revelries. It is only more recently that orgy has taken on its explicitly sexual meaning, describing uninhibited group sex.

orientation. Today this is a fashionable word to describe the ideas, beliefs and directions to which an individual is naturally drawn. We may, for example, say of someone that he is arts-orientated or science-orientated, indicating a natural talent or predilection for one or the other. Originally, however, orientation involved facing only one direction, east – *oriens* being the Latin for 'east' – and described the placing of the eastern window of a church due east so that when the sun rose it fell directly on the altar.

Oscar. The name given to a bronze-gilt statuette awarded annually for outstanding achievement in various fields of the film industry by the American Academy of Motion Picture Arts and Sciences. The statuettes were first awarded in 1927 but they did not acquire the name Oscar until 1931. A chance remark in that year by Mrs Margaret Herrick, an official later to become secretary of the Academy, that the statuette reminded her of her uncle Oscar just happened to be overheard by a newspaper columnist. The columnist's paper the following day reported that 'Employees have affectionately dubbed their famous statuette "Oscar",' and the name stuck.

ostracise. Ostracism was a mechanism of social democracy used in Ancient Greece to prevent unpopular or dangerous people from gaining power. Each year the citizens of Athens participated in a vote, writing down on a piece of broken pottery or tile the name of a prominent person they would like to see banished from the city. These pot shards were known as *ostrakon*, which means literally an oyster shell and alludes to the size and rough shape of the broken pottery. Having written the name, the citizens deposited their votes in ancient ballot boxes. If six thousand votes were cast against an individual

he was banished, and this act of banishment was known as *ostrakismos*. From this source we get the verb to ostracise, meaning to banish someone socially, to exclude them from something.

out of one's pram. *See* OFF THE WALL.

out of one's tree. *See* OFF THE WALL.

out of touch. To be out of touch with someone means to lose track of them. The phrase is also applied to those who lose contact with the latest ideas, technology, news, fashion etc. The expression originated on the military parade ground where, in the 18th century, a popular method of drilling required soldiers to march so closely together that their elbows brushed. Any soldier who stood too far from his marching companions was deemed to be out of touch.

out to lunch. *See* OFF THE WALL.

out to pasture. Horses who were too old to pull a load or carry out useful work were, if they were lucky, put out to pasture. Applied to humans rather than horses, this phrase describes retirement. It is often used in a faintly negative way to imply that someone is too old to be of further use.

outplacement. The business term for services offered to an employee who is to be made redundant or fired. These services can include financial and psychological advice and assistance in helping the employee find a new job. An outplacement agency is a company which provides such advice and assistance. A recent development in the USA is 'hidden outplacement'. When an employer wishes to dispense with the services of an employee without having to pay compensation, he may secretly contact an outplacement agency and instruct them to find the employee a new position. The agency finds a suitably lucrative and attractive job and, apparently in secret, offers it to the employee. He accepts it and apologetically offers his resignation to the employer, who accepts it with a show of regret. Despite the duplicity, this would seem to be a more humane version of getting rid of someone than merely LETTING THEM GO. *See also* TO BE GIVEN ONE'S CARDS and TO HEADHUNT.

outro. In the music world an outro is the opposite of an intro. It is the ending of a song, the final few bars that fade away at the end of a record or performance.

over the moon. Delighted. This cliché originated in the late 1970s. It is particularly associated with television sports commentaries, and the remarks made after a match by players, managers or commentators. The phrase was quickly seized on and worked to death by comedy impressionists and by the satirical magazine *Private Eye*.

over the top. Beyond what is customary or proper; outré. The phrase originated in the trench warfare of World War I, when it referred to charging over the parapets lining the trenches in order to attack the enemy. The phrase passed into show business usage with its current meaning. In 1982 an outrageous television comedy series was entitled *O.T.T.*, whence these initials came to be a widely-used alternative to the full expression.

overture and beginners. The cry 'Overture and beginners' is broadcast backstage in a theatre to warn those performers who appear on the stage as the curtain goes up that they should take their places.

own goal. A self-inflicted injury or impediment. Originally football jargon, referring to a player knocking the ball into his own team's goal, thus conceding a point to the opposing team. The expression is now widely used in a figurative sense.

Oxbridge. Widely used, as noun or adjective, in reference to the two old-established English universities, Oxford and Cambridge. In some contexts it is used merely as a convenient shorthand for 'Oxford and Cambridge'; in other contexts it conveys overtones of upper-class privilege or academic remoteness from 'real life'. The expression was first used by W. M. Thackeray in his novel *Pendennis* (serialised 1848–50) as the name of his hero's university. The name did not come into general use until it was revived by Virginia Woolf in her book *A Room Of One's Own* (1929). For the American equivalent of Oxbridge *see* IVY LEAGUE.

Oyez! Oyez! Oyez! This phrase was originally introduced to the English language by the Normans and is traditionally used by town criers and court officials to summon attention. Oyez! is the Old French imperative for 'Hear ye!'.

P

Ps and Qs, mind your. There are at least three explanations of this phrase, but only one generally accepted meaning; to behave politely and carefully. It is said by some authorities that the expression derives from the old practice in inns and public houses of giving regular customers credit and chalking up their bills on a slate – this being the origin of the phrases 'chalk it up' and 'put it on the slate'. On the slate was written P for pints and Q for quarts of ale consumed. When the time came to total up the account the customer had to mind his Ps and Qs to ensure that he was correctly charged. A second theory relates the phrase to the elaborate dances performed at the court of Louis XIV. At the time huge wigs were in fashion and dancing masters would warn their pupils to mind their Ps (*pieds*, feet) and Qs (*queues*, wigs). The third and least colourful of these derivations, and according to Brewer the most likely, is that the phrase is simply a school-room reminder to children to take care in distinguishing the difference between the letters p and q.

Paddy. (1) A colloquial term for an Irishman, derived from the common Irish forename Patrick. Among American blacks, however, Paddy is sometimes used to refer to any white man. (2) Paddy, as in the expression 'paddy field', comes from a Malay word, *padi*, meaning rice in the husk.

Paddy wagon. In America, a colloquial term for a police patrol wagon or BLACK MARIA.

page three girl. A female photographic model who poses nude or topless. The expression derives from the *Sun*, a British daily publication, on page 3 of which a picture of such a model is a regular feature.

pageturner. A word used in the publishing industry to describe a book with such a gripping story that readers keep turning the pages, unable to put it down until they reach the end.

paint the town red. This phrase is American in origin, though American scholars have yet to pinpoint its exact derivation. Some speculate that it refers to the red flames of burning buildings left behind them as Indians went on a wild spree of destruction. Others relate it to the wild drinking-parties held by cowboys. Another suggests that it may refer to the way in which a drunk's nose turns red after a night out on the town. Whatever the precise origin, the expression means to have a good time, to go on a noisy, riotous spree.

Pakistan. Although the state of Pakistan was not formed until 1947, the name was devised by Chaudrie Rahmat Ali in 1933, anticipating future independence. It is an acronym formed from the names of the constituent territories: P for Punjab, A for Afghan border states, K for Kashmir, S for Sind, and Tan for

Baluchistan. The name thus formed also consists of a Persian root, *pak*, meaning pure or holy, and an Urdu root, *stan*, meaning 'land'. Pakistan may thus be translated as 'land of the holy'.

pale horseman. *See under* GRIM REAPER.

paleface. Anyone who watches westerns may be forgiven for thinking that paleface is a word coined by North American Indians to describe a white man. The evidence indicates, however, that the word was invented by novelist James Fenimore Cooper, author of *The Last of the Mohicans*.

palimony hit the headlines in 1979 when American actor Lee Marvin was taken to court by his ex-lover, Michelle Triola Marvin, who demanded a settlement. The term was coined by combining the words 'pal' and 'alimony' and immediately caught on as a description of the financial share-out when an unmarried couple separate.

Palladium. The original Palladium was a wooden statue of the goddess Pallas Athene which fell from heaven to Troy and became the spiritual guardian of the city. While it remained there the city was safe, but when Odysseus stole the Palladium Troy fell. According to legend the statue was taken to Rome and had the same effect there, keeping the place safe from invasion. Because of this the word Palladium came to mean anything on which the safety and well-being of a nation depended; a constitution, good law, freedom of the Press etc. When at the beginning of this century cinema owners were wondering what to call their splendid picture palaces they lighted on a number of words that carried overtones of classical grandeur. Thus many cinemas were named the Hippodrome, the Coliseum and, for no reason other than its classical allusions, the Palladium.

palm something off. This expression refers to the way in which a conjuror makes something appear to vanish by concealing it in the palm of his hand. Today we use the phrase to describe getting rid of something unwanted or worthless by persuading someone else to buy it or take it on. To do this we may conceal from them the fact that the item is worthless or unwanted, much as the conjuror conceals what he doesn't want his audience to see.

pamphlet. Various suggestions have been put forward to explain the origins of pamphlet, a word describing a booklet only a few pages long. Most trace it back to a love poem written in the 12th century by Pamphilus which was a 'best-seller' of its day and was extremely popular throughout the Middle Ages. It seems likely that copies of this short poem were known as 'pamphilets' and that the word came to be applied to any similar short work. Dr Johnson, however, suggested that the word derives from the French phrase *par un filet*, meaning 'by a string', this describing the way in which the pages were held together. Whatever the origin, a pamphlet is, technically speaking, an unbound or paperbound book of less than a hundred pages. The two-page advertising handouts we often call pamphlets should in fact be known as leaflets.

pan out. American gold prospectors coined this verb, usually used in a negative sense to indicate that something has failed to work or been a flop. It alludes to the shallow pan in which prospectors separated sand and gravel from flakes of gold. When gold wasn't found they would say that it 'didn't pan out'. The phrase was taken up by critics who declared that a play or book 'didn't pan out' and this came to known as panning –

which is why we say when a new play or film or other work of art is declared to be a flop that it has been panned by the critics.

panama hat. These don't come from Panama; they were originally manufactured in Ecuador and Peru. Their name isn't a geographical error, just a corruption of 'palmata hat', the palmata being the tree from which the hats were made. And even that isn't what it seems, for despite its name the *Carludovica palmata* is *not* a true palm tree.

Pandora's box. According to legend Pandora was the first mortal woman, sent by Zeus as revenge upon man for accepting fire stolen from heaven by Prometheus. She brought with her a box in which were sealed all the ills of the world and which she had been told not to open. But curiosity got the better of her, she opened it and out flew all the evils that now trouble mankind. Only one thing was left in the box, and that was hope. Today we use the phrase 'a Pandora's box' to describe an issue or a situation which seems superficially innocuous but which, if broached, may lead to all kinds of unforeseen problems.

panhandle. This American expression has two distinct and unrelated meanings. (1) A strip of territory stretching out from the main area like the handle of a pan – as in northern West Virginia, northern Texas or western Oklahoma. (2) To beg – derived from the practice of beggars holding out tin pans to solicit money from passers-by.

panic. The Greek god Pan is the source of the word panic, describing a sudden and uncontrollable sense of terror. It was perhaps panic that his mother experienced at his birth, for he is said to have been born with goat-like feet, legs, ears and horns and covered in black fur. Later in his life he took pleasure in terrifying people by appearing and vanishing without warning. According to legend he did this at the battle of Marathon, causing the Persian army to flee in blind, irrational fear – which is exactly what panic is.

panic button. *See under* CHICKEN SWITCH.

pansy. A male homosexual or simply an effeminate, weak or cowardly man. The derivation is unknown; the word was probably applied because flowers are considered to be feminine, unsuitable for a MACHO man to be involved with.

pantechnicon. In its original Greek, it meant 'belonging to all the arts' – which was why, when in the 19th century a bazaar selling works of art was opened in Belgrave Square, it was known as the Pantechnicon. Unfortunately it went out of business and the building in which it had been housed was turned into a furniture store. Soon the name pantechnicon had been transferred to the huge removal vans that visited the place and today the term is loosely applied to any large vehicle. *See also* JUGGERNAUT.

pants. The word pants, meaning trousers to Americans, underpants to the British, is derived from the name of a 4th-century saint, St Pantaleone. He was a Christian doctor who was martyred by the Romans and later became the favourite saint of Venice. In the 15th century the saint's name was adopted by one of the characters in the *commedia dell'arte*. This character, known as Pantaloon, was always portrayed wearing baggy trousers – which in turn came to be known as pantaloons. The word was imported to America in the 18th century and was soon shortened to pants. *See also* BLOOMER.

pants – to be caught with one's pants down means to be taken at a disadvantage. There are two schools of thought about the origins of this phrase, which has only been traced back to 1920. The first and most likely is that it refers to a man caught *in flagrante delicto* with another man's wife – the stuff of a hundred farces. An American theory, however, points to a pioneer caught unawares by an Indian as he answers the call of nature. Whichever derivation one prefers, one can be sure that illicit sex, the call of nature and the inevitability of men being caught with their pants down dates back much further than the 1920s.

paparazzi. Freelance photographers who specialise in trailing the rich and famous and taking candid pictures of them, often at revealing or embarrassing moments. This aggressive form of photo-journalism first started in Rome twenty years or so ago. The annoyance they caused was such that they became known as paparazzi, from the Italian for 'buzzing insects'.

paper-shuffler. A lowly bureaucrat or office worker whose job involves processing paperwork. As the number of NON-PAPER transactions increase paper-shufflers and their pen-pusher colleagues may find that their days are numbered.

paper over the cracks, to. To use a temporary, superficial measure to make something look better in the short term. The expression was used by Bismarck in 1865 to describe the Convention of Gastein, aimed at establishing some kind of reconciliation between Austria and Prussia over their territories. History does not record whether Bismarck had recently had an unsatisfactory experience with interior decorators, but that is where the phrase comes from. It alludes to the way in which a COWBOY decorator just papers over the cracks rather than putting the deeper damage to rights.

paper tiger. A person or thing that appears menacing and powerful but is in fact weak. This is a literal translation of an old Chinese expression, *tsuh lao fu*, which was popularised by the Chinese leader Mao Tse-tung (1893–1976). Speaking to an American interviewer in 1946 he said:

All reactionaries are paper tigers. In appearance, the reactionaries are terrifying, but in reality they are not so powerful.

par for the course, meaning 'about average', is a golfing expression. Par comes from the Latin word for equal, *par*, and defines the number of strokes an averagely good player might be expected to take to complete a round. Thus anything or anyone described as par for the course, whether on the golfcourse or not, performs about as well as expected. *See also* BOGEY.

paraphernalia. In Roman law paraphernalia were the personal possessions of a bride that were not included as part of her dowry. From this sense of personal belongings we get the modern meaning of bits of equipment or apparatus or even just the items we use in everyday life.

Parkinson's Law or *The Pursuit of Progress* was published in 1958 by Cyril Northcote Parkinson, a British academic. Parkinson's Law states that

Work expands so as to fill the time available for its completion

with the corollary

Subordinates multiply at a fixed rate regardless of the amount of work produced.

parting – to fire a parting shot. The original parting shots were fired by the mounted archers of the Parthian army who were famed for their ability to fire arrows backwards at the enemy as their horses retreated at a gallop. These tactics, which made the Parthians almost invincible, give us the phrase 'to fire a parting shot'.

We use it figuratively today to describe the action of someone who, at the end of an argument, when everything seems to be over, makes one last comment before walking away.

party plan. A method of selling merchandise aimed particularly at women. Kitchen equipment, cosmetics and clothing are the goods most frequently sold in this way. A salesperson encourages a woman to hold an informal party for her friends at which the goods are demonstrated. Under pressure to prove their friendship and support for the hostess, the guests are induced to buy the goods. When the party is over the hostess receives a payment related to the value of items sold.

pasteurise. Louis Pasteur was a 19th-century French chemist who discovered and propagated a process for sterilising milk. The process, called pasteurisation in his honour, prevented such diseases as bovine tuberculosis and brucellosis being spread by infected milk. He also invented a number of vaccines, including one against rabies.

patsy. A victim, a FALL GUY, a dupe or a person who takes the blame for a crime on someone else's behalf. It came into use in the USA at the turn of the century but its origin has not been conclusively identified. Various sources suggest that it is derived from the Italian word *pazzo*, meaning a fool, the word being introduced to America by Italian immigrants. Incidentally, *pazzo* got its meaning because in the 15th century the Pazzi family were foolish enough to oppose the all-powerful Medicis – with the result that most of the family were killed. Another source suggests the Italian name Pasquale as the origin of patsy. The name Pasqualino, the diminutive of Pasquale, is applied to any weak or vulnerable man, this perhaps because in Italian 'Easter' is known as *Pasqua* and is associated with the sacrifice of the Pascal lamb. By association a *pasqualino*, like a patsy, is a lamb for slaughter.

payola. A form of bribery offered to disc jockeys and those in the pop music industry in return for airplay and publicity. After payola scandals in the 1960s and 70s it was said to have been wiped out, but such is the money to be made from a hit record that now other inducements are offered to willing disc jockeys. These may include a share in the royalties earned by the song or inducements in the form of gifts, holidays, meetings with pop stars and so on. The -ola suffix is of Italian origin, usually added to make a word sound more important.

peace in our time. This is the promise made by prime minister Neville Chamberlain on his return from a meeting with Adolf Hitler at Munich on 30 September 1938. World War II started, of course, the following year. The phrase is actually a quotation from the Anglican prayerbook: 'Give peace in our time, O Lord'.

peace with honour. This is what prime minister Benjamin Disraeli claimed to have achieved when he returned in 1878 from the Congress of Berlin, which had been convened in order to settle 'the Balkan question'.

pearls – to cast pearls before swine. This expression is taken from the Bible.

Give not that which is holy unto the dogs, neither cast ye your pearls before swine, lest they trample them under their feet, and turn again and rend you (Matthew 7:6).

To cast pearls before swine means to offer something of value to people who cannot appreciate it.

pecking order. Scientists have observed that chickens kept together in a coop establish a rigid social order among themselves. At the top of the order is a hen who can peck any other in the run. Below her in the pecking order is a hen that can peck any of the others except the one at the top – and so on, until at the bottom of the order there is an unfortunate hen who is pecked by all but can peck none back. Human society has similar chains of authority which, because of the similarities, are also known as pecking orders.

pedestal, to set on a. To idolise someone, worship them as something superhuman, unflawed by normal human failings. Inevitably the individual who has been put up there shows some sign of humanity and falls off. The expression derives from the fact that statues of saints and other revered figures were placed on pedestals. According to a feminist joke, the reason men put women on pedestals is so they can have a better view up their skirts.

pedigree. When medieval genealogists prepared a family tree they would indicate the line of descent with arrowlike marks. One scholar with, it might be supposed, an interest in ornithology, spotted a similarity between these marks and the bones in a crane's foot and christened them *pied de grue*, meaning 'crane's foot'. From *pied de grue* we get the modern pedigree.

peeler. Rarely used today, the slang expression peeler means a policeman and is derived from the name of the man who founded the Irish constabulary, Sir Robert Peel. In 1829, as British Home Secretary, he founded the Metropolitan Police. They, too, were given a nickname based on Sir Robert's name and became known as BOBBIES.

peeping Tom. A voyeur – one who gets his kicks from watching people who are unaware that they are being observed, particularly if they are naked or engaged in sexual activity.

The expression is said to have been coined in the year 1040 when Leofric, Lord of Coventry, imposed a tax on the people of the town. When there was an outcry at this he said he would repeal the tax if his wife, Lady Godiva, rode naked through the streets on a white horse. This the philanthopic lady agreed to do, on the understanding that everyone would keep their doors closed and their windows covered as she went by. Everyone did as she asked except one man, a tailor called Tom, who couldn't resist taking a peep. As he did so he was struck blind – or, according to an alternative ending, was killed by the more honourable residents of Coventry.

peg, to take someone down a. In the 17th century a ship's flags were raised and lowered by means of a system of pegs. The higher a flag was flown, the greater the honour; thus someone whose flag was taken down a peg had their rank publicly diminished. Today an arrogant or egotistical person may be taken down a peg, i.e. humbled or humiliated.

peg out, to. To peg out, meaning to die, is derived from the game of cribbage in which players move their pegs until they achieve a winning score, at which they are said to peg out and the game ends. Cribbage also gives us the phrase to peg away, meaning to keep going at something persistently, alluding to the movement of the peg each time the score increases.

pennies – look after the pennies and the pounds will look after themselves. *See* PENNY WISE, POUND FOOLISH.

penny for your thoughts. When someone says 'A penny for your thoughts' they are asking, in an indirect way, what you are thinking. This expression goes back a long way – it occurs in Thomas More's *Four Last*

Things of 1522 and in John Heywood's *Proverbs* of 1546.

penny wise, pound foolish. This is said of someone who is thrifty over small matters but careless over larger ones. It implies that it isn't enough to be careful with the pennies – the pounds require attention too. As so often happens, this is in direct contradiction to another proverb, **look after the pennies and the pounds will look after themselves**. This means that if you take care of the minor things, the major issues will resolve themselves. Both sayings have an element of commonsensical truth; whatever the situation, one or other is bound to fit the bill.

Pentagonese. The language spoken by American politicians and famed for its euphemisms and vagueness. A speaker of Pentagonese will never use one word when six will do; thus a simple question requiring a yes or no answer will be greeted with, 'The answer to that is in the negative' and the word 'now' has been banished and replaced by 'At this moment in time . . .' General Alexander Haig is acknowledged to be one of the most fluent users of Pentagonese and had no trouble in coming up with phrases such as 'an additional number of augmentees'. *See also* GOBBLEDY-GOOK.

peppercorn rent. Anyone lucky enough to occupy premises at a peppercorn rent pays a token rent, one so small that, like a peppercorn, it is of no appreciable value. Peppercorn rents were more common in the Middle Ages than they are today.

Pepsification. This word first appeared in the British press in 1988 to describe American-style commercialisation of unlikely places. It was applied particularly to the burgeoning number of American-style fast food outlets being established in Moscow, where pizza, hamburgers and Pepsi and Coke are now available.

perestroika means literally 'rebuilding' or 'reform' and refers to the changes set in motion by Russian leader Mikhail Gorbachev. His aim, revealed in his book entitled *Perestroika: Our Hopes for Our Country* published in 1987, includes fundamental reform of the presidency, the Supreme Soviet, the legal system and the vast bureaucracy that has stifled individual initiative and enterprise. The new mood of self-reliance and motivation he hopes to create in the USSR bears a surprising resemblance, some have noted, to that propounded by the British Conservative party under Margaret Thatcher. Perestroika has been rapidly adopted into the English language and, though it is sometimes confused with GLASNOST, generally means the same as it does in Russian – positive, timely change. *See also* GLASNOST.

performance medicine. A relatively new branch of the medical profession which deals with the problems experienced by musicians as a result of playing their instruments. Among the conditions reported were bagpiper's lung (caused by fungal infections lurking in the watertight bellows of the pipes), guitarist's nipple (soreness of the nipple caused by the friction of the instrument against the chest) and violinist's neck (a painful crick caused by the position in which the violin is played). Other pastimes and professions have also yielded fascinating medical problems; we all know about housemaid's knee and tennis elbow, but what about jogger's nipple, typist's wrist, honeymoon nose and cyclist's balls?

perfume dynamics. For several years supermarkets have been using artificial scents of baking bread and freshly-made coffee to whet the appetites of shoppers. Perfume dynamics are a recent development of this, being the deployment of scents and aromas to make an environment or workplace more pleasant. In the office or factory the right perfumes are said to boost output and efficiency. In hospitals patients recover quickly when a mildly bracing scent is used.

peter out. There are a number of alternative theories about the origin of the phrase to peter out, meaning to fade away, to slowly disappear. One source suggests that it derives from the French verb *péter*, meaning to fart. Another guess is that it might have been derived from gold-mining operations, where an explosive mixture of saltpetre, charcoal and sulphur was used to blow away rock and expose the gold. This mix was known as 'peter' and when the gold it had revealed had been mined the vein was said to have petered out. The third suggestion is that the phrase refers to St Peter, whose faith failed him when Christ was arrested. Three times he denied knowing Jesus, his courage gradually petering out.

Peter Principle, The. *The Peter Principle: Why Things Always Go Wrong*, written by Laurence J. Peter and Raymond Hull, was published in 1969.

My analysis of hundreds of cases of occupational incompetence leads me to formulate *The Peter Principle*: In a Hierarchy Every Employee Tends to Rise to his Level of Incompetence.

petticoat. The first petticoats (literally a 'small coat') were worn by men. They were light coats or shirts worn under chain mail or beneath a doublet. No one is certain about when exactly the petticoat ceased to be a male garment and became instead a woman's underskirt, but the transformation must have occurred by the 18th century, when petticoat

was a slang word for a woman. From it we get the phrase 'petticoat government', applied to situations in which women 'wear the trousers'.

Philadelphia lawyer. This is an American expression for a lawyer of outstanding ability, extremely skilful at finding the weakness in an adversary's case, and with an uncommon grasp of the law's intricacies. There was at one time a saying that three Philadelphia lawyers were a match for the devil. The origin of the expression goes back to 1735 when a particular Philadelphia lawyer, Andrew Hamilton, defended New York printer John Peter Zenger in a case of criminal libel. Hamilton obtained his client's acquittal despite the strength of the case against him, and he charged no fee. The case has been hailed as the first blow in the struggle for freedom of the press in America.

Philistine. The Philistines were a warlike people who lived in ancient Palestine and were a thorn in the side of the Israelites until Saul and David conquered them. Though they were undoubtedly barbaric their name would probably not have passed into the English language had it not been for an incident in 17th-century Germany. In 1689 (or 1693, according to various sources) the city of Jena was the scene of a violent town-and-gown riot in which several people were killed. The university preacher responded by giving a sermon on the value of education and its importance for the citizens, beginning it with the words, 'The Philistines be upon thee . . .' As a result of this the students began calling the uneducated locals *Philisters*, that being the German for Philistines. In 1869 the poet and educationalist Matthew Arnold used the English version of the word in his book *Culture and Anarchy*, defining a Philistine as someone uncultured, illbehaved, boorish:

The people who believe most that our greatness and welfare are proved by our being very rich, and who most give their lives and thoughts to becoming rich, are just the very people whom we call Philistines.

phony. There has been some controversy over this word, which all sources agree is an Americanism dating from the turn of the century. The only derivation offered for it is the obsolete word *fawney*, used by criminals to describe brass rings which con-men would pass off as gold to unwary purchasers. Though the link between the two words seems possible, no one has yet shown the progress of the word from the English underworld to American slang, and for that reason many experts remain sceptical.

picket. Originally a pointed stake, being derived from the French word of the same meaning, *piquet*. These stakes were used for tethering horses and tents and, with their visible end sharpened to a point, were also utilised as a barrier round an army encampment. Small bands of troops on the lookout for the enemy would go as far as the picket and soon became known as pickets themselves. In 1867 the word was first applied to groups of trade unionists stationed around a factory perimeter during a strike to keep a lookout for strikebreakers.

pidgin English. A language invented by early traders in China; a simplified version of English which employs phonetic spellings and no formal grammar. It takes its name from the way in which the Chinese pronounce the word 'business', which comes out 'bijin', and proved so popular that it was widely adopted throughout the Pacific and developed in new forms in some parts of Africa.

pie in the sky. The illusory prospect of future benefits. This phrase, dating from the early 1900s, comes from a song written by the trade union organiser and WOBBLY martyr Joe Hill. The song is a parody of the Ira Sankey hymn *The Sweet By and By*:

You will eat, by and by,
In the glorious land above the sky!
Work and pray,
Live on hay,
You'll get pie in the sky when you die!

See also the WOBBLIES.

pièce de résistance. Translated as 'piece of resistance' this was originally the main course of a meal – usually a roasted joint or other type of meat dish. This was the highlight, the most substantial part of the meal. From this idea the phrase passed into more general use to describe anything that stands out from the rest – the best, the thing that is worth waiting for.

piece of the action. A share of something, particularly business or potential gains. This American colloquialism dates from the 1920s and was originally gamblers' jargon, 'action' being a slang term for gambling.

pig. A contemptuous term, originating in the American counterculture of the 1960s, for a policeman.

pig in a poke. A blind bargain; something that is bought without the purchaser seeing it or being sure of the quality. In olden days one had to be wary if one went to market to buy a young pig. It was a common trick of unscrupulous dealers to display a fine young pig as a sample and to hand over to the purchaser one already tied up in a sack or 'poke'. Only when the buyer got home did he discover that the poke contained not a pig but a cat. The same sharp practice is the origin of the phrase LET THE CAT OUT OF THE BAG.

pigeonhole. It has been calculated that in the Middle Ages pigeons were the main source of meat for the ordinary people. This may explain the surprising size and complexity of old dovecotes, which included small individual nesting holes for dozens, sometimes hundreds, of pigeons. When, at a later date, desks with small compartments or filing racks were constructed, the small sections were known as pigeonholes. From this we get the verb to pigeonhole, meaning to classify someone or something. The term refers to the way in which someone filing papers or mail in pigeonholes classifies their material before inserting it in the correct space.

pile, to make one's. This phrase originated in the goldfields where it meant simply that if a man dug enough out of the ground, thus making his pile, he would be rich enough to retire. The phrase has the same meaning today.

pillar to post, from. It is widely believed that this phrase was originally 'from post to pillar' and that it derives from the old game of tennis (known as Real, Royal or Court tennis) which was played indoors. The net was suspended from a post and attached at the far end to one of the building's pillars. It seems to have been a favourite tactic for opponents to hit long volleys from one end of the net to the other and from this came a saying current in the 15th century, 'from post to pillar tossed', used to describe anything thrown a long distance. A century later the phrase had evolved into the more mellifluous from pillar to post, meaning to and fro, from one thing to another and back again. An alternative theory suggests that the expression derives from punishments meted out in the Middle Ages. It speculates that medieval criminals were humiliated in the pillory before being taken to the whipping post and lashed, this giving us 'from pillar to post'. Though this sounds plausible, the weight of evidence is in favour of the first explanation.

pilot scheme. An experiment, a try-out that leads the way for others to follow later. Pilot is derived from the French, which in turn is derived from the Italian for 'rudder'.

pin money. In the Middle Ages pins were manufactured under a Crown monopoly and were both expensive and scarce – so much so that in the 14th century they were allowed to be sold only on the first two days of the year. For this reason husbands would give their wives a sum of money with which to buy the pins they would need for the rest of the year. This became known as pin money, and though at a later date pins became more widely available the phrase remains to describe a sum given to a woman by her husband or earned by her own efforts and used to buy items for her personal use.

pinch hit. To take someone's place as a substitute in an emergency. This American expression comes from the game of baseball. A pinch hitter is someone who comes to bat in place of another player.

pinch of salt. When a person is promised something but doubts that the promise will be kept, or is told an item news but doubts that it is true, they may be said to take it with a pinch of salt. That is, they greet it with scepticism or reservations. This expression dates back to the time of ancient Rome, when sceptics received promises *cum grano salis*, with a grain of salt. The phrase derives from the fact that a grain or pinch of salt added to an unappetising meal makes it taste better and thus easier to eat. A metaphorical grain or pinch of salt makes it easier to swallow news we don't believe or promises we don't expect to be kept.

ping-pong. (1) Originally a trade name for the game of table tennis, now often used as a synonym (though not by those who take the game seriously). The name was apparently chosen for its onomatopoeic quality – though it has been pointed out that the name would be more suggestive of the sounds made by the game if the letters were turned round to give 'gnip-gnop'. (2) In the medical profession in the USA, to ping-pong means to refer patients to other doctors in a reciprocal arrangement to maximise medical fees.

ping-pong diplomacy. This phrase was coined to describe the attempts by China and the USA to re-establish their links in the 1970s. The USA initiated the contact by sending a national table tennis (known as PING-PONG) team to play in the People's Republic – hence the expression ping-pong diplomacy. It has since been applied to other means of indirect diplomatic contact.

pink-collar. A word used by those in the employment industry to describe the kind of low-paid, low-status jobs usually carried out by women. These include nurses, secretaries, nannies, infant school teachers, cleaners, hairdressers and shop workers. The expression was coined in analogy to BLUE-COLLAR and white-collar; blue-collar refers to unskilled and semi-skilled staff, mainly male, who are employed in manual labour and characterised as wearing blue overalls. White-collar defines skilled, non-manual workers who wear a white shirt and probably a tie to work.

pipe down. Be quiet; stop making a noise. This expression is of naval origin, referring to a signal the boatswain would give on his pipe or whistle to indicate 'hands turn in' or 'lights out'.

pipe dream. A fantasy or an unattainable illusion of the kind experienced by those who smoke opium. The phrase originated in America during the last decade of the 19th century.

Pippy. A Person Inheriting Parents' Property, coined as yet another variation on YUPPIES, DINKIES, GLAMS and so on. Inheriting one's parents' property is nothing new, of course, but with a growing proportion of home-owners and the property boom of the 1980s, an increasing number of middle-aged people are finding themselves with a massive increase in wealth. Such people were quickly categorised as Pippies by the marketing men who were anxious to help this new socio-economic group find ways of disposing of their legacies. *See also* YUPPIES etc.

pissed as a newt. *See under* BRAHMS AND LISZT.

pitched battle. The earliest pitched battles were formal affairs where the opposing sides selected a mutually agreed battleground and pitched their tents beforehand. Today we use the expression to refer to a situation in which two sides are locked in intense and dangerous conflict. The modern use of the phrase continues to acknowledge the seriousness and intent of the original; a pitched battle, whether in a war or in figurative use, is more than just a skirmish.

pits, the. A terrible place, the worst situation imaginable. The phrase originated among drug-addicts who were forced to inject drugs into their armpits, having burned out the veins in more accessible areas. The armpit is a sensitive area and an injection there is painful. Because of this the pits came to stand for anything terrible.

pixel. One of the many illuminated elements that form the picture on a television or VDU screen. This piece of computer and electronics jargon, dating from the late 1960s, derives from the words 'picture element'.

pizzazz. Energy; force; vitality; pep. The derivation of this American colloquialism is unknown, though it seems to have originated among people working in show business and the media, *c.*1930. The *Supplement to the Oxford English Dictionary* has the following quote from *Harper's Bazaar* of March 1937:

Pizzazz, to quote the editor of the Harvard *Lampoon*, is an indefinable dynamic quality, the *je ne sais quoi* of function; as for instance, adding Scotch puts pizzazz into a drink.

plain as a pikestaff, as. Something that is glaringly obvious, impossible to mistake. Two derivations have been proposed. The first is that the phrase was originally 'as plain as a packstaff', a packstaff being the staff or stick on which a pedlar carried his pack of wares. A well-used packstaff, according to this theory, was worn smooth and 'plain'. The second and more convincing suggestion identifies the weapon known as a pike as the source of the expression. A pike was a long pole – sometimes measuring as much as sixteen feet – tipped with a sharp, spearlike end. It doesn't take much imagination to see that such a weapon could not be easily concealed; that, in fact, it stuck out as plainly as a pikestaff.

plain brown wrapper or **under plain cover** are phrases used today to reassure those who are tempted to send away for mail-order pornography but are nervous of their neighbours discovering the contents of the package. The expression came into use at the end of the last century, when American mail-order companies began operations and undercut the business of local retailers. These retailers were naturally aggrieved to see packages bearing the name of their mail-order rivals being delivered to their customers and would sometimes vent their spleen on the unfortunate purchaser. To avoid this, the mail-order companies began delivering goods in plain brown wrappers, guaranteeing anonymity to nervous customers.

plain sailing. Something described as plain sailing is straightforward and troublefree. The expression is derived from the nautical phrase 'plane sailing', which is a means of plotting on a flat plane and not on the rounded surface of the globe. This method of 'plane sailing' makes plotting positions a simple task – hence the meaning of the phrase.

plain white wrapper. Citizen's band radio jargon for an unmarked police car.

plastic. A coinage (forgive the pun!) of the 1980s, referring to credit cards or charge cards used for purchases in place of cash.

platonic love. Named for the Greek philosopher Plato, who expounded the theory that it was possible for two people to love each other deeply without being sexually attracted or entangled. Plato's original concept of sexless love was based on the love of men for each other, not for a woman. It wasn't until the 17th century that platonic love was used to describe a heterosexual relationship. Today we use the phrases platonic friendship or platonic relationship to describe a deep but non-sexual relationship.

play fast and loose. To be untrustworthy or unfaithful; to fail to keep one's promises; to act in a shifty manner. The origin of this phrase lies in the name of a game with which sharpers cheated innocent victims at village fairs, perhaps as far back as the 14th century. Fast and Loose, otherwise known as Prick the Belt, Prick the Loop, or Prick the Garter, was played with a belt or strap folded and coiled in an intricate manner on a table. The victim was invited, for a wager, to push a stick into the coils so as to hold the belt 'fast' to the table when it was uncoiled. The sharper then uncoiled the belt so that it came 'loose' from the stick – which, of course, he was always able to do – and the victim lost his wager.

play possum. To feign death; to dissemble. A possum (or, to give it its proper name, an opossum) when under threat will lie, with closed eyes and limp muscles, as if it is dead.

play the field. *See under* FIELD.

play the sedulous ape. To model oneself on others. Robert Louis Stevenson (1850–94) coined this phrase when he wrote in *Memories and Portraits* (1887):

I have played the sedulous ape to Hazlitt, to Lamb, to Wordsworth, to Sir Thomas Browne, to Defoe, to Hawthorne, to Montaigne, to Baudelaire and to Obermann . . . That, like it or not, is the way to learn to write.

play things close to the chest, to. A prudent card-player ensures that his opponents cannot see his hand by keeping it close to his chest. Used figuratively, to play things close to the chest means to keep them secret, to give away very little about one's position or plans.

plebeian. The Latin for 'the common people' was *plebs*, from which we derive the word plebeian, meaning an ordinary citizen.

plenty more fish in the sea. *See under* FISH.

plenty more pebbles on the beach. *See* PLENTY MORE FISH IN THE SEA *under* FISH.

plonk. Cheap wine of inferior quality. This expression is thought to have originated in World War I, and to be a semi-humorous corruption of the French *vin blanc*. It was probably coined by Australian soldiers, since plonk was recorded as current Australian slang in 1919, whereas it was much later before it was generally used in Britain.

ploughman's lunch. The very thought of a ploughman's lunch inspires a vision of genial ploughmen in country smocks tucking into a wholesome meal of farmhouse bread and cheese, washed down with a flagon of the local brew. This was exactly the kind of image that the English Country Cheese Council wanted to create when they invented the Ploughman's Lunch in the 1970s and they have succeeded with a vengeance. Now it seems as if almost every British pub offers a Ploughman's (known in anti-sexist establishments as a Ploughperson's), consisting of bread and cheese with a variety of trimmings. They may also offer a French Ploughman's, consisting of French cheese or pâté, a Huntsman's, comprised of bread and cold meat, or a Fisherman's, which includes fish or seafood.

plugumentary. In the last year or two avid television viewers will have spotted a new type of programme on the box. These are usually documentary-style films about the making of a movie or a play. *Shanghai Surprise*, starring Madonna, and *A Fish Called Wanda* were both given this documentary treatment shortly before they arrived in the cinemas. Such television programmes are categorised as plugumentaries – programmes which are apparently objective 'behind the scenes' documentaries but which in fact are aimed at 'plugging' (i.e. publicising) their subject.

Plumber. A member of a White House special group, during the 1969–74 administration of President Richard Nixon, with the responsibility of investigating leaks of government secrets. This group came to the attention of the public when it was revealed that they had engaged in a number of illegal activities including burglary and installing concealed bugging devices. *See also* WATERGATE.

plumb the depths, to. Since the

Middle Ages and probably long before, a lead weight tied to the end of a string and used to test the depth of water has been known as a plumb or a plumb line (from the French *plomme* for a lead weight). Hence anyone who uses a plumb for this purpose may be said to be plumbing the depths. The expression has been used figuratively since the 1500s to refer to someone who, like the lead weight, has sunk as low as they can possibly get in despair or unhappiness.

podunk. A name used to represent a typical small American country town. There are in fact several places in New England with this name, which was originally an Algonquian place name meaning 'a neck or corner of land'.

point, to stretch a. It has been suggested that this phrase, meaning to make allowances, alludes to the way in which clothes were once held together by laces. These laces, tagged with a metal tip to make it easier to thread them through the appropriate holes, were known as points. Perhaps after a particularly good meal it was the habit to let out these laces and stretch a point, even though it was not strictly good manners to do so.

point-blank. In French the white bull's-eye of a target is known as the *point blanc*; this became anglicised as point-blank and in the 16th century an archer who scored a bull's-eye was declared to have shot a point-blank. Later, when cannon were used and trajectories were better understood, it was applied to a shot where the angle of sight is parallel to the horizontal and the ball travels in a straight line over a relatively short distance to the target. This kind of shot was effective and caused great destruction, which explains why today we use the expression to refer to a definite, uncompromising response. To say that someone refused to do something point-blank means that they refused outright, without the slightest possibility of deviation from the decision – rather as a point-blank shot goes undeviatingly to its target.

point of no return. Originally, the point in an aircraft's flight at which it no longer has sufficient fuel to return to its point of departure and therefore must proceed. Hence the figurative use to mean the point, as in a course of action, beyond which there is no turning back.

point-to-point. A cross-country race on horseback in which competitors have to race directly from one visual point – usually a landmark – to another. *See also* STEEPLCHASE.

poison pill. A poison pill, usually cyanide, is carried by spies or undercover agents so that they can kill themselves, if necessary, rather than be captured alive. Hence the figurative meaning in business and financial circles, dating from the 1980s – a poison pill being any strategy used by a company to make it unprofitable or impractical for others to make a takeover bid for it.

Poll Tax is the popular name for the COMMUNITY CHARGE, which was introduced to Scotland in 1989 and to the rest of Britain in 1990. It replaced the old rating system by which local taxes were assessed on the basis of the size and situation of the property occupied by an individual or family. The Poll Tax is unrelated to property and is instead levied on each adult resident in the area; it is, literally, a 'head tax', poll being an archaic word for 'head'. Though greeted as a fair and equitable development by single occupants of large houses, who will benefit financially from it, the Poll Tax is unpopular among those large families living in small homes who will have to foot a bigger bill. The long-term effects of this new taxation system remain to be seen.

Pollyanna. The name of the heroine of children's books by the American author Eleanor Hodgman Porter (1868–1920), characterised by her unquenchable happiness and optimism, and noted for her skill at 'the glad game' – finding cause for happiness in the most disastrous situations. Hence the epithet Pollyanna is bestowed on anyone who is irritatingly cheerful or who achieves happiness through self-delusion.

pom or **pommie** as it's sometimes known, is an Australian term for an Englishman. No generally accepted derivation has been traced but several suggestions have been offered. One speculates that pom is derived from the French word *pomme*, meaning an apple and referring to the red and white colouring of an Englishman newly-arrived down-under. According to Australian tradition it relates to the word POHM (Prisoner of His Majesty) that early convicts had stamped on their clothing when they were transported. A third suggests that it was coined by the convicts who described themselves as Prisoners of Mother England.

poodle-faker. A ladies' man or womaniser; one who cultivates female society, especially for the sake of self-advancement. The expression originated in the British army in India around the turn of the century. The reference is to someone who behaves in the manner of a lapdog.

poor as a church mouse. When someone is described as such they are very poor indeed, for in a church, which has no kitchen and no food left around, a mouse has a very lean time of it.

poppycock. In common use a few decades ago to describe ridiculous chatter or nonsense. It was a respect-able word, which indicates that its origin was not widely known. Poppycock can be traced directly to the Dutch word *pappekak*. This in turn is derived from the Latin words *pappa* for food and *cacare*, to defecate – which in modern translation might give us shit or, perhaps, bullshit, which is exactly what poppycock is.

popular capitalism. The kind of capitalism practised by the British Conservative government over the last decade. It aims to make capitalists (and thus guaranteed Tories) of a large segment of the population – an aim which has been achieved by selling off to the public various nationalised industries (gas and steel, for example) and encouraging share-ownership, profit-sharing and the formation of small businesses.

pork barrel. Since the Reconstruction era in the aftermath of the Civil War, 'pork' has been an American slang term, particularly in the context of Congressional politics, for favours or financial benefits obtained by means of graft or patronage. Later the term pork barrel came into use when Federal funding became available for projects such as river or harbour improvements or public buildings, and such funds were allocated to a particular distinct to buy the allegiance of the congressman for that district or to reward him for services rendered.

pork chopper. American term for a union official whose sole concern is the amount of money he can make for himself by abusing the power his position confers.

pornography. The word pornography is Greek for 'the writing of prostitutes'; it has been speculated that it referred originally to obscene stories and tracts about the activities of prostitutes.

posh. Wealthy travellers making the journey to India and back on a P&O

steamship would, at considerable expense, book a portside cabin for the outward journey and a starboard one on the homeward. This arrangement ensured that they were always accommodated on the shadier side of the ship and therefore had a more comfortable journey. This kind of booking was recorded as POSH (Port Out, Starboard Home), which soon became a word to describe first-class passengers and, by association, anyone smart or grand.

post-haste. To do something as quickly as possible. The phrase derives from the days when mail was transported by messengers on horseback. Teams of fast horses were kept ready at intervals along the route, often at inns. When the messenger came galloping into the inn yard he would shout 'Post haste', which gave him priority over other travellers waiting for horses.

pot. One of the most common slang terms for the drug marijuana. The name probably derives from the Mexican-Spanish word *potiguaya*, meaning marijuana leaves, but there may also be some association of ideas with the word 'tea', another slang term for marijuana.

pot, to go to. To go to pieces, to disintegrate, to fall apart. The expression probably originated in a medieval kitchen and, more specifically, a medieval stewpot. It is an allusion to the fact that meat for a stew is first chopped into pieces, then cooked in a pot for a long time until it begins to disintegrate. An alternative theory traces the phrase back to a nameless tailor who dropped a stone into a pot for every funeral he saw pass by on its way to the nearby cemetery. When his time came to make the journey, someone is said to have commented that he had gone to pot.

pot luck. This phrase originated at a time when every household had a pot simmering over the fire. Unexpected visitors would be told if they wanted to eat they would have to take pot luck, i.e. take a chance with whatever there was in the pot, good or bad. Today, despite the microwave and the deep-freeze, we still use the same phrase to mean exactly the same thing.

pot shot, to take a. Originally to take a quick, spontaneous shot at any creature with the aim of bagging it for the cooking pot. It is used more generally today to describe an opportunistic attack of any kind, verbal as well as physical, on someone who is unprepared and unarmed.

The word **snipe** has developed along similar lines. A snipe was originally a long-billed bird found mainly in marshy areas. From this came the verb to snipe, describing at first the way in which snipe were hunted and shot and being later applied to a concealed marksman. And from this, rather like pot shot, we also get the figurative sense of sniping as being a barbed verbal attack.

potato. The word derives ultimately from the Haitian word *batata* for a sweet potato. When in the 16th century the Spanish discovered the sweet potato in the West Indies they brought it back to Europe where it soon became known as a *patata*. Later, when Spanish explorers found a similar plant growing in Peru they assumed it was just another variety of *patata*. So it was that the new vegetable came to be known in England as the potato, despite the fact that it had practically nothing to do with the original *batata*.

potboiler. A work of art or literature, usually of inferior quality, which is produced merely for the sake of the money it will provide 'to keep the pot boiling' – that is, to secure the necessaries of life.

poteen. Irish whiskey that is illegally distilled and thus escapes duty. The name comes from the Irish *poitin*, meaning a little pot.

poverty trap. A CATCH 22 situation in which poor families and individuals who receive state benefits are discouraged from finding work. If they do get a job (almost inevitably a low-paid one) they lose their right to benefit and thus end up worse off than they would have been had they remained unemployed.

powder, to take a. This Americanism means to race off or leave a place suddenly. The origin has yet to be traced but that has not prevented a number of theories. Flea powder has been proposed as one source, with the phrase alluding to the speed with which fleas quit their host when the powder is applied. Another suggests that 'powder' alludes to the dust that rises in the road as someone disappears up it at speed. A third, that the 'powder' was a laxative whose results required the taker to make a quick dash to a lavatory. Take your pick.

power dressing. A style of dress adopted by female executives and managers to emphasise their authority and seriousness. The fashion originated in America but has become widely adopted elsewhere. Power dressing started with the female business suit, cut on the same lines and of the same fabric as the traditional male suit. Shoulder pads, sober colours and discreet designer labels are all part of the image, designed to distinguish the high-powered businesswoman from other more frivolously dressed and lower-status female workers. *See also* POWER LUNCHING.

power lunching. The practice of clinching a major deal over a midday meal is known as 'power lunching'. It usually takes place in fashionable and expensive restaurants to underline the status and influence of the participants. A power lunch may involve the ingestion of 'power food', which varies with changing culinary fashion but has in the past included the minimal *nouvelle cuisine*, with its implication of fitness and perfection, and raw steak or fish, with its overtone of the predatory carnivore. The truly dynamic also hold power breakfasts and the phenomenon of power teas has recently been reported, though quite how one can promote an aggressive and serious image while eating cream cakes and balancing a teacup is not absolutely clear.

praise the Lord and pass the ammunition. This is the title and chorus line of a song by Frank Loesser that became popular in America in 1942. The phrase is said to have actually been used by a Navy chaplain as an exhortation to the ship's gunners during the Japanese attack on Pearl Harbour in 1941. As to the name of the chaplain there is some confusion. Some credit the saying to Lieutenant Howell M. Forgy, chaplain of the USS *New Orleans*; others to Captain W. H. Maguire who at first denied using the phrase but later conceded that he might have done so.

pre-owned and **pre-used** are euphemisms for 'second-hand'. They were coined by car dealers in the USA, for whom 'second-hand' is a dirty word. The image of the second-hand car dealer is a shady one; they are seen, rightly or not, as crooks. When opponents wished to discredit Richard Nixon they asked simply, 'Would you buy a second-hand car from this man?' The answer was a resounding no.

prequel. When a book or film proves itself to be a best-seller publishers and movie companies immediately start planning the sequel. This can be difficult if, in the original story, the author foolishly killed off his characters. In this case, or when a sequel has sold well and the publisher feels that the source can be tapped further, the author may be asked to produce a prequel – a novel or film script that tells about the early lives and adventures of the characters who appeared in the previous book.

press gang. For several hundred years sailing was considered such an unpleasant and dangerous career that captains were obliged to forcibly recruit a proportion of their crew. To this purpose they employed a press gang who carried out the job of *impressment*, searching for sailors in portside taverns and offering them *prest* or *imprest* money (from the French verb *prêter*, meaning 'to lend') to join up for a voyage. Until 1830 the Royal Navy relied on this method of recruitment too; after that time pay and conditions were so improved that voluntary enlistment became the order of the day. Today we use the phrase to indicate that we have been forced to do something against our will or better judgement, for example, 'I only did it because they press-ganged me into it.'

prima donna. Literally, in Italian, this means 'first lady'. It came to be used of the principal female singer in an opera company. Because such singers have gained a reputation for being full of self-esteem, touchy, temperamental and jealous of possible rivals, the term 'prima donna' has come to be applied to anyone, of either sex, who displays such traits.

private eye. A private detective. The Pinkerton detective agency used an open eye as its symbol, together with the slogan 'We never sleep'. To criminals and others the Pinkerton agency was known as The Eye. Some authorities claim that this is the origin of the term 'private eye'. Others say that it just derives from the initials P.I. for Private Investigator. Whatever the origin, the expression was popularised in the 1930s by crime writers such as Raymond Chandler.

processorrhoea. A kind of verbal diarrhoea suffered by people who use word processors. The word processor allows a writer to go back over their work and add extra words and phrases that they wouldn't have bothered with if they had been using a typewriter. As a result, some people who used to write clearly and concisely now turn out long, tedious, elaborately constructed sentences that no one wants to read.

professional foul. A calculated offence; an illegal act committed to prevent an opponent from scoring in some way. The expression was first used to describe the cold-blooded fouls committed by football players. It is now used more generally to describe deliberate spoiling tactics employed not only in sport but in business, too.

pronto. Quickly; at once. This word was taken unchanged from Spanish. It is the equivalent of the English word 'prompt'.

propaganda. The word comes from the title of a committee set up in Rome in 1622 by Pope Gregory XV. Known as the *Congregatio de propaganda fide* (translated as College for propagating the Faith), it had the job of overseeing missionary activities and ensuring that the Catholic religion was disseminated to all corners of the world. In Britain the committee was known as the Propaganda and British Protestants viewed its missionary work as the spreading of lies. Hence, over the years, propaganda has come to mean deliberate DISINFORMATION designed to influence the way people think or feel.

protection. A euphemism for extortion and usually operated by a protection racket – a gang who threatens to smash up or ruin a business if its owner refuses to pay bribes, known as protection money. The only protection on offer is from the racket itself.

psychedelic is defined by the *Supplement to the Oxford English Dictionary* as follows:

Of a drug: producing an expansion of consciousness through greater awareness of the senses and emotional feelings and the revealing of unconscious motivations . . . producing an effect or sensation held to resemble that produced by a psychedelic drug . . . having vivid colours, often in bold abtract designs or in motion.

The derivation is from two Greek words meaning 'soul-clearing' but usually translated as 'mind-expanding'. The term was first proposed by H. Osmond in a letter to Aldous Huxley in 1956, but did not come into widespread use until the late 1960s when there was a great deal of experimentation with drugs such as cannabis and LSD.

Psychobabble. A dismissive term for psychological and quasi-psychological jargon, often tedious or meaningless except to the person who uses it. Psychobabble is particularly associated with 'alternative' Californian lifestyles of the 1970s and 80s and inspired a number of satires. Those who use such language are interested in analysis and therapy and enjoy talking about their feelings and motives.

public school. The use of this phrase to denote a private, fee-paying educational establishment has been a source of confusion for many years. A public school is what the Americans, quite sensibly, call a private school.

pukka is derived form the Hindi word *pokka*, imported to England from India in the late 17th century. The original word was applied to anything mature, ripe or ready. The English version has a slightly different slant, being applied to anything that is genuine, honest, reliable, socially acceptable.

pull out all the stops. This expression, meaning to give one's all or exert one's best efforts, originated among church organists. An organ's stops are used to change its sound and by pulling them all out, an organist could produce a truly eardrum shattering noise.

Pullman. Strictly speaking, a luxuriously fitted railway sleeping-carriage, named after its American designer, George Pullman (1831–97). The name is often used loosely for any luxury railway carriage or train or even a motor coach (for road transport).

pumpkin time is an American phrase which refers to the story of *Cinderella*, whose coach turned back into a pumpkin at the stroke of midnight. Used metaphorically, pumpkin time refers to the moment when a period of artificial or unusual prosperity ends and things revert to the way they were originally; that moment when the golden coach turns back into a plain old pumpkin.

Punch, pleased as. Someone who is very self-satisfied may be referred to as pleased as Punch, the allusion being to the character Punch in a Punch and Judy show. When these shows originated in Italy in the 17th century Punch was known as Pulcinello and was a vain, self-important character. In the English version of the show his name was shortened to Punch but he retained his pompous characteristics, particularly when he was gloating in satisfaction over his evil plans to defeat Judy.

punch drunk. Boxers who have been on the receiving end of too many hard punches may end up with brain damage that, typically, causes slurred speech, slow thinking and bad coordination. As a result they may seem to be drunk, which is why the expression punch drunk was coined around the year 1915 to describe this phenomenon.

pundit. A learned man; an authority on some subject. The word comes from the Hindi *pandit*, meaning a person learned in Sanskrit literature, law, religion, etc.

punk. In Shakespeare's day a punk was a prostitute; indeed it has been speculated that the word is a variation of spunk, slang for sperm. In gangster movies of the 1930s and 40s it was often used as a term of abuse to a man: 'You dirty, no-good punk'. By the late 1970s punk had become a British youth movement and punks, with their multi-coloured Mohican haircuts, bondage trousers and safety-pins through their noses, were the latest symbols of youthful rebellion and alienation. They made it their business to flout ordinary social values and prided themselves on being dirty, rude and ugly. Punk music was deafeningly loud and played by groups who boasted that they knew only three chords. For a brief time the movement looked truly anarchic, but then fashion caught up with it. With Sex Pistols' records in the charts, the King's Road punks posing for tourist photos and tartan trousers on sale in chain stores it became just another in a succession of short-lived youth cults.

pup, to be sold a. *See under* CAT – TO LET THE CAT OUT OF THE BAG.

purple patches. The term is applied to any gushing, ornate, overwrought passages in a longer piece of literary work. If the entire work is written in this way then it may be described as **purple prose**. The expression purple patches was coined by the Roman poet Horace, who advocated that all such passages be cut.

push, to be given the. *See under* CARDS, TO BE GIVEN ONE'S CARDS.

pussyfoot. This verb alludes to the way in which cats walk silently and delicately about, cunningly avoiding pitfalls. Applied to humans, pussyfooting means to behave evasively or hesitantly. Someone who is told to 'Stop pussyfooting around' is instructed to behave more openly and with less caution.

puzzle palace. Originally US Army slang for any military headquarters, including the Pentagon. Extended, in civilian use, to refer to any place where important decisions are made in secret.

Pyrrhic victory. The original Pyrrhic victory occurred at Asculum, in the third century BC, when king Pyrrhus of Epirus led his army against the Romans. He won the battle but in the process so many of his men were killed that he was unable to sustain his attempts to conquer the Western world. As a result a Pyrrhic victory means a hollow victory – one in which the winner loses so much that he is no better off than the vanquished.

Q

Q.E.D. The abbreviation of *quod erat demonstrandum*, Latin for 'which was to be proved', a phrase used by the ancient Greek mathematician Euclid at the end of his theorems to indicate that he had solved the problem set out or made the point he had intended to demonstrate. We use the phrase in much the same way today, applying it when a problem has been solved or a difficulty overcome.

QT, on the. Something which is mentioned on the quiet, QT referring to the first and last letters of 'quiet'. The derivation of the phrase has not been identified, but the expression was used in a number of popular ballads at the end of the last century. Perhaps the best-known of these is 'Ta-ra-ra-boom-de-ay' which contains the lines:

> A sweet Tuxedo girl you see,
> Queen of swell society,
> Fond of fun as fun can be
> When it's on the strict Q.T.

quack. A charlatan; a familiar, disparaging term for any doctor. This is a contraction of 'quacksalver' – a term for an itinerant medical charlatan who hawked his nostrums to credulous rustics and 'quacked' in praise of his 'salves' or remedies.

Quaker. A member of the religious sect the Society of Friends, founded by George Fox (1624–91). There have been a number of religious sects – such as Shakers, Rollers, Jumpers – whose name derives from the physical contortions they exhibit in their excess of religious fervour. The name Quaker had some years earlier been applied in this way to a different group of religious enthusiasts. But it was first applied to the Society of Friends by Justice Bennet at Derby when Fox was on trial before him and Fox bade him and others to quake and tremble at the voice of the Lord.

quality control. A method of inspecting goods as they are manufactured so that any mistakes or poor-quality samples can be weeded out. Part of the great manufacturing success of the Japanese in recent years has been as a result of their rigorous application of quality control.

quality time. A phrase used by American parents, and an increasing number of British ones, to describe the time they spend with their children. It means intensive, valuable time in which the parent concentrates entirely on the child. Quality time tends to be a vogue concept among busy working parents who employ others to care for their children and who see them for perhaps only an hour or two each day. When time together is so limited, it has to be quality time.

quango is defined by the *Oxford English Dictionary* as

a semi-public administrative body outside the civil service but financed by the exchequer and having members appointed by the government.

The term is an acronym which originated in the USA in the mid-1960s and became popular in the UK in the mid-1970s. With regard to what the acronym stands for, there are a number of variations: Quasi non-government(al) organisation; Quasi-autonomous non-government(al) organisation; Quasi-autonomous national government(al) organisation. The acronym has also spawned the coinages 'quangocrat' and 'quangocracy'.

quantum jump or **quantum leap.** A sudden large advance or increase; a 'breakthrough'. In physics, a quantum jump is the transition of an atom from one of a limited number of possible states to another. The non-technical and metaphorical use of the expression dates from the mid-1950s.

quarantine. A period of compulsory isolation or segregation to prevent the spread of contagion or infection. The expression comes from the Italian *quarantina*, meaning forty days. When ships came to Venice from the plague-ridden east they had to wait offshore for forty days. Only after that time, on condition that there were no signs of plague on board, were the crew and passengers allowed ashore.

quark. One of a group of hypothetical sub-atomic particles (originally three in number) carrying a fractional electric charge and conceived as being a constituent of known elementary particles such as electrons. The term was coined by the American physicist Murray Gell-Mann (born 1929), using a word invented by James Joyce in his *Finnegans Wake* (1939), where it occurs in the sentence: 'Three quarks for Muster Mark!'

quasar. This is a shortened form of 'quasi-stellar radio source' – a very distant celestial object that resembles a star but emits usually bright blue and ultraviolet light and powerful radio waves. The word quasar first appeared in print in a paper by H. Y. Chou in *Physics Today* in 1964.

Queensberry rules. A code of rules for the sport of boxing, originally drawn up in 1867 and remaining in effect until 1929, when they were superseded by rules issued by the British Boxing Board of Control. The rules took their name from John Sholto Douglas (1844–1920), the eighth Marquis of Queensberry, who took a keen interest in the sport.

queer. The word has had a number of colloquial and slang uses. In old-fashioned criminal slang it means 'base' or 'worthless'. In Ireland it may mean 'eccentric'. In English colloquial use it may mean 'ill' or 'poorly'. These uses have tended to be driven out by the use of queer as a pejorative term for 'homosexual'. This usage seems to have originated in the USA *c*.1920 and to have been current from the UK from the 1930s.

queer street, to be in. To be in debt or in other financial difficulties. This expression is said to be a punning one, based on the practice of a tradesman putting a query – ? – next to the name of any customer whose financial soundness was doubtful.

qui vive, on the. This phrase, still occasionally heard, is based on the challenge traditionally used by French sentries. *Qui vive?* means 'who lives?', a Gallic version of 'Who goes there?' The phrase entered the English language in the first quarter of the 18th century and is sometimes heard today in the expression 'on the qui vive', meaning 'on the lookout'.

quibble. This term derives from the Latin word *quibus*, meaning 'whom or which', scribbled by lawyers in the margins of documents to query an ambiguous legal point. The resulting disputes gave rise to the word 'quib' for a NITPICKING argument. In the

17th century this became quibble – a petty dispute over minor details.

quick, cut to the. Someone who is deeply hurt, literally or figuratively. The 'quick' is the body's most tender flesh and derives from the Anglo-Saxon word *cwic*, meaning 'living' (as in the biblical phrase 'the quick and the dead'). Traditionally the most sensitive flesh is that beneath the fingernails, known as the 'quick'.

quid pro quo. A rather grand version of TIT FOR TAT. It is the Latin phrase for 'something for another' and means simply that for something rendered an equal return is required.

quisling. A traitor. Vidkun Abraham Quisling (1887–1945) was a Norwegian politician. He was Defence Minister in the Norwegian government from 1931–3, but resigned and later formed a minority right-wing party, the Nasjonal Samling (National Unity) party. When the Germans invaded Norway in 1940 they installed Quisling as a puppet prime minister. Though hated by most of his people, Quisling remained in power until the Germans surrendered in Norway in 1945. He was then arrested, tried for treason, and shot by firing squad in October 1945.

quixotic. Someone who has impossibly high ideals and lofty ambitions, characteristics embodied in Miguel de Cervantes' fictional hero Don Quixote whose life was spent pursuing adventure and romance. In the middle of the 17th century an enthusiastic, visionary person was named a Quixote after the famous Spanish knight and more than a hundred years later, in 1791, the adjective quixotic came into use.

quiz. A test of one's knowledge, general or otherwise, often as an entertainment; an informal questionnaire. This is the common meaning nowadays. In former days it has meant: an eccentric person; any odd-looking person or thing; a piece of banter or playful mockery; a mocking look; a hoax; a monocle. There is an amusing (but almost certainly false) story that purports to account for the origin of this word. According to the story, a Mr James Daly, the manager of a Dublin theatre, sometime about 1780 made a bet that he could introduce a new word into the English language within twenty-four hours, and furthermore that this word would be completely meaningless. He then employed all the urchins he could find to go round Dublin chalking the word 'quiz' on every wall in the city. As a result the curiosity of the citizens was aroused and they were soon all asking one another what the mysterious word meant. Thus Mr Daly won his wager and the word passed into the language. In fact, all major dictionaries concur that the origin of the word is not known. Its first appearance in print dates from 1782 in the diary of Madame D'Arblay, otherwise known as Fanny Burney, and here it is used with the meaning 'an eccentric person'. It is possible that it is somehow derived from the Latin *quis*, meaning 'who?' or 'what?' or from the words 'inquisitve' or 'inquisition'.

quonset hut. A pre-fabricated building of corrugated iron on a bolted steel foundation. It is the American equivalent of the British NISSEN HUT, and takes its name from Quonset Point, Rhode Island, where these buildings were first made *c*.1942.

R

Rs, the three. Sir William Curtis is widely attributed with coining this phrase. A biscuit merchant, MP and Lord Mayor of London, he took up the cause of education at the turn of the 19th century – a cause which some have suggested he was unsuited to support, being illiterate himself. The three Rs that he promoted are reading, writing and arithmetic, which he presented as ''Riting, Reading and 'Rithmetic'. Whether he was truly illiterate or whether he simply knew a good phrase when he saw one remains something of a mystery.

rabbit. In Cockney rhyming slang to rabbit means to talk. The original phrase was 'rabbit and pork' but only the shortened version, evoking the constantly nibbling jaw of the rabbit, has survived.

Rachmanism. Exploitation of slum tenants by unscrupulous landlords. Under the Rent Act of 1957 rents were controlled at an artificially low level compared to the value of the property being rented, so long as the original tenant remained in occupation. This led to a situation in which an unscrupulous person could buy property with such sitting tenants at an advantageous price, harass the tenants to force them to leave, and then sell the property at a much higher price or re-let it at a much higher rent. Peter Rachman (1920–62), a Polish immigrant, operated in such a way in the Paddington area of London, and Rachmanism became a major scandal and political issue in 1962–3.

rack – to go to rack and ruin. The 'rack' in this phrase was originally 'wreck', which given us a clue about the meaning of the expression. Someone whose vessel or goods were lost in a shipwreck was likely to be ruined by the disaster, which is why to go to rack and ruin means to be brought to complete destitution, to have one's fortune destroyed.

rack one's brains, to. It is widely agreed that this expression refers to the instrument of torture known as the rack, introduced to English dungeons in the 15th century from Germany and still to be seen in places such as Warwick Castle. The victims of this machinery had their hands and feet tied to rollers at each end of the frame and were gradually stretched until their joints dislocated. The rack was normally used to gain information or a confession from a suspect and it's not difficult to imagine how the mental effort of a torture victim, trying desperately to find the right answer to the torturer's questions, gave us the phrase to rack one's brains.

racket. The word, meaning a noise or disturbance, was first recorded in 1565 and was probably coined in imitation of the noise to which it was applied (as were 'bang' and 'crash', for example). By 1812 racket had come to mean a trick or ruse, perhaps because pickpockets and other criminals used firecrackers or created noisy disturbances to distract the attention of their victims. This sense of the word fell into disuse until it was revived again in the USA in 1928 to describe the criminal activities of organised gangs during Prohibition.

radar. A device, originally developed in the USA *c.*1941, to determine the presence and location of an object by measuring the time for the echo of a radio wave to return from it and the direction from which it returns. The word is an acronym – from 'radio direction and ranging'. It is also rather apt that the word is palindromic.

rag, to chew the. *See* CHEW THE FAT.

ragtime. Rhythm marked by frequent syncopation, as is common in black American piano music from the late 19th century and early 20th century; music using such a rhythm. The expression, probably a slurring of the phrase 'ragged time', referring to the then unconventional syncopation, was popularised and perpetuated by the Irving Berlin tune *Alexander's Ragtime Band* of 1911. In 1912 a show at the London Hippodrome was entitled *Hello Ragtime*. One of the principal ragtime composers was Scott Joplin (1868–1917), whose work enjoyed a revival in the 1970s.

rails, off the. When a young person gets into trouble with authority they may be described by their despairing elders as having come off the rails. The allusion is to a train or some other kind of transport that involves rails or tracks. A train that comes off the rails has deviated from the straight and narrow and becomes useless, a disaster, as a result.

railroad, to. This verb originated in the USA and was inspired by the speed and disregard with which railroad companies laid their tracks across forests, mountains and anything else that got in their way. By the end of the 19th century to railroad meant to hustle someone or something through with unseemly haste and without regard to the proper formalities.

rain cats and dogs, to. To rain very heavily. There are several theories to account for the origin of this common expression, but none is convincing. One theory is that the expression originated in days when street drainage was so bad that a heavy downpour was quite capable of drowning cats and dogs that were caught in it. Another theory has it that in Norse mythology cats were supposed to have great influence on the weather, and dogs were symbolic of the wind. Yet another theory is that the phrase derives from the Greek word *catadupa*, meaning a waterfall. The first recorded literary use of the expression is in Jonathan Swift's work *A Complete Collection of Polite and Ingenious Conversation* (1738). But much earlier, in 1653, Richard Brome had written a play, *The City Witt*, in which he used a variant of the expression:

it shall rain . . . Dogs and Polecats.'

raincheck, to take a. If rain forces the cancellation of an outdoor sporting event in the USA, ticketholders may be offered a raincheck – a free pass to a future game. From this practice came the expression 'to take a raincheck', used by those who have to refuse an invitation but want to make it clear that they would be glad to accept another time. The phrase has been used so often in American films and TV programmes that British audiences know its meaning if not its origin.

raise Cain. To create a disturbance, nuisance or trouble. This is a reference to the story in the Book of Genesis of Cain and Abel. Cain's jealousy and violent anger led him to kill his brother Abel. Thus for someone to raise Cain is to revive the spirit of this murderer.

rake-off. A share in money that is acquired illegally or unethically. This American slang expression originated in the late 19th century. Originally it meant the percentage of each pot or stake taken by a gambling house or casino, and refers to the rake used by croupiers to gather in payments on a gaming table.

Ramada socialist is a modern variation on the traditional champagne socialist. The phrase originated in 1987 when the Labour Party conference was held in Brighton and the leaders of the party were booked into the Ramada Renaissance, one of a new chain of expensive hotels. This aroused the wrath of Labour MP Dennis Skinner, a left-winger known for his objections to the softening-up of the party. He found the luxury of the Ramada at odds with the tenets of socialism and coined the expression Ramada socialism as a term of abuse. It was aimed at those Labour supporters who believe that to have any chance of gaining power the party must shift its policies to appeal to the growing middle class – a middle class swelled by the newly-prosperous working-class people who have traditionally supported Labour.

Rambo. Someone who behaves in a mindlessly aggressive manner. The expression comes from the name of the character John Rambo, played by Sylvester Stallone in a series of violent movies produced in the 1980s. The name has also given rise to the adjective 'Ramboesque' and the noun 'Ramboism'.

ramshackle. There are at least two contenders for the source of this word, describing something that is run-down or falling apart. The first is the old word *ranshacle* meaning 'wrecked by plundering'. The second is the Icelandic word *ramshakkr*, meaning 'twisted'.

rap music, sometimes known simply as rap, is a song (often improvised) that is spoken rather than sung to the rhythm of a heavy electronic beat. Rap is part of the HIP HOP youth culture and songs refer to the kind of issues that concern black youth. In modern black slang to rap more generally means to talk or chat.

rapture of the deep. This romantic-sounding phrase is used by divers to describe the light-headed, ecstatic feelings caused by breathing in compressed air that contains large amounts of nitrogen. It is known rather more prosaically as nitrogen narcosis.

raspberry. A sign of disapproval – a noise produced by blowing hard with the tongue between the lips. This is the British equivalent of what is called in the USA a BRONX CHEER. It is cockney rhyming slang: raspberry tart = fart.

rat race. The struggle for success, particularly in one's career, fiercely competitive and often unscrupulous. This phrase, an example of the word 'rat' used to express contempt, originated in the USA *c.*1930.

read between the lines. *See under* LINES.

Real McCoy, The. *See under* MCCOY.

realpolitik. A word of German origin, realpolitik describes the kind of politics that are dominated by the day-to-day needs of a situation and not by ideology; practical politics based on the best interests of a party or a nation and not on any higher moral or social objectives.

rebirthing. A therapy developed by Otto Rank for resolving the traumas caused by the stress of birth. Rebirthing enthusiasts believe that emotional and physical problems experienced in adult life can be traced back to birth, and that by re-experiencing the moment of birth adults can rid themselves of the distress and problems they have carried into later life. The organisation that promotes this therapy is known as Theta.

received pronunciation. At a time when dialects and regional accents were frowned on, 'received pronunciation' was the only kind of English heard on British radio or television. Known also as Oxford English, BBC English and standard English, received pronunciation is the kind of educated upper-middle-class English spoken by people in the south-east of England. Though it is now more common to hear regional accents on the radio and TV, a recent survey by one Professor Honey has shown that there is still prejudice against them and that people who speak 'received pronunciation' have a better chance of achieving success in their career than those who speak with accents.

red – like a red rag to a bull. This expression is based on the erroneous belief that the colour red has an enraging effect on bulls, which is why matadors carry cloaks lined with red into the bullring. Experiments have proved that it is not the colour that infuriates the bull but the constant swishing and flicking movement of the cape. Whatever the truth, the belief will probably persist as long as the phrase is in use to describe anything that is calculated to incite rage. Those who enjoy country rambles and worry about coming across bulls in fields may be interested to know that other experiments show that bulls take little interest in people with no clothes on. The message is clear; don't just remove that red sweater – take everything else off too!

red, to paint the town. *See under* PAINT.

red-eye. Originally airline operators' jargon to describe a flight that takes off late at night and arrives very early the next morning. Its passengers, deprived of sleep, emerge red-eyed and exhausted. The phrase was picked up by the businessmen who travelled on the red-eye and came to wider notice when it was mentioned in a 1988 television advert promoting an airline. The advert featured a group of hard-faced businessmen planning to sabotage a rival's chances of success by booking him on the red-eye to London in the anticipation that he would arrive in no fit state to take them on. They are confounded when he arives fresh and relaxed after a comfortable journey across the Atlantic courtesy of the airline's wonderful new services.

red-handed, to be caught. To be caught in the act of committing a crime. The expression alludes to the murderer caught with his victim's blood still on his hands.

red goods. In advertising and marketing circles 'red goods' are products purchased on a regular basis, consumed quickly and then replaced again. Prime examples are fresh foods, fruit, vegetables and so on. *See also* WHITE GOODS and BROWN GOODS.

Red Guard. The name given to a revolutionary youth movement, or a member of this movement, in China during the Cultural Revolution of 1967–77. The term had earlier been used to describe a member of an organised detachment of workers during the Russian revolution of 1917, and to members of other revolutionary groups in Finland in

1918 and in China during the civil war of 1927–37, and may nowadays be applied loosely to any fanatical revolutionary activist.

red herring. Anything that serves to divert attention from the main issue. In the literal sense, a red herring is simply one that has been dried and smoked – a process that changes the colour of the fish from white to a reddish hue. Herring, cured in this way, has a persistent odour, and it was at one time used by huntsmen when training their hounds to follow a scent. But a red herring, if drawn across the path of a fox, could be used by anyone who wished to spoil the sport, so as to divert the hounds from the chase.

red letter day. Any memorable day or date. This expression derives from the practice, which has lasted since the 15th century, of distinguishing feast days and saints' days in calendars and almanacs by marking their dates in red ink as opposed to the black ink used for other dates. The figurative use of the expression goes back at least as far as the 18th century. In Fanny Burney's novel *Cecilia* (1782), she wrote

Today is a red-letter day, so that's the reason for it.

red light district. The infamous Dodge City is said to have been the first place to have a red light district – not that this particular district offered anything new, for cities the world over have had their official and unofficial brothels and areas of prostitution for thousands of years. But Dodge City was the first, according to repute, to have its brothels and pleasure-houses lit by red-tinted lamps.

red tape. Excessive and punctilious attention to formality and routine; bureaucratic procedures. It has been claimed that this phrase was coined by Charles Dickens – but it appears that Dickens was anticipated by the American writer Washington Irving, who used the expression in the early 1800s.

redbrick. A term used to denote some British universities, as distinct from the older institutions of Oxford and Cambridge, the ancient Scottish universities and some of the London colleges, and from the more modern institutions established since the 1960s. The term is applied particularly to those univerisities established at the end of the 19th century and early in the 20th century in industrial cities such as Leeds, Manchester, Birmingham, Liverpool, Sheffield, Reading, etc. The phrase was coined by 'Bruce Truscot' – the pseudonym of Professor E. Allison Peers – in his book *Redbrick University*, published in 1943.

redneck. A crude, bigoted person, typically a poor white American from the Southern states; a PHILISTINE, entrenched in right-wing philosophy. Two theories have been put forward explaining the origin of the phrase. The first is that rednecks tend to be angry about encroachments on what they see as their liberties and that anger makes their necks red. The second and more interesting theory is that poor Southern whites are prone to a disease known as pellagra which can produce scaly red dermatitis around the neck.

reefer. A cigarette containing marijuana. This American expression originated in the 1920s and probably derives from the Mexican–Spanish word *grifo*, meaning marijuana.

reggae. Popular music of Jamaican origin, that combines elements of BLUES with a strongly accentuated off-beat and often a prominent bass. The origin of the name is not known, but may be connected with the Jamaican colloquial expression *rage-rage*, meaning a quarrel or row.

Remember the Alamo! The Alamo

was the name of a garrison head-quarters where in 1836 a small force of 160 US soldiers were reputedly massacred by a force of 4,000 soldiers under the command of General Antonio Santa Ana, president of the newly-emergent independent Mexico. The Americans had their revenge later that year when US troops under General Sam Houston defeated the Mexicans at San Jericho. 'Remember the Alamo!' was used as a rallying cry on that occasion. It was used as a rallying cry or as a warning on subsequent occasions by US troops, but it eventually degenerated into a mere catchphrase, and is nowadays never used except in jest.

rent boy. A young homosexual prostitute who can be 'rented' for a client's enjoyment. That, at least, is one theory to explain the phrase. Another suggests that these boys are often homeless and are driven into prostitution in an attempt to earn enough money to rent a place to live.

rich as Croesus, as. Phenomenally rich. It derives from the story of King Croesus, the last king of Lydia, who gathered a fortune so huge that his name became synonymous with vast wealth. At his court he gathered famous philosophers and wise men, including Aesop and Solon. Croesus was known to be a happy man and one day he asked Solon whether he had met anyone happier. 'Call no man happy until he is dead,' was Solon's reply, by which he meant that even the happiest and wealthiest of men could experience disaster. As it turned out, Solon was proved correct. Cyrus the Great invaded Lydia and took Croesus captive, condeming him to be burned to death. As the king was escorted to his execution he called out to Solon three times and Cyrus, on hearing the explanation of this, was moved to spare his life.

ride, to take someone for a. Today we use this phrase jokingly to describe someone who is tricked or fooled by another, but in the early decades of this century being taken for a ride was a method of killing and not at all amusing. Hymie Weiss, a Chicago gang member, is reputed to have developed the technique of pushing someone into the front seat of a car, driving them to a suitably desolate spot and shooting them. The body was often thrown out of the car as it sped away. This method of disposing of opponents was also used by the Nazis in Germany.

ride one's hobby-horse, to. Before a hobby came to mean a favourite pastime it referred to a small horse. From this in turn came the hobby-horse, a basket-work frame with room for a man inside, covered in a fabric skirt and with a horse's head. This extraordinary creature cavorted in Morris dances and other ancient fun and games and gave us the phrase 'horsing around', meaning to mess about. A child's toy horse was also known as a hobby-horse. One or other of these probably gave us the word hobby to describe an enjoyable pursuit; playing with its horse was the child's favourite hobby, while adults favoured the entertainment provided by the larger hobby-horse. When we refer to someone these days as riding or getting up on their hobby-horse we usually mean that they are dwelling at length on their favourite obsession.

ride roughshod, to. To ride rough-shod over someone is to disregard their feelings or interests; to treat them with contempt. 'Roughshod' horses wore shoes from which nail heads or points projected, thus enabling them to keep their grip in bad weather. A passerby who was kicked or trodden on by a roughshod horse might well feel that their safety had been disregarded by the owner for his own convenience. One authority has also suggested that in the 17th century horses were ridden into battle equipped with spiked shoes intended to inflict damage among enemy foot-soldiers. Whether or not this is accurate, it is easy to see how the expression 'to ride roughshod' got its meaning.

rider on a pale horse. *See under* GRIM REAPER.

riffraff. There is wide agreement that the term riffraff is derived from the French phrase *rif et raf*, but there the consensus of opinion ends. Some interpret *rif et raf* as meaning 'every last bit' and thus referring to rubbish; from there it is an easy progression from literal trash to the human kind. Others suggest that the verbs *rifler* (from which we get the English verb to rifle, meaning to ransack) and *raffler* (meaning to grab or snatch) are at the root of *rif et raf* and that people who habitually ransack or snatch things are correctly classified as riffraff. An alternative theory notes that in the Middle Ages the phrase 'riff nor raff' meant 'nothing' and proposes that it developed into riffraff, applied to people who had nothing. Whether disagreement exists about the derivation of the word, all authorities agree that it is applied to people who are undesirable members of the rabble or the MOB.

right-brain thinking. *See* LEFT-BRAIN THINKING.

right-hand man. The right side is always the place of honour and so it is quite logical that one's most trusted and loyal assistant should take that position. What is more, such a trusted servant would be as indispensable to his master as a right hand. These two points together are enough in themselves to explain why a valued assistant is known as a right-hand man. *See also* TO GET OUT OF BED ON THE WRONG SIDE.

right on. Originating among black Americans, this is an exclamation expressing approval, encouragement or agreement. The expression began to spread beyond the bounds of the black community in the 1960s, but it was current at least as far back as 1925 when it was recorded by Howard W. Odum and Guy B. Johnson in *The Negro and His Songs*:

Railroad Bill was a mighty sport,
Shot all buttons off high sheriff's coat,
Den hollered 'Right on, Desperado Bill!'

righteous. This black American expression, originating among jazz musicians in the 1930s, has two different meanings. On the one hand it may mean 'excellent' or 'genuine'. On the other hand it may mean 'typical of white people or of white society'.

Riley (or Reilly), to lead the life of, means to live luxuriously. The origin of this expression is a comic song called *Is That Mr Reilly?* It was written by Pat Rooney, and was popular in the USA in the 1880s. The song described what Reilly would do if he 'struck it rich', and had a chorus that went as follows:

Is that Mister Reilly, can anyone tell?
Is that Mister Reilly that owns the hotel?
Well, if that's Mister Reilly they speak of so highly,
Upon my soul, Reilly, you're doing quite well.

ring true, to. One test for identifying counterfeit coins was to drop them on a flagstone. Silver coins would emit a pure ringing tone while the fakes would just land with a flat thud. From this practice comes the expression to ring true, meaning to give indications of authenticity or genuineness. It is also the origin of the phrase to ring false, meaning exactly the opposite.

riot – to read the Riot Act. Under the Riot Act of 1715 magistrates were obliged to disperse riotous gatherings of twelve or more people by reading a proclamation. The opening lines of the proclamation went:

Our Sovereign Lord the King chargeth and commandeth all persons being here assembled immediately to disperse themselves, and peaceably to depart to their habitations or to their lawful business . . .

Anyone found to be rioting an hour later was liable to be arrested and sentenced to imprisonment or even death. Such sanctions are not invoked today but memories of the 1715 Act linger in the phrase to read the Riot Act, meaning to scold or warn an individual for their bad behaviour.

rise – to get a rise out of someone. This phrase originated among anglers who knew how a fish 'rises to the bait' and applied the same expression to a person who could be lured into becoming the butt of a practical joke. From this we get the phrase to get a rise out of someone, meaning to trick them into doing something that gives other people a laugh.

ritzy. The word was coined for Swiss hotelier Cesar Ritz who in the 19th century managed several of Europe's grandest and most famous hotels and who founded the Paris Ritz in the 1880s. His hotels were famed for their food (the chef Escoffier was a colleague) and their style. He never achieved his ambition to have a hotel in London and it was four years after his death that the London Ritz opened its doors. It soon became the meeting place for the most glamorous and famous people of the day and the word 'Ritz' became synonymous with style and chic – hence the word ritzy, applied these days to anything glamorous and costly. The title of the Irving Berlin song 'Putting on the Ritz' has also entered the language. **Putting on the Ritz** describes dressing up or preparing a place for a glittering occasion worthy of the Ritz.

river, to sell down the. This expression means to betray someone. The phrase originated in the USA when owners of domestic slaves sold them to Southern plantation owners, notorious for their brutality. A household slave who had been sold would be sent down the Mississippi to the plantations, hence the phrase to be sold down the river, meaning to be let down by a trusted person.

rob Peter to pay Paul, to. According to legend this phrase originated in 1540 when the Abbey Church of St Peter in Westminster was made a cathedral with its own diocese. Only a decade later it was absorbed into the diocese of St Paul's and many of its estates were used to pay for repairs to the older cathedral. Unfortunately the expression was already in common use by 1380 when John Wycliff wrote in his *Selected Works*:

How should God approve that you rob Peter, and give this robbery to Paul in the name of Christ.

Robbing Peter to pay Paul probably alludes to an even old Latin saying whose origins have not yet been uncovered, but whatever its ultimate derivation it refers to the practice of borrowing money from one person in order to pay off a debt owed to another.

robot. An automaton with humanlike intelligence and capabilities. This word was coined by the Czech novelist and dramatist Karel Čapek (1890–1938), whose play *R.U.R.* (*Rossum's Universal Robots*) was first produced in 1922, and played in London the following year. The play forecast a world in which machines would perform the work of humans. The word robot is derived from the Czech word *robota*, meaning forced labour or drudgery.

rock and roll. A type of popular music, characterised by a heavy beat and simple melodies, and containing elements of BLUES, folk and country music. The name, as well as the music it represents, was popularised by the American disc jockey Alan Freed (1922–65) in the early 1950s. However, the expression had been in use earlier. It was used as the title of a song in 1934, and it is believed to have derived from a black American slang expression for the sexual act.

rockabilly. A type of popular music, originating in the south-eastern USA *c.*1956, and so called because it combines elements of ROCK AND ROLL with elements of hillbilly music.

roger. No one knows the identity of the Roger after whom this verb was coined, or even if it was based on an individual's name. What *is* known is that to roger is current English slang for the sexual act. *See also* BONK.

roman à clef. Translated from the French 'roman à clef' means 'novel with a key' and refers to novels which feature well-known people thinly disguised as fictional characters. Once aware of the 'key' the reader is able to find deeper, often satirical meaning in the plot. The first examples of the roman à clef appeared in France in the 17th century. Among the best-known English examples are *Brave New World* and *Point Counter Point* by Aldous Huxley.

Roman culture. *See* ENGLISH CULTURE.

Rome . . ., when in. The full version of this expression is 'When in Rome do as the Romans do', though familiarity has led to its abbreviation. It was in fact the advice given to St Augustine when he became confused about the day of the week on which the Romans fasted, which

was different from the day he was used to. Its meaning is obvious; when abroad, follow the local customs – which is still good advice for enterprising travellers.

rose by any other name would smell as sweet, a. This cynical expression is based on a quotation from Shakespeare's *Romeo and Juliet*. It is Juliet who asks:

What's in a name? that which we call a rose
By any other name would smell as sweet;
So Romeo would, were he not Romeo call'd.

The phrase, meaning that the name of a thing is irrelevant to its quality, is often used sarcastically to imply the exact opposite of Shakespeare's original intention.

rose is a rose, a. This phrase is often used when something is incapable of definition or explanation. It is a quotation, and like a number of popular quotations, it is a *mis*quotation. The phrase comes from a poem, *Sacred Emily*, by the American writer Gertrude Stein (1874–1946). What Gertrude Stein wrote was

Rose is a rose is a rose is a rose

It was a reference to the English painter Sir Frederick Rose, whose work she admired.

round robin. A petition or other paper or letter having the signatures arranged in a circular manner so as to conceal the order of signing; any petition or letter signed by a number of people. Round robin has no connection with birds. It comes from the French words *rond*, meaning 'round', and *ruban*, meaning 'ribbon'. The expression is said to derive from 18th-century France. When a petition was presented to the king, the petitioners would sign their names on a strip of ribbon which was then joined at the ends and affixed to the petition. Thus it was impossible for the king to identify who had signed the petition first, and so presumably was guilty of instigating it, and they were able to escape the full measure of his wrath.

rub up the wrong way, to. To annoy someone by tactless or off-hand behaviour. Various elaborate origins have been speculated, the most convincing being that the phrase alludes to rubbing a cat's fur in the wrong direction, something guaranteed to annoy the cat. The weaving industry has also been suggested; fabric with a pile has to be carefully rubbed in the right direction if it is to look neat and smooth, otherwise it looks messy and unkempt as, perhaps, someone who has been rubbed up the wrong way looks. And an American source traces the expression back to Elizabethan cleaning methods, speculating that oak floorboards had to be mopped in the direction of the grain if they were not to become streaky. It may be, however, that the expression comes originally from the game of bowls where a 'rub' was the term applied when two bowls collided and threw each other off course. By the 16th century a rub had come to mean an intentional blow to the feelings of another person or an unpleasant encounter.

rubberneck. In the tourist trade, a disparaging description of people who travel on coach tours and see the world from behind the glass windows of their bus. The phrase comes from the kind of commentary offered on such a tour: 'On your right you can see . . . on your left there is . . .' The passengers have to keep turning their heads to see what is happening – a process that requires a rubberneck. In the USA the word means to gawp or stare at something. Also from the tourist trade comes the word **grockle**, used to describe visitors to the countryside or to a wildlife or nature park, who turn up wearing inappropriate clothing and walk around without understanding what is going on.

rule of thumb. This phrase is probably based on the fact that the upper joint of the thumb measures roughly one inch across. Knowing this, for hundreds of years people have used their thumbs to work out rough measurements. From this practice we get the phrase 'rule of thumb' meaning a guessed measure; something broadly accurate but subject to variation.

rule the roost. To lord it; to predominate. If asked to account for the origin of this expression, I expect most people would explain it in terms of a cock lording it over the hens in a farmyard. In fact, the expression is a fairly modern corruption of the expression 'rule the roast', which goes back at least as far as the 15th century and refers to the lord of a manor who takes precedence at table and presides over the roast of meat.

Rumpie. A Rural Upwardly Mobile Professional – a country YUPPIE. An increase in the number of rumpies has been reported, thanks mainly to the new high-speed rail networks that enable commuters to travel into cities from areas once considered inaccessible.

run amok (amuck), to. *Amoq* is the Malay word for a state of frenzy, applied to Javanese opium smokers who in the 16th century were reported to run down streets, crazed by drugs, attacking and killing those they met. They were known as *Amuco* and from this word we get the term amok or amuck and the phrase to run amok (or amuck), meaning to run riot, to attack with frenzied violence.

run it up the flagpole. *See under* FLAG.

run the gauntlet. *See under* GAUNTLET.

259

run to seed, to. This expression has been in use for around four hundred years. It refers to the fact that plants that are allowed to run to seed do not produce useful fruit; seeded plants may also become large and unattractive. Shakespeare uses a variation of the phrase in one of Hamlet's soliloquies:

Fie on't! O Fie! 'tis an unweeded garden
That grows to seed; things rank and gross
    in nature
Possess it merely.

Used figuratively it may describe a person or place that has developed in an undesirable or unpleasant way, often due to neglect. From the same horticultural source we also get the word **seedy**, meaning run-down, neglected, dirty, unpleasant.

running dog. One who does someone else's bidding; a lackey; in communist terminology, someone who is subservient to capitalist or counter-revolutionary interests. Running dog is a literal translation of the Chinese expression *zou gou*. It was a phrase used on several occasions by the Chinese leader Mao Tse-tung, and became popularised in American and British English in the 1960s by those opposing American involvement in the Vietnam war.

Ruritania. A fictional kingdom of Central Europe; the name is frequently used allusively for any small state where court romance and intrigue are rife, or for any petty kingdom. The kingdom of Ruritania was the invention of Anthony Hope. Here he set his novels *The Prisoner of Zenda* (1894) and *Rupert of Hentzau* (1898).

Russian roulette. According to one source Russian roulette gets its name because it was originally played by drunken officers at the Czar's court. The 'game' involves inserting a single bullet in a revolver and spinning the chamber; 'players' then take the gun in turn, point it to their heads and pull the trigger.

S

S.O.S. The internationally-recognised Morse Code distress signal. The letters S.O.S., contrary to popular belief, are not an abbreviation. They do not stand for 'save our souls', 'save our ship', 'stop other signals', 'sink or swim' or anything else. The letters were chosen as a distress signal at an international conference in 1908, simply because in Morse Code S.O.S. is three dots, three dashes and three dots – a sequence that is easily remembered, easily transmitted and easily recognised.

sabotage. Striking French railwaymen have given us the word sabotage, to maliciously destroy, to secretly undermine and ruin something. The original saboteurs removed the iron 'shoe', known as a *sabot* (French for 'clog'), from beneath the railway lines, thus making it dangerous for trains to pass.

saccharine manner. A person who puts on artificial sweetness or coyness in their voice and manner may be described as saccharine sweet. The phrase is derived from the chemical sweetener discovered at the end of the last century and used by millions of slimmers ever since. Saccharine is named from the Latin word *saccharum*, meaning 'sugar', and although it bears some resemblance to true sugar it can also have a nasty, bitter taste – hence the fine meaning of saccharine sweet or saccharine manner as something which resembles the genuine article but is actually artificial, sickly and ultimately rather nasty.

sack. To sack someone means to dismiss them from their job, to fire them. The expression dates from the early days of the Industrial Revolution when workers provided their own tools. When they were dismissed they were given a sack in which to carry their belongings home. *See also* OUTPLACEMENT.

sacred cow. An individual or institution held in such high esteem that they are exempt from any kind of criticism or attack. The expression probably derives from the Hindu belief that cows are sacred, which is why in India they roam the streets freely, in little danger of being turned into steaks. Like their Indian counterparts, human sacred cows can do or say what they like without fear of harm.

sadism. Sexual pleasure gained through the infliction of pain or humiliation on others. The word was coined for the Marquis de Sade, an 18th-century French nobleman who became infamous for the sexual scandals in which he was involved and for his novels. These included *Justine* and *120 Days of Sodom*, written while he was in jail, which describe hundreds of variations on the sexual act, many of them sadistic. De Sade

261

died in a mental hospital in 1814 but the lust for cruelty exhibited by his life and works ensured the immortality of his name.

salad days. The phrase evokes an image of something green and fresh, which is pretty much what it means. Someone in their salad days is 'green' – young and inexperienced. The expression was coined by Shakespeare in *Antony and Cleopatra* and is used by Cleopatra herself to describe her youth.

salt, to be worth one's. In ancient times salt was a valuable and scarce commodity and soldiers of the Roman army received a special allowance called a *salarium* (from the Latin *sal* for 'salt') to buy it. This eventually gave rise to the English word salary meaning 'pay'. Though these days no one is paid in salt, the phrase worth one's salt, means 'worth one's salary'.

samizdat. The system developed in the USSR for the clandestine printing and distribution of literature which is suppressed by the government; an underground press; literature printed and distributed in this way. This is an abbreviation of the Russian word *samizdatelstvo*, meaning 'self-publishing house', and it passed into English usage in the mid-1960s. It might be hoped that with the advent of perestroika in the 1980s, samizdat will become an obsolete term in its country of origin.

sandwich. The sandwich was not, as is widely believed, invented by the Earl of Sandwich; it was simply that he formalised this ancient meal and, in doing so, gave his name to it. Sandwich was a notorious gambler and often refused to leave the card table for meals at the appointed hours. During one twenty-four-hour session in 1762 he sent his servant away to fetch him slices of beef between pieces of toasted bread, a concoction that could be eaten easily, using only one hand. His fellow players nicknamed this handy snack a sandwich, a name which has stuck. The sandwich was nothing new, of course. The Romans had something similar which they called an *offula* and for centuries people had been eating meals of bread wrapped around various fillings. But by giving it a name and establishing it as a replacement for a proper meal, the Earl defined its concept.

sang froid. This phrase is French for 'cold blood'. The French use it to imply that someone is lacking emotion and depth of feeling. The British, on the other hand, use it as a compliment to describe those who are cool-headed and emotionally detached – a fact which says an awful lot about the differences between our two nations.

sanitised violence. The kind of glossy, stylised violence that can be seen almost every night on the television or at the cinema. Examples might include carefully choreographed fights where punches are thrown but no one bleeds; stabbings and shootings in which victims die cleanly, quietly and attractively; or vicious attacks from which the hero emerges unharmed and usually unmarked. As well as the actual physical representation of violence and its effects, camera angles, lighting and other film techniques may be employed to DENASTIFY scenes – to remove all the horror from them. Film and programme-makers argue that through these means they minimise the danger of corrupting or influencing those watching. Many critics of sanitised violence think the opposite and argue that showing violence in such an unreal and acceptable way encourages viewers to believe that it is like that in real life. They cite the horror and complaints with which 'unsanitised' scenes of real violence are greeted when they are shown on the news as proof of just how radically sanitised violence has affected our responses.

sapfu. Incredibly botched. This slang expression, formed along the same lines as SNAFU, originated among American troops in World War II. The acronym stands for 'surpassing all previous fuck-ups'.

sardonic laughter. The word sardonic is derived ultimately from Sardinia, where the poisonous plant *herba Sardonia* (named after the island) grows. When eaten this plant induces convulsions which, to the Greeks, seemed to make the faces of the victims go into terrible grins before they died. This the Greeks christened 'Sardinian laughter', which in French became *rire sardonique* and thus, in English, sardonic laughter, a phrase we use today to describe laughter with a bitter or unpleasant ring to it.

Saturday night special. In the USA, a small, cheap, mail-order revolver carried by those who, after a few drinks on Saturday night, tend to use it to settle their old scores. In medical jargon Saturday night specials are either alcoholics or tramps who come into accident departments feigning illness in the hope that they will get a bed over the weekend, or patients suffering from stab injuries, the majority of which occur on Saturdays after a night's drinking.

saved by the bell. Rescued at the last minute. The expression derives from the sport of prize-fighting, and refers to a boxer who is in danger of being beaten and is reprieved by the bell ringing to end a round.

sawbuck. American slang for a ten-dollar bill. This expression has been in use since about 1850. Originally a sawbuck was another name for a sawhorse, a movable frame for holding wood that is to be sawn, and which consisted of a crossbar with legs on each side, projecting above the crossbar so that they formed the shape of an 'X' on either end. This resemblance to an 'X' – the Roman numeral for 10 – led to a ten-dollar bill being called a sawbuck.

saxophone. Invented by Adolphe Sax and patented in 1846, it was originally intended for use in military bands but has become one of the principal jazz instruments.

say it with flowers. This advertising slogan has had a long life. It was coined in 1917 by two Americans: Henry Penn, chairman of the National Publicity Committee of the Society of American Florists, and Major Patrick O'Keefe, the head of an advertising agency.

scally or **scallywag** is an American term coined originally to describe undersized cattle and in the 19th century applied to minor criminals and other rogues and rascals. The derivation of the word remains a matter of dispute. One theory proposes that it comes from one of the Shetland Isles, Scalloway – the Shetland Isles being famous for small-scale ponies (Shetland ponies) and cattle. An old Scottish word *scurryvaig*, meaning a beggar, has also been implicated. Though scallywag (or scalawag as it is sometimes spelt) is rarely heard these days, in current Liverpool dialect a scally is a young rascal, an individual who lives off his wits and beats the system.

scapegoat. A person who is made to carry the responsibility for another's mistakes or sins. The idea comes from the Bible where, in the Book of Leviticus, we learn that one part of the ritual for the Day of Atonement involved selecting a goat from a pair and sending it into the desert, where it symbolically bore away the sins of the people. The word 'scape' is shortened version of 'escape'.

schlemiel. An awkward, clumsy person; someone who is 'born unlucky' and for whom everything always goes wrong. There are two possible derivations of this Yiddish expression. It may derive from the name of a biblical character: Shelumiel, the son of Zurishaddai, was the leader of the tribe of Simeon, and according to the Talmud he came to an unhappy end. Alternatively it may derive from the name of the eponymous hero of a German fable published in 1814 by A. von Chamisso, *Peter Schlemihls wundesame Geschichte* – The Wonderful History of Peter Schlemihl.

schlep (or **schlepp** or **shlep**) comes from the Yiddish verb *shleppen*, meaning to drag. To schlep around means to drag something around or to walk as if dragging something around.

schlockmeister. Schlock is junk – inferior, worthless, lowbrow stuff, often used to describe BLOCKBUSTER novels and movies written with no intention other than being wildly popular and making money. A schlockmeister is a person skilled at turning out such rubbish and it is applied as an insult – though schlockmeisters tend to take it as a compliment. Schlock is Yiddish for shoddy, cheaply-made goods and meister is the German word for 'master'.

schmaltz. Blatant sentimentality; emotionalism; music, writing, etc. of a cloyingly sweet or maudlin sort. The use of this expression in American English originated among jazz musicians *c.*1935. The literal meaning of the Yiddish word is 'melted chicken fat' or 'grease'.

schmuck. A stupid or naïve person; an idiot; a contemptible or objectionable person. This word in Yiddish literally means 'an adornment', but in vulgar use means 'a penis'.

scorched earth policy. No one knows when the first scorched earth policy was put into practice, but it was certainly a very long time before this phrase was invented. Such a policy dictates that a retreating army burns the land in its path, leaving nothing for its pursuers to live off. It got its current name in 1937, when the Japanese invaded China.

score an own goal, to. This expression comes from the game of football, where a player who scores an own goal puts the ball into the wrong net and scores a goal against his own team. The meaning is obvious; anyone who scores an own goal makes an error that gives his opponent the advantage. *See also* TO CUT OFF ONE'S NOSE TO SPITE ONE'S FACE and TO SHOOT ONESELF IN THE FOOT.

scot-free, to get off. A 'scot' was a local or municipal tax paid to bailiffs, sheriffs or landowners. There are records of 'scots' being levied from the 12th century until the 18th. Someone who managed to avoid paying these taxes was said to have got off scot-free, hence our use of the phrase to describe someone who escapes unharmed from a dangerous or difficult situation.

scotch a rumour, to. To put an end to it, to prove it wrong. The expression has nothing to do with Scotland or its national tipple, deriving instead from the Old French word *escocher*, meaning 'to cut'.

Scottish play, The. Also known as *that* play, the Caledonian tragedy and 'the unmentionable'. All four are euphemisms for *Macbeth* and ways of overcoming an old superstition that the title should never be mentioned within a theatre.

scratch, to start from. To start something with no advantages or advanced preparation; to begin from the very beginning. It has been suggested that the phrase was originally a horse-racing term, where a scratch race is one in which there are no handicaps or allowances made for weight, age etc. and all horses start from the same point, the scratch or line on the ground.

screw – to have a screw loose. This expression, dating from the early 1800s, draws a parallel between a machine malfunction caused by a loose screw and someone whose mind is not working as it should. The phrase is used to describe a wide variety of mental aberrations, so a person described as having a screw loose could be merely irresponsible or eccentric or, at the opposite extreme, clinically insane. *See also* TO LOSE ONE'S MARBLES *under* LOSE.

screw, to put on the. Thumbscrews were just one of a number of methods of torture used to extract information from those who would rather not give it, and the memory of them persists to the current day in this expression. To put the screw on someone means to put pressure on them; to force them, usually by unfair or illegal means, to pay money or do something they don't want to do. From this idea we also get the phrase 'a turn of the screw', a metaphorical tightening of the grip which increases the victim's distress.

screwball. An eccentric or erratic person. This American expression, dating from the 1930s, is a metaphor derived from the sport of baseball. The literal meaning is a ball that is pitched in an unconventional manner so that it is impossible to predict the path that it will follow.

scuba. An acronym for 'self-contained underwater breathing apparatus'. The name, and the equipment it describes, originated in the USA *c.*1950.

scuzzball. This American slang word to describe a disgusting or despicable person is probably a combination of 'screwball' or 'oddball' with the word 'scuzzy', derived from 'disgusting'.

seamy side of life. The tough side, the unglamorous underside of life. Various suggestions have been proposed to explain the phrase's origins. It has been suggested that it refers to garments which may look wonderful from the outside but, if one inspects the inside, are covered in rough seams and odd stitches. It has also been suggested that it alludes to carpets and tapestries used as wall-hangings. The nobility would see only the attractive, finished side of the fabric but the servants, would be aware of the seamy side of life.

second – to play second fiddle. In an orchestra the first violins often have a showier, more complicated score to play than the second violins who support and follow them. Thus we get the phrase to play second fiddle, meaning to take a subordinate, secondary position behind someone else. Also from the musical world comes the phrase second string to describe a person held in reserve and, by implication, not quite as good as the first string. Musicians who play stringed instruments sometimes keep a spare string in reserve in case one of the originals breaks during use.

secretary. The first secretaries were men who carried out confidential business in medieval Europe. Such a man was known as a *secretarius*, from the Latin for 'secret'. It was not until the 19th century that secretary became the name for an office assistant, and it was not until the 20th century that the term became practically synonymous with 'woman' and, in some circles, BIMBO.

See you later, alligator. The phrase 'See you later' was in use in the USA as a form of farewell by the 1870s. The rhyming addition was a JIVE usage of the 1930s. The conventional response to 'See you later, alligator' was the parallel rhyming phrase 'In a while, crocodile'. These expressions had a revival in the world of popular music in the 1950s, when the song *See You Later, Alligator* was sung by Bill Haley and his Comets in the film *Rock Around The Clock* of 1956.

seedy. *See* TO RUN TO SEED under RUN.

segue, pronounced seg-way, is a vogue word among disc jockeys. It comes from the Italian for 'now follows' and describes the way DJs or musicians move from one piece of music to the next without an obvious or forced break or, in the case of disc jockeys, with a few well-chosen words linking the two.

settle a bargain. In the past many homes and most public houses would have had a settle by the fire, this being a long, high-backed wooden bench in which people would 'settle' for the evening. The word settle comes from the Anglo Saxon *setl*, meaning a seat. It was also the place where people would sit when they had a quarrel or a bargain to settle, i.e. a quarrel or a bargain to sort out.

seven-year itch. Since the 17th century to itch for someone has meant to have sexual desire for them, but according to one authority the phrase seven-year itch had no sexual innuendo when it was coined. It was, apparently, originally applied to an itch that went away after seven years' treatment. At a later date the sexual meaning asserted itself and seven-year itch came to describe a man's urge to look for other partners after seven years of marriage.

seventh heaven, to be in. Followers of Islam believe that heaven has seven different grades to which dead souls are sent according to the way they have conducted themselves in life. The ultimate grade is seventh heaven, a place of indescribable light and bliss where all the inhabitants continually chant the name of Allah. Thus to be in seventh heaven is to be in ecstasy, as happy as it is possible to be.

sexism refers to prejudice and discrimination against women based purely on the grounds of their sex. Sexist behaviour includes sexual harassment, by which a man makes unwanted and persistent advances towards a woman, and sexual stereotyping by which men categorise women according to traditional female roles. These usually include 'mother', 'wife', 'mistress', 'secretary', 'prostitute' and so on.

shaggy dog story. During the 1940s there was a vogue for long and intricate jokes involving lots of SPOOF detail and repetition and often featuring a shaggy dog. After the laborious telling the joke would end with an excruciating pun or a twist that came as a complete anti-climax. This kind of tale became known as a shaggy dog story and the phrase is sometimes used to describe a real situation which looks promising but fails to fulfil its build-up.

shamateurism. World-class athletes and sportsmen and women sometimes find themselves in a CATCH 22 situation. To compete in their sports international competitions they have to be amateurs; but by virtue of their fame they are able to command vast fees through sponsorship, appearances and advertising. As a result of this various means have been found to enable the 'amateurs' to take the money *and* continue to compete. These methods include trust funds, in which payments are invested and locked up until the sportsman retires, and the payment of large fees for 'expenses' to sports stars who attend particular competitions. As a result of these measures in some sports the concept of amateurism has been so badly tarnished that it is known to the cynical as shamateurism.

shambles. Today the term is applied to a mess, a scene of untidyness, but originally it referred to a place where meat was put out for sale. Visitors to York can still walk down the charming medieval street known as The Shambles which today houses a variety of tourist-orientated shops that were originally slaughterhouses and butchers' shops.

shanghai, to. In the days when PRESS GANGS combed ports looking for suitable 'recruits', many a sailor was drugged or stupefied with alcohol before being forced aboard a ship. By the time he came round he was on his way to Shanghai or some other distant port. Those to whom this happened described themselves as shanghaied and before long the word was applied to any abduction in which someone was taken unwillingly away.

Shangri-La. An earthly paradise. Shangri-La was the name of a Tibetan utopia in James Hilton's novel *Lost Horizon*, published in 1933. A film version of *Lost Horizon*, starring Ronald Colman, was very popular and helped to popularise the expression.

Shanks's pony, to ride or to go by Shanks's pony means to walk, 'shank' being an old word for leg.

shark repellent. A company under threat of takeover from a 'raider' may employ shark repellent to ward them off. The repellent can take many forms but often involves making provision for GOLDEN PARACHUTES or creating POISON PILLS.

shebang, the whole. Everything. In 19th-century American slang, a shebang was a shanty or hut. Thus, in certain contexts, the whole shebang might originally have meant one's hut and all its contents, that is, all one owned.

sheep in sheep's clothing, a. Someone who appears to be, and is, ineffectual. This is a satirical variation of the proverbial expression 'a wolf in sheep's clothing'. It has been attributed to Winston Churchill, describing the man who succeeded him in 1945, the Labour prime minister Clement Attlee. Churchill himself denied describing Attlee thus, but said he might have applied the expression earlier to another Labour prime minister, Ramsay MacDonald. It is believed, however, that the expression may have been originated in the 1930s by the journalist J. B. Morton, who was better known by his pseudonym of Beachcomber.

sheep – One night as well be hanged for a sheep as a lamb. This phrase, meaning 'if you're going to do a minor wrong and get into trouble for it, you might as well do something even worse and suffer the same fate', dates from the time when the death penalty was imposed for stealing almost any kind of livestock. As the risk in stealing both sheep and lambs was the same, a thief might just as well go for the bigger prize as the smaller. No precise date can be offered for the saying because laws dealing out the death penalty for such crimes were in use for hundreds of years, right up to the beginning of the 19th century.

sheep – to separate the sheep from the goats. This phrase, describing the separation of the good from the bad, the worthy from the unworthy, is based on a biblical reference in Mathew 25:32:

. . . and he shall separate them one from another, as a shepherd divideth his sheep from the goats.

In modern use the expression denotes any separation between those who are capable, deserving or whatever and those who are not.

shelf, to be left on the. Said of unmarried women of more than average marriageable age, this expression alludes to goods in a shop; some are popular and are snapped up at once, others are never sold and remain on the shelf. If nothing else, the phrase acknowledges the 'market' aspect of love and marriage. It is also applied to those employees or projects put aside because they are deemed to be of no further use. Putting them on the shelf implies putting them in storage, so that perhaps at a later date they can be taken down from the shelf and reinstated.

shell out. To pay for something, to **stump up**. The allusion is to shelling peas or broad beans, opening the pod and extracting the seed. Stumping up is an Americanism meaning to pay, derived from the word 'stumpy', slang for cash. This in turn got its name because it could be put down on the spot, maybe on a convenient tree-stump – an American version of CASH ON THE NAIL.

ship – when one's ship comes in. Everyone at some time or other plans what they'll do when their ship comes in, i.e. when they suddenly become rich. The phrase was originally used by merchants who quite literally spent their time waiting for their ship to come in, laden with a profitable cargo which could be worth enough to make their dreams come true.

ships that pass in the night. This phrase comes from the poem *Tales of a Wayside Inn* by Longfellow and describes the way in which people, like ships, encounter each other by chance, enjoy a brief moment of communication or recognition and then lose sight of each other

Ships that pass in the night, and speak each other in passing,

Only a signal shown and a distant voice in the darkness;
So on the ocean of life we pass and speak one another,
Only a look and a voice, then darkness again and a silence.

In use today 'ships that pass in the night' is often applied to strangers who meet and have a brief romance in the knowledge that they can never have a permanent relationship.

shiver my timbers. This nautical-sounding exclamation or oath was never used by any flesh-and-blood sailor. It was invented in 1834 by the author Frederick Marryat for use in his nautical yarn *Jacob Faithful*. Marryat wanted an oath that would sound authentic but would not offend the sensibilities of his most prudish reader. Thus in *Jacob Faithful* we may read:

'I won't thrash you, Tom. Shiver my timbers if I do.'

shoddy. An Americanism describing something that is cheap or badly made. It was coined during the American Civil War when Union troops were supplied with uniforms made of cheap fabric known as 'shoddy' which soon began to fall apart. Not surprisingly the men concerned applied the word shoddy to anything else that failed to work as it should, and it was only a matter of time before it had entered the language.

shoes, to occupy another man's. To take the place of another person or represent him. The phrase may derive from an ancient north-country custom by which an adopted son put on his adoptive father's shoes to indicate acceptance into the new family.

shoestring, on a. Someone who survives on a shoestring gets by on an extremely tight budget. A small business may also be said to run on a shoestring, meaning that it has very little capital behind it. The phrase, which seems to have come into use around the turn of the century, is probably based on the idea that people living or running a business on a shoestring have just enough cash to buy a shoelace and nothing more.

shoot oneself in the foot, to. *See under* FOOT.

shooting gallery. American slang expression for a place where narcotics users gather to inject themselves ('shoot') with drugs.

short – to be held by the short and curlies. In this phrase short and curlies refers to the pubic hair. The expression describes a situation in which one person has complete control over another, perhaps through coercion, blackmail or some other dirty trick. One authority argues that as it's literally impossible to get a firm grip on another by grabbing their pubic hair, the phrase is more likely to refer to the short hairs of the beard – and there is indeed an old saying, 'to hold someone by the beard', that means something similar. However, it is far more likely that to be held by the short and curlies is a euphemistic way of saying 'got' or 'held by the balls' – balls in this case meaning the testicles and aptly describing a situation in which there is no option but to go along with the person who has such a powerful grip.

short – to give short shrift. Shriving is one of the sacraments of the Roman Catholic Church in which a believer makes his confession and receives a penance and absolution. Known as 'shrift', it has been a custom since medieval times. The expression to give short shrift dates from the Elizabethan period when condemned prisoners often had only a matter of minutes between receiving the death sentence and going to their execution. At such times Catholics received shrift but the priest might be

limited to a shortened form of the ceremony. This was known as giving or getting short shrift, i.e. doing or being on the receiving end of something hurried and unsatisfactory. The phrase has exactly the same meaning today; we use it when we are dealt with quickly, without attention, or when we treat others in the same way.

shotgun wedding. A forced marriage, usually when the bride is pregnant. It alludes to the image of the bride's father standing behind the groom at the ceremony, shotgun at the ready in case the man tries to back out.

shoulder – to put one's shoulder to the wheel. The exact origin of this old saying is unknown, but it's quite likely that ever since the invention of the wheel men have been putting their shoulders to it. In the days before motors, when everything was carried on carts and coaches and barrows, people were used to pushing vehicles out of ruts. It required a considerable amount of strength to do so, which is why now, when we want to urge someone to make a major effort, we may instruct them to put their shoulder to the wheel.

shutterbug. An American slang term for a photographer, particularly an enthusiastic amateur.

shyster. A crook, a professional CON-MAN who makes his living by acting unscrupulously. The word is an eponym, named for a 19th-century American lawyer called Scheuster who was known for his UNDERHAND deals and QUIBBLING.

side-track. To side-track someone is to divert them from what they were saying or doing, whether intentionally or not. The expression was first used by those working on the American railroad, when a train would be diverted onto a side-track to allow another through.

silent majority. The majority of the population, who are more or less content with the policies of the government and with the status quo, but who attract less attention than the minority of voluble protesters. This expression gained wide currency after its use by President Nixon in a speech that he made on the Vietnam war on 3 November 1969. Although the phrase is always associated with Nixon, he did not originate it – it had been used in a similar sense by the British historian J. M. Thompson in his *Lectures in Foreign History*, published in 1925. *See also* THE MAN IN THE STREET, MIDDLE AMERICA.

Silicon Valley. The Santa Clara valley south of San Francisco in California. The expression derives from the concentration of high-technology manufacturing plants in this area, particularly those concerned with the production or use of silicon chips.

silly season. In the days when newspapers relied on Parliament and the law courts for the majority of their news, the silly season was the description attached to the summer months when both MPs and lawyers took their holidays. To fill their pages newspapers had to turn to stories of monsters and Martians, blowing trivial incidents into 'major' features. Today, of course, it is the silly season all year round and popular journalists live in dread of the time when trivial stories dry up and they have to resort to using tedious political and legal stories to fill the gaps between the adverts and the PAGE THREE GIRLS.

silver wheelchair. *See under* GOLDEN PARACHUTE.

Simon Legree. A cruel, unsympathetic person; a tyrannical superior; a slave-driver. The expression derives from the name of a character in the novel *Uncle Tom's Cabin* (1852) by Harriet Elizabeth Beecher Stowe.

sing for one's supper, to. This phrase, these days meaning to earn one's reward, whether it be food or a salary, alludes to itinerant minstrels who literally sang (and played) for their supper. It has been immortalised in the nursey rhyme 'Little Tommy Tucker', which goes:

> Little Tommy Tucker
> Sings for his supper.
> What shall we give him?
> Brown bread and butter.

Interestingly, **tucker** is the Australian slang for food, particularly one's daily rations. Dictionaries of Australian English do not give a derivation for the word, so it may be worth speculating that tucker alludes to this old nursery rhyme and, further, to the medieval troubadour's method of earning his bread.

sing like a canary, to. A criminal who is arrested by the police and proceeds to give details about the crime and his accomplices is sometimes said to sing like a canary. The phrase is derived from association with the canary, a yellow bird whose chirpiness has contributed to its popularity as a pet. Many people quite naturally assume that the Canary Isles, which is where these birds are found, is named after them – but in fact the opposite is true. The largest of the Canary Isles was named Canaria (from Latin *canus* for dog) for the packs of wild dogs that early explorers found there. When trade in the native birds started they were known as 'the bird from the Canary Islands', which was gradually shortened to canary.

single. *See under* ALBUM.

sirloin. Henry VIII, James I and Charles II are all credited with having knighted a particularly tasty loin of beef, thus making it sirloin, but alas the stories are extremely unlikely to be true. Sirloin is derived from the French *surloin*, meaning 'above the loin' which is the place from which this particular joint of meat is taken. English misspelling made the word sirloin and the English love of puns did the rest.

sitcom. An abbreviation of the phrase 'situation comedy' – a radio or television series involving a regular cast of characters in a succession of unconnected self-contained episodes. The first occurrence of the word sitcom recorded by the *Oxford English Dictionary* is in *Life* magazine in September 1964.

six hundred pound gorilla. A slang phrase for a person so powerful they can do anything they want, for example a major movie star who can virtually name his or her own price. The expression is based on a terrible old joke that goes something along the lines of, 'Where does a six hundred pound gorilla sleep?' The answer is 'Anywhere he likes.'

$64,000 dollar question. Asked a question it is impossible to answer, many people still reply, 'Now *that's* the $64,000 dollar question.' The phrase comes from a series of quiz shows in which contestants answered questions to win money. The first, called 'Take It or Leave It' and broadcast on the radio, offered prizes of $64 and was so popular that in the 1950s a television show called *$64,000 Question* was established. Of course the $64,000 dollar question was an extremely difficult one, guaranteed to flummox most of the contestants, and thus it is that the phrase is used today, long after the programme's demise, to describe a real poser – a question on whose answer a great deal depends.

skeleton at the feast (or sometimes a spectre, a ghost) at the feast is a term for someone who by their mere presence reminds others of the problems and troubles of life; a natural wet blanket or spoiler. The Egyptians are responsible for the phrase, for whenever they held a banquet it was the custom to place a skeleton at the table as a reminder to the guests of their mortality. Whether this served to dampen high spirits or to invoke an 'eat, drink and be merry' atmosphere is impossible to say, but a modern skeleton at the feast certainly does the former. The alternative phrase 'spectre at the feast' may allude to the scene in *Macbeth* when Banquo's ghost makes its return during a banquet, reminding the Macbeths of their guilt. Macbeth's reaction certainly puts an end to any party spirits.

ski trip. An American slang expression for the taking of cocaine or for a dose of cocaine. The expression is a doubly punning one, based on the drug-user's meaning of the words SNOW (a name for cocaine) and BAD TRIP.

skid row. Any run-down or derelict area of town, frequented by vagrants, beggars, alcoholics, etc. The phrase is a variant of 'skid road' which started out in the late 19th century as American lumberjacks' jargon for a forest track over which logs were hauled. Hence it came to be a slang expression used by lumberjacks, hoboes and criminals for any street or district of cheap shops and bars or for any disreputable area of a town.

skin – by the skin of one's teeth. To avoid something by the skin of one's teeth means to have the closest of shaves, to escape by a hair's breadth. The phrase comes from the Old Testament *Book of Job*, 19:20.

My bone cleaveth to my skin, and to my flesh, and I am escaped with the skin of my teeth.

skinflint. An old saying, now seldom heard, compares someone who drives a hard bargain with one who skins a flint, i.e. one so mean that they would try to pare the skin from a flint stone. From this saying we get the word skinflint for a miser.

skinny-dip. To swim naked (i.e. in one's skin); a naked swim. This slang expression originated in the USA in the early 1960s.

skylarking. *See under* LARK.

sleeper. *See under* DEEP COVER.

slipshod. In the 16th century male FASHION VICTIMS could be seen padding about the streets in *slipshoes*, loose, slipper-type shoes into which the feet slid without any effort – the ancient equivalent of slip-ons or loafers. Those with a more traditional sense of dress thought these slipshod individuals looked untidy and uncouth, and eventually slipshod came to mean something done carelessly or sloppily.

Sloane Rangers. UPPER-CRUST young women who live in the fashionable area surrounding Sloane Square in London. The term was coined by Peter York in an article in *Harpers and Queen* entitled 'The Sloane Rangers', published in 1975, and was followed by the successful *Sloane Rangers' Handbook*, which gave the low-down on the Sloane LIFESTYLE. Sloane Rangers are typically young, well-bred and educated single girls who share flats with their friends and use their time in London to find a suitably upper-class mate. They dress conservatively in navy blue outfits, sensible shoes and Gucci and Hermès headscarves. They tend to work (not because they have to, but because it gives them a social life) as secretaries in smart companies, in high-class estate agencies, as CORDON BLEU cooks preparing directors' lunches or, as Lady Diana Spencer did before her marriage to Prince Charles, as nursery school teachers. Sloanes are by definition jolly, cheerful and outgoing, brought up with traditional values and outlooks. They go out with HOORAY HENRYS and YOUNG FOGEYS and when they have found a suitable partner often leave London and go and live in the country, leaving room for the next generation.

slogan. A distinctive catchword or catchphrase used by a party, class, organisation or person. This word, generally associated with either politics or advertising, comes from the Gaelic *sluagh-ghairm*, meaning a war-cry (literally, 'host outcry').

slopperati. This word was recorded in 1986 and describes young people from wealthy backgrounds who deliberately dress and behave in an untidy, casual, couldn't-care-less manner. Had they not rebelled in this way, members of the slopperati might have become HOORAY HENRYS or SLOANE RANGERS. The expression is coined by association with GLITTERATI.

slurb. An area of unplanned surburban development, characterised by drearily uniform, and often poorly constructed, housing. The expression originated in the USA in the early 1960s, and is a combination of 'sl-' for 'slum' (or alternatively for sloppy, sleazy, slovenly, slipshod) and 'suburb'.

slush fund. In politics and big business a slush fund is a secret fund of money, often undeclared and sometimes illegal as a result, used to pay for those services and activities that the organisation does not want to be public knowledge. Payment from ordinary funds would need to go on the record; payment from the slush fund can be kept from public scrutiny. The expression is probably derived from the idea that the money in such a fund, and the things on which it is spent, are not as pure as the driven snow – in fact they are distinctly grey and murky, like slush. The echo of 'hush' ('hush money' being money paid to someone to keep them quiet) may also have contributed to the term.

Smart Alec(k). No one knows who the original Smart Alec was, though some authorities point the finger in the direction of a 16th-century scholar and general know-all called Alexander Ross. Unfortunately there is no written record of Smart Alec for another three centuries, not until it was noted in America in the 1860s. Whatever its origin, it is widely agreed that the phrase refers to someone who is infuriatingly conceited and who thinks they know everything.

smokeism was coined by journalist Keith Waterhouse to describe discrimination against smokers; the persecution they experience at the hands of the non-smoking lobby. Smokist attitudes have resulted in the banning of smoking on much public transport, in certain restaurants and in an increasing number of public places. The expression is coined by analogy with ABLEISM, SEXISM etc.

smoky bear. Citizen's band radio jargon for a policeman or a police patrol car. This expression derives from the fact that many state highway patrol police wear, as part of their uniform, a broad-brimmed ranger's hat, similar to that worn by the ursine symbol of the US Forest Service.

snafu. Good-humouredly cynical American armed forces slang from World War II, this is an acronym for 'situation normal, all fucked up' – the last two words sometimes being bowdlerised as 'fouled up'.

s'n'f. An abbreviation of 'shopping and fucking', s'n'f is the polite way of referring to a particular genre of women's fiction which features impossibly glamorous, incredibly rich women who spend most of their time either shopping for the latest DESIGNER clothes or engaged in torrid sex. *Scruples* is often cited as the classic s'n'f book but authors such as Jackie Collins and Shirley Conran are also famed for their contribution to the genre.

snipe. *See* TO TAKE A POT SHOT under POT.

snob. Like NOB, snob was originally a term added after the names in lists of Cambridge students. While those of noble birth were noted as NOBS, those of ordinary rank were categorised as s. nob, from the Latin phrase *sine nobilitate*, meaning 'without nobility'. So the original snobs were not the titled and privileged members of the nobility but the commoners. There is evidence, too, that the townspeople of Cambridge were called snobs by the members of the university. It was not, perhaps, until Thackeray used snob with reference to George IV that the word took on its current meaning. By calling the king a snob Thackeray meant that he was pretentious and lacked true nobility – which is pretty much what we mean by snob today.

snooker. *See under* BEHIND THE EIGHT-BALL.

snow. An American slang expression, dating from the early 1900s, for the drug cocaine. The expression derives from the physical appearance of the drug.

soap or **soap opera.** The term soap opera was first used in the USA in the 1930s, referring to popular melodramatic radio serials. There was nothing particularly operatic about them but they were all sponsored by soap manufacturers. By the 1980s the soap opera was extremely popular television fare, covering a wide range of styles – from the gritty *Coronation Street* and *EastEnders* in the UK to the ultra-chic and glamorous *Dynasty* in the USA – and was generally referred to simply as soap.

sob sister. An American colloquial expression, dating from the 1920s, for a female journalist who specialises in sentimental 'human interest' stories.

social mountaineer. A social climber *par excellence*: one whose sights are set on achieving the very highest social echelons and who approaches the task with commitment and professionalism.

sock – to put a sock in it. This phrase dates from the early days of sound recording and refers to the way in which the volume of a phonograph could be muffled by stuffing a sock or other similar item in the horn. Someone whose phonograph annoyed other people might be told to put a sock in it, and though it wasn't long before volume controls were fitted to the machines the phrase stuck. Today it is most often used to warn someone to be quiet or keep their voice down.

Sod's Law. *See under* MURPHY'S LAW.

soft soap. *See under* BANANA OIL.

Soho. The name of an area in London; also an area in New York City. Although the names of these two city areas are the same they have different origins. 'Soho!' (like 'tally-ho!') is an exclamation once used by huntsmen. The London area got its name from this hunting-cry when it was still an area of open fields popular with huntsmen. The name of the New York area is a sort of acronym – it is the area *south* of *Houston* Street.

son of a gun. A jocular way of referring to a man. The expression is usually regarded as being inoffensive, sometimes expressing affectionate regard, but may also be used as a term of contempt. In this respect it is like the word 'bastard' when used figuratively. This word too, depending on context, may express affection or contempt – and in fact 'bastard' is more or less what son of a gun means. In the 18th century, if a pregnant woman was being carried on a warship and she was ready to go into labour, the place traditionally made available to her was between two gun-carriages. There she would have some measure of privacy and would not obstruct the work of the crew. A child born in such circumstances, particularly if the identity of the father was not known, was called a son of a gun.

song, going for a. Something that is going cheap. This expression dates back to the 16th century when the poet Edmund Spenser wrote his long poem *The Faerie Queene*, an allegory that celebrated and praised Elizabeth I. Elizabeth was, understandably, charmed by it and ordered Spenser to be rewarded with a gift of £500 from the treasury. The treasurer, Lord Burghley, disliked Spenser and thought this was an outrageous sum to pay for a mere 'song'. Through his influence Spenser's fee was cut to £100, so inspiring the phrase 'going for a song', meaning to be sold for a surprisingly low price.

sorts, out of. Someone who is in an irritable frame of mind or feeling slightly UNDER THE WEATHER. Two explanations for the origin of this phrase have been put forward. The first theory traces it to printing jargon, where in the days of hot metal printing a 'sort' was a piece of type showing an individual letter of the alphabet. If a typesetter ran out of sorts he ran out of a particular letter – a situation quite likely to make him irritable. The second definition points to the card table, where the deck was 'sorted' before a game to ensure that all the cards were present. If there was a card missing the deck was declared out of sorts, i.e. not fit for anything – pretty much as a person out of sorts is unfit for anything.

sound-bite. In television and radio, a unit of time related to the average concentration time of viewers. News and current affairs programmes and advertisers aim to present information in convenient chunks or sound-bites so that the main points of it are absorbed without any great effort from the viewer. American research indicates that the attention span of the average person is diminishing, mainly due to the influence of television which has taken people away from pursuits such as reading, which require a longer period of attention. For this reason American sound-bites, standing at the moment at around fifteen seconds, are scheduled to become shorter and shorter. *See also* KIDULT.

sour grapes. The act of pretending to despise something, only because one cannot have it. The expression comes from the fable by Aesop in which a fox persuaded himself that the grapes he could not reach were sour.

sozzled. *See under* BRAHMS AND LISZT.

spade – to call a spade a spade. This may be said of someone who is a plain-speaker and doesn't mince his words, i.e. reduce the effect of his words with politeness. It is the proud boast of Yorkshiremen that they always call a spade a spade, which may go some way to explain why to other people they sometimes seem insensitive and rude.

Spaghetti Western. A cowboy movie made by Italian producers and directors, often with Italian actors too, but for an international market. There was a spate of such movies in the early 1970s.

Spanish practices. Restrictive practices, usually in industry. Although not commonly heard, the expression was used to describe the traditional union restrictions in the British newspaper industry when, a few years ago, they were ended by upheavals in Fleet Street. The phrase dates back further than the founding of the trades unions, however, and refers to the practices of the Spanish Inquisition. *See also* DUTCH.

spanner – to throw a spanner in the works. A spanner thrown into a moving piece of machinery is likely to bring the whole thing to a grinding halt. Thus to throw a spanner in the works means to create a problem that holds something up or causes it to break down temporarily.

Spartan. The citizens of ancient Sparta were widely renowned for their tough, cold-blooded approach to life. The Spartan army was rigorously trained to withstand incredible hardships and Spartan mothers saw their grown sons off to war by giving them a shield and telling them to return home either with it or on it, i.e. dead. Thus when we call someone Spartan today we mean that they are tough and can do without many of the 'necessities' of life. A Spartan room is one with few furnishings and no frills; a Spartan diet is a very limited, rationed diet; and a Spartan regime, perhaps in a prison, is a tough, uncompromising one.

-speak. This is one of the most widely-used suffixes of recent years, added to any number of words to describe a particular language or manner of speech.

speakeasy. In the USA, a place where alcoholic drinks were sold illegally in the Prohibition era between 1919 and 1933 – so called because it was advisable to speak in a quiet voice to the doorman when seeking admission.

Speed. American drug-users' slang, dating from the mid-1960s, for an amphetamine, particularly that marketed under the trade name of Methedrine.

spendaholic. An individual who cannot control their spending; who spends money compulsively in order to satisfy some unrecognised emotional need. The word is coined along the lines of 'alcoholic' and is just the latest in a succession of terms referring to compulsive or obsessive behaviour. These include 'workaholic', describing someone who spends most of their life working, and 'chocoholic', an individual addicted to chocolate.

Sphinx, the riddle of the. According to ancient Greek legend the Sphinx (who, unlike the famous Egyptian sphinx, had the head and shoulders of a woman, a lion's body and paws, the wings of of a bird and the tail of a serpent) posed a riddle to everyone she met. Those who answered went free, those who failed she killed. The riddle was, 'What has four feet, then two feet, then three feet but only one voice?' The answer, given by Oedipus, was man – who crawls on all fours as a baby, walks on two legs when grown but in old age walks with a stick.

spick and span. Originally applied to something brand new, a *spic* being a nail and a *span* being a chip. We still use the phrase today but with a slightly different emphasis, not so much on the newness of something but on its neat and tidy appearance.

spinster. Today the word is applied to a woman who has been LEFT ON THE SHELF; one who has gone beyond the normal marriageable age without being wed. Originally, however, it referred to any single woman who spent her time spinning, whether she was young or old. According to ancient tradition a woman was not worthy of becoming a wife until she had spun a set of bed and table linen and created her own wardrobe of petticoats and personal items. Thus some of the most hard-working spinsters were probably young women, anxious to complete this task so that they could be married. *See also* DISTAFF.

spitting image. This phrase has been traced back to the beginning of the 15th century, when it meant pretty much what it does today – an exact likeness of a person, as if one of them had been spat out of the other's mouth. From this idea of spitting we get phrases such as 'the dead spit of his father', meaning the exact image. Some authorities have suggested that spitting image might originally have been 'spirit and image', meaning not just that the two people looked like each other but that they shared the same character as well.

spleen, to vent one's. These days most of us wouldn't know where our spleen is, let alone its function, but for hundreds of years it was believed to be the source of melancholy and ill-temper. Thus someone who was depressed or bad-tempered was said to be 'splenetic' and when they gave vent to this ill-temper they were said to be venting their spleen.

splice the mainbrace. *See under* MAINBRACE.

sponge, to throw in the. This phrase comes from boxing, when a coach would toss his sponge (used to mop down the fighter between rounds) into the ring to indicate when his man had taken enough punishment. A coach equipped with a towel instead of a sponge would throw the towel into the ring, hence the phrase **to throw in the towel**, meaning exactly the same thing – to give in, to show the white flag.

spoof. To hoax; a hoax; a parody or pastiche. This word was coined by a British comedian, Arthur Roberts (1852–1933), as the name of a card game which he invented *c.*1890. The card game has elements of humour and hoaxing.

spoon – born with a silver spoon in one's mouth. *See under* BORN.

spoonerism. The Reverend W. A. Spooner was Warden of New

College, Oxford around the turn of the century and achieved fame for his habit of transposing the initial letters of words. This led to some extremely amusing blunders. One of the most famous, uttered to a disgraced undergraduate who was being dismissed from the college, was, 'You have deliberately tasted two whole worms, and now you can leave Oxford on the town drain.' During his lifetime Spooner protested that many so-called spoonerisms were wrongly attributed to him. Nevertheless, examples such as these ensured that his name lives on to describe any accidental transposition of letters or even, on some occasions, words:

'You have hissed my mystery lecture.' 'Yes, indeed, the lord is a shoving leopard.' 'Give me a well-boiled icicle.' 'A toast to the queer old Dean.'

spot, to put someone on the. This expression is generally acknowledged to have originated in the USA, though no source gives a date for it. The phrase refers to the widely-held superstition that the ace of spades is an ill omen or even a symbol of death. The card depicting the ace of spades has one black symbol or 'spot' in its centre. In the past it was sent as a death threat by criminals and pirates; in *Treasure Island*, for example, Robert Louis Stevenson has one of his characters living in fear after receiving 'the black spot.' He, or anyone else who received it, was put on the spot, i.e. put into a difficult and dangerous situation from which there wasn't much chance of escape. These days the phrase has a less sinister impact but we still use it to describe someone in an uncomfortable situation – being grilled for information, perhaps, or having to explain a mistake. The expression also means to be ready, prepared, in place. We use it in such

phrases as 'on the spot reporter' (referring to a journalist who happens by chance or design to be on the spot when a news story breaks) or an 'on the spot answer', a reply given immediately, without hesitation.

spots – to knock the spots off someone means to defeat them easily. The expression originated in America where it has been suggested that it refers to shooting matches where marksmen would attempt to shoot the 'spots' – the red or black symbols – from playing cards. Anyone good enough to knock the spots off the card succeeded in defeating his opponent.

spout, up the. Pawnbrokers' shops once contained a hoist or 'spout' up which items were sent for storage and down which they came when they were redeemed. When something went up the spout it was normally an indication that times were hard and people were in trouble. Thus when something goes wrong or there is some kind of disappointment people may still say that things are up the spout. The phrase has to be used with a little care for it also means to be pregnant. In this case it is not entirely clear whether the expression is a vague physical description or whether it simply means 'in trouble'.

spread a technicolor rainbow. *See under* CHUNDER.

spurs, to win one's. In the great days of chivalry a man who wished to become a knight had to show his valour and skill in battle, in this way proving himself worthy of the honour. Having passed this test he would be knighted and presented with a pair of silver spurs. Today when we describe someone as having won their spurs we mean that they have proved themselves at whatever endeavour they were aiming at; they have been recognised as experienced and responsible practitioners.

sputnik. A man-made earth satellite. This was the name given to the first such satellite, launched by the Soviet Union on 4 October 1957. In Russian the word *sputnik* means 'travelling-companion'.

squeaky wheel. According to a traditional American saying, 'the squeaky wheel gets the grease.' From this we get the expression squeaky wheel to describe a person whose constant squeaks of complaint eventually result in them getting their own way.

stag. In Stock Exchange parlance, a stag is someone who applies for new shares in order to sell them again immediately at a profit. *See also* BEAR and BULL.

stagflation. A 'portmanteau' expression, coined in the mid-1960s, for a state of the economy in which stagnant demand is combined with severe inflation.

stalking-horse. Anything put forward to mask plans or efforts; a pretext. This expression dates back at least as far as the 16th century. At first it was an actual horse beside or alongside which a hunter concealed himself while hunting his quarry. The expression is used in the figurative sense by Shakespeare in his play *As You Like It*:

He uses his folly like a stalking-horse and under the presentation of that he shoots his wit.

stamping ground. When someone decides to make a return visit to a place where they grew up or where significant events in their life occurred, they may describe it as visiting their old stamping ground. It was originally a place where horses or other animals gathered, and it has been suggested that this American phrase derives from the stamping mating dance of prairie chickens or perhaps the stamping of stallions. Either way, it came first to mean a place where people congregated and then to describe familiar territory, a place one knows well.

stand aloof, meaning to keep one's distance or maintain one's reserve, started life as a nautical term meaning 'to bear to windward'. The word loof is derived from luff, itself adapted from the Dutch word *loef*, meaning 'windward'. Carrying out this manoeuvre necessitated turning the bow of the ship out of the wind, and from this action of turning away the phrase took on the more widely-used meaning of 'keeping away from.'

stand pat. To refuse to change; to carry on as one is. This expression comes from the game of poker, in which it means to retain the cards one is dealt instead of exercising the option to exchange some of them, when one is dealt a 'pat hand' – the word 'pat' here meaning 'exactly suited to the purpose'.

Star Wars. The unofficial name for a system of national defence for the USA proposed in the 1980s and championed by President Reagan – the official name being the Strategic Defense Initiative (or SDI for short). SDI or Star Wars involves the use of laser-beam weapons orbiting in space to shoot down hostile guided missiles. The name Star Wars derives from the name of a very popular science-fiction movie of the 1970s.

starkers. An abbreviated version of the expression **stark naked**, in use since around 1530. There is some dispute about the derivation of stark in this phrase. Its most obvious meaning is 'bare', but some sources suggest that the expression was originally 'start-naked', 'start' meaning 'tail', and that therefore 'start-naked' and 'stark-naked' mean 'naked to the tail'. Another source accepts that the phrase was originally start-naked but goes on to suggest that this may have been an allusion to the nakedness in which we start life –

someone who is as naked as the day they were born.

state-of-the-art. Something described as the most up-to-date thing in its field, the most advanced of its kind.

steal a march. This expression, meaning to get the upper hand over someone by anticipating his actions, has a military origin. In the days when armies marched long distances in order to fight each other, a commander would try to calculate when his rivals would arrive at a given destination. Then he would make his soldiers march through the night so that, if the calculations were correct, they were ready and waiting to surprise enemy troops. A 'march' being the daily distance covered by troops, a leader who managed to get two marches out of his men in a day and thus steal time from his rivals was said to have stolen a march.

steam, to let off. To express pent-up feelings or physical energy in an emotional outburst or bout of exercise. The phrase dates from the early days of steam power when steam engines had no safety valves. It was the job of the engineer to prevent the pressure within the engine rising to an explosive level by pulling a lever. This released a blast of steam and enabled the engine to go on running safely. The analogy between the steam engine and an angry person is obvious. From the same source we get the expression steamed up, meaning 'furious', and the idea that an outburst of temper is an emotional safety valve.

steep, that's a bit. An expression of disbelief, used in response to an exaggerated story or to a demand for a ridiculously high price. According to unproved tradition, the phrase arose when George IV boasted that he had ordered a cavalry troop to charge down the side of Devil's Dyke, a ravine near Brighton, Sussex, where he built his flamboyant Royal Pavilion. The Duke of Wellington, overhearing this and believing not a word of it, commented dryly, 'Very steep, sir, very steep.'

steeplechase. According to an old story, this word was coined one day in 1903 when a party of Irish huntsmen decided to hold a race in a straight line across country to a distant church steeple. The original steeplechase involved a scramble over natural obstacles such as ditches and hedges and these barriers are recreated as jumps on the specially prepared racecourses where steeplechases are now held.

stetson. A man's hat, with a broad brim and a wide, high crown, once common in the western USA. The hat gets its name from the name of the manufacturer, John B. Stetson (1830–1906), whose hat-making company was founded in Philadelphia in 1865.

stick in the mud. *See* FUDDY-DUDDY.

stitch in time saves nine, A. This old proverb is a warning to pay attention to a problem as soon as it starts, the implication being that if it is left it will get much worse. The expression highlights the fact that when a thread in a piece of sewing breaks, it can be easily mended with a single stitch. If, however, it is left unmended it unravels further and requires more work to put right the damage.

stone – to leave no stone unturned. This phrase dates back to the 5th century BC, when Polycrates went searching for the treasures of the Persians, believed to have been left on the plains of Plataea after the Persians had been vanquished by the Greeks. Unable to find them he consulted the Delphic Oracle, who told him to leave no stone unturned. Once more he returned and this time took up the floor under the tent of the defeated Persian general, where he found the treasure hidden. Hence to leave no stone unturned means to search with the utmost thoroughness. In show business the phrase is reversed and becomes a SPOONERISM to describe a bad audience who 'leave no turn unstoned'.

stonewall. This comes from cricket, where a defensive batsman was described as blocking every ball as though with a stonewall. To stonewall something therefore means to block it, perhaps by stubbornly keeping silent and thus to refuse to give one's opponent an opportunity for attack.

stool-pigeon. A police informer. This American slang expression is a figurative use of a term used literally by American hunters in the early 19th century. A stool-pigeon, in the literal sense, was a bird fastened to a stool or perch, thereby serving as a decoy to entice other birds to a trap set for them by the hunter. The expression 'stool-crow' was used in the same sense.

strafe. This verb, meaning to rain machine-gun bullets at ground troops from a low-flying plane, is taken directly from the German word *strafe*, meaning 'punish'. During World War I the phrase *Gott strafe England*, meaning 'God punish England', was a favourite in Germany. When the English learned of it they borrowed *strafe* and applied it to the new form of warfare.

streak. Streaking was all the rage in the 1970s, when exhibitionists seemed to take any opportunity to rip off their clothes and dash around in public. The streaking phenomenon is said to have started at either the University of Texas or Memphis State University, but whichever of the two institutions gets the honours, the term is derived from the fact that,

once undressed, practitioners have to move like a streak of lightning if they want to evade capture.

streak, to talk a blue. This is an American expression and refers to a blue streak of lightning. Someone who talks a blue streak talks quickly and, usually, for a long, long time.

street credibility. To have this, also known as street cred, is to be *au fait* with urban youth culture – the culture of the streets. A street credible person will know the latest fashions, music and jargon of the street. They will also be **street smart** or **streetwise**, i.e. aware of the ways of getting by on the streets – the tricks and dodges employed by those with street credibility. Those who lack street cred and are nervous of walking in the city may take steps to get themselves street-proofed, perhaps as a defence against the streetwise. Street-proofing means learning self-defence and other techniques as a means of protection against molestation on the street.

string – to have more than one string to one's bow. The English longbow was one of the most formidable weapons in use in the 14th century and English longbowmen were highly-skilled and highly-paid troops. No longbowman WORTH HIS SALT would have dreamed of going into battle without a spare bowstring in case his first broke – and thus originated the expression to have more than one string to one's bow, meaning to be versatile, ready for anything. *See also* TO PLAY SECOND FIDDLE under SECOND.

stump up. *See under* SHELL OUT.

suck – Don't teach your grandmother to suck eggs. *See under* EGG.

sugar daddy. An older man who keeps a young and often illicit mistress. The phrase can also be used to describe an older man who takes a non-sexual pleasure in caring and buying gifts for a younger woman.

sunlighting. Sunlighting is a variation on MOONLIGHTING, describing someone who doesn't simply do two jobs but manages to do them both at the same time. As many people experience difficulty in fulfilling one job at a time, one presumes that sunlighters are talented, not to say hard-working people.

sunrise industry. Industries of the future; the new, high-tech manufacturing industries which use computers, robots and modern factories to produce the kind of modern, electronic goods that everyone seems to want to buy. Such industries are so called because it is over them that the sun can be seen to be rising. The phrase may also be connected with the fact that many sunrise industries are dominated by Japan, the Land of the Rising Sun. *See also* SUNSET INDUSTRY.

sunset industry. Those traditional industries that have been the backbone of the economy since the Industrial Revolution but which are now being overtaken by new technological advances, are known as the sunset industries. Steel, coal, textiles, shipbuilding – all are facing dramatic cutbacks and are widely agreed to have reached the twilight of their years. Hence the adjective sunset, graphically describing their fading glory. *See also* SUNRISE INDUSTRY.

surly. Our modern word surly is a good example of a term that means entirely the opposite of the original, *sirly*, which was an adjective applied to knights and high-born gentlemen in medieval times. Then *sirly* meant noble, knightly, chival-

rous. These knights obviously behaved in a high-handed, careless fashion because *sirly* soon changed to surly, meaning arrogant and haughty, and finally to mean what it does today – rude and discourteous.

survival of the fittest. This expression essentially encapsulates the evolutionary theory of Charles Darwin, but the phrase was originated not by Darwin but by Herbert Spencer in his book *The Principles of Biology* (1867).

Svengali. *See* TRILBY.

swan song. One's last work, utterance or achievement before one's death or retirement, supposedly the culmination of one's career. Swans in fact never sing, but there is a very old belief that they burst into glorious song at the onset of death. According to the ancient Greeks this was because the swan, sacred to Apollo, the god of music and poetry, was about to join the god it served. It was also believed that the soul of a singer or poet passed after death into the body of a swan.

swat team. An American expression, dating from the 1960s, for a special police unit organised on military lines, with military-style uniforms, assault weapons, etc. and used for assignments requiring coordination and force beyond that capable of being provided by ordinary police officers. The word 'swat' here is an acronym, standing for 'special weapons and tactics'.

Sweeney, The. The Flying Squad, a division of the Metropolitan Police Force, or a member of this squad. In full, Sweeney Todd, this is cockney rhyming slang. Sweeney Todd, a barber who murdered his customers, was a character in a popular play by George Dibdin Pitt (1799–1855).

Sweet Fanny Adams. *See under* FANNY.

swing both ways, to. To be bisexual, to engage in sexual practices with both men and women. Since the 1960s swinging has been a euphemistic description of the sex act, with the result that promiscuous or sexually experienced individuals were known as **swingers**. Though the phrase **swinging single** is sometimes used to describe a person who is happily single and enjoys a busy social life, it can also imply a degree of sexual promiscuity.

sword of Damocles. Any impending danger or evil. The expression comes from an ancient Greek legend. Damocles, a courtier in Syracuse, was wont to talk irreverently of the wonderfully easy life led by kings. In order to teach him a lesson his king, Dionysius, invited him to a banquet, at which Damocles was seated under a sword hanging by a single thread. Understandably, Damocles found this rather disturbing and was unable to enjoy the banquet. This was supposed to teach Damocles that the privileges of kingship are not without their accompanying responsibilities and perils.

synergy. A current BUZZWORD, the search for synergy being a modern preoccupation – but what is it? It describes the way in which two separate, complementary businesses or interests are combined to make something that is bigger, better, more productive or more profitable than the simple sum of the two. In a basic mathematical analogy, synergy is when $2 + 2 = 5$.

T

T, to suit to a. Something that is exact or perfect for its purpose – be it a dress or a job – can be said to suit someone to a T. Some sources identify the 'T' as a draughtsman's T-square, but as the phrase was in use before this device was developed it has been suggested that 'T' is an abbreviation of 'tittle'. A tittle described a carefully placed dot or an exact stroke of the pen, and thus 'to a tittle' meant 'precisely' while 'a jot and tittle' meant a tiny amount. Someone who was suited to a tittle was therefore precisely suited, and in time the tittle was abbreviated to become a 'T'.

table d'hôte. *See under* À LA CARTE.

tables, to turn the. It used to be the custom to turn a chess or draughts board around in the middle of a game so that the situation of the two players was entirely changed. This habit generated the phrase to turn the tables, meaning to reverse the position completely. To turn the tables on one's opponents means to take them by surprise by transforming a losing situation into a winning one.

Taffy. American journalists coined this expression along the lines of YUPPIE to describe the Technologically-Advanced Family. Taffies (or perhaps Taffys) tend to be middle-class, middle-income, well-educated families who encourage their children to use all the latest technological equipment.

tail – to go home with one's tail between one's legs. A whipped or frightened dog cowers with its tail between its legs before slinking back to its kennel. This idea is applied metaphorically to a person who, having undergone some frightening or humiliating experience, races back home, shoulders hunched and head down in despair or shame.

take the high jump. *See under* CARDS, TO BE GIVEN ONE'S CARDS.

talking heads. The name given to any TV programme which features people talking in close-up and nothing much else. This kind of programme tends to be very static and usually features academics or 'experts' talking at length about their particular specialism, which makes for HIGHBROW minority entertainment and can lead to the TELECIDE of the people concerned.

tall poppy syndrome. An American phrase describing the way in which individuals who achieve anything out of the ordinary are resented and eventually **cut down to size.** The image is of a field of wheat in which a few poppies stick their heads up above the general level, only to have them chopped off.

tally, to keep. Until 1826 tallies were part of the Exchequer's way of calculating money received. The tally was a wooden stick into which was cut a notch to acknowledge that a sum had been paid to the treasury. On other sides of the stick were noted the name of the person who had paid the money and the date. The tally was then halved lengthways and the lender took one while the Exchequer held the other. At a later date, when payment was required, the lender brought his half of the tally back, the two pieces were matched and, if everything was in order, he received his cash. In 1834 all the old tallies, a wealth of history, were used as fuel to heat the House of Lords. It was while they were being disposed of that the furnace overheated and caused a fire which burned the place down – so destroying even more of our history. Anyway, from this old practice we get the phrases to tally, meaning to correspond or match up, and to keep tally, meaning to keep score.

tandem. We use the word today to indicate two people, items etc. working together – on a tandem bicycle, perhaps. Originally tandem described two horses pulling a carriage, one horse in front of the other. Whoever coined the word must have had a sense of humour, for it is derived from the Latin *tandem* meaning 'at length'.

tantalise. In Greek legend Tantalus was the king of Lydia, son of Zeus and a nymph, and a prosperous and respected man until he made the mistake of revealing the secrets of the gods to mortal men. As punishment Zeus had him placed up to the chin in the river Hades, whose waters receded each time he tried to drink, while above his head there hung a tree covered in fruit that bobbed temptingly just out of his reach. From this tale comes the verb to tantalise, meaning to raise excitement and then disappoint. From this in turn comes a **tantalus**, the name given to a locked box in which bottles of spirits are kept. A would-be drinker is tempted by the sight of the bottles but cannot open them to take a tipple.

taper off. A taper is the traditional word for a candle, made by dipping the wick in molten wax time and time again until the requisite thickness was achieved. Tapers made in this way had a broad base that gradually diminished, becoming narrower at the top. From this shape we get the verb to taper off, meaning to diminish, to get smaller – until, perhaps, nothing is left and the item has tapered away.

tarred – to be tarred with the same brush. A person who is implicated in the crimes of another or who shares the same faults with another may be said to be tarred with the same brush. Authorities offer a number of different suggestions for the origin of this verb, the most common being that it refers to the way in which tar was applied to sheep sores. The sheep of a single flock would all have their sores tarred with the same brush, hence the association of ideas. Still on the sheep theme, another source suggests that the expression refers to the way in which the members of a flock would receive a special mark, applied with the tar brush, to indicate their owner. Another proposes that the phrase refers to the practice of tarring and feathering in which offenders were stripped, daubed with hot tar and covered in feathers as a form of public humiliation. Perhaps those people known to have associated with the victim or to have been peripherally involved in the crime could be said to have been metaphorically tarred with the same brush.

tarmac. A shortened version of tarmacadam, a mixture of tar and stone chippings, developed by John McAdam. His invention was used to surface roads and paths and made a great contribution to the speed of transport in his native Scotland and elsewhere.

tarpaulin. *See under* JACK TAR.

tawdry is a corruption of the name of St Audrey who retired to live at Ely (then an island surrounded by marshes) and built a monastery there. She died in 679 AD of a tumour of the breast and blamed the cancer on the fact that as a child she had worn jewelled necklaces. As a result of this silk necklaces became fashionable and were sold annually at St Audrey's fair, held on the date of her death, 23 June. (Though according to other sources, it was St Audrey's lace, not necklaces, that bec. me popular.) Also sold at the fair were any manner of cheap and cheerful ornaments and decorations, so that eventually anything bright and garish but ultimately worthless came to be known as tawdry.

taxi. The first taxis were meters installed in French horse-drawn cabs some years before motorised cabs hit the streets. These contraptions were originally known as taximeters and when motor-cabs took over from horses, they too were fitted with them, thus becoming known as taxis.

technofear describes the dread and panic some people experience when faced with new technology of even relatively undemanding kinds – an automatic cash dispenser or a word processor, for example. Many sufferers adopt an aggressive anti-technology stance to conceal their basic fear, insisting that there's nothing they can do on a computer or word processor that they can't already do with a pencil, paper and manual typewriter. *See also* LUDDITE and TECHNOPEASANT.

technofreak. *See* TECHNOPHOBIA.

technopeasant. A woman who has no understanding of new technology. According to Kathy Keeton, author of *Women of Tomorrow*, published in 1985, they are women who are

as ignorant of technology as medieval serfs, overwhelmed by the changes taking place around [them] and helpless to direct [their] own future.

See also TECHNOFEAR.

technophobia. Like TECHNOFEAR, technophobia is a dread of new technology, particularly computers. Technophobes are the precise opposites of **technofreaks**, those people who have no fear at all of technology and can be persuaded to spend their money on any clever gadget that boasts of being 'the latest technology'. *See also* TECHNOPEASANT.

teddy-bear. The first teddy-bears were made in Germany by Margaret Stieff, who ran a cottage industry making toy bears for the local children. They became extremely popular and her brother Richard went to America to set up a factory and sell bears there. He was given a major marketing boost when President 'Teddy' Roosevelt took a hunting trip in the Mississippi area. Anxious to find a bear for him to shoot, his aides dragged a bearcub into camp and suggested he take aim – but this Roosevelt refused to do. His act of compassion inspired the best-known cartoonist of the time, Clifford Berryman, to draw a picture of the scene. Instead of depicting the real bear he drew one of the Stieffs' toy bears, and when the cartoon was published, teddy-bears, as they were soon known, became all the rage. Now there can be scarcely a child in the western world who doesn't have a bear of its own.

teddy-bear syndrome. Sociologists have coined the expression teddy-bear syndrome to describe the way in which many people enter marriage or long-term relationships not for positive reasons but because they do not want to be alone. According to these experts as many as four out of ten people use their partners as a kind of human teddy-bear – something to cuddle and provide comfort at difficult times but not much more than that.

teetotal. There is disagreement over the origin of this word. American sources trace it back to 1807 and suggest that it is derived from the record books of turn-of-the-century temperance societies. When a drinker took the pledge to abstain totally from all kinds of alcohol his name was registered with a 'T' in the book, 'T' standing for 'total abstinence'. Such reformed drinkers were known as 'T-for-totals', which soon became 'teetotal'. British sources date the word to around 1833 and unequivocally credit Dick Turner, an artisan from Preston, Lancashire as its inventor. Indeed, his tombstone bears this inscription:

Beneath this stone are deposited the remains of Richard Turner, author of the word *Teetotal* as applied to abstinence from all intoxicating liquors, who departed this life on the 27th day of October, 1846, aged 56 years.

Could the word have developed independently on either side of the Atlantic? Until one of the theories is proved wrong or a link between them discovered, we'll keep an open mind.

telecide. From America, telecide is televisual suicide – the result of someone making a television appearance and going down very badly, with the result that they have no future on the box.

telecommuter. A person who works from home using a computer, a telephone and other electronic devices. Their homes are known to those in the computer business as electronic cottages, probably because of the amount of gadgetry the telecommuter uses. Among his methods of communicating with the outside world he may have an electronic mail system, a terminal by which he can send and receive messages.

telethon is a television event staged to raise money for charity. It is a television 'marathon' (hence the derivation of the word) lasting as long as twenty-four hours, during which normal broadcasting is suspended and replaced with a series of guest interviews, stunts, auctions, live events, specially-made features and so on. During the period of the telethon viewers are encouraged to phone in and pledge their charitable donations. Though chaotic and often tedious to watch, each year they succeed in raising millions of pounds for charity.

tenterhooks, to be on. Tenterhooks were hooks on which freshly woven and washed cloth was stretched and dried, so-called because the frames from which they hung were known as 'tenters'. Both terms are derived from the Latin *tendere*, meaning 'to stretch'. Someone who is said to be on tenterhooks is, like the stretched fabric, in a state of tension and suspense, with their nerves strained to the limits.

terminological inexactitude. A lie. The phrase is ascribed to Winston Churchill who used it in a 1906 speech. Parliamentary procedure forbids MPs from calling each other liars. More recently Sir Robert Armstrong popularised another euphemism for lying when he revealed during the *Spycatcher* trial in Australia that he had been ECONOMICAL WITH THE TRUTH.

testify. When Greek and Roman men were required to swear an oath or give evidence it was the practice for them to place their hand over their testicles, this act symbolising their belief that if they lied they would become sterile or impotent. In Latin 'witness' is *testis*, which is why testify and testicles have the same root. This is a fact that galls some feminists who object to giving testimony in court on the grounds that they have no testes and that the male obsession with fertility and potency has nothing to do with them.

tête-à-tête. A conversation between two people, usually a private or intimate conversation. The phrase is French, meaning literally 'head to head'.

thinking cap. *See under* CAP.

third degree, to give someone the. The Third Degree is the highest rank a Mason can achieve and to do so he has to undertake a series of demanding tests. It is probably from this source that we derive the expression to give someone the third degree, meaning to cross-examine them, to question them exhaustively and therefore, to give them a hard time.

thorn in the flesh. It has been recorded in the Talmud that in ancient times there existed an ultra-strict sect of Pharisees who placed thorns in their garments so that as they walked their legs were pricked. It is perhaps this sect to whom St Paul referred in II Corinthians when he used the phrase a thorn in the flesh to describe a source of constant irritation and annoyance. Today we use the expression, and a variation, a thorn in one's side, to describe anything that continually makes our lives uncomfortable or difficult.

thrash something out, to. To settle a disagreement but not, as one might imagine, by fighting it out. Thrashing, or threshing as it is more commonly called, involves hitting or flailing corn so as to separate the wheat from the chaff. Metaphorically, thrashing something out involves sorting out the relevant details

from the irrelevant; getting down to brass tacks.

three sheets in the wind. Someone described as three sheets in the wind is very drunk. The expression is a nautical one, a sheet being a rope attached to a sail. If the sheet is not tied down to secure the sail it flaps freely in the wind. The phrase 'a sheet in the wind' is applied to someone who is tipsy; one who is three sheets in the wind has had significantly more to drink.

throw the book at someone, to. It isn't difficult to imagine a judge literally hurling the law-book at a particular nasty defendant in the dock, but if this *has* ever happened it has not been recorded. Metaphorically speaking, however, many judges could be said to have thrown the contents of the book at a criminal by finding them guilty of every possible offence and then levying the harshest justifiable penalties. These days this expression is used outside the legal sphere to describe the comprehensive application of any kind of discipline or punishment.

thug. The modern-day thug can trace his etymological ancestry all the way back to the 13th century when the thugs were a fanatical Indian religious sect who proved their dedication to the goddess Kali by committing indiscriminate acts of murder. Notorious for the way in which they strangled or garrotted their victims, the name thug has continued in use despite the fact that the sect was dispersed and its leaders executed in the 1830s. Today thug is applied to a wide variety of criminals and ne'er-do-wells, from relatively harmless bully-boys through to professional killers.

thumbs – to give the thumbs down. The citizens of ancient Rome liked nothing more than to watch Christians being eaten by lions or a good fight-to-the-death between gladiators. If any of the gladiators failed to please they would show their disappointment by calling for his execution and giving him the thumbs down, i.e. making the sign that today means 'no' or 'bad' but in those days had a rather more drastic effect.

thunder, to steal someone's. To take credit for someone else's accomplishments; to appropriate another person's claim to fame. This expression is said to derive from an incident involving the English dramatist John Dennis (1657–1734). He wrote a play called *Appius and Virginia*, which he presented in 1709. The play was a flop and was withdrawn by the theatre-manager, but one feature was highly praised, for as part of the production Dennis had devised a novel method of creating a realistic sound effect of thunder. A little later Dennis went to see a production of *Macbeth* at the same theatre and discovered that his thunder sound effect had been employed without his permission.

'My God,' he exclaimed, 'the villains will play my thunder but not my plays!'

Time heals all wounds. This proverb made its first appearance in the work of the comic Roman playwright Terence. In its original Latin it was a somewhat more cumbersome saying: *diem adimere aegritudinem hominibus.* An equally reassuring modern variation, 'Time wounds all heels', has been variously credited to such diverse wits as Dorothy Parker and W. C. Fields.

tin-tack is British YUPPIE rhyming slang for the sack. The people most likely to be tin-tacked are those working in the City and in finance and insurance – these being typical YUPPIE occupations. *See also* OUT-PLACEMENT.

tip. In the 16th and 17th centuries to tip meant to hand over a small gift of money – that, at least, is one story and the most likely of all the derivations. Others include the suggestion that the word was written on a box passed round by apprentices, shop-workers and so on at Christmas. According to this theory, on the side of the box were written the initials T.I.P. meaning 'to insure promptness'. Another theory has the same three letters written on boxes set on coffee house tables, the idea being that a tip would speed the service. This is, perhaps, a custom we should revive today. After all there's nothing more galling than to receive sluggish service and then to be expected to give a tip. If by tipping first one could ensure quick attention it would be a significant improvement.

tit for tat means to give like for like or blow for blow – which is exactly what an old English phrase 'tip for tap' meant. Some authorities like to take a sophisticated line and suggest that tit for tat emerged from this source due to the influence of the Dutch phrase *dit vor dat* or the French *tant pour tant*. It is certainly not beyond the bounds of imagination that they contributed to the change, but it seems equally likely that, the letter p sounding very much like a t, it arose as a natural result of blurred pronunciation.

Titan. *See under* URANUS.

tizzy. Used as an adjective, tizzy describes any annoying, buzzing sound – such as the annoying sound leaked by personal stereos, enough to drive anyone into a more traditional tizzy.

toady. A creep, an obsequious, cringing person. The word has an extraordinary background, dating from the time when toads were believed to be poisonous. A toady or toad-eater was usually a boy who would accompany a quack medicine-seller to country fairs where the boy would swallow (or maybe just pretend to swallow) a toad. The audience would look on aghast as the boy swayed and pretended to be in his death throes. Then the quack would step forward, administer a dose of the medicine he was selling – and Hey presto! the toady would be miraculously on his feet, living proof of the medicine's wonderful properties. From this we get the term toady, still occasionally used today, meaning someone who will do or say anything, no matter how low or disgusting, in order to make a living or get on in the world. *See* YES-MAN.

toast. The verb to toast derives from the old practice of putting a piece of toast in a tankard of beer to improve its flavour. A story told in *The Tatler* recounts how in the time of Charles II one of the most famous beauties of the day was taking a dip in one of the baths at Bath when an admirer took a glassful of the water in which she was immersed and drank her health. Another admirer, who had had too much to drink, promptly riposted that though he didn't like 'the liquor he would have the toast' – by this meaning the lady. Hence, it is said, to toast means to raise one's glass to someone. Toasting is also a kind of music usually performed by West Indian DJs in clubs. They take a basic background beat from a reggae song and perform their own lyrics over the top of it. The words are often witty and usually reflect current events. *See also* RAP.

toe the line. *See under* LINE.

toff. A NOB, a POSH person, a member of the upper classes. The term originated in Oxford where the noble students at the university – the aforementioned nobs – wore a distinguishing gold tassel or tuft dangling from their caps. Toff is a corruption of tuft and was eventually applied to the wearers themselves.

togs, British slang for 'clothes', comes from the Roman toga, a semi-circular white cloak wrapped round the shoulders and body and worn by most Roman citizens. From this we also get the phrase togged out, meaning dressed up smartly.

tokenism. Business, government, the media and many organisations practise tokenism, the placing of a limited number of women, blacks, handicapped individuals and those from other racial minorities in a few 'token' jobs, while the vast majority of employees remain white, middle-class and male. Such 'tokens' are used for purely cosmetic purposes – perhaps to create a certain impression for customers or to satisfy employment laws – but actually do nothing to change attitudes.

Tom, Dick and Harry means everyone, every ordinary person in the street. Similar phrases with the same meaning have been in use for hundreds of years, the main variation being the names. The earliest version of every Tom, Dick and Harry involved Dick, Tom and Jack, those three names being the most common of their time. American authorities date Tom, Dick and Harry to 1815; Brewer says the expression is Victorian. It's equally likely that Tom, Dick and Harry, or a variation on their names, have been around far longer than that.

top drawer. Someone described as such is UPPER CRUST, born to the highest social class. The allusion is to a chest of drawers in which the top drawer signifies the highest social degree and the bottom drawer the lowest. **To put something in one's bottom drawer**, incidentally, is not a comment on social class. It means to put something away for the future and alludes to the custom, still practised, of putting away items for a girl's trousseau.

topless radio refers to radio phone-in programmes where the subject under discussion is sex; X-rated radio. The phrase was coined because of the sexually explicit nature of the problems discussed.

topsy-turvy. A very old phrase meaning upside down. It is a construction of 'top' and the Old English word *tearflian*, meaning to roll over.

Tortilla curtain. Coined by analogy to the IRON CURTAIN or BAMBOO CURTAIN, the Tortilla curtain is a joking reference to the fence that has been erected along parts of the US-Mexico border to keep illegal immigrants from Mexico out.

Tory. How many of today's Tories are aware that their name derives from a band of Irish thieves and outlaws who harassed the English in Ireland during the 17th century? During the reign of Charles II the name was applied to a group who supported the Crown and who, after the revolution in 1688, took up the Jacobite cause and became a political force. It was not until 1830 that the word Tory, with its less than honourable history, was scrapped and the party became the Conservatives.

touch wood. Some woods, such as oak, hazel and hawthorn, are said to have magical or sacred properties and to protect those who touch them. Thus touching wood – touching one of these trees or something made from them – was a way of warding off problems. Gradually the phrase itself began to supersede the actual wood-touching, though the superstitious still look round for something wooden to tap and, if they can find nothing, may resort to tapping their head instead.

towel, to throw in the. *See under* SPONGE.

toyetic. This extraordinary word has been coined by toy manufacturers to describe a television or film character who can be translated well into toys. To be toyetic a character must have a distinct and unmistakable look – which is why Mr T of *The A Team* fame is toyetic and the cast of *Dallas* are not.

tracks, to make. To set off on a journey. 'Let's make tracks' means simply 'Let's go.' The phrase is said to come from the wagon tracks left across the snowy or dusty American landscape by wagon trains carrying early pioneers. Even though they were out of sight it was, apparently, possible to tell their destination from the direction of the tracks.

trade winds. Most authorities agree that trade winds are winds that have, since time immemorial, blown 'trade' across the world's oceans. In the northern hemisphere they blow from the northeast, in the southern hemisphere from the southeast, helping to speed sailing vessels on their journeys. There is at least one dissenting voice, however, which protests that 'trade' in this phrase is derived from the Anglo-Saxon word *treadan* meaning to tread a path, make a trail. Thus trade winds were winds that set a course for ships and had nothing whatsoever to do with the idea of carrying goods from one place to another for trading.

tragedy, that most noble of all dramatic forms is, wait for it, derived from a Greek goat song. This mystery has bothered academics for many years. No one can shed much light on the subject except to suggest that perhaps the earliest tragedies featured men dressed in goatskins like mythical saytrs, or that ancient choral competitions offered a goat as the prize for the most moving writer. We will probably never know which, if either, is true.

trailblazer. The original trailblazers were men who established a path through an unknown area by marking the trees with a notch. This left a white mark for those behind to follow and this mark was named for its similarity to the white 'blaze' or spot between a horse's eyes. Thus, the early trailblazers. The word is used today to describe those who cut a trail through metaphorical new ground; people who make their own paths and show the way for others to follow.

travelogue. This expression, originally referring to a lecture on foreign travel or foreign parts illustrated with pictures, was invented by the American lecturer Burton Holmes at the beginning of the century. It was later applied to films which have travel as their subject.

treacle has an intriguing and strange history, meaning originally an antidote against animal bites. In ancient times the name was applied to a number of different concoctions but came eventually to describe just one, Venice treacle, a salve made of honey into which were mixed more than sixty different kinds of herb and medicine. It retained this meaning until the 18th century, when the word came to be applied to the syrupy substance made of boiled sugar.

triffid. We call a large, ugly plant or a rampant weed a triffid, borrowing the term from John Wyndham's science fiction novel *The Day of the Triffids*, published in 1951. His original triffids were huge, bulbous plants with a poisonous sting; they could move around on their own and also had a degree of intelligence. After the book had been dramatised on the radio any particularly ugly and malevolent-looking plant became known as a triffid.

trilby. Hats, made of felt and with a dented crown, which get their name from the heroine of a novel by George du Maurier. It tells the story of an artist's model called Trilby who falls under the influence of a hypnotist called Svengali. Through hypnotism he turns her into a great singer who achieves fame and fortune, but on his death her talent deserts her and she eventually dies of despair. From this novel we also get the word Svengali, describing a person with a forceful personality and vision, who guides and shapes others' success.

trompe l'oeil. A painting that fools the eye into thinking it real. The expression is based on the French phrase meaning 'to trick the eye' and refers to pictures painted with a three-dimensional effect and often intended to give the impression of a landscape.

trumpet, to blow your own. To boast about oneself. The phrase may go back to medieval times and beyond, when monarchs, members of the aristocracy and other figures of authority kept heralds who blew trumpet fanfares to 'herald' their approach. An ordinary person who wanted to seem important had to blow his own trumpet.

trumps, to come up. To be more helpful than anticipated in assisting someone else out of difficulties. The phrase derives from the gaming table, where a trump (from the French *triomphe* meaning 'triumph') is an unbeatable card that can save a disastrous hand. **It's on** (or **in**) **the cards**, meaning 'It's extremely likely to happen' is derived from the Tarot cards used for fortune-telling. Also from the card table comes the phrase 'He's a card' to describe someone who enjoys fooling around – the card in question being the Joker.

tsunami. This Japanese word means a tidal wave. It was adopted into English at the turn of the century and though rarely heard seems to be gaining in popularity in recent years.

tucker. *See* SING FOR ONE'S SUPPER.

tucker, best bib and. In the 17th and 18th centuries women wore wide lace collars around the neck and shoulders of their dresses. These were known as tuckers and a bib was a shirtfront. From these two garments we get the phrase best bib and tucker, meaning to be dressed up in one's best, to look clean and tidy.

tune, to change one's. To change one's opinion or behaviour. The expression dates back to the 14th century which has led one scholar to speculate that it originally referred to travelling minstrels who would change their songs – and perhaps the 'political' content of the words – to suit different audiences. It's an intriguing suggestion and one which is as unlikely to be disproved as proved.

turkey, to talk. This is another phrase which has an interesting but probably untrue story at its heart. It is said that a hunter and his Indian tracker went out shooting one day and brought down a number of crows and an equal number of turkeys. At the end of the day the hunter divided the spoils, giving the Indian a crow and putting a turkey in his own bag saying, 'A crow for you, a turkey for me.' This he continued to do, until he had all the turkeys and the Indian had all the crows – at which point the Indian turned on him and said, 'You talk turkey all for you, not for me. Now I'm going to talk turkey to you.' From this tale, which is widely told but has never been authenticated, is said to come the expression to talk turkey, meaning to talk seriously, to quit larking about and get down to the real business. No one seems to have been able to explain why the term turkey should have such negative meanings; in the film business, for example, a turkey is a total flop; in the drugs trade it describes fake drugs, substances that look like the real thing but turn out to be sugar or talcum powder. The turkey is, after all, a useful and delicious bird, though somewhat stupid and faint-hearted – which is perhaps why its name has become synonymous with failure.

turtle, to turn. When the natives of the Caribbean came across a turtle laying eggs they would turn her over on her back; in this position she was helpless and they were able to do what they wanted with ease. This habit was noted by British seamen who later applied the expression turned turtle to a capsized ship floating helplessly upside down. This phrase caught on quickly and was later applied to anything upside-down. *See also* TOPSY-TURVY.

tuxedo. What the British know as a dinner jacket, Americans know as a tuxedo. It is named after the Ptuksit Indians whose name the American settlers found impossible to pronounce. They called them the Tuxedos and the area they inhabited, just forty miles or so from Manhattan, became known as Tuxedo. In the 19th century a country club was established there and the men were required to wear a tailless dinner jacket to the functions. This was known as a tuxedo coat and when trousers were added to the outfit it became known simply as a tuxedo.

twitcher (or **ticker**). *See* BIRDER.

two-faced, or double-faced, is applied to a hypocrite – a person who says one thing and thinks another. Such a person may also be known as a **Janus**, Janus being a Roman god with two faces, one looking backwards, one forwards. It is after Janus that the month January is named, because January is the month that looks back at the old year and forwards to the new one.

two shakes of a lamb's tail, in. This delightful phrase, which originated in the USA in the 19th century, simply means 'very quickly', 'in a trice'. Whether lambs shake their tails more rapidly than other animals has yet to be discovered. So, too, has the link between this expression and the English phrases 'in two shakes' or 'in a brace of shakes', for which no derivation has been offered.

two sticks short of a bundle. Someone who is described as such is lacking in intelligence or common sense; they may be said to be 'not all there'. There are a number of other phrases constructed along similar lines and meaning the same thing. For example, 'tuppence short of a shilling', 'ninepence to the shilling' and 'fifty cards in the pack'.

U

U and Non-U. It is to Nancy Mitford that we owe the terms U and Non-U, which mean 'upper class' and 'non-upper class'. She contributed an article to a book entitled *Noblesse Oblige*, published in the mid-1950s, in which she popularised an existing theory that people could be divided into U and Non-U by the vocabulary they use. In particular she demonstrated how two words with the same meaning could be distinguished as upper class and non-upper class. Thus 'mirror' was Non-U and 'looking glass' was U; 'serviette' was Non-U and 'napkin' was U; 'toilet' was Non-U, 'lavatory' was U – and so on. As fashions in vocabulary change, this theory is perhaps more interesting as a commentary on the British class system than anything else. However, the terms U and Non-U continue to be applied, usually by the Us, to distinguish the upper class from the ordinary. *See* POSH and SNOB.

Ugandan discussions. The satirical magazine *Private Eye* is responsible for this euphemism for sexual intercourse. It was coined after the *Eye* reported that a senior Ugandan diplomat had been caught in the act and tried to explain it away by insisting that all he and his partner were doing was 'discussing Ugandan affairs'.

ugly duckling. Hans Christian Anderson's tale of 'The Ugly Duckling' tells of a cygnet who thinks he is a duckling and who is socially ostracised because he doesn't look like other ducklings. After undergoing various humiliations, to everyone's amazement he turns into a beautiful swan. From this the figurative phrase ugly duckling is applied to an unattractive or unpromising child who turns, against expectations, into a beautiful or admirable adult.

umbrage, to take. *Umbra* is the Latin word for 'shadow'. From it are derived a number of words such as umbrella (which gives shade) and the phrase 'to take umbrage', meaning to take offence. This alludes to the fact that someone who is overshadowed by another is likely to feel slighted.

umpteen. An indefinite number but a very large one all the same; like zillion it is an exaggeration used to make a point: 'I've told you umpteen times not to do that!' The term originated in Army Signallers' slang, perhaps because the letter M was known as 'umpty' and umpty came to mean 'a lot'.

unacceptable face of capitalism, The. This phrase came into popular use after Edward Heath had used it on 15 May 1973 in a speech condemning the bad habits of big businesses. Among the things he criticised was the practice of exploiting legal loopholes to avoid paying tax – loopholes which ordinary individuals had no hope of using. The phrase 'The unacceptable face of . . .' has since been adapted by many people to include their particular bugbear.

Uncle Sam. American sources show admirable unity in naming Samuel Wilson, a 19th-century New York store-owner who supplied meat to US army, as the source of the phrase Uncle Sam. One of Wilson's suppliers was called Elbert Anderson and his salted meats came in barrels stamped with the initials E. A. U.S. A soldier once asked what the initials stood for and was jokingly told Elbert Anderson's Uncle Sam. The idea caught on and soon Uncle Sam was to Americans what John Bull is to the English. It has to be said that some authorities, the most vehement of them British, discount Samuel Wilson entirely and argue that Uncle Sam is just a pun on the initial letters of the United States.

Uncle Tom. In Harriet Beecher Stowe's phenomenally popular novel *Uncle Tom's Cabin* the eponymous hero, a black slave called Uncle Tom, was characterised as a simple, servile man who was grateful for whatever life gave him. The author had intended him to be a noble, almost Christ-like figure who is killed at the end of the story by the wicked plantation owner, and the book certainly aroused American opposition to slavery and led, ultimately, to its abolition. However Uncle Tom's attitude towards his white superiors was too subservient for later black activists and the phrase Uncle Tom was coined to describe a black person who is over-respectful towards white authority.

unclubbable. This term was coined by Dr Johnson and is still heard in certain quarters to describe a person who lacks social graces or is unable to mix easily with others. Such an individual was therefore not a good candidate for membership of one of the many gentlemen's clubs of the time. Today there are fewer clubs but the word is still applied to those who lack the urbanity necessary for membership.

under the table. *See* ABOVE-BOARD.

under the weather. *See* ONE DEGREE UNDER.

underclass. Thomas Carlyle used the phrase 'under class' in 1839 to describe the people at the bottom of society. It disappeared in the meantime but resurfaced again in the mid-1980s to describe those people at the very bottom of the heap; the underprivileged, uneducated, impoverished individuals who suffer the worst of all circumstances and lack the personal ambition or means of escaping their situation.

underhand. *See under* ABOVE-BOARD.

Up the wooden hill to Bedfordshire. *See under* LAND OF NOD.

upper-class twits. *See under* CHINLESS WONDER.

upper crust. In households of the past, the most honoured guests were served with the upper crust of a loaf at mealtimes, this being thought to be the best part of the bread. The phrase was first cited in a book entitled *The Sayings and Doings of Samuel Slick of Slickville* by Canadian humorist Thomas Haliburton in 1836. He defined the upper crust as being the most wealthy and noble ten thousand of the population.

upper hand, to get the. This expression, meaning to obtain mastery over someone or something, has generated a number of explanations. One refers to an old game in which a stick was thrown and a number of men seized it, each laying their hands on it until one of them managed to get the upper hand, thus winning the contest. Another and less complex proposal is that the phrase comes from the sport of arm-wrestling, in which opponents face each other across a table, their elbows resting on the surface and their hands clasped. The aim is to force the opponent's forearm down flat on the table, and in doing so the victor's hand is always on top, giving him the upper hand.

upstairs, to kick someone. When a British politician becomes an embarrassment to his party he is sometimes promoted to the House of Lords, socially a more elite and rarefied place than the Commons but without quite the same political power. From this old Parliamentary custom, infinitely preferable to being kicked downstairs, i.e. kicked out of political life altogether, we get the expression 'to kick upstairs', used in business institutions to describe what is ostensibly a promotion but which is done just to get rid of someone and leave them powerless.

uptight. *See* HANG LOOSE.

Uranus. In Greek mythology Uranus was the personification of heaven. His children were the giants known as the Titans, from whose name we obtain the word **Titan** to describe anything huge (such as the infamous ocean liner the *Titanic*) and the element titanium. Uranus was the name given to the planet discovered by Herschel in 1781 and for centuries was unashamedly pronounced 'your-anus' with the emphasis on the second syllable. In recent years, however, a certain prurience has crept into the astronomical world and when a space probe was launched to explore the planet, news coverage of its progress pronounced the planet as 'Ure-a-nus', the emphasis firmly on the 'Ure' and the 'a' virtually ignored.

utilise the facilities. *See under* FACILITY.

Utopia. The name given to an imaginary island in Thomas More's book of the same name, published in 1516. More uses this perfect construct to illustrate just how good a well-thought-out system of law, politics and morals could be, and by contrast how bad the contemporary situation was.

V

valentine. Valentine's Day and a valentine, meaning a sweetheart, are both derived from the name of a Christian martyr. At least two St Valentines are recorded, one of them a doctor and the other the bishop of Terni, and both met nasty ends. The physician was clubbed and then beheaded on 14 February in the year 270 or thereabouts, according to the *Lives of the Saints*, and by luck more than judgement 14 February became St Valentine's Day. It is sometimes said that this date was chosen as the day to celebrate romance because it is a time when there are signs that spring is drawing near – which is simply not true. February is often the coldest month of the year and a young man's thoughts are more likely to turn to a mug of hot soup and a warm blanket than to romance. More probably St Valentine's Day coincided with the ancient Roman feast of Lupercalia, introduced to Britain by the Romans and still observed at the time Christianity arrived. Lupercalia was marked by giving gifts and generally having a good time and it seems likely that clever Christian leaders simply imposed St Valentine's Day onto an existing celebration.

value-added. A marketing term that describes the way in which the basic value of something is enhanced to boost profits on a product. This often involves tampering with it or processing it, which explains the proliferation of JUNK FOOD on our supermarket shelves. For example, a piece of meat sold over the counter achieves so much profit; but by processing that meat, bulking it out with other, cheaper, products, adding colouring and flavouring and presenting it in a tin can, i.e. with value added, manufacturers can significantly boost their profit margin.

vamoose means go, get out, scram, and is derived from the Spanish word *vamos* meaning the same. It came into use in the south-west states of the USA having travelled north from Mexico. From it, it has been suggested, comes the verb to MOSEY.

vampire is derived from the old Magyar word to describe a member of the walking dead, a creature who sucks the blood of others, and was introduced to the English language in the 18th century. It was popularised by Bram Stoker's classic horror story *Dracula*, published in 1897, and is sometimes used figuratively to describe a person who sucks someone dry, a parasite.

vandal. In the 5th century the Vandals were a greatly feared tribe of fierce warriors originating from the area that is now East Germany. Their name meant 'the wanderers' and wander they did, conquering much of France, Italy, Spain and North Africa. In 455 they took Rome, deliberately destroying many of its artis-

297

tic, literary and sacred treasures in the process. It is from this behaviour that the word vandalism derives, referring to wanton, pointless destruction.

Vatican roulette. This expression, a pun on RUSSIAN ROULETTE, refers to the rhythm method of contraception which requires couples to calculate the time when it is safe to make love. It is so-called because the Vatican continues to outlaw birth control, though in these Aids-conscious times it has been reported that some Catholics are using condoms – having first made some holes in them.

Venetian blinds were not invented by the Venetians but by the Persians. Venetian traders brought the idea for these slatted blinds back to Italy, where they are known as 'Persian blinds' to this day. Unfortunately the rest of Europe was under the impression that they had been invented by the clever Venetians, which is why they still carry that city's name.

Venezuela. When the first Spanish explorers reached the country we now know as Venezuela they thought that some of the canals along which inhabitants in certain areas lived were a little like Venice. Thus the new country was christened Venezuela, meaning 'little Venice' – which is not to be confused with the English 'Little Venice', an area of canals in the Maida Vale area of London.

veni, vidi, vici. Generations of schoolchildren have grown up sure in the knowledge that this phrase was uttered by Julius Caesar, boasting about his invasion of Britain. In translation they mean 'I came, I saw, I conquered.' Only one problem; according to some experts, Caesar probably never said the words.

ventilator. This is US theatrical jargon for a play that's so bad the audience depart before the end and leave nothing but fresh air in their places.

venture capital. An expression from the financial world to describe money offered by investors to buy shares in new or developing businesses. It is one of the more risky ways of investing money but can pay off spectacularly.

vice versa means 'and the reverse is also true' in, for example, a sentence such as, 'When George is on duty, Frank is off duty – and vice versa, of course.' The expression derives from the Latin words *vicis* meaning 'change' and *versa*, meaning 'turned'.

vicious circle. A chain of events or circumstances in which every effort made to improve the situation ends up creating a new or worse one. *See* CATCH 22.

vino veritas, in. Translated from the Latin this expression means 'in wine there is truth', i.e. that when people have drunk too much they are unable to conceal the things that, at other times, they keep secret.

virago. When, several years ago, a new publishing company dedicated to reviving the novels and writing of neglected female authors looked for a name, they chose Virago. We must assume that they had the original sense of the word in mind, for in its oldest form virago described a heroic woman, one who in some ways was man-like. Viragos were strong-willed and decisive, qualities which men came to distrust and which they soon redefined as shrewish and unfeminine. For this reason, since the 14th century a virago has been a nagging woman, a hussy, a man-hater – an image that the Virago publishing imprint has had some success in destroying.

vital statistics. The phrase referred originally to statistics based on life – hence the 'vitality' of the phrase from the Latin *vita* for 'life'. These included birth, marriage, divorce, health, death and so on. The expression was also jokingly applied to a woman's measurements at the bust, waist and hips, and women's measurements being infinitely more interesting than marriage statistics, the meaning stuck.

vodka. In Russian vodka means 'water', probably because of its clearness and thus its resemblance to water but also, it is said, because it was once believed to be as necessary to life as water. This is a belief that the present Russian administration is doing its best, against some opposition, to counteract.

vogue. The French verb *voguer* means to be moved across the water by sail or to go with the tide. It is from this sense of the verb that we get the meaning of following fashion, being in the current, moving along with things. To be in vogue means to be up-to-date with the latest influences in fashion, thought, art, literature etc. And of course, those who are in vogue often end up in *Vogue*.

voodoo has caused some disagreement among word experts. Some say that it derives from the African word *vodun*, meaning 'guardian spirit', but others trace it back to a 12th-century French religious leader, Peter Waldo, who led a group called the Waldensians in Lyons. They believed in basing their lives on the teachings of the Gospels and accordingly gave away their possessions. They were also accused and found guilty of various heresies and excommunicated. The Waldensians were also known by the French name Vaudois, and when French missionaries encountered black magic and witchcraft during their work in the West Indies they applied the name to this new phenomenon. In the course of time Vaudois became voodoo, a kind of magic that is still practised today in countries such as Haiti.

W

wagon, fall off the. *See under* FALL *and* BRAHMS AND LISZT.

walking on rocky socks. *See under* BRAHMS AND LISZT.

wall, the writing is on the. When someone refers to 'the writing on the wall' they point to an unmistakable sign of impending disaster. The saying alludes to the biblical story of Belshazzar's feast, during which a mysterious hand appeared and wrote a message on the wall. When translated it predicted the death of Belshazzar and the downfall of his kingdom, both of which came true.

wall, to go to the. This phrase is derived from the old self-protective habit of backing up against a wall during an attack in the street. Today a mugger's victim might be advised to avoid the wall and walk near the traffic, but in the Middle Ages someone who was set upon would retreat to the wall to be sure of covering his back. Thus to go to the wall, or have one's back to the wall, was to be in a desperate situation, in danger of losing everything. These phrases mean much the same today. They describe anyone in deep trouble and facing a financial or physical disaster.

wallflower. It has been suggested that this term is derived from the plant known as the wallflower which blooms in early spring and is hardy enough to grow on or against walls. Maybe, but as a human wallflower is an individual, usually a girl, who sits by the wall at a dance or party and is never invited to take the floor, it may just be that the phrase was a combination of the wall she sat against and a common endearment for a woman, 'flower'. 'Flower' is still in use in Yorkshire and is the rough equivalent of the southerner's 'dear' or 'dearie'. Another botanical phrase meaning pretty much the same thing is 'petal', which has a sympathetic ring when used in a sentence such as, 'What's wrong, petal?'

walls have ears. In the days before bugging several rulers are on record as having had listening devices implanted in the walls of their palaces. Catherine de' Medici is said to have had some rooms in the Louvre constructed in such a way that what was said in them could be heard in another room and Dionysius, a Greek ruler of Syracuse, had a listening tube that ran from his room to the prison below so that he could listen to the prisoners talking. Today's more sophisticated equipment is monitored by people who shun the -er ending of their profession and prefer to be known as buggists.

wally. Someone who makes a fool of themselves. Wallies always wear the wrong clothes, have the wrong haircuts, drive the wrong cars, say the wrong things and take the wrong actions – but the defining characteristic of the wally is that he does all these things in blissful ignorance and thinks of himself as a super-cool character. *See also* WIMP.

Walter Mitty. The main character of a story written by humorist James Thurber. Mitty lived a life of fantasy, imagining himself in all kinds of guises and achieving all kinds of goals. When the story was made into a film starring Danny Kaye it was instantly popular, with the result that the name Walter Mitty passed into the language to describe any person who lives in a day-dream.

Walter Plinge. In the British theatre Walter Plinge was the pseudonym traditionally taken by an actor who appears in two roles. It was long thought that the name was originally that of a stage-struck pub landlord whose premises in Drury Lane were frequented by actors. By calling the fictional 'extra' Walter Plinge the landlord got his name in the programme and probably reciprocated with free drinks. However, in 1981 Norman A. Punt claimed that it was invented by a certain H. O. Nicholson whose sister enjoyed a long career on the stage. This doesn't seem to have been authenticated, so the story of the star-struck landlord should be allowed to stand – at least for the moment. The American equivalent of Walter Plinge is George Spelvin.

Waltzing Matilda. A Matilda is an Australian term for a swag or sleeping roll or a roll of belongings that tramps carried around with them. Waltzing was originally 'walking' and no one seems yet to have discovered how or why the change occurred. To go waltzing Matilda was to be a swagman and cut a romantic figure in the Australian bush, wandering at liberty and settling down for the night at any convenient billabong (or for non-Australians, a waterhole). Hence the fact that the song 'Waltzing Matilda'

is virtually the national anthem of Australia.

wampum. Still heard occasionally referring to money, wampum was a shell currency used by American Indians. When the first white settlers arrived there were in fact a number of different currencies based on shells but all of them, except wampum, became obsolete.

wannabee. A derogatory expression that originated in the USA but has recently been introduced to the UK, a wannabee is a person who models themselves on someone or something else; a person who wants to be like another. Often applied to pop fans who want to be just like their heroes and heroines, the expression is dismissive, implying that the wannabee doesn't have enough individuality or imagination to 'create' themselves.

war paint. Today we use the term war paint pejoratively to describe the look of an over-made-up woman who, in seeking to outdo her rivals, has applied her cosmetics too thickly. The phrase originally referred to the war paint applied by American Indians and other tribal people, particularly in Africa, before they went on the warpath. To put on one's war paint is a metaphorical expression meaning to prepare oneself for the fray, to get oneself psyched up.

warnography. Constructed on the same principle as pornography, warnography is the term applied to films and other material that glorify war and violence and arouse aggression in consumers. Examples include glossy magazines full of pictures of weapons, and the *Rambo* films which relentlessly glamorised killing and which led to a spate of vicious attacks that, according to the police, could be traced back to incidents shown in the movies.

wash one's dirty linen in public, to. To make public embarrassing or disgraceful things that are normally kept private. The origin is not known.

wash one's hands of something, to. The Bible tells how Pontius Pilate, the Roman governor of the area, gave the chief priests and elders the choice of pardoning either Christ or a noted criminal, Barabbas. They 'out of envy' according to Matthew xxvii:18, called for the release of Barabbas. Pilate had been warned by his wife that she had had a dream that Christ was innocent and and that her husband should have nothing to do with condemning him, so he repeated his offer to free him – and again the elders and priests called for the release of Barabbas and the crucifixion of Christ. Matthew goes on:

When Pilate saw that he could prevail nothing, but that rather a tumult was made, he took water, and washed his hands before the multitude, saying, 'I am innocent of the blood of this person: see ye to it.

From this incident derives the phrase to wash one's hands of something, meaning to deny responsibility for something or to publicly disown something in which one has been involved.

Wasp. An acronym for White Anglo-Saxon Protestant, a term coined in the USA in the 1960s to describe the members of the nation's ruling class, the people most likely to make it to the top. Wasp is often applied pejoratively to someone who has all the advantages when it comes to success; someone who holds conventional middle-class values.

Watergate. The Watergate, a block of flats, offices and a hotel in Washington, USA, housed the headquarters of the US Democratic Party for the 1972 election. In June that year five men were discovered in the act of bugging the Democrats' offices and subsequent investigations revealed that they were in the pay of the Republican 'Committee for the Re-Election of the President', an organisation known as CREEP. Their trial the following year set off a far-reaching series of disclosures that implicated President Richard Nixon and eventually led to his resignation. The scandal came to be known simply as Watergate and in recent years the suffix -gate has been a byword for any political scandal involving corruption and secret deals. In the USA Oliver North became a national hero in conservative circles after his involvement in **Irangate**, a scheme for supplying arms to Iran and then channelling the profits from that deal to aid the Contras in Nicaragua (this after Congress had refused to finance the right-wing Contras). Though both President Reagan and his Vice-President, George Bush, were alleged to have been involved in this scheme, both managed to survive the furore. In Britain the Westland helicopter scandal hit headlines in 1986 and was quickly christened **Westlandgate**. Michael Heseltine, then Defence Secretary, supported the sale of the troubled Westland helicopter firm to a European consortium; Leon Brittan, then Trade Secretary, supported its sale to the American Sikorsky company. In January 1986 a letter criticising Heseltine was leaked via the Department of Trade and Industry, with the result that he resigned. Two weeks later it was revealed that the letter was deliberately leaked by Brittan's office to discredit his rival. Brittan was forced to resign too, but though obviously shaken the Conservative government quickly re-established its equilibrium.

weakest go to the wall, the. This expression is said to derive from the time when most people attending church had to stand throughout the service, for until comparatively recently only the wealthy and powerful enjoyed the luxury of their own pew. It was customary to place benches along the walls so that the elderly, injured or infirm could sit down. After the 17th century fixed pews were added to most churches and the entire congregation was seated.

weasel words. The language of politicians is heavily sprinkled with weasel words, words and phrases which, though they sound impressive, mean nothing or have the effect of removing much of the impact of the statement. Thus a phrase such as 'The unemployed should be given support' becomes 'The unemployed should be given due support', that single word qualifying the meaning and giving the speaker a chance to 'weasel' or waffle out of any responsibilities implied in it. The weasel is commonly thought to be a sly, cunning creature, hence the origin of the phrase; it may also be related to the idea that weasels suck the contents of an egg cleanly, leaving nothing except the empty shell.

weaving, to get. *See* TO GET CRACKING.

well-heeled. A poor or shoddily-dressed person may be described as down at heel, i.e. with their shoes in a poor state of repair. Someone who is well enough off to keep their shoes in better condition is, therefore, known as well-heeled. That, at least, is one explanation for the phrase. Another, from the USA, suggests that in America well-heeled was slang for having plenty of guns and weapons, this deriving from 'heeled', meaning to be armed with a gun, and ultimately from the description of a fighting cock equipped with spurs at its heels. How the phrase came to be associated with money is less clearly explained, but there's no doubt that on both sides of the Atlantic today well-heeled means to be wealthy.

Wellington. Wellington boots, commonly known just as wellingtons, were named for the Duke of Wellington. Whether he would approve of the modern plastic or rubber boots that go under his name is a MOOT POINT, for his own famous footwear was made of leather and came up above the knee at the front. They were worn by the army and by followers of fashion in all weathers; Wellington wore them even in the Houses of Parliament, where they would be much frowned on now. Other things named after him included the Wellington bomber and a giant fir tree, known as *wellingtonia*.

welsh on someone, to. To betray a person, reveal a secret or back out of a deal. The phrase seems to have been applied originally to bookmakers who welsh on the bets placed with them. There has been much speculation about the phrase's derivation, the English insisting that welshing is so-called because it is typical of Welsh behaviour and citing the old rhyme, 'Taffy was a Welshman, Taffy was a thief' as proof. The Welsh retaliate by persistently citing the name of a 19th-century bookmaker called Bob Welch from Epsom, Surrey, who was apparently inclined to welsh on his clients. Other authorities speculate that the phrase is much, much older than Mr Welch. This one looks like running and running.

west, to go. To die or retire, or to lose one's chances of achieving a goal. The phrase alludes to the setting sun which sinks slowly in the west and disappears from view, taking with it one's hopes, life etc. Not to be confused with **Go West, young man**, an injunction to young ambitious men who arrived on the Eastern seabord of the USA to travel westwards and seek their future – the West being seen as a land of opportunity.

Westlandgate. *See* WATERGATE.

wet blanket, a. A person who makes a habit of spoiling the pleasure of others; someone who acts as a dampener on fun and high-jinks. Wet blankets were used to smother smoke and flames, so in a perverse sort of way they were useful, if unexciting, things to have around.

wet – to be wet behind the ears. The babies of most mammals are born wet behind the ears, but this phrase is said to refer specifically to foals and calves, whose ears were believed to be the last part of their bodies to dry after birth. We use the phrase figuratively to describe someone for whom allowances have to be made because they are young and have a lot to learn.

wet sell. This is cynical salesman's jargon for the trick of taking a customer out to lunch and getting him drunk before negotiating an order.

Wets. Wet probably began its life as an insult in the playground, where it was applied to weak, sensitive children who were reduced to tears by their more boisterous playmates. It is also commonly applied to spineless adults, and has become particularly associated with the Conservative government under Mrs Thatcher. Those members of her party or Cabinet who refused to go along wholeheartedly with her hardline monetarist policies she defined as Wets, implying both that there was something weak and cowardly about them and also that their presence diluted the efficacy of her policies. *See also* DRY.

What the dickens? Any suggestion that this expression refers to Charles Dickens is inaccurate, for the phrase originated long before his time – indeed it was used by Shakespeare in *The Merry Wives of Windsor*. Most of the authorities agree that dickens is a euphemism for the devil and that 'what the dickens?' is a polite way of saying 'what the devil?'

wheel, to reinvent the. In the business world this phrase is used to refer to wasted effort. New bosses who want to scrap old systems and reinvent new ones similar to those they have disposed of are accused of reinventing the wheel.

wheeler-dealer. American sources trace wheeler-dealer back to the gambling saloon or casino, where someone who placed a lot of money on the spin of the roulette wheel or a hand of cards dealt him, came to be known as a wheeler-dealer. Such a man was a major player, one who made his money by luck and skill. From all these associations we get the modern meaning, applied to an individual of some importance and power who improvises and negotiates deals, playing by his wits. Also implicit is a sense that the wheeler-dealer cannot be trusted, that he is only out for himself.

whipping boy. A boy kept in royal palaces so that when a young prince misbehaved the whipping boy could be punished in his place – it being considered unsuitable (and probably illegal) to smack or chastise the noble child himself. Edward VI, who by all accounts was a very pious boy and didn't cause a lot of trouble, had a whipping boy named Barnaby Fitzpatrick. Charles I's was Mungo Murray. Today royal children are just as likely to receive a telling-off and maybe even a smacking as their ordinary counterparts, but the phrase whipping boy lives on, used metaphorically to describe someone who takes the rap for another's misdeeds.

whistle-blower. An employee in government or private industry who finds evidence of corruption and, unable to persuade the company or department to investigate the matter and put it right, exposes the situation to the press. In several celebrated cases whistle-blowers have uncovered frauds worth millions; sadly some of them have also discovered that after publicly displaying their honesty, no one else will employ them.

whistle, to wet one's. It's impossible to whistle with a dry mouth and lips, hence perhaps the origin of this phrase meaning to have a drink. People were wetting their whistles, and the mouth was known as a whistle, in the 12th century and probably some time before that. Various ornate tales have been 'discovered' to explain the origin of the phrase, one of them involving a magical drinking vessel which made a whistling noise whenever it was empty and could only be silenced by wetting the whistle. Truth is probably, in this case, less strange than fiction.

whistle for it, to. Someone who demands something unreasonable may be turned down with the admonition, 'Well, you'd better just whistle for it'. The expression dates from an old nautical superstition that when a ship was becalmed a wind could be raised by whistling for it. This was greeted with scepticism by LANDLUBBERS and the phrase retains that sarcasm today, meaning roughly 'You can ask what you want, but you have about as much chance of getting it as whistling up a wind.'

white-collar. *See* PINK-COLLAR.

white elephant. An unwanted item, often a gift or an expensive mistake, that cannot be easily disposed of. The expression originated in Siam, now Thailand, where white elephants were once venerated. To rid himself of a courtier he no longer favoured, the king of Siam would give the man a white elephant. This precious beast had to be gratefully received and then fed and cared for, which usually led to the financial ruin of the unfortunate courtier.

white goods. *See under* BROWN GOODS.

white lie. A 'good' lie or a conventional excuse; a relatively minor TERMINOLOGICAL INEXACTITUDE, often uttered for the best of reasons – perhaps to spare someone's feelings or extricate oneself from a difficult situation. A black lie is altogether more serious, being a major and knowing deception, a reversal of the truth calculated for selfish reasons.

white knight. A Stock Exchange term for a bidder who comes to the rescue of a company which has been threatened with an unwelcome takeover by a BLACK KNIGHT.

white man's burden. When heard today this phrase is usually applied with heavy irony, for the white man's burden was his duty to civilise, govern and educate the 'backward' black races who inhabited the white man's empires. Rudyard Kipling used the phrase as the title of a poem that today makes many a reader blush at its patronising tone. Among the lines are:

> Take up the White Man's Burden –
> Send forth the best you breed,
> Go bind your sons to exile
> To serve the captives' need.

whited sepulchre. A hypocrite. In Matthew, 23:27 Christ says:

> 'Ye are like unto whited sepulchres, which indeed appear beautiful outward, but are within full of dead men's bones, and of all uncleanness.'

He was alluding to the Jewish tradition of painting their sepulchres a conspicuous and brilliant white so that passers-by had no difficulty in identifying them and thus avoided defiling the dead by coming too close. Today we apply the expression to someone who gives the appearance of virtue and charm but who is, underneath, something else entirely.

whodunit (sometimes spelt whodunnit) is a mystery or crime novel in which the reader tries to work out the identity of the villain as the plot progresses. The very apt term whodunit, describing this kind of book, was probably coined in 1930 in the *American News of Books* – 'probably', because at least two individuals claim to have been the inventor of the phrase.

wholefood. A wholefood diet is one based on unprocessed natural foods. For example, wholefood enthusiasts eat breat made from wholemeal flour, i.e. wheat that includes the natural outer husk or covering of the grain, which provides fibre. The flour used for popular white bread has not only been separated from the husks but may also have been bleached and processed before being baked and has therefore lost much of its natural value. Wholefoods include whole grain cereals, beans, pulses, fresh and dried fruits and vegetables and other 'natural' products. Increasingly, people who consume wholefood are requiring it to be organically grown, i.e. produced without the use of chemical fertilisers and sprays. In the past those who have lived on wholefood have been considered to be somewhat freakish. In recent years, however, with a succession of food scares and medical reports condemning processed food, more and more people have adopted wholefoods into their diet. *See also* MACROBIOTICS and MUESLI-BELT MALNUTRITION.

wicked. In modern teenage parlance something described as wicked is impressive wonderful, amazing, clever. Though it would be easy to classify it as just another modern inversion, it is interesting to note that wicked was being used in this approving way in the USA in the early 1900s. *See also* BAD.

wicket, to bat on a sticky. This is a cricketing term, originally referring to a soft, damp wicket or pitch which created difficulties for the batsmen. Today professional wickets are covered overnight and when it rains, which has solved the original problem. Despite that, the phrase continues in general use to describe a precarious situation, one in which great care and caution need to be exercised if success is to be achieved.

widow's peak. One can be born with a widow's peak or acquire one, for this term describes the way in which the hair comes down to a point in the centre of the forehead and recedes at the sides, creating a V-shaped effect. Some people are born with this kind of hairline but many men develop it as their hair recedes. The name is based on the kind of close-fitting black cap which was cut so that the band dipped in a point at the centre of the brow.

wild goose chase, a. A waste of time, an absurd attempt to achieve something. English sources say merely that trying to catch a wild goose is a near-impossible task and leave the explanation at that, but an American authority alludes to a 16th-century game played on horseback and called wild goose chase. This involved one rider taking an erratic and random course and leaving the other competitors to try and imitate each twist and change of direction. It is suggested that the name of the game is based on the idea of wild geese flying in formation behind the leading bird. As the game sounds pretty impossible and pointless, it may explain why today's wild goose chase means what it does.

wimmin. Coined originally by feminists who wanted to get the 'men' out of 'women', wimmin has now been turned on them with a vengeance and is used by the right-wing and unsympathetic to satirise everything that the radical women's movement stands for. H. G. Wells actually used the word wimmin well before wimmin took it up, applying it not to feminists but to indicate a certain rather twee, down-market accent. That, perhaps, is where the women's movement went wrong, for it is impossible to pronounce wimmin (and make it sound distinct from 'women') with dignity. Instead, it tends to emerge with a kind of nasal whine – and plays straight into the hands of those who seek to knock it.

wimp came into use in the USA in the 1970s and entered Britain English rather later. It has been suggested that it is derived from the character Wimpy in the *Popeye* cartoons or from the verb 'whimper' – whimpering being what the average weak, non-MACHO wimp does when faced with trouble.

wind, to sail close to the, whether actually or metaphorically, is a dangerous business. It literally describes sailing a boat almost directly into the wind, dangerous because a single gust can send the vessel heeling over. Metaphorically the expression refers to someone whose activities are just this side of legal or acceptable; someone who lives in danger of being exposed or getting into real trouble.

windfall. Medieval forest law dictated that peasants could pick up branches they found on the ground and pull down those they could reach with a stick, but they were not allowed to cut down a tree or higher branches. When a strong wind brought down extra timber the peasants thought themselves lucky to have had a windfall. To this day we use the term to describe an unexpected bit of good luck, particularly a surprise sum of money. *See also* BY HOOK OR BY CROOK under HOOK.

windmills, to tilt at. In Cervantes' famous novel *Don Quixote*, the Don attacks a windmill under the erroneous impression that it is an evil giant. In his attack his lance gets caught in a sail and he is whirled into the air before coming down to earth with a bump. *Don Quixote* was an instant success when it was published in 1605 and the windmill episode caught the contemporary imagination so thoroughly that soon the phrase 'to tilt at windmills' was coined. It means to waste one's efforts attempting to fight imagined enemies or evils and is usually used in the sense of 'Don't go tilting at windmills.' *See also* QUIXOTIC.

wing, to take under one's. The allusion here is to the way a chicken shelters her chicks under her wings. The expression is used figuratively to describe someone who offers protection or support to another, often younger or inexperienced, person.

wobbly, to throw a. Someone in a fit of uncontrollable rage shakes their head and hands in a violent, unco-ordinated, wobbly manner; that, at least, is the supposed derivation of the phrase to throw a wobbly, meaning to be extremely angry. The phrase is said to have originated in the early 1980s in London and is now in general use.

Wobblies, the. Members of the Industrial Workers of the World, a radical American labour organisation that was formed in 1905. It was formed largely of dockers, farmers and textile workers, and though the First World War reduced its importance, it remained a potentially revolutionary movement into the 1920s. The word 'Wobbly', applied to a member of the IWW, is said to come from the Chinese-American pronunciation of W as 'wobble'.

wolf in sheep's clothing, a. The Bible is full of warnings against hypocrisy and deception (see, for example, WHITED SEPULCHRE) and this is another of them. A wolf in sheep's clothing is someone who appears harmless and innocent but beneath the skin is dangerous and cunning. The reference is Matthew 7:15:

Beware of false prophets, which come to you in sheep's clothing, but inwardly they are ravening wolves.

wolf, to cry. Once upon a time there was a young shepherd who liked to make fun of the local people by crying, 'Wolf!' and watching the stir it caused. Then one night a wolf really did appear on the hillside and the shepherd yelled and yelled – but, thinking it was yet another practical joke, no one believed him and he was eaten. Variations on this story are told around the world. When we accuse someone of crying wolf we mean that they have given a false alarm or made a fuss over nothing.

wood – to be unable to see the wood for the trees. This phrase, which dates back to 1546, is used to describe a situation in which one is so enmeshed by details that it is impossible to see the whole issue clearly. Americans use 'woods' instead of 'wood'.

wooden – up the wooden hill to Bedfordshire. *See* THE LAND OF NOD.

wool, dyed in the. A textile trade phrase referring to fabric that is dyed after the spinning stage but before it has been woven. Wool dyed in this way was deeply dyed and kept its colour better than that which was dyed after weaving. We use dyed in the wool today to describe those people whose habits or character are so deeply ingrained that they can never be changed – a dyed in the wool Liberal, perhaps, or a dyed in the wool criminal.

wool – to pull the wool over someone's eyes. The exact origin of this phrase has not been traced but it has been speculated that 'wool' was a slang term for the large wigs worn by gentlemen in the past. One suggestion is that pickpockets and other criminals attacked these BIGWIGS by pushing the wig over the wearers' eyes and then robbing them. It is an intriguing, if unproven, idea.

woolgathering. We describe someone engaged in trivial, time-wasting pastimes or work as woolgathering because for several hundreds of years woolgathering has been a trivial, half-hearted occupation somewhere between work and play. The original woolgatherers were the poor who would walk in the countryside, picking bits of fleece off fences and bushes as they went. The scraps of wool collected in this way weren't worth much and it is easy to imagine how quickly the outings developed into an excuse for mucking around. From this we get the modern use of the word and its application to someone who is absent-minded, dreamy or inattentive.

working women. *See under* BODY WORKER.

write like an angel. When an author is praised for 'writing like an angel' it is most usually his style that is being complimented. The phrase should in fact refer to the quality of the handwriting, for it derives from the name of Angelo Vergece who was a famous 16th-century calligrapher at the court of Francis I of France.

wrong side of the blanket. *See under* BASTARD.

WYSIWYG stands for What You See Is What You Get, a computer term meaning simply that what one sees on the screen will be what one gets when the page is printed up.

X

X marks the spot. Used to mean 'this is the exact position', this expression originated with 'Spot the Ball' competitions which featured sporting photographs with the ball removed. Competitors had to mark the spot where they thought the ball was with an X and the nearest guess won.

Xmas. The abbreviation of Christmas to Xmas is considered by many to be a nasty modern invention but it in fact dates back more than four hundred years. And even then Xmas was following an ancient tradition, for as early as the 12th century X was used as a routine replacement for 'Christ'.

Y

Yahoos. In Swift's *Gulliver's Travels*, Yahoos are brutish people who love nastiness and dirt. They are governed by intelligent, reasoning horses known as Houyhnhnms, Swift using this device to throw an entirely new light on the world of his day. We use the word Yahoo to describe a brutish, unthinking person but the ultimate derivation has not been found. Various suggestions have been put forward, including one that it comes from a pun on a Greek word meaning 'sleepy' or 'dopey' and that it is based on either a Brazilian tribe known as the Yahos or an African tribe with a similar-sounding name.

Yankee. The most widely accepted derivation of the word Yankee, which to those outside America refers to all Americans, but which to Americans usually refers only to Northerners or New Englanders, is that it comes from the name Jan Kee, a contemptuous English nickname for Dutch sailors. With time the term was transferred to seamen working from New England and became spelled Yankee. Today Yankee is a little outmoded and Americans abroad are better known as Yanks.

yellow goods. Items such as cars, washing machines etc., that have a decent profit margin but are bought infrequently. Some yellow goods can also be filed under the WHITE GOODS category. *See also* BROWN GOODS, RED GOODS.

yellow press. This expression is derived from a 19th-century circulation war between two American newspapers, William Randolph Hearst's *New York Journal* and Joseph Pulitzer's *New York World*. Hearst boosted his sales by introducing a comic strip feature called 'The Yellow Kid' and this was immediately termed yellow journalism by his rivals, who accused him of down-market popularism. The phrases yellow press and yellow journalism are still used today to describe the antics and sensationalism of the tabloid newspapers, which concentrate more on trivial entertainment than they do on hard news.

yen, to have a. The Chinese word *yen* means opium smoke, which was something that drug addicts longed to taste. From this we get the expression to yen for, meaning to want something badly, to have a strong desire for it.

yes-man. A worker who always agrees with his boss, whatever the boss says, and is therefore considered to be a creep and a TOADY by his colleagues. The phrase may be based on the German word *Jaherr* describing a person who was always saying 'Yes, sir'. If it was, it didn't catch on until a 1913 newspaper cartoon which showed a sports editor looking through the latest edition, surrounded by assistants all loading him with praise. The phrase took hold in Hollywood where assistant directors were christened yes-men and from there was adopted into wider use.

yo-yo. Invented in the Philippines where it was not a toy but a hunting weapon, used for hitting and lassoing prey. As a toy it became popular in the Middle East and the sheer number of people who spent their time yo-yoing in Damascus led to a yo-yo ban there. We use the verb 'to yo-yo' today to indicate something that is rising and falling dramatically – for example, 'Stock Market prices were sent yo-yoing by the news last week'. In business parlance to yo-yo is for a company to keep its suppliers on TENTERHOOKS by ordering large quantities of supplies at one time and small ones the next. The aim of these tactics is to keep the supplier on his toes and to ensure that goods are supplied at a highly competitive rate – something which tends to lapse when company and supplier have too cosy a relationship.

yob stands either for Youth Of Britain or 'boy' spelt backwards. Given that a yob is a loud-mouthed, coarse, loutish young man the latter derivation seems more likely. From this we get the word yobbism to describe a breaking-down of civilised behaviour in all walks of life – not just on urban streets but in rural towns where 'lager louts' cause disruption and in such hallowed institutions as Parliament, where formality and courtesy have given way to rough speech and spoiling tactics.

yokel. There are at least two confident derivations for this term, meaning a peasant. The first is that it can be traced to the name Jacob, which in Bohemia was spelt Jokel and pronounced 'yokel'. As the name was particularly common in the countryside, city-dwellers adopted it as a contemptuous nickname for rural people. The second proposes that the green woodpecker found in the English countryside was christened yokel after its call, which sounded something like 'Yo-Kel'. Later the people who lived in the areas where yokels dwelled came to be known as yokels themselves, the implication being that they were country bumpkins.

yomping came into public awareness at the time of the Falklands War when British Royal Marines were reported to have yomped their way across miles of difficult countryside. By all accounts yomping is not for the faint-hearted. It involves carrying packs and weapons that can total as much as 120 lb, often over long distances and through the worst imaginable conditions, in the knowledge that when the destination is reached battle may commence immediately. No one has yet succeeded in tracing a derivation for the word, though it has been suggested that it might be linked to a similar verb used by Norwegian skiers to describe crossing an obstacle.

young fogey. A recently identified species of British origin. The old fogey, set in his ways, deeply conservative, unquestioningly patriotic and profoundly dull and respectable, has long been recognised. But only since the development of Thatcherism, with its emphasis on a return to Victorian values, has the young fogey made an appearance. Young fogeys are, like their elders, concerned with tradition, stability and old-fashioned middle-class values. They are aged under thirty, mainly male and public school educated, and likely to be staunch Conservatives. Like YUPPIES they strive for material success, but they disapprove of the Yuppies' flashy modernism and deeply distrust anything labelled 'progress'. Young fogeys like things that are old and reliable. They wear tweed jackets and corduroy trousers, read *The*

Times, dream of owning a country estate and prefer to work in the respectable world of finance rather than that vulgar newcomer, industry. *See also* SLOANE RANGER.

Young Turks. The original Young Turks were a party of political reform, supported by students and young radicals, who staged a revolt in Salonika in 1908 and succeeded in overthrowing the ruling Sultan Abdul Hamid. The party was dissolved at the end of World War I. The expression Young Turks is used figuratively to describe almost any ambitious, young, rebellious individual or faction with a desire to reform and change the established order.

Yuppie. A Young Urban Professional. The Yuppie phenomenon is said to have started in America in 1983 when *The Yuppie Handbook* gave a definition and identity to large numbers of young, affluent, city-dwelling professionals in their twenties and thirties. Yuppies the world over can generally be identified by their ruthless ambition, confidence and conspicuous consumption. Status symbols associated with the Yuppie lifestyle include BMW and Golf GTI cars, Rolex watches, portable telephones and Filofaxes. Yuppies love gadgets, particularly if they are expensive and come in matt black. The classic Yuppie works in finance, business or in advertising, but others can be found wherever there is serious money to be made. They have a pioneering spirit, and in many cities have colonised areas in which BMWs and Rolexes were once rarities. The advent of wine bars, fitness centres and shops selling sushi and Perrier water in previously working-class districts is an indication that Yuppification is underway. Yuppies are by nature conformist and materialistic. Both sexes wear designer-label suits to enhance their money-making image, and the women are exponents of POWER DRESSING. In Britain both men and women buy their clothes from stores like Next, which exist to supply everything a Yuppie needs – from boxer shorts to espresso coffee machines. Following in the footsteps of Yuppie came a vast number of related phrases, all of them defining social groups. Among them are Black Urban Professionals, identified as Buppies, and young working couples without children, known as Dinkies (Double Income, No Kids Yet). Families with children and only a single wage packet coming in are termed Oiks – One Income and Kids. At the opposite end of the age range, wealthy pensioners have been defined as Woopies, Well Off Older People, though one letter to *The Times* suggested that they might more appropriately be known as Wotchas – Wonderful Old Thing Considering His/Her Age. There were also Swells (Single Women Earning Lots of Loot). And finally, there was even a term for those Yuppies who failed to make the grade and dropped out – Droppies, standing for Disillusioned Relatively Ordinary Professionals. *See also* HOORAY HENRY, YOUNG FOGEY and SLOANE RANGER.

Z

zany. In the Italian *commedia dell'arte* the zany was a clown or buffoon. The word zany is from the Italian *zanni* meaning a clown, a word which in turn derived from the diminutive of the Italian name Giovanni. Today someone described as zany is a bit crazy, full of strange ideas.

zapping. A relatively new phenomenon that has developed since the introduction of hand-held remote control devices. These make it possible to change a television channel without the inconvenience of getting up and crossing the room to do so. Zapping involves using one of these devices to move quickly among the channels, stopping to watch a couple of minutes here or there and moving on again as soon as the attention wavers. Advertisers worry about this because people tend to zap away to another channel as soon as the adverts come on. For this reason the advertising agencies are forever trying to devise more exciting and tight-knit commercials which will 'hook' viewers. *See also* SOUND-BITE and KIDULT.

zeppelin. We owe the word zeppelin to Count Ferdinand von Zeppelin who devoted the second half of his life to developing the first airships. The idea was adopted by the Germans in World War I and zeppelin bombing raids soon imprinted the word on the minds of the Parisians and Londoners who suffered their attacks. Though too slow and cumbersome to be of great use in war, the zeppelins maintained their popularity into the 1930s. By that time aeroplanes were coming into their own and this, combined with the tragic crash of the *Hindenberg*, led to the demise of the airship.

zero. The word zero did not enter the English language until the 1600s and is, even today, regarded as being something of a vulgar Americanism. It is derived from the Arabic word *cifr* which was adopted into Italian as *zefiro* and thence into English as zero.

Zero option. One of President Reagan's pet theories, the Zero option proposed that the USA would not deploy cruise missiles in Europe if Russia withdrew its SS-20s. Though not yet fully adopted, we could see the Zero option coming into force before long.

zilch. The expressions 'zilch', 'zero zilch' or 'zilch zero' mean 'nothing' or 'nil' and gained wide currency in the late 1960s. Eric Partridge suggested that zilch was a portmanteau word combinin 'zero' with 'nil' and the Yiddish word *nich*, but a more likely derivation is from the name Joe Zilsch, a term used in 1910s and 20s to describe an insignificant figure, a Mr Nobody. In 1931 the American humorous magazine *Ballyhoo* introduced readers to a family of Zilches: Charles D. Zilch was Chairman of the Board, Otto Zilch was Treasurer and Henry P. Zilch, the President, made his début in a cartoon in which he was seen floundering in the swimming pool. From the water's edge a solicitous secretary murmurs, 'Mr Zilch, you don't often stay in so long,' to which the boss retorts, 'No, I don't often lose my bathing trunks.'

zip. The word zip was an onomatopoeic word coined around 1875 to describe the noise made by a speeding bullet, fabric ripping (or maybe a speeding bullet ripping through fabric) etc. By 1900 it had taken on the meaning of speed and energy and someone very active was described as having plenty of zip. In 1893 Whitman L. Judson invented what he called a 'Universal Fastener' of interlocking metal teeth. This was used under a variety of names (including C-Curity for trouser flies) until in 1921 a footwear manufacturer decided to incorporate the new invention into shoes, saving the inconvenience of fiddling with buttons. The marketing department looked around for a name that would demonstrate the speed and ease of use of this development and came up with zipper, based on zip and soon abbreviated to zip by users.

zit. Among teenagers a zit is a spot or mark on the skin. It refers particularly to a pus-filled spot or a blackhead that can be squeezed. The origin of the word hasn't been traced but maybe it derives from the gentle popping sound that occurs when a blackhead is squeezed.

zizz. To snooze. The term derives from the gentle snoring noises made by someone asleep.

zoid. American slang for a nonconformist, someone who doesn't fit into accepted roles. Zoid may be derived from the word 'schizoid', a person suffering from schizophrenia whose illness may well make them seem strange.

zombie. Originally a god worshipped in West Africa, the cult surrounding it was taken by slaves to the West Indies and most notably to Haiti. The word zombie was also applied to dead bodies brought back to life by VOODOO ceremonies. These zombies, favourites of horror movie makers and thriller writers, were robot-like beings under the control of the person who had resurrected them. It is also a term of abuse aimed at someone who is stupid or just slow and sleepy-headed, unable to think for themselves.

zombie food. This is an American slang term for JUNK FOOD, highly-processed and nutritionally worthless food of the kind eaten by people who GRAZE. Whether the phrase implies that it is only unthinking zombies who eat such food, or whether it turns people into zombies, is not absolutely clear.

zoo daddy. An American phrase for a divorced or separated man who sees his children rarely and, when he does, takes them to the zoo. *See also* DISNEYLAND DADDY.